Understanding Market Reforms in Latin America

Understanding Market Reforms in Latin America

Similar Reforms, Diverse Constituencies, Varied Results

Edited by
José María Fanelli

First published 2007 by
PALGRAVE MACMILLAN
Houndmills, Basingstoke, Hampshire RG21 6XS and
175 Fifth Avenue, New York, N.Y. 10010
Companies and representatives throughout the world

PALGRAVE MACMILLAN is the global academic imprint of the Palgrave
Macmillan division of St. Martin's Press, LLC and of Palgrave Macmillan Ltd.
Macmillan® is a registered trademark in the United States, United Kingdom
and other countries. Palgrave is a registered trademark in the European
Union and other countries.

ISBN-13: 978–0–230–50057–0   hardback
ISBN-10: 0–230–50057–9   hardback

This book is printed on paper suitable for recycling and made from fully
managed and sustained forest sources. Logging, pulping and manufacturing
processes are expected to conform to the environmental regulations of the
country of origin.

A catalogue record for this book is available from the British Library.

Library of Congress Cataloging-in-Publication Data

Understanding market reforms in Latin America : similar reforms, diverse
constituencies, varied results / edited by José María Fanelli.
    p. cm.
  Includes bibliographical references and index.
  ISBN-13: 978–0–230–50057–0 (cloth)
  ISBN-10: 0–230–50057–9 (cloth)
    1. Latin America–Economic policy I. Fanelli, José María.

HC125.U52 2007
338.98—dc22   2006053452

10   9   8   7   6   5   4   3   2   1
16   15   14   13   12   11   10   09   08   07

Printed and bound in Great Britain by
Antony Rowe Ltd, Chippenham and Eastbourne

To Ana, Paula, and Sebastián

Contents

List of Figures

List of Tables

Notes on Contributors

Carlos H. Acuña holds a PhD in Political Science (University of Chicago) and an MA in Research Methodology. He heads the MA in Public Policy at Universidad de San Andrés, Argentina. He taught as Visiting Professor at the University of Chicago and the University of Notre Dame. Author of numerous articles, his books include *Los Derechos Humanos y la Justicia en la Política Argentina* (co-authored), *Latin American Political Economy: Theoretical Perspectives in the Age of Neoliberal Reforms*, and *Democracy, Markets and Structural Reforms in Latin America* (co-authored).

Regis Bonelli holds a BSc degree in Engineering (Pontifical Catholic University of Rio de Janeiro, 1965) and a PhD in Economics (University of California at Berkeley, 1975). He held executive positions in agencies of the Brazilian government such as BNDES (the Brazilian Development Bank) and IPEA (Institutito de Pesquisa Econômica Aplicada (IPEA). He is presently Director of ECOSTRAT, a consultancy firm, and Research Associate at IPEA, both in Rio de Janeiro, and has authored studies in the areas of economic development, growth, and productivity.

Dionisio Borda is the Director of Centro de Análisis y Difusion de la Economia Paraguaya (CADEP), Paraguay. He received his PhD in Economics from the University of Massachusetts-Amherst in 1992 and has written extensively on the Paraguayan economy. He was Finance Minister in Paraguay (2003–05).

Daniel Buquet is Doctor in Political Science (FLACSO-Mexico). He is currently Professor and Researcher in Political Science at the Universided de la República, Uruguay and has held Visiting Professor positions at different institutions in Uruguay and abroad. His main academic focus is on electoral systems and party politics in Latin America. He is consultant in public opinion, elections, and Uruguayan politics for private companies and international organizations. He is the co-author of *Fragmentación Política y Gobierno en Uruguay: Un Enfermo Imaginario?* and several articles in books and journals.

Armando Castelar Pinheiro holds a PhD in Economics from the University of California, Berkeley. He is a Senior Researcher at IPEA, a think-tank linked to Brazil's Ministry of Planning, and a Professor of Economics at the Federal University at Rio de Janeiro (UFRJ). Formerly, he was the Head of the Economics Department of BNDES, Brazil's National Development Bank.

Rómulo Chumacero holds a PhD in Economics from Duke University. He is currently Senior Economist at the Research Department of the Central Bank of Chile, and he is also Professor and Academic Director of the PhD Program in Economics of the University of Chile. His areas of interest are econometrics and macroeconomics.

José María Fanelli has a PhD in Economics from the University of Buenos Aires. He is currently Senior Researcher at CEDES, Argentina and former Director of the Economics Department at the University of Buenos Aires. He has been actively involved in the establishment of research networks in the Latin American region, and has worked as a consultant for ECLAC, IDB, the G-24, UNCTAD, GDN, and IDRC (International Development Research Centre). He has published extensively on macroeconomic and financial problems in Latin America and market reforms in developing countries.

Alvaro Forteza holds a PhD in Economics from Gothenburg University, Sweden. He is Professor of Macroeconomics at the Universidad de la República, Uruguay and former director of the Department of Economics, Universidad de la República. He has published papers in the *Journal of Policy Reform*, the *Journal of Macroeconomics*, the *European Journal of Political Economy*, and the *Journal of Applied Economics* among others. He has been Visiting Professor at the universities of Cergy (France), Antwerpen (Belgium), Aarhus (Denmark), and Murcia (Spain), and consultant for the World Bank, ECLAC, and the ILO.

Rodrigo Fuentes holds a PhD in Economics from UCLA. He is a Senior Economist at the Research Department of the Central Bank of Chile. His areas of interest are economic growth and banking.

Sebastián Galiani is Associate Professor of Economics at Washington University in Saint Louis. He obtained his PhD in Economics from Oxford University and works in the areas of development economics and applied microeconomics, with special interest in labor economics, health economics and public policy. He has published papers in the *Journal of Political Economy*, the *Quarterly Journal of Economics*, the *Journal of Development Economics*, *Labour Economics*, *Regional Science and Urban Economics*, *International Tax and Public Finance*, *Economics and Human Biology*, *Fiscal Studies*, and *Emerging Markets Review* among others.

José Alberto Garibaldi studied Law and Economics at the Catholic University of Peru, gained his PhD at Essex University, and Master in Public Policy from Georgetown. He is currently Professor at Instituto Tecnológico Autónomo de México. He is co-author of *Corruption and Change* (1999) and of a number of papers on institutional economics. He has been adviser to several European, Asian, and Latin American governments and institutions on governance and environmental issues.

Marino González holds a PhD in Public and International Affairs from the University of Pittsburgh, Graduate School of Public and International Affairs (GSPIA). He is Professor at Universidad Simón Bolívar, Department of Economics and Administrative Sciences. He specializes in the analysis of intergovernmental health systems in Latin America and the Caribbean, the institutional performance of the public sector, and social security reform in Venezuela.

Mario Ibarburu holds a degree in Industrial Engineering (Universidad de la República, Uruguay), a Master of Science in Planning of Energy (Universidad Federal de Río de Janeiro), and a Master of Science in International Economics, Universidad de la República, Uruguay. He specializes in energy economics, regulatory economics, and industrial organization.

Jorge Lanzaro has a Doctorate in Political Science and is Professor and Researcher in Political Science at Universidad de la República, Uruguay. He is former director of the Political Science Institute and Coordinator of the Doctorate Program in Political Science (Universidad de la República). He had Visiting Professor positions in several universities of Latin America, the United States, and Europe. He is the author of *La izquierda uruguaya: entre la oposición y el gobierno* and *Tipos de Presidencialismo y Coaliciones Políticas en América Latina*. He is currently coordinator of the CLACSO (Latin American Council of Social Sciences) group on left-wing parties in Latin America.

Rolf Lüders holds a PhD in Economics from the University of Chicago. He is a Professor of Economics at the Catholic University of Chile. He was Chilean Minister of Finance and Minister of the Economy (1982–83). His areas of interest are economic history and macroeconomics.

Francisco Monaldi holds a PhD in Political Science (Political Economy) from Stanford University and has a Masters in International and Development Economics from Yale University. He is the Director of the International Center for Energy and Environmental Studies at the Institute for Advanced Management Studies, IESA, Venezuela, and Professor at Andrés Bello Catholic University. He has been a consultant to the Andean Development Corporation (CAF), the Inter-American Development Bank, and the World Bank, among other public and private institutions. He has recently collaborated in the IDB study *The Politics of Policies*.

Andrés Pereyra has an MSc in Economics (Université Catholique de Louvain, Belgium) and is currently Assistant Professor of Microeconomics, Universidad de la República, Uruguay. He specializes in the economics of regulation, telecom, and transport economics, and the evaluation of transport, water, and environmental projects. He is consultant to the World Bank and the IADB and has published papers in *El Trimestre Económico, Estudios Económicos*, and *Estudios Públicos*.

Donald G. Richards is Professor of Economics at Indiana State University in Terre Haute, Indiana. He received his PhD in Economics from the University of Connecticut in 1983. He is the author of several articles on the Paraguayan economy.

Germán Ríos received a Master's Degree in Economics from Johns Hopkins University and is currently a PhD candidate (George Washington University). He is an Assistant Director at the Andean Development Corporation (CAF, a multilateral financial institution which promotes sustainable development and regional integration). Previously, he served as Director of Public Investment at the Ministry of Development and Planning of Venezuela, and as a Country Analyst in the Brazil Department at the World Bank in Washington, DC. He has worked as a consultant for the World Bank, the Inter-American Development Bank, and the UN Economic Commission for Latin America. Mr Ríos is author of several publications on the Venezuelan economy and on Latin American growth.

Ben Ross Schneider is Professor of Political Science at Northwestern University. His publications include *Reinventing Leviathan: the Politics of Administrative Reform in Developing Countries* and *Business Politics and the State in 20th Century Latin America*. He has also written on economic reform, democratization, technocracy, the developmental state, and comparative bureaucracy. His current research revolves around two projects, the first on the institutional foundations of capitalist development in Latin America, and the second on market-oriented reform in health and education.

Eduardo Siandra received a PhD in Economics from the University of California, Los Angeles. He is currently Professor of Economics of Banking and Finance at Universidad de la República, Uruguay. He has taught and done research at the University of Tilburg (the Netherlands), the University of Cambridge, and University College London. He has been actuarial, economic, and financial consultant for the World Bank, the Central Bank of Uruguay, and the largest domestic pension fund in Uruguay (República AFAP).

Mariano Tommasi (PhD in Economics, University of Chicago, 1991) is Professor of Economics at Universidad de San Andres, Argentina. He was President (2004–05) of the Latin American and Caribbean Economic Association. He specializes in political economy and institutional economics, with a focus on developing countries. He has published several books and articles in journals such as *American Economic Review, American Journal of Political Science, American Political Science Review, Journal of Development Economics, Journal of Monetary Economics, International Economic Review, Economics and Politics, Journal of Policy Reform, Economic Inquiry, Journal of International Economics*, and *Journal of Law, Economics and Organization*. He has held visiting positions at Harvard, Tel Aviv, UCLA, and Yale.

Marcel Vaillant holds a PhD in Economics from Universitaire Faculteiten Sint-lgnátius Antwerpen, Belgium. He is currently Economic Consultant in the MERCOSUR Secretariat, and Professor of International Trade at Universidad de la República. He is former Director of the Department of Economics, Universidad de la República and has published several articles in his field of specialization. He has been adviser to multilateral institutions including IDB, ECLAC and so on.

Joaquín Vial holds a PhD in Economics from the University of Pennsylvania. He is the Chief Economist of the Global Trends Unit of the Economic Research Department at BBVA (Banco Bilbao Vizcaya Argentaria). He has been National Budget Director in Chile (1997–2000) and Chief Macroeconomic Adviser to the Finance Minister (1992–94). His areas of interest are macroeconomics and political economy.

Ricardo Villasmil holds a PhD in Economics from Texas A&M University and a degree in Agronomic Engineering from the Universidad Central de Venezuela. He is currently Professor at the Universidad Católica Andrés Bello (Venezuela) and researcher at Instituto de Investigaciones Económicas y Sociales (IIES). He specializes in political economy and has written several articles on Venezuelan development problems.

List of Abbreviations

ACEPAR	Aceros del Paraguay (Steelmakers of Paraguay)
AD	Acción Democrática (Venezuela)
AFP	Administradora de Fondos de Pensiones (Retirement Fund Administrator) (Peru)
Anatel	Agência Nacional de Telecomunicações (National Telecom Agency) (Brazil)
ANCAP	State-owned enterprise operating in oil (Uruguay)
Aneel	Agência Nacional de Energia Elétrica (National Electric Energy Agency) (Brazil)
ANP	National Port Administration (Uruguay)
ANS	Agência Nacional de Saúde (National Health Agency) (Brazil)
ANTEL	State-owned enterprise operating in telecommunications (Uruguay)
ANVISA	Agência Nacional de Vigilância Sanitária (National Sanitary Vigilance Agency) (Brazil)
APAL	Administración Paraguaya de Alcoholes (Paraguayan Alcohol Administration)
APRA	Alianza Popular Revolucionaria Americana (Peru)
ATNs	Contributions from the National Treasury (Argentina)
BANXICO	Banco Central de México
BCP	Banco Central del Paraguay
BCRP	Banco Central del Perú
BCV	Banco Central de Venezuela
BNDES	Banco Nacional de Desenvolvimento Econômico e Social (National Development Bank) (Brazil)
BW	Bretton Woods
CANTV	Compañía Anónima Nacional Teléfonos de Venezuela
CAPASA	Cañas Paraguayas S.A. (Alcohol producer)
CEDES	Center for the Study of the State and Society
CEPRI	Comisión Ejecutiva de Privatización (Executive Privatization Commission) (Peru)
CET	Common External Tariff (MERCOSUR)
CGE	General Economic Confederation (Argentina)
CGT	General Labor Confederation of the Argentine Republic
CIEPLAN	Corporación de Estudios para Latinoamérica
CLAD	Centro Latinoamericano de Administración para el Desarrollo
CNA	Comisión Nacional del Agua (National Water Commission) (Mexico)

CNBV	Comisión Nacional Bancaria y De Valores (National Banking and Securities Commission) (Mexico)
CNE	Consejo Nacional Electoral (Venezuela)
CNV	Comisión Nacional de Valores (National Securities Commission) (Paraguay)
COFETEL	Comisión Federal de Telecomunicaciones (Federal Telecommunications Commission) (Mexico)
CONATEL	Comisión Nacional de Teléfonos (National Telephone Commission) (Paraguay, Venezuela)
Concertación	Coalition of Political Parties in power since the return of democracy (Chile)
COPEI	Comité de Organización Política Electoral Independiente (Independent Committee for the Organization of Electoral Policy) (Venezuela)
COPRE	Comisión Presidencial para la Reforma del Estado (Presidential Commission for Reform of the State) (Venezuela)
COPRI	Comisión para la Privatización (Privatization Commission) (Peru)
CORDIPLAN	Oficina Central de Coordinación y Planificación (Central Office for Planning and Coordination) (Venezuela)
CORFO	Corporación de Fomento (State-owned and managed development corporation) (Chile)
CORPOSANA	Corporación de Obras Sanitarias (Sanitary Works Corporation) (Paraguay)
COSENA	Consejo de Seguridad Nacional (National Security Council)
CPI	Consumer price index
CRE	Comisión Reguladora de Energía (Energy Regulatory Commission) (Mexico)
CTV	Confederación de Trabajadores de Venezuela (Worker's Confederation of Venezuela)
CVM	Comissão de Valores Mobiliários (Brazil's security and exchange commission)
DE	Desarrollo Estabilizador (Development with Stability) (Mexico)
DGC	Dirección General de Contribuciones (General Contributions Direction) (Peru)
DIPRES	Dirección de Presupuestos (Budget Office) (Chile)
DL	Decreto Ley (Decree Law) (Chile)
DNAEE	Departamento Nacional de Águas e Energia Elétrica (National Department of Water and Electric Energy) (Brazil)
DNU	Decree of 'necessity and urgency' (Argentina)
ECLAC	Economic Commission for Latin America and the Caribbean

EEC	European Economic Community
Eletrobrás	Centrais Elétricas Brasileiras (Federal Holding Company in electricity sector)
ENNIV	Encuesta Nacional Ingreso Gasto (National Income Expenses Survey) (Peru)
EnTel	National Telecommunications Company (Argentina)
FCCAL	Ferrocarril Central Carlos Antonio López (Carlos Antonio López Central Railway) (Paraguay)
FDI	Foreign direct investment
FEDECAMARAS	Federación de Cámaras y Asociaciones de Comercio y Producción de Venezuela (Federation of Business and Industrial Boards and Associations of Venezuela)
FIDES	Fondo Intergubernamental para la Descentralización (Intergovernmental Fund for Decentralization) (Venezuela)
FLOMERPASA	Flota Mercante Paraguaya (Paraguayan merchant fleet)
FMM	Fernando Martínez Mottola
FOBAPROA	Fondo Para la Protección del Ahorro (Savings Protection Fund) (Mexico)
FREDEMO	Frente Democrático (Democratic Front) (Peru)
FTA	Free trade agreement
GATT	General Agreement on Tariffs and Trade
GDN	Global Development Network
GDP	Gross domestic product
GSLT	General Sale and Luxury Tax (Venezuela)
IDB	Inter-American Development Bank
IESA	Instituto de Estudios Superiores de Administración (Institute for Higher Studies in Administration) (Venezuela)
IFE	Instituto Federal Electoral (Federal Electoral Institute) (Mexico)
IFI	International financial institution
IIE	Institute for International Economics
IMF	International Monetary Fund
IMPI	Instituto Mexicano de la Propiedad Intelectual
INDECOPI	Instituto Nacional de la Competencia y la Propiedad Intelectual (Peru)
INEI	Instituto Nacional de Estadística e Informática (Peru)
INP	Instituto Nacional de Planeación (National Planning Institute) (Peru)
ISI	Import substitution industrialization
IU	Izquierda Unida (United Left) (Peru)
LA	Latin America
LAPSA	Líneas Aéreas Paraguayas (Paraguayan Airlines)

MAS	Movimiento Al Socialismo (Movement to Socialism) (Venezuela)
MEF	Ministerio de Economía y Finanzas (Ministry for Economy and Finance) (Peru)
MEP	Movimiento Electoral del Pueblo (Electoral Movement of the People) (Venezuela)
MERCOSUR	Mercado Común del Cono Sur (Southern Cone Common Market)
MINPRE	Ministerio de la Presidencia (Ministry for the Presidency) (Peru)
MVLL	Mario Vargas Llosa
NAFTA	North America Free Trade Agreement
NGD	Nueva Generación Democrática (New Democratic Generation) (Venezuela)
NGO	Non-governmental organization
NIC	Newly industrializing country
OAS	Organization of American States
ODEPLAN	Oficina de Planificación (Planning Office) (Chile)
OECD	Organization for Economic Co-operation and Development
ORA	Partido Nacional Organización Renovadora Auténtica (Venezuelan political party)
OSE	State-owned enterprise operating in water and sewage (Uruguay)
OSINERG	Órgano de Supervisión de La Inversión en Energía (Peru)
OSIPTEL	Órgano Supervisor de la Inversión en Telecomunicaciones (Peru)
PA	Procedural approach to development
PAN	Partido Acción Nacional (National Action Party) (Mexico)
PAYG	Pay-as-you-go
PCV	Partido Comunista de Venezuela
PDVSA	Petróleos de Venezuela Sociedad Anónima (Petroleum Company of Venezuela)
Petrobrás	Petróleo Brasileiro S.A. (State-owned oil company)
PEMEX	Petróleos Mexicanos
PFL	Partido da Frente Liberal (Liberal Front Party) (Brazil)
PFP	Policía Federal Preventiva (Federal Prevention Police) (Mexico)
PIT-CNT	Central trade union (Uruguay)
PJ	Peronist Party (Argentina)
PMDB	Partido do Movimento Democrático Brasileiro (Party of the Brazilian Democratic Movement)
PND	Programa Nacional de Desestatização (Brazilian Privatization Program)

PPC	Partido Popular Cristiano (Popular Christian Party) (Peru)
PRD	Partido de la Revolución Democrática (Democratic Revolution Party) (Mexico)
PRI	Partido Revolucionario Institucional (Institutional Revolutionary Party) (Mexico)
PROMCOPRI	Comisión para la Promoción de Inversiones (Investment Promotion Commission) (Peru)
PS	Predatory state
PSDB	Partido da Social Democracia Brasileira (Brazilian Social Democrat Party)
PT	Partido dos Trabalhadores (Workers' Party) (Brazil)
SA	Substantive approach to development
SAFP	Superintendencia de Administración de Fondos de Pensiones (Retirement Fund Administration Superintendency) (Peru)
SAL	Structural adjustment loan
SAT	Sistema de Administración Tributaria (Tax Administration System) (Mexico)
SBS	Superintendencia de Banca y Seguros (Bank and Insurance Superintendency) (Peru)
SCT	Secretaría de Transportes y Comunicaciones (Secretary for Communications and Transport) (Mexico)
SECAL	Sector adjustment loan
SECOFI	Secretaría de Comercio y Fomento Industrial (Secretary for Commerce and Industrial Promotion) (Mexico)
SECOGEF	Secretaría de Contraloría General de la Federación (Secretary for Comptroller General's Office) (Mexico)
SEDUE	Secretaría de Desarrollo Urbano (Secretary for Urban Development) (Mexico)
SEGBA	Electric Services for Greater Buenos Aires
SEMIP	Secretaría de Minas e Industria Paraestatal (Secretary for Mines and SOE) (Mexico)
SG	Secretaría de Gobernación (Ministry for the Interior) (Mexico)
SHCP	Secretaría de Hacienda y Crédito Público (Secretary for Finance and Public Credit) (Mexico)
SIDOR	Siderúrgica del Orinoco (Orinoco Steel Company) (Venezuela)
SME	Sindicato Mexicano de Electricistas (Mexican Union of Electricians)
SNRE	Secretaría Nacional de Reforma del Estado (National Secretariat of State Reform) (Paraguay)
SOE	State-owned enterprise
SOMISA	Steel Mixed Society Argentina

SP	Shining Path (Peru)
SPP	Secretaría de Programación y Presupuesto (Secretary for Programs and Planning) (Mexico)
SSS	Servicio de Seguridad Social (State-run Social Security Service) (Chile)
SUNAT	Superintendencia Nacional de Administración Tributaria (National Tax Superintendency) (Peru)
Telebrás	Former state-owned telecom monopolist (Brazil)
TEM	Título de Estabilización Monetaria (Monetary Stabilization Paper) (Venezuela)
TESOBONOS	Bonos del Tesoro (Treasury Bonds) (Mexico)
UCAB	Universidad Católica Andrés Bello (Venezuela)
UCD	Democratic Center Union Party (Argentina)
UCR	Radical Civic Union Party (Argentina)
URD	Unión Republicana Democrática (Venezuelan political party)
UREE	Regulatory offices for electrical energy (Uruguay)
URP	Understanding Reform Project
URSEA	Regulatory Unit for Energy and Water Services (Uruguay)
URSEC	Regulatory offices for communications (Uruguay)
USAID	United States Agency for International Development
UTE	State-owned enterprise operating in electricity (Uruguay)
VAT	Value added tax
VIASA	Venezolana Internacional de Aviación Sociedad Anónima (Venezuelan airline)
WB	World Bank
WC	Washington Consensus
YPF	Fiscal Petroleum Fields (Argentina)

1
Understanding Market Reform in Latin America: Similar Reforms, Diverse Constituencies, Varied Results

José María Fanelli

1.1 Introduction

Latin America has gone through a period of intense market reforms in the last twenty-five years. In contrast to the initial enthusiasm in the late 1980s and early 1990s, a vivid debate currently exists as to whether market reforms have been instrumental in fostering development and whether reforms should be deepened or reversed. Those who favor a deepening consider Chile as the successful flagship signaling the path to follow. Those who favor alternative strategies argue that the Argentine crisis or the transformations in the Venezuelan polity well illustrate the vulnerabilities that the market-friendly programs can create. This debate has an importance that goes far beyond academic circles to the extent that the arguments and conclusions will undoubtedly influence future development strategies to be adopted not only in Latin America but also in other developing regions. This book seeks to contribute to this debate. It presents a set of case studies of market reforms in Latin America (LA) produced within the framework of the Understanding Reform Project (URP), which comprises a larger set of case studies of market reforms in developing countries embracing all regions in the world.[1] The case studies in this book are authored by researchers drawn from the respective Latin American countries who are familiar with the institutional and political peculiarities of their own countries. All of the studies are comparable, given that they all derive from the same closely coordinated research project.

The research work discussed here has a number of distinctive features that are particularly relevant to the current policy debate. To begin with, the country studies comprise the most frequently cited reform cases in Latin America, both successes and failures. These are Argentina (Chapter 2), Brazil (Chapter 3), Chile (Chapter 4), Mexico and Peru (Chapter 5), Paraguay (Chapter 6), Uruguay (Chapter 7), and Venezuela (Chapter 8). The studies explicitly tackle questions that are central to the policy debate, such as: Why reform? What was reformed? Were the results in line with expectations? And, why did similar

1

reforms work differently? The units of analysis in the case studies are not particular reforms (for example, trade or financial reforms) but the market reform processes as a whole, conceived of as instances of institutional change that call for intensive policy implementation. The research methodology assigns a central role to the analysis of the specific initial conditions and the details of the processes by which reforms were reached and implemented. Unlike most existing analyses, which tend to focus on economic outcomes, the authors view market reforms as exercises in institution-building embedded in specific economic, political, institutional, and cultural contexts. With the aim of disentangling the details of the process, the project utilized case-study methodology and adopted a multidisciplinary approach which combines economic, institutional, and political analysis to structure the narratives of the reform experiences.

The main aim of this introductory chapter is to present an overview and to assess the research findings of the country studies contained in the book. It focuses on the issues that are at center stage in the current policy debate on reforms in Latin America[2] and the chapter is structured accordingly. From the analytical point of view, the discussion relies heavily on the empirical and analytical results of the Understanding Reform Project, which are presented in Fanelli and McMahon (2005a, 2006a). Furthermore, this chapter must be read as a complement to the article that Forteza and Tommasi (2006) produced for the URP on Latin America. In the remaining part of this section we briefly discuss the conceptual side of such results. Section 1.2 presents the most salient features of the eight reform experiences analyzed, describes commonalities and differences between these experiences, and identifies stylized facts concerning initial conditions and outcomes of reform in the countries under analysis. Section 1.3 addresses the problematic side of reforms. It focuses on implementation, sustainability, and the legitimacy of the reforms. With the guidance of the conceptual framework, we pinpoint several unsolved questions, which basically have to do with the determinants of institutional persistence and change under structural conditions such as those in Latin America: conditions that include macro volatility, crises and external vulnerability, highly skewed wealth distribution, and a polity in transformation from authoritarianism to democracy. Section 1.4 concludes the chapter and draws policy implications

A brief look at the conceptual approach

We will now summarize the essential features of the conceptual framework (for a more detailed discussion see Fanelli and McMahon, 2005b and 2006b).

Market reform

A market reform is defined as the implementation of changes in the rules of the economic game by a legal authority to widen the role of markets and the private sector and to make the entire economy more open. This definition has implications for the analytical approach to understanding reforms. The most relevant dimensions are scope, depth, and consistency; effectiveness; sustainability; distributional conflict and political economy; uncertainty and learning; and the features of the policy.

Scope, depth, and consistency

Reforms primarily affect the formal rules of the game of the institutional structure. Since the institutional structure consists of rules pertaining to different hierarchies in diverse social domains that show varying degrees of formality, the scope and depth of a specific reform package will largely depend on the hierarchy of the rules to be modified and the domains involved.[3] Furthermore, the functional linkages between hierarchies, domains, and informal institutions will pose consistency constraints on reforms; dysfunctional reforms will likely lead to unsustainable institutional changes.

Effectiveness

To be effective (to permanently change constraints and incentives) the changes in the rules of the game must be designed, executed, and enforced. An effective state and the quality of the pre-existing organizations and institutions are central in this regard. The first generation of papers on reform focused on the analysis of the factors that induce the initiation of reforms (crises, attrition wars and so on) to the detriment of the factors that contribute to making reforms sustainable. Most LA countries have been able to launch reforms, but only a small number of the reforms were sustainable.

Sustainability

The factors that impinge on sustainability are not easy to grasp because sustainability raises the problem of the determinants of institutional permanence and change, which analytically is still in swaddling clothes.[4] Three issues are worth highlighting: first, an institution can be self-enforcing in its domain but dysfunctional with regard to the rest of the domains or rules of upper hierarchies; second, path-dependence is central to understanding institutional evolution, placing idiosyncratic factors at center stage; and third, since exogenous shocks can change the parameters of the institutional game, the features of the shock-generating stochastic process matter to sustainability.

Distributional conflict and political economy

Reforms result from a conscious choice to change the rules of the game and can affect the income, wealth, and political power of varied social groups. For example, different Pareto-efficient outcomes entail different resource distributions and, hence, forward-looking agents will take the probable distributional effects into account. Since market reforms impinge on rules pertaining to different social dimensions and hierarchies, they affect groups of individuals and organizations of varying sizes, who will play different roles as stakeholders to different transactions ruled by the governance structures that will be affected by reforms. The ability for collective action of a given group of individuals or organizations can differ substantially depending on the character of the transactions and governance structures that are at stake. It follows that the ability to solve collective action problems and distributional conflicts is an essential component of reforms and is not independent of the type of reform involved.

Uncertainty and learning

Uncertainty makes it difficult to anticipate what the reform path will be. Hence, the ability to change the rules under uncertainty, to learn, and to rectify are all factors influencing the reform path. Important variables in this respect are the ways in which political decisions are made; the features of the shock-generating stochastic processes; state and organizational effectiveness; and the ability for institutions and organizations to learn (that is, to change beliefs). Macro instability is inimical to cooperation and learning to reform because it increases uncertainty, feeds distributional struggles, and typically induces a short-term bias in decision-making.

The features of the polity

The polity enters the picture because a legal authority must implement the changes in the rules of the game and reforms must be supported by a suitable political coalition and an effective state. The way in which legal authority is legitimized, authority is exerted, and coalitions are built is primarily determined by the characteristics of the polity (that is, whether it is authoritarian or democratic; whether it is liberal or illiberal; whether the state is predatory or developmentalist). Political institutions are key to processing conflict among various stake holders without resorting to violence or civil disobedience. However, we cannot assume that these institutions are completely exogenous to reform; inter-temporal agreements depend on 'state' variables such as the distribution of political power (political institutions), the distribution of resources, and relevant beliefs. In this regard, it is important to determine whether reforms are imposed by special interests, whether the gains are widespread, and whether state capture phenomena are present. These elements impinge on the legitimacy of the reform.

The eight reform experiences analyzed in this book are rather dissimilar; therefore the studies do not necessarily deal with the same aspects of reforms, pinpoint the same set of empirical issues, or embrace all the dimensions covered by the above concepts. We will next summarize each of the country studies and pinpoint the issues that they emphasize.

1.2   Eight Latin American reforms: similar packages, varied results

The design of the reforms in each of the eight countries was essentially inspired by the Washington Consensus (WC) and – to varying degrees – by the ensuing 'generations' of reform blueprints.[5] In light of this fact, the variety of reform results – moving from clear successes (Chile) to outright failures (Argentina, Venezuela, Paraguay) – is at first striking. The evidence provided by the set of case studies included in this book can help account for this fact. The studies reveal that, indeed, the specific reform packages present different scopes and depth, ranging from gradualism to big bang and from orthodoxy to pragmatism. They cover a wide gamut of policy initiatives, implementation problems, and outcomes. The first part of this section summarizes the content of the country studies. The second part presents some stylized facts that we have identified concerning initial conditions, goals, and outcomes.

Summary of the country studies

Argentina

The study comprises the market reforms implemented in the 1990s. The scope and depth of the policy packages were far-reaching, embracing several tiers in the institutional hierarchy and the economic domain. One salient feature of the Argentine strategy of reform was the bundling of measures, such as privatization and market deregulation, with stabilization (convertibility or currency board). The reform process was particularly intensive in the early 1990s. Despite significant early success, it ran into serious difficulties at the end of the decade, ultimately leading to a full-blown economic and political crisis. The Argentine experience vividly illustrates the fact that the effective implementation of legal changes is not sufficient to ensure reform sustainability. The following points are worth highlighting. (a) Although the 1989 hyperinflationary crisis did foster reforms, the Argentine case suggests that crises do not necessarily produce good-quality policies; crisis-induced institutional, distributional, macroeconomic, and political disarray created path-dependence effects that severely constrained society's institution-building ability. (b) After hyperinflation, it was necessary to build institutions to ensure sustainable macroeconomic fundamentals. 'Convertibility' (the currency board implemented in 1991) was an institutional shortcut towards the building of such institutions but it did not work. Budget disequilibria primarily associated with favors to over-represented provinces ultimately dominated the currency board regime. (c) The characteristics of the polity influenced sustainability. President Menem – who led the country from 1989 to 1999 and implemented most of the reforms – resorted to clientelistic political machineries, which, in turn, harmed the quality of institutions and eroded the political legitimacy of the whole process. (d) Under these circumstances, the idiosyncratic distribution of political power and the ability for collective action of some interest groups (powerful provincial governors, some union leaders and conglomerates that participated in the privatization process) hindered the quality of the reformed institutions. (e) Argentina was envisaged as the poster child of the Washington Consensus reforms and the reforms were explicitly supported by multilateral organizations and market participants. After the demise of the reforms, not only the government's legitimacy but also that of the international players weakened. It is no wonder that the ensuing government adopted an anti-reform discourse.

Brazil

The study embraces the entire period of reform from the first stabilization and trade liberalization initiatives of the 1980s. The authors classify the experience as gradualist because market reforms in Brazil are essentially a loosely coordinated process of partial state retrenchment that spans the last twenty years. Since the initiation and deepening of reforms were frequently motorized by the goal of reducing macro instability, initiatives of institutional change were often bundled together with other urgent or popular policies to facilitate their approval. They were not enacted as a coherent, overall change in development strategy, but as an incomplete, flexible, mostly disconnected reform process. The study stresses that what stands out in Brazil's reform process, in comparison with other developing countries, is not so much the depth and nature of the reform, or the main contextual factors encouraging it, but rather the 'why' and 'how' of reform. A democratic polity carried out the reforms; democracy was restored in 1985 after a two-decade authoritarian military government. The fragmented character of the political system, together with the importance of the federal states favored pragmatism and negotiations about reform initiatives. Ideology and partisan politics played a lesser role in fostering market reforms in Brazil than in other countries of the region. Therefore, reforms in Brazil tended to be contested, piecemeal, and pragmatic, in that they largely targeted specific problem-solving. The Brazilian state has been particularly effective at transforming some areas largely thanks to the quality of the bureaucracy it inherited from the previous interventionist regime. For example, the authors call attention to the intensive participation of the BNDES – the Brazilian development bank – in the privatization process. The outcomes are mixed. Reformers succeeded in widening the participation of private players, enhancing productivity in certain sectors, and reducing the inflation rate. They also induced higher trade and financial openness, but were unable to accelerate growth or induce a substantial change in the skewed distribution of income. The achieved growth rates are not comparable to those observed during the import-substitution industrialization period. Indeed, reduced state intervention in the economy was more the result of a pragmatic reaction of the political elite to external pressures and a lack of alternatives than the outcome of a newfound ideological conviction.

Chile

The Chilean market reforms had ample scope and depth; they were a large-scale exercise in institution-building that radically changed Chile's institutional landscape. On the basis of the findings analyzed, it is only natural to classify Chile as a reform success. In the last twenty years it has transformed itself from an 'average' Latin American country into a dynamic economy that now exhibits accelerated growth rates and decreased volatility. This experience has played a prominent role in LA in that, first, it pioneered the implementation of pro-market policies and, second, several countries tried to emulate Chilean reforms. The market-oriented reforms were initiated in the early 1970s and were generated by the demise of the previous regime, which had a socialist orientation and had undergone a severe macroeconomic crisis in the period immediately preceding the *coup d'état* that General Pinochet led in September 1973. The case study describes the entire reform process with emphasis on the political economy and incentives behind the two main political regimes that undertook them: the authoritarian government of General Pinochet between 1973 and 1989 and the democracy that succeeded it. Despite the positive outcomes, the process went through periods of severe disequilibria during the implementation stage. The most important occurred in the early 1980s as a consequence of both domestic policy mistakes – induced by the wrong sequencing of trade and financial reforms and misleading macroeconomic policies – and external shocks, triggered by the debt crisis. Despite this, the authoritarian government was able to implement measures to set the market reforms on track once again. The currency was devalued substantially and the authorities intervened intensively in the banking sector to bail out the system. The acceleration of growth after 1985 played a central role in making reforms sustainable and encouraging the first democratic government – the opposition won the election – to maintain the course of reforms. Other important factors in this regard were the negative 'demonstration effects' provided by the deep macroeconomic disequilibrium that the first government of the newly recovered Argentine democracy experienced in the 1980s and the collapse of the socialist system and the fall of the Berlin Wall. Beyond the important economic outcomes of the reform, what is most significant from the point of view of our analytical interest is that: (a) the transformations in the polity reinforced reforms – the changes in the upper-level institutions of the hierarchy reinforced rather than debilitated the functionality of economic institutions; and (b) Chile managed to overcome a sizable crisis in the 1980s that was largely due to the ill-designed implementation of market reforms; in other countries this type of crisis stalled or reversed reform attempts.

Mexico and Peru

The chapter on Mexico and Peru presents a structural reform process as an attempt to change the institutional setting in which the economy operates, a transaction between agents within a central policy domain so as to alter the pattern of interaction between political and economic rules for the purpose of improving the economy's performance. Peru and Mexico are taken as contrasting examples of the way in which reformers solve complex implementation and sustainability problems. Peruvian and Mexican reformers operated under different formal and informal institutional settings, although they shared similar difficulties and used informal enforcement mechanisms to push the reform process. The chapter argues that the institutional environment provides the setting and means to reject, abort, or enforce the proposed deals in the reform process. The authors emphasize the role of the mental models that agents employ. The reform process in Mexico was gradual and spanned almost twenty years from its beginning in 1982, following the debt crisis and the abandonment of the populist policies associated with oil discoveries and high prices in the 1970s. The chapter distinguishes a number of different groups relevant to policies, embracing technocrats, PRI politicians, and other political forces. Both the PRI and the technocrats lost power after the Tequila Crisis in 1994. The corruption scandals associated with Salina's presidency also ultimately contributed to this result. The weakening of the PRI and the strengthening of new players in Congress and the regions resulted in the stalling of reforms. Growth acceleration did not occur despite Mexico's signing of the NAFTA agreement in 1993 and the reduction of macroeconomic imbalances. Before launching reforms in the 1990s, Peru went through deep macroeconomic disequilibria. The most important indicator was the acceleration of inflation that took the country to the brink of hyperinflation. On the political front, the democratic polity faced the challenge of the Shining Path guerrilla movement. Fujimori's strategy in the 1990s was a kind of shock-therapy, bundling structural reforms with stabilization. The government adopted an increasingly authoritarian stance, which included a self-promoted *coup d'état* and a modification of the constitution to allow Fujimori's re-election. His regime collapsed in late 2000 when corrupt political agreements were revealed. The reform process lost momentum and legitimacy. The ensuing government was not effective at deepening the reforms. The authors conclude that corruption is associated with the lack of strong and operative formal institutional channels to make reforms effective. This raises the importance of 'parallel' or informal institutional channels and results in the hijacking of the reform agenda and corruption. This problem was more severe in Peru than in Mexico. They also argue that the ability to strike intertemporal agreements in Mexico favored gradualism and sustainability. In Mexico, PRI's lengthy tenure provided a longer horizon and coordination capacity. With a long horizon a gradual reform process is more credible as specific transactions can be advanced gradually. In Mexico, successive presidents insisted on including PRI's opposition in the reform negotiations and the central administration provided the means to deliver the presidents' promises. Fujimori, on the contrary, tried to destroy any opposition.

Paraguay

The scope of the reforms implemented in Paraguay was narrower than in other countries of the region, although Paraguay had been traditionally open to trade. Privatizations were not important and financial liberalization resulted in two financial crises. In explaining the failures, the authors emphasize path-dependence effects associated with the predatory character of the state under Stroessner's dictatorship. The demise of this predatory state occurred as a consequence of the exhaustion of the traditional sources of rents (the expansion of the agricultural frontier and the construction of large dams in association with Argentina and Brazil). The reform process began in the early 1990s within the context of the transition toward democracy but the new polity failed to replace the institutions of the predatory state with new development-friendly institutions. A central proposition of the case study is that successful policy reform in Paraguay has been impeded by the poor quality of the political institutions the country inherited from the old regime. The lack of an effective bureaucracy and the increasing demands of workers, peasants, and civil society during the transition to democracy were additional obstacles. The existing institutions could neither protect the property rights of actual and potential investors and provide political stability, nor ensure that political elites (particularly the Colorado Party) faced effective, formal constraints on their behavior. Neither could these same institutions promote the participation of a broad cross-section of society in either the formal economy or in the political life of the nation. Given the importance of path-dependence, the authors undertake a brief analysis of Paraguay's political history to highlight a set of elements and events that contributed to the failure of institution-building and policy reforms, such as authoritarian personalities, two bloody wars, and a political culture where interpersonal relations based on kinship, friendship, and partisan allegiances prevailed regularly over impersonal relationships, rules, and obligations. The case study illuminates, in this way, the importance of cultural factors and transactions that are governed by rules of the game in the shadow of the law. These factors render the changes in the legal structure immaterial and the reforms ultimately produced a set of mostly dysfunctional institutions. Since the polity also failed to strengthen the legitimacy of the process, it is not surprising that the reforms proved to be unsustainable.

Uruguay

Like Brazil, Uruguay can also be classified as a gradual reform process. The case study covers the extended period of structural reform that has been taking place in Uruguay since democracy was restored in 1985. The authors adopt a wide approach to market reform. The analysis deals not only with the reforms as they have been summarized in the WC, but also with political reform and the consolidation of democracy. The general goal is to understand reform in a broad economic and political sense. The study does not merely assess the reforms implemented, but also tries to understand why the market-friendly reforms moved faster in some areas than in others, who promoted and who opposed reform, and how the political process shaped the reform. One main point that the study highlights is that civil society played a central role; plebiscites approved or rejected specific initiatives, which decisively affected the content and timing of reforms. They also pinpoint that pluralism was a central feature of the polity. Indeed, Uruguay is a paradigm of how political economy variables affect the implementation and sustainability of reforms. The ultimate outcome of such a process is an amalgam of rules of the game corresponding to different regimes. The authorities advanced substantially concerning trade and financial liberalization, but there has been little progress concerning labor markets and privatization because of the stakeholders' opposition. The reform process has also been affected by the country's external vulnerability. As in the case of Brazil, although a left-wing party won the last elections, there have been no reform reversals. The authors conclude that reformists have not won the battle for public opinion in most policy areas in Uruguay. The disappointing economic performance of the country in recent years and Argentina's collapse contributed to discrediting pro-market reforms. However, at the same time, social and political unrest in Uruguay have been very limited during the crisis, and the political system still appears to be strong. The authors conclude that political pluralism explains the puzzle; the institutions provided channels and legal means (plebiscites) for vocal groups to express disagreement. This strengthened political legitimacy. The cases of Brazil and Uruguay suggest that gradualism and pragmatism can reduce the speed and scope of reforms, but can also strongly benefit sustainability.

Venezuela

The study comprises *El Gran Viraje* (The Great Turnaround), an ambitious agenda of macroeconomic and structural reforms led by President Carlos Andrés Pérez during his second presidency (1989–93) and the *Agenda Venezuela*, which was implemented during the Caldera administration in 1996. From the evidence discussed it follows that Venezuela's limited but revealing experience with market-oriented reform can be classified as a failure. The authors state that although Venezuela's failure to reform may be surprising in light of its massive oil revenues, it is not the case once institutional and political economy variables have been taken into account. They stress that oil revenues allowed policy-makers to maintain an 'illusion of harmony' for an extended period of time by financing an increasingly subsidized and distorted economic system managed through an even more complex patronage-based political system. When the government found itself financially unable to prolong this state of affairs in 1989, the public and the polity reacted harshly. Cultural attitudes generate path-dependence and cannot be changed overnight but the Pérez administration did not take this into account and adopted a big-bang shock therapy based on a textbook version of the WC, which generated popular unrest (the Caracazo) and ultimately undermined political stability. The reforms either reversed or stalled during Caldera's government. The current regime, led by Hugo Chavez, has adopted a strong anti-neoliberal stance. One central implication of the research work is that the general failure of the two reform initiatives that took place between 1989 and 1998 illustrates the overriding importance of political, cultural, and institutional constraints in determining the outcomes of the economic reform.

This is in line with the empirical institutional literature. The experience of resource-rich nations with reform indicates that policy-makers in these countries tend to face stronger opposition in their attempts to reform, suggesting that the political economy of resource wealth has a strong and negative effect on institutional development, promoting rent-seeking behavior and generating untenable expectations based on shared beliefs that are difficult to change.

On initial conditions, goals, and outcomes

One main conclusion of the URP (Fanelli and McMahon, 2006b) is that initial conditions and the overall political context are central determinants of the reform path and that this fact contributes to explaining why similar reform packages frequently result in markedly different outcomes. Table 1.1 presents data concerning a set of initial conditions and contextual dimensions that are highlighted in the eight studies: the level of macro volatility; whether a crisis preceded the launching of reforms; the growth performance under the previous international and policy regime; the extent and quality of the integration in the global economy; social disparities; and the characteristics of the polity and the institutional infrastructure.

High volatility was a common feature characterizing the pre-reform scenario. To a certain extent, this is not surprising because macro volatility is a standard trait of developing countries. The literature shows that there is an inverse relationship between the volatility of the growth rate and per capita GDP; likewise, consumption tends to be more volatile than income in poorer countries.[6] It is worth noting, however, that the kind of macro instability described in the case studies is often extreme; for example, Argentina underwent hyperinflation and others were on the brink of it in the 1980s (for example, Brazil). Figures 1.1a and 1.1b show that the countries under analysis can be classified as volatile even if we take developing countries as our standard. The countries in our sample tend to be above the volatility/per capita GDP regression line (Figure 1.1a) and almost all of them display higher consumption than output volatility (Figure 1.1b).

As Table 1.1 shows, sizable crises occur in all cases in the period preceding the implementation of reforms and, in some countries, additional crises transpired during the implementation of the reforms. Chile, the leading reformer, launched the program of structural reforms after the economic breakdown that accompanied the fall of the socialist government in 1973 and had to endure a second period of financial and aggregate turbulence in the early 1980s. The vulnerabilities created by an ill-designed sequencing of market liberalization policies impeded the authorities from insulating Chile from the 'debt crisis'. Indeed the long-lasting recessionary and inflationary consequences triggered by this latter crisis affected the entire region, giving rise to the so-called 'lost decade'.

The studies clearly show that the deep disequilibria of the 1980s created a propitious environment for policy innovation. The Chilean reformers

Table 1.1: On the initial conditions

Country	Macro volatility	Crisis	Growth under BW–ISI regime	Integration with global economy	Social disparities	Polity characteristics
Argentina	Very high	Debt crisis and hyperinflation	Disappointing	Deficient	Moderate, worsening fast	Recovered democracy
Brazil	Very high	Debt crisis and very high inflation	High	Deficient	Very high	Recovered democracy
Chile	Very high	Socialist regime demise and debt crises	Disappointing	Deficient	High	Authoritarian/ recovered democracy
Mexico	High	Debt crisis	Good	Deficient	High	PRI semi-democratic regime
Paraguay	Moderate	Exhaustion of rents (Itaipu effect)	Moderate	Moderate	High	Recovered democracy
Peru	High	Debt crisis	Good	Deficient	High	Recovered democracy
Uruguay	High	Debt crisis and failed liberalization	Disappointing	Deficient	Good, reasonably stable	Recovered democracy
Venezuela	High	Struggle over rents	Moderate	Deficient	High	Democratic regime

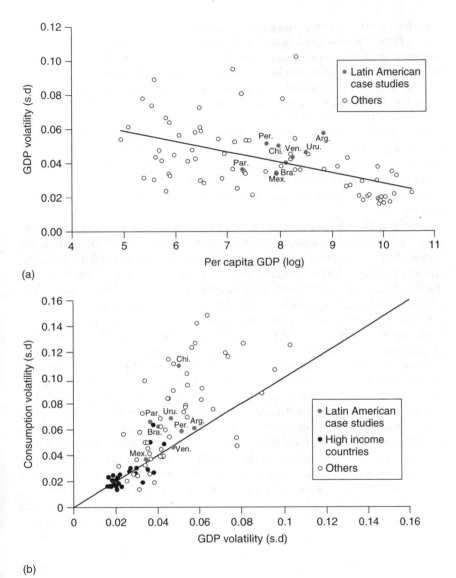

Figure 1.1 (a) GDP volatility and per capita GDP, 1960–2002; (b) Consumption volatility and GDP volatility, 1960–2002
Source: World Development Indicators, World Bank.

introduced significant changes in the reforms that had been implemented in the 1970s while most of the countries under analysis – Argentina, Brazil, Mexico, Peru, and Uruguay – introduced structural reforms as part of the policy efforts to overcome the effects of the debt crisis. The only country that deviates somewhat from this general pattern is Paraguay. The crisis in this case is basically associated with the exhaustion of the sources of rents – the completion of the Itaipu Dam – that had sustained the predatory state. The Venezuelan crisis is also closely associated with struggles over oil rents.

Other relevant commonalities during the pre-reform period are the widespread and systematic inability to exploit the opportunities provided by the international economy, the presence of important social disparities – although the size of these disparities was much lower in Argentina and Uruguay – and the fact that all these countries were undergoing a period of transition from authoritarian polities to democracy when major reforms were launched. The main exception in this regard is Chile, where the reforms were initiated by an authoritarian government, and then deepened substantially by democratic governments.[7]

Growth performance under the previous regime shows much less commonality. The growth data concerning the 1950s, 1960s, and 1970s – when the Bretton Woods (BW) regime and the import-substitution industrialization (ISI) strategy policies ruled – confirm this fact. Table 1.2 indicates that there was a substantial contrast between the remarkably good evolution in Brazil and Mexico, the largest economies in the region, and the exceedingly poor performance in Argentina, Uruguay, and Chile. The differences in the growth rate under the BW–ISI regime were, nonetheless, important for another reason: they created path-dependence. This occurred to the extent that, first, the growth memory influences the public opinion's perceptions of policy options; and second, initial conditions were, *ceteris paribus*, better in those economies that had been growing over a long period. Brazil is a good case in point. The authors highlight that growth success during the BW–ISI favored less orthodox approaches to policy-making and the public bureaucracies associated with the ISI period conserved their effectiveness and were able to contribute to the success of reforms (as is the case of the BNDES participation in the privatization process or the role of the technocracy in Mexico). These path-dependence effects are at the root of the more pragmatic approach to reform in Brazil and gradualism in Mexico. In the case of poorer performers, such as Chile and Argentina, the commitment to 'old' policy views was weaker and, hence, reformers tended to favor approaches more akin to the new WC orthodoxy.

We must take into account, notwithstanding, that independently of evolution during the BW–ISI period, all the countries in our sample went through a period of stagnation or, at least, substantial growth deceleration in the 1980s. The figures corresponding to the 1980s in Table 1.2 are clear in this respect. At the end of the 'lost decade', there was thus a wide consensus that the previous growth strategy was exhausted and that a deep change in the domestic rules of the game would be necessary if the countries were to take advantage of globalization. As the policy and analytic debate on this change unfolded, the proponents of market-oriented reforms tended to prevail. Two experiences played a highly exemplary role in this regard: the 'export-led growth' strategy

Table 1.2: Latin American growth

	Latin America		Argentina		Brazil		Chile		Venezuela	
	GDP	GDP per capita	GDP	GDP per capita	GDP	GDP per capita	GDP	GDP per capita	GDP	GDP per capita
1950/59	4.9	2.1	2.4	0.6	6.5	3.3	3.8	1.5	7.7	3.68
1960/69	5.7	2.8	4.4	2.9	6.2	3.2	4.5	2.2	5.4	1.92
1970/79	5.6	3.1	3.0	1.4	8.6	6.0	2.0	0.3	4.9	0.98
1980/89	1.7	-0.4	-0.6	-2.1	2.9	0.8	3.2	1.6	0.0	-2.55
1990/99	2.8	1.0	4.2	2.9	1.8	0.3	5.4	3.9	2.4	0.12
2000/05	2.6	1.1	1.8	0.8	2.3	0.9	4.3	2.1	2.8	0.66

	Mexico		Uruguay		Paraguay		Peru	
	GDP	GDP per capita	GDP	GDP per capita	GDP	GDP per capita	GDP	GDP per capita
1950/59	5.9	2.9	2.1	0.7	2.3	0.0	4.2	1.9
1960/69	7.1	3.8	1.5	0.7	4.0	1.2	5.4	2.4
1970/79	6.5	3.3	2.3	1.6	7.9	4.7	4.6	2.0
1980/89	2.1	0.0	1.0	0.3	4.0	1.0	0.3	-1.9
1990/99	3.6	1.8	3.2	2.5	2.2	-0.5	3.4	1.6
2000/05	2.6	1.1	0.6	-1.3	1.6	-1.1	3.9	1.8

Source: ECLAC.

of the Asian Tigers and the Chilean success at overcoming volatility and restoring growth after having been severely hit by the debt crisis in the first half of the 1980s.

In sum, except for the remarkably positive fact that democracy was returning to the region, the pre-reform picture was highly discouraging. It is no wonder, then, that the goal of implementing decisive changes in the initial conditions appears at center stage in the reform programs analyzed in the studies. Indeed, the studies indicate that pro-market coalitions prevailed in the political arena because public opinion – or, at least, the leaders who won the elections – perceived that market-oriented reforms were the best instrument to overcome both the sizable macro disequilibria that were being observed in the 1980s and some of the key traditional obstacles to development in LA. More specifically, the debates that preceded the intensification of reform efforts and the evidence in the case studies indicate that structural reforms were intended to:

1. *Reduce aggregate volatility and the frequency of crises.* A number of the WC measures aimed to achieve macro stability.
2. *Improve the degree and quality of the integration with the global economy.* It was central in the diagnosis of the failure of the ISI experience that Latin American countries' trade and capital accounts were too closed and financial markets too repressed.
3. *Accelerate growth.* This would be the consequence of abandoning market-repression in favor of market-friendly policies and institutions (privatization, deregulation, and secure property rights). Specifically, heterodox measures to accelerate growth were banned either explicitly or by default.[8]
4. *Ameliorate social problems.* The redirection of public expenditure towards primary health care, primary education, and infrastructure was the WC's main instrument; the ensuing generations of reforms recognized that specific policies were necessary, especially concerning poverty alleviation and the goal of empowering the poor.
5. *Contribute to strengthening democratic institutions.* This was not in the WC. However, the political discourse more or less suggested that liberal democracy and markets were complementary and the accent of the second-generation blueprint on institutions would naturally include the role of upper-level institutions.
6. *Promote a new market-friendly culture.* Informal institutions were not in the WC, but entered the picture hand-in-hand with the increasing emphasis on the need to reform the formal rules of the economic game. By opening new opportunities, a deregulated environment would change informal cultural patterns, strengthening entrepreneurship and investment and empowering the poor (for example, via land titling).

Given the centrality of these goals on the reform agenda, it is only natural that, for better or worse, public opinion and the political elite's perception of the reforms' degree of success is heavily influenced by the judgment on the degree to which reforms were effective at achieving these goals, although, of course, growth and macro stability have played the most prominent roles in the outcomes versus goals debate.

Although the late 1980s were by no means promising, growth has recovered in the last fifteen years – when major reforms were implemented. This recovery, however, shows four main weaknesses. First, the performance under the newly defined domestic institutional setting is far from impressive when assessed on the basis of the performance of the Latin American economies in the 1950s, 1960s, or 1970s, when the ISI policies and state interventionism were the rule rather than the exception (see Table 1.2). Second, although there are cases of great success (for example, Chile), in several cases the growth processes were unstable and substantial crises occurred (for example, Argentina, Venezuela, Mexico, Uruguay). Third, although these crises were in part associated with failures in international capital markets, the international financial architecture proved to be inefficient at either preventing the occurrence of crisis or at managing its consequences (see Prasad et al., 2004). It is no wonder, consequently, that both domestic and international institutions are being blamed for not helping to recover growth and some authors suggest that there is reform fatigue. Fourth, there was no substantial progress concerning distributional issues and social inclusion. The income distribution indicators show that distribution has not changed much in the last two decades (although it worsened substantially in Argentina), while poverty indicators improved and unemployment worsened (ECLAC, 2006). Social inclusion and poverty have been a problem in LA in the past, and they are still a problem.

To be sure, from the analytical point of view, comparing goals and outcomes is not the best way to determine how instrumental market-friendly reforms were in restoring growth and stability. For one thing, we need to control for the influence of other exogenous variables that impinged on reform results. It is one thing to describe what happened after the initiation of reforms and quite another to attribute the outcomes to specific policy initiatives. One important conclusion of the URP (Fanelli and McMahon, 2006b) is that it is very difficult to identify the policy–outcome linkages. However, although this is somewhat obvious at the academic level, it is not necessarily so at the polity and public-opinion levels. The coalitions supporting Washington Consensus-like policies presented reforms as a way to restore a sustainable growth process and not much effort was devoted to discussing the subtleties of the policy–outcomes linkages. Therefore, even recognizing the difficulties in assessing the policy–outcome linkages, an examination of the degree to which structural constraints have changed in the 'post-treatment' period is relevant from the political economy point of view because citizens have to vote and investors and politicians have to make policy decisions in a world devoid of counterfactuals.[9]

1.3   The problematic side of reforms: implementation, sustainability, and legitimacy

The preceding review reveals four important facts: one, all countries have been able to initiate substantial market-oriented reforms; two, the implementation difficulties were more complex than had been expected; three, the sustainability of the newly-instituted market rules is far from guaranteed in several cases; and four, weak substantive results have produced a certain 'reform fatigue' in the region (Lora et al., 2004) and, as a consequence, the legitimacy of the process is under scrutiny.

Why was it 'easier' than expected to initiate pro-market reforms? The evidence in the studies assigns a critical role to crises and favors the hypothesis that crises beget reforms. The periods of deep macro and financial disequilibria – particularly those associated with the debt crisis – were instrumental in tearing down the political economy equilibrium corresponding to the ISI regime. The transformations in the international scenario also contributed to accelerating institutional changes; in particular, the exchange rate instability and financial deregulation in developed countries and the positive demonstration effect of 'export-oriented' policies in Asia. The ISI policy regime and the postwar shared beliefs about development strategies that had been functional to the BW order became increasingly anachronistic under globalization, which made outward orientation more appealing and weak macro policies more painful. Hence, both the changes in the environment and the endogenous forces associated with the exhaustion of the ISI regime called for institutional changes. While the endogenous evolution of the 'quasi-parameters' defining the ISI political economy ultimately produced a crisis, the characteristics of the changes in the international parameters help to explain why the orientation targeted deregulation and opening.

These developments account for three salient characteristics of reform implementation. First, given that reforms were fostered by macro instability, the bundling of stabilization and structural reforms was the rule rather than the exception in the case of LA. Policy bundling additionally reflected a mounting consensus concerning the fact that achieving macro stability was a requisite to restore sustainable growth. Nevertheless, the studies suggest that policy bundling techniques were not particularly well known. For one thing, in some instances (notably Argentina) policy bundling became an important obstacle to deepening structural reforms because public opinion perceived the failure of stabilization as the failure of the reform package as a whole. This is only natural to the extent that the reformers' rhetoric generally emphasized the importance of bundling structural change and stabilization policies. This rhetoric was not based on a sound knowledge of ways to build institutions under volatile conditions, that is, about ways to sustain structural reforms if the stabilization of the economy were to take longer and demand a greater effort. Indeed, the contrast between the successful Chilean experience and the Argentine and Uruguayan performances in the 1980s suggests that the Chilean positive evolution partly had to do with the ability to keep reforms going even in the face of a crisis, which to a degree resulted from policy mistakes concerning sequencing. Argentina and Uruguay incurred similar sequencing mistakes but were unable to maintain the reform momentum during the lost decade. Second, trade and capital account opening, together with a dramatic relaxation of controls on foreign direct investment, was the first reform implemented and has shown significant progress; the indices of reform progress in trade and liberalization show the best performance (Lora et al., 2004; Forteza and Tommasi, 2006). To be sure, the studies document that the opening occurred at different speeds and reversals have occurred. But the current overall degree of financial and trade openness cannot be compared with the ISI period. The most revealing example in this regard is the significantly higher degree of opening that Mexico and Brazil currently show, two economies that grew substantially during the ISI years. In addition, when reversals did occur, they were mostly temporary and triggered by deep balance of payments crises. Chile in the 1980s is a good case in point. But even Argentina and Uruguay, which underwent sizable crises, were able to sustain an open economy. Third, the progress of external liberalization contrasts with the difficulties on the domestic side of structural reforms. The country studies document numerous cases of delay, stalling, and reversal. Delay is the rule rather than the exception concerning the second-generation proposals for upper-level institutional changes (the judiciary, regulatory bodies), but first-generation reforms such as privatization, tax reforms, the deregulation of financial intermediation, and increasing labor market flexibility also show little progress or sustainability problems.

These facts indicate that political economy factors have been a primary determinant of the observed implementation path to the extent that the content and timing of reforms depended on the way in which the authorities solved the tension between the opposing forces of globalization and pro-market orientation, on the one hand, and political and stakeholders' pressures on the other. Furthermore, the studies document that the characteristics of the policy choices were heavily dependent on the specific features of the constituencies involved and the economic situation. Those reforms that implied substantial political conflict or had strong distributional implications, but were not strictly required to maintain trade and financial opening in the short run or to stabilize the economy, tended to be delayed or stalled, as was the case of labor market reform. In other cases, the authorities could not avoid the implementation of measures with hard distributional consequences. This was typically the case of stabilization programs, which were difficult to postpone because global markets are intolerant of macro disequilibrium. This process eventually led to the emergence of dysfunctionalities between the rules of the game that were effectively implemented in different domains.

One indicator that the implementation difficulties have frequently been severe is that the case studies report that all the countries underwent post-reform crises, although the ability to control the consequences differed significantly. The reforms in Argentina, Venezuela, and Paraguay were the interlude between two macroeconomic crises. In the cases of Chile, Peru, Mexico, Uruguay, and Brazil, on the other hand, the post-reform turbulences did not lead to a collapse. Chile was the only case in which the polity deepened institutional transformations following a post-reform crisis. Indeed, the size of the crisis and the polity's ability to manage the consequences were primary factors in determining the overall sustainability of reforms.

For a reform to be sustainable, two conditions should be met: first, the emerging institutional structure should be robust to (exogenous) changes in the relevant environment; second, the self-enforcing outcomes that the new rules generate should not cause (endogenous) modifications in the parameters that result in the demise of the institution. In light of these conditions, the post-reform institutional outcomes analyzed in the studies can be classified into three categories: sustainable (Chile), weakly sustainable (Uruguay, Peru, Mexico, Brazil), and unsustainable (Argentina, Paraguay, Venezuela).

Both endogenous and exogenous factors were important threats to sustainability. Concerning the latter, two primary sources hindered sustainability. The first was the international economy. The studies document that external vulnerability was important. The Tequila, Asian, and Russian crises severely affected the reform path. In the case of Uruguay and Paraguay, the Brazilian devaluation in 1999 and the Argentine default in 2001 were also key determinants. The second was the democratization of the polity. The changes in the international scenario with the end of the Cold War were functional to democratization because the 'communist threat' ceased to 'legitimize' dictatorships. The process of democratization was the cause of domestic shocks that were exogenous to economic institutions, whose different consequences on reforms depended on the characteristics of the constituencies involved.

As to the endogenous factors that impinged on sustainability, the evidence in the studies suggests that *institutionalization* played a central role. The characteristics of institutionalization were endogenously determined by the interactions between the quality of the blueprint, state effectiveness, and political economy factors. Since these elements differ from country to country, the ultimate outcomes of the process – the instituted rules – show a wide variance and diverse degrees of functionality. In some cases the outcomes were basically in line with expectations, but in others they differed substantially. We have seen that the changes were significant in those areas where the pressure exerted by globalization forces was strong (trade, foreign investment, and financial flows). Conflictive areas, in contrast, show less progress. Therefore, the current institutional frameworks are amalgams of formal and informal institutions corresponding to the old (ISI) and new (market-oriented) regimes – including mutant institutions resulting from reversals – combined in different proportions. The Argentine experience with convertibility is a good illustration of the way in which a dysfunctional institutional structure can undermine sustainability. The Argentine authorities implemented a currency board regime, which is a very effective but extremely rigid strategy to curb high inflation. By prohibiting monetary emission originating in domestic sources, it was assumed that the fiscal deficit would be checked and that the labor market would become more flexible because the currency board was incompatible with a loose fiscal policy and rigid nominal prices. Of course, the downside was that the dysfunctionality between the rigid rules of the currency board and the existing institutions in the fiscal and labor markets led to a macroeconomic breakdown. The important point is, however, that the fiscal and labor formal and informal rules of the game dominated the currency board rules and the macroeconomic crisis spilled over into other domains, making the entire reform attempt unsustainable.

The implementation and sustainability problems documented in the studies show that reformers did not fail to initiate the reforms, but to institutionalize them. Indeed, one key weakness of the market-reform approach was that it conceived of institutionalization as a 'comparative static' rather than a dynamic exercise. The Chilean polity and state bureaucracy have been very effective at institutionalizing the reforms, to the extent that a functional structure of market-friendly institutions emerged from the process. In Mexico and Peru, the new rules of the game have been effectively introduced in many areas, but the functionality of the structure as a whole is not as good as that of Chile. In addition, the transformations in the polity in these two countries also hindered the quality of reforms. In Brazil and Uruguay, the new institutional amalgam includes rules pertaining to both the market-oriented and the older paradigm. Furthermore, in these two countries the path-dependence constraints highlighted by cognitive institutionalists (Denzau and North, 1994) are highly relevant. In Uruguay, deeply-rooted shared beliefs about the role of the state in the economy led to the rejection of reforms in plebiscites that stakeholders had pushed. In Brazil, trade liberalization and privatization did not displace the shared beliefs about the importance of industrial policies inherited from the ISI period. BNDES is a good example of the hybrids that resulted; while BNDES played a significant role in the privatization process, it still allocates a huge amount of credit using non-market criteria. In Paraguay, cognitive path-dependence was also relevant, although the problem lay in the upper-level informal institutional framework. The polity was unable to sustain the new institutions because many of the predatory practices of the previous political regime persisted. On the other hand, even in the cases of overall failure, it is possible to identify areas in which the new rules of the game were effectively introduced. In sum, the evidence indicates that achieving a minimum of functionality is not an easy task and the threat of getting caught in a political-economy trap is always latent.

Public discussion basically overlooked the institutionalization process. To be sure, macroeconomic stability was considered a critical element in guaranteeing reform sustainability and it was stressed that it was central to ensuring budgetary equilibrium, to checking for moral hazard in banking, and to enhancing price flexibility. It was also diagnosed that the roots of these problems were institutional disarrays and, accordingly, a good part of the first and second generation of reforms consisted of blueprints for fiscal accounts (from taxes to privatization), prudential regulation, and labor market flexibility. But surprisingly, no systematic analysis was made of the factors determining institutional change and the sustainability of the rules recommended. In the pre-reform period, the political economy analysis stressed ways to create the conditions (that is, to build a pro-reform coalition) to initiate reforms. The case studies suggest that more attention should be paid to the post-reform political economy.

In view of the problems with institutionalization, it is surprising that the issue is still largely overlooked. Current debates mainly revolve around the substantive (specifically, the growth rate and equity) rather than the institutional output of reforms. Indeed, an evaluation focusing on growth and distributional results is not entirely correct in terms of the market reform's analytical underpinnings. In effect, the WC proposals – especially the second-generation reforms – are based on a procedural rather than a substantive approach to development.[10] In the WC view, implementing the right institutional framework will allow the economy to achieve its highest growth potential; it does not say that such a potential will necessarily be high or equitable. Hence, reforms should in the first place be assessed by their effectiveness at institutionalizing the correct rules of the game.

Is the current emphasis on outcomes rather than rules misleading? This conclusion is difficult to sustain. To begin with, the reformers' political discourse emphasized that the new policies would stabilize the economy, accelerate growth, and alleviate poverty. It was of course easier to transmit a message based on expected substantive results to the relevant constituency. It was clearer to public opinion what growth and lower inflation meant than what 'successful' institutional change was. There is, however, an additional difficulty: the proponents of the WC did not explicitly state at the analytical level how the degree of success of institutional changes should be assessed. For example, it is unclear whether the occurrence of an exogenous shock, say, the Russian crisis, can justify discouraging results. Ex ante, reformers had stressed that the changes in the rules of the game would make the economy more resilient to shocks. But they did not specify ex ante what kind or size of shock we should expect to be 'filtered' by the more resilient rules and policies implemented and what kind or size of shock we should not. This was a central issue concerning the assessment of the performance of several Latin American economies after the 1998 Russian crisis, which gave rise to a period of high instability and stagnation. And finally, reforms coincided with democratization, a period in which various segments of the population gained the right to voice their demands. One central requisite for democracy to gain legitimacy was precisely to show that it would effectively strike a balance between contradictory demands without jeopardizing stability and growth. In this critical historical juncture, the choice of the rules of the economic game was to a large extent perceived as the choice of a regime that could match the needs for legitimacy of the new democracies. This is another reason why substantive growth and distributional outcomes mattered to reforms. In many of the instances analyzed in the studies, the reforms' outcomes far from fulfilled the new democracy's need to strengthen legitimacy. When the outcomes did fulfill such requirements, as in the case of Chile, institutionalization was successful.

In sum, why did the results of Latin American reforms vary so widely across countries if they were based on similar blueprints? The studies suggest the hypothesis that this was due to the fact that the blueprint had to become institutionalized and that institutionalization is embedded not only in the realm of the economy, but also in society and the polity. Hence, the blueprint mattered, but the idiosyncratic features of the constituency mattered too. Indeed, sustaining reforms may have been harder than initiating them because too much emphasis had been placed on the efficiency-enhancing properties of market institutions and too little on the process by which a blueprint becomes a functioning institution that is legitimately enforced by the polity. It can be argued, then, that no one-size-fits-all blueprint exists that can work independently of the context.

1.4   Conclusions and policy implications

Chile is the only case that can undoubtedly be classified as a reform success. The other cases show that reforms have only partially achieved the desired goals (Mexico, Peru, Uruguay, and Brazil) or resulted in outright failure (Argentina, Paraguay, and Venezuela). For reforms to deliver their expected outcomes, several observers currently argue that it would be necessary to deepen and complete the process based on a second-generation (or even third-generation) blueprint aimed at improving the rules of the game in various areas. The basic hypothesis is that the disappointing outcomes are associated with poor institutional frameworks. Other researchers who have been following the process closely, however, are not optimistic about the possibility of deepening reforms in the future because of 'reform fatigue' affecting both public opinion at large and all the major players in the game of economic reform (Lora et al., 2004). Reform fatigue is defined as the lack of public support, the loss of confidence in the benefits of pro-market reforms, and/or a less proactive stance towards reforms. After assessing several hypotheses that can account for reform fatigue, Lora et al. conclude that the increased rejection of reforms is associated with growth slowdowns in many countries in the region and that an eventual recovery would not facilitate the re-initiation of the process because of two obstacles: first, the fragmentation of the political system, partly resulting from the reform process; second, public opinion's negative perception of the market-oriented reform strategy.

These views well reflect the current disenchantment with the outcomes of 'market-oriented' reforms in LA but are of little help concerning policy guidance. The second-generation reform agenda is institution-building intensive. Although LA institutions undoubtedly present important flaws, the remedy is somewhat paradoxical in light of the evidence. If the existing polities were unable to create a suitable environment for the (simpler) first generation of reforms, why would they be able to institutionalize new and sophisticated rules of the economic game? This view tends to overlook the 'technical' complexities of institutionalization that we pinpointed – crises, an amalgam of institutions of different vintages creating dysfunctionality – and the political economy constraints on reforms, such as state capture, clientelism, or the existence of patrimonialistic polities. In fact, the second-generation agenda more or less implicitly assumes the existence of a benevolent 'institutionalizer' and therefore leaves the political economy question unsettled. The reform fatigue diagnosis does take into account political economy variables in explaining why reforms have stalled. However, it falls short of fully characterizing the fatigue situation from the analytical point of view. Lora et al. (2004) state that the region was caught up in a low-growth equilibrium trap but the analysis is not particularly informative about how this situation evolved. It is necessary to develop hypotheses as to what exogenous/endogenous forces could break this equilibrium, and what policy initiatives could help the authorities to overcome the trap and restore a growth process that public opinion considers legitimate.

We believe that the reform fatigue equilibrium will not persist and that the present reform hiatus reflects the search of Latin American leaders and public opinion for new strategies that can sustain a new coalition in the polity domain. The way in which the fatigue equilibrium will evolve towards the next stage, however, is not irrelevant to the goals and policies to be adopted. One way in which the status quo can change is via a period of crisis. As we have seen, crises are double-edged swords. They open windows of opportunity not only for better policies but also for political opportunism. In addition, crises have path-dependence effects that can hinder institutionalization. So, if the low-growth equilibrium is displaced by a sizable crisis, it will become more difficult to anticipate the content of the new strategies. For example, there could be a significant reversal in the reforms, as in the case of Venezuela. An alternative to overcoming the fatigue equilibrium is to reform the reforms without generating a crisis. In any case, the first necessary step to definitively supersede the status quo is to find a strategy to accelerate growth and to persuade the relevant constituencies that the structural obstacles to sustainable growth will be effectively addressed. The successful Chilean evolution indicates, however, that no precise and detailed blueprint exists for the transition towards sustainable growth. The path is largely context-specific, uncertain, and very demanding in terms of collective action at different levels.

On the basis of the evidence provided by the case studies, we can draw some lessons that may be useful to policy design. More specifically, it follows from the evidence discussed that the way out of the status quo requires policy-makers:

(a) To accelerate growth, taking into account the distinction between initiating and sustaining growth.
(b) To design context-informed policies.
(c) To establish economic institutions that are both growth-friendly and functional with respect to other components of the pre-existing institutional structure.
(d) To ensure the political legitimacy of the process.

Point (a) highlights the need to accelerate growth in the sense of Rodrik (2005). The reforms have largely failed in doing so. Although the growth rate of the last fifteen years has exceeded the growth rate during the lost decade of the 1980s, the reforms were as a rule unable to accelerate growth. On average, the post-reform observed growth rate has been lower than the pre-lost decade period. A closely associated and disappointing fact is that traditional obstacles to sustained growth in Latin America, such as a markedly skewed income distribution, sluggish productivity growth, or external vulnerability were unaffected. The studies indicate that Chile is the only country in which substantially higher growth resulted from reforms. In the other seven countries the periods of growth were short and followed by substantial decelerations and, in some cases, by sizable crises. To be sure, it would be wrong to ignore the influence of variables other than domestic reforms on growth. Volatile financial markets, in particular, characterized the international scenario, and the developed countries' protectionist stance showed a bias against products in which the region enjoys comparative advantages, such as agricultural products. We should not overlook, nonetheless, that reforms were expected to create a flexible economy that would not only take advantage of globalization's opportunities but would also become more resilient to external shocks. Chilean reformers – and to a certain extent the reformers in the countries classified as weakly sustainable – performed better, even though they have also had to deal with the globalization hazards.

According to Rodrik (2005) growth accelerations are feasible with minimal institutional change, while the deeper and more extensive institutional reforms required for long-term convergence take time to implement and mature. It seems that Latin American countries still need to find a way to strike a balance between 'heterodox' means to accelerate growth and ways to ensure the institutionalization of the rules of the game to procure sustained long-run growth. The analysis of the economic policies to initiate growth is not the goal of this book, which focuses on institutional change. But we do want to emphasize two points: first, the acceleration of growth is central to ensuring the political legitimacy of any process of institutional change; second, the measures specifically oriented to ignite and accelerate growth should take into account the sizable experience accumulated during both the ISI and the market-reform periods in LA. One important fact to consider is that the details of the Latin American institutional and political economy context matter for any type of policy. The evidence in this book suggests that the Chilean specific advantage – and that of other successful reformers (see Fanelli and McMahon, 2006b) – has had primarily to do with the ability to manage the process of institutionalization and with strengthening the political legitimacy of the process.

Point (b) on designing context-informed policies calls attention precisely to the role of contextual factors. Fanelli and McMahon (2006b) summarize and discuss the elements of the context that have typically influenced the reform path in the 31 countries covered by the URP. Here, we would like to pinpoint the role of four phenomena that repeatedly appear in the LA studies and are important in explaining why expected outcomes have frequently departed from the blueprint's path: crises, structural changes, macro volatility, and distributional tensions. More specifically:

- *All reform experiences were preceded by sizable crises and crises also occurred as part of the reform processes.*   The crises examined in the case studies illustrate how they often open Pandora's Box. They often destroy existing institutions, induce important wealth redistribution, increase macro volatility and, as a consequence, exacerbate income struggles and make way for political opportunism. The occurrence of a crisis in the post-implementation period should be conceived of as one of the largest downside risks of reform attempts. The policy implication is straightforward: it is important to assess the probability that a certain reform path leads to a crisis. Reformers should ideally perform exercises along the lines of the value-at-risk exercises that bank risk-managers perform routinely. To be sure, we do not know what the precise characteristics of the stochastic process generating crises are, but we need to develop methods to evaluate the downside risks of reforms.
- *Structural changes were sizable and created substantial disequilibria during the reform stage.*   Permanent shocks were associated with three primary sources: globalization, the transformation of the post-World War II institutions inherited from the ISI period, and the democratization of the polity. These sources of shocks will likely persist. Globalization will continue to be a source of exogenous shocks to which domestic institutional structures will have to adapt. Likewise, democracy is far from settled in the region and the upper-level institutions of the polity will be a source of both negative and positive shocks affecting the rules of the economic game.
- *By international standards, Latin American countries are highly volatile.* Although some variables, such as inflation, have shown a downward trend

and macro policies are now more orthodox, this structural feature has not disappeared; consumption, investment, and income continue to show high variance. With the exception of Chile, the reforms did not substantially reduce volatility. Hence, macro volatility will remain at center stage. The methods to initiate and to sustain growth – which call for institutional deepening – must be robust to aggregate volatility. Beyond the effects on economic incentives and financial intermediation (which are not the focus of our analysis) we must take into account that volatility hinders the institution-building ability. It hinders the willingness to cooperate in that it shortens the horizon for decision-making and exacerbates income struggles.

- *Distributional struggles were a source of tension during the reform process.* This is no wonder given that the pre-existing highly unequal income distribution has shown no weakening as a consequence of reforms and the changes in the rules of the game per se have generated winners and losers.

The channels through which these elements have influenced the reform path vary across countries and from one stage of the reform to another. Indeed, one important contribution of the country studies has been the detail and analyses they have provided with respect to the way in which policy-makers and the polity managed unexpected developments. Beyond diversity, however, the evidence indicates that these four elements will continue to play a major role in Latin America, even if it is also likely that their relative significance will change as reforms evolve. For example, we expect that the more successful the initiation of growth and institutionalization, the less important the risks of crises and macro volatility will be; but structural changes will still be important, as will distributional tensions. Hence, if reforms are exercises in building sustainable institutions, it is critical to take into account the constraints that these four elements pose to institutionalization strategies.

Point (c) on growth-friendly and functional institutions underscores how important the degree of functional compatibility is between the rules of the economic game and the different segments of the overall institutional framework. The overall framework that resulted in most of the countries is an amalgam of old (ISI) and new (market-oriented) – formal and informal – rules of the game. This amalgam is highly idiosyncratic. In each country it resulted from the implementation of (mostly first-generation) reforms, specific initial conditions, 'exogenous' forces – the pressure of globalization, idiosyncratic external shocks, democratization – and the outcomes of distributional conflicts that occurred in the process. It is not surprising, then, that in several cases the emerging structure was dysfunctional and did not produce the expected policy and economic outcomes. The studies provide a wealth of illustrations about the dysfunctional outcomes produced by: (i) financial liberalization within a context of weak supervision and volatile capital flows (Chile, Uruguay, Argentina); (ii) exchange rate regimes that are inconsistent with price rigidities and the political economy of the fiscal accounts (the Argentine currency board); (iii) price liberalization that triggered distributional effects that could not be handled by the institutions that were meant to manage distributional conflicts (the Caracazo); and (iv) privatizations that fed market power because they preceded the establishment of suitable regulatory bodies (repeatedly documented in various LA countries).

A set of rules designed to induce Pareto optimality may be dysfunctional with respect to other domains (that is, cultural legacies, legal traditions, macro instability) or the resulting equilibrium can be considered unjust and therefore illegitimate. This indicates that there can exist relevant trade-offs between economic efficiency, political legitimacy, and overall functionality that the polity must assess. Likewise, it is likely that growth acceleration and the amendment of undesired outcomes produced by a dysfunctional institutional structure will call for discretional policy decisions (such as the establishment of a highly competitive exchange rate or capital controls in Chile). It follows that policy-makers must be empowered with some degree of discretion to change the outcomes so as to ensure that a given function is performed and the overall functioning of institutions is ultimately growth-friendly. This means that one central role of the polity during the institutionalization process will be, precisely, to define the boundaries within which policy-makers can exert constrained discretion. Of course, to pose constraints on discretion and isolate the authorities from rent-seekers and patrimonialistic and clientelistic politicians is a daunting challenge.

This is a challenge that few polities have faced successfully. But it is inevitable. The experiences covered in this book show that the first generation of reforms attempted to widen the room for rules (rather than discretion) and was also highly vulnerable to opportunistic politics and rent-seeking. Indeed, the experience of unsustainable and weakly sustainable countries suggests that an improper assessment was made of the downside risks entailed by some reforms that were being implemented within a context in which structural changes could introduce dysfunctional elements. It seems that managing reforms calls for a risk management approach in line with the principles successfully adopted in other policy areas. For example, in managing monetary policy, 'The risk-management approach has gained greater traction as a consequence of the step-up in globalization and the technological changes of the 1990s, which found us adjusting to events without the comfort of relevant history to guide us' (Greenspan, 2005: 3).

Point (d) stresses the political legitimacy of the process. The authors of the Chilean study emphasize that one of the reasons for Chile's success lay in the polity's ability for consensus-building, especially after democracy was recovered. They also state that the process was facilitated by the substantial acceleration of growth. This second point suggests that achieving positive results at an early stage is central, independently of whether the 'best' rules of the game have already been implemented. The Chinese experience with reforms is a good case in point (Fanelli and McMahon, 2006b), but there are good illustrations in the Latin American cases too. The authors of the Brazilian and Argentine studies stress that in these highly volatile countries, the achievement of rapid results concerning inflation was instrumental for the first reforms that Cardozo and Menem implemented to gain momentum and legitimacy. In addition to growth and macro stability, rapid advances concerning poverty alleviation and social inclusion may also have contributed to legitimizing a subsequent process of institutional deepening.

The rapid initiation of a growth process is important for another reason. In a highly volatile and thus uncertain context, the materialization of 'good' states of nature has informative content for the public opinion in general. Positive results are tangible signals that the benefits are worth the effort; in addition, given that there can be multiple equilibria with very different distributional implications, results that improve the situation of a broad cross-section of society signal that the power elite is not redefining the rules of the game in its favor, as was the case with state capture and the patrimonialistic and predatory states.

We have emphasized the importance of some phenomena, such as structural shocks, volatility, and distributional consequences. However, even in more stable countries, prudent policy-makers keep these factors in check. Reflecting on monetary policies, Greenspan (2005: 3) makes this point clearly:

> Given our inevitably incomplete knowledge about key structural aspects of an ever-changing economy and the sometimes asymmetric costs or benefits of particular outcomes, the paradigm on which we have settled has come to involve, at its core, crucial elements of risk management. In this approach, a central bank needs to consider not only the most likely future path for the economy but also the distribution of possible outcomes about that path. The decision makers then need to reach a judgment about the probabilities, costs, and benefits of various possible outcomes under alternative choices for policy.

In sum, the challenges posed by the current 'reform fatigue' bring the issue of procedural versus substantive approaches to development to the fore. To a certain extent, the Chilean success can be interpreted as the product of a remarkable ability to strike the balance between the substantive and procedural approaches and between the sometimes contrary short-run requirements of growth acceleration and pro-growth institutionalization. If a new pro-development coalition that can overcome the 'reform fatigue' trap takes shape in the region, we believe that it will likely combine the substantive and procedural approaches to development, and policy-makers will likely adopt constrained discretion to manage the risk originating in reforms and globalization hazards. Yet, it is unlikely that any reform attempt be successful if, as Sen (2004) has emphasized, the main legitimizing question cannot be answered: Why reform? In the case of Latin America, one can safely say that most agree on the answer: to overcome underdevelopment.

Notes

1. The project was developed and first organized by the Global Development Network (GDN) with funding from the World Bank, the Government of Italy, and the Government of Austria. It was coordinated by the Center for the Study of State and Society (CEDES), Buenos Aires, and GDN. This book is highly complementary to the other volumes containing the results of the project that Palgrave has been publishing; see Fanelli and McMahon (2005a, 2006a).
2. Two recent papers that well illustrate the analytical issues at stake and public opinion as reflected in Latinobarómetro are Lora et al. (2004) and Panizza and Yañez (2006); see also Forteza and Tommasi (2006).
3. On hierarchies, domains, and institutions, see Aoki (2001), Dixit (2004), and Tommasi (2002).
4. To answer the question of why and how institutions change, two questions are central according to Greif and Laitin (2004): How does an institution persist in a changing environment? How do processes that it unleashes lead to its own demise? On institutional change, also see Aoki (2001) and Denzau and North (1994).
5. On the Washington Consensus, see Williamson (1990) and the discussion in Fanelli and Popov (2005).
6. On the stylized facts concerning the volatility of developing countries, see Aizenman and Pinto (2004).
7. It should also be mentioned that military governments, in the mid-1970s, also launched the first market liberalization attempts in Argentina and Uruguay.
8. There is, however, a somewhat intriguing reference to the need for a 'competitive' exchange rate in the WC.
9. On the role of counterfactuals in political and institutional analysis, see Przeworski (2004).
10. This distinction is based on Fanelli and Popov (2005). According to these authors, the approaches to development can be classified into two categories, substantive approaches (SA) and procedural approaches (PA). A reformer sustaining SA will tend to specify the substantive goals to be achieved by reform (that is, a given reduction in poverty, certain types of technological upgrade, a minimum growth rate) and, hence, the results of the reform could, in principle, be assessed on such a basis. A reformer adopting PA, in contrast, will focus on building and improving the rules of the game. The SA emphasizes the final destination of the journey toward development; the PA focuses on the construction and improvement of the tracks that are supposed to lead the economy toward the best economic outcome.

2
Understanding Reform: the Case of Argentina

Carlos H. Acuña, Sebastián Galiani, and Mariano Tommasi

2.1 Introduction

Throughout the 1990s Argentina underwent a very intense process of transformation of some of its policies and economic institutions, constituting until fairly recently the 'poster child' for the implementation of what is known as the Washington Consensus. Yet, more than a decade later, the experiment reached an inflection point, under the effects of a dramatic economic, social, and political crisis. It is nowadays common to hear critics of the so-called 'pro-market reforms' refer to the Argentine case as irrefutable evidence that such reforms lead to disastrous outcomes not only in terms of inequality and exclusion, but also in terms of aggregate economic performance.

The Argentine case presents an important analytical challenge in order to distill lessons about the interactions of economics and politics, and about the interactions of internationally construed reform packages with the idiosyncrasies of domestic political institutions, political practices, and historical heritages. This chapter is one attempt to deal with that challenge.[1]

The reform-cum-convertibility process achieved some spectacular macroeconomic results in the early part of the 1990s. We are still watching the unfolding of the post-convertibility economic and political dynamics. It is too early to have very set conclusions about the 'final outcome' of the reform process. Our very tentative reading of the Argentine reform experience is as follows.

We conjecture that several areas of reform (such as trade liberalization and some transformations of the structure of the public sector) are likely to remain broadly in place. On the other hand, the very negative reading of the reform experience that seems dominant in public opinion and political discourse suggest the potential for (at least partial) reversions in some areas.

Beyond the broad strokes of what was done and not done, what might stay and what might be reversed, we believe that some aspects of the reform policies were colored and shaped by historical and permanent characteristics of the Argentine polity. A history of ill-resolved distributional conflicts and macroeconomic mismanagement, as well as some characteristics of the political system and policy-making process, cast a long shadow on the policies and outcomes of the period. Indeed, there are some examples in the Argentine reform experiences in which reforms following the standard recipe did not lead to the desired behavioral outcomes because of a lack of deeper institutions.

In the real economy, the reforms of the 1990s have left a modernized productive structure, with substantial heterogeneity. Some firms have been able to bring their operations closer to the international frontier; there has been substantial product and process innovation throughout the decade; and there was a huge increase in exports even under a severe exchange rate appreciation. Nowadays, economic and (to a lesser extent) social indicators show recovery from the crisis. Yet, many relevant economic actors are still following a wait-and-see strategy, and the credibility necessary for adequate intertemporal behavior is not there yet. Also, poverty and income inequality are quite high compared to Argentine historical standards.

The chapter is organized as follows. Section 2.2, 'The political economy of reforms in Argentina', constitutes the core of the chapter from the point of view of the comparative project. It aims at answering *why, by whom* and *how* reforms were made for the Argentine case. It contains a synthesis of the historical politico-economic background that led to reforms (*why . . .*); an analysis of the options, motivations, and understanding that lay behind the strategic decision and design of the reforms (*who . . .*); and an explanation of the logic that characterized the implementation of reforms, paying particular attention to (a) the way reforms were presented and legitimized vis-à-vis society and markets, (b) the politico-institutional resources that made the reforms possible, and (c) the political steering of the reforms through building coalitions and neutralizing the opposition within the complex realm of political and economic actors affected by the reform process (*how . . .*). Section 2.3 describes some of the main economic and social outcomes of the reform decade. Section 2.4 provides some parting thoughts.

2.2 The political economy of reforms in Argentina

2.2.1 Background: the road to structural reforms

Even though Argentina grew at a reasonable rate up to 1974, the overall performance of the economy during the import-substitution industrialization (ISI) period was disappointing when put in comparative perspective. As predicted by notions of growth convergence, other poorer Latin American countries were catching up with Argentina. However, Argentina was diverging from more developed countries such as Australia, Canada and the United States, to mention just a few (see Figure 2.1).

In the post-World War II period Argentina adopted an extreme version of the ISI model. Industrialization was promoted using the whole set of ISI instruments. First, the relation between internal and external prices was distorted to protect the

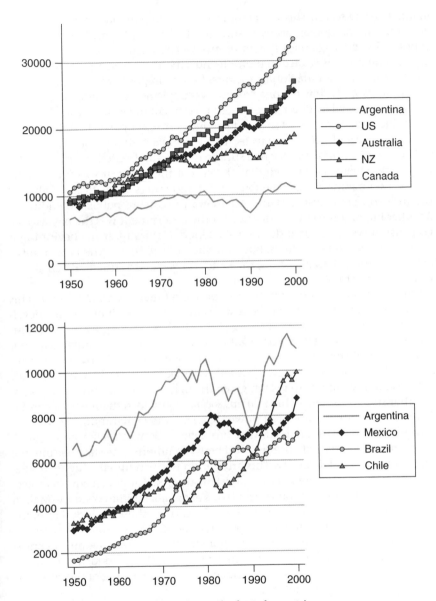

Figure 2.1 GDP per capita, Argentina and selected countries
Note: Series in 1996 PPP-adjusted dollars.
Source: Penn World Tables, 6.1.

manufacturing sector. This was achieved by building up protectionist barriers via tariffs, import quotas, licenses, and prohibitions, and by taxing agricultural exports. Second, a complex system of investment incentives (via subsidies and tax exemptions) was created to promote industry. There were several reimbursement regimes for non-traditional exports. Certain imports were exempted from paying tariffs, and a 'buy national' regime was implemented. Third, industrialization was promoted by direct government investment in key industries. User fees for utilities were normally set so as to favor industrialization. Finally, interest rates were regulated and credit was directed to the manufacturing sector.

The Argentine public sector had suffered a structural deficit since the 1930s. Up to the hyperinflation period at the end of the 1980s, it was financed by diverse non-traditional revenue sources. Inflation was systematically high, and the inflation tax played a significant role in financing public expenditures. Another important source of finance for the government was the pay-as-you-go pension system created during this period. Naturally, at the beginning it operated under large surpluses. But from the mid-1970s on, when the number of retired workers began to grow, the system developed a structural deficit that worsened over time.

Strong oligopolies arose within the protected manufacturing sector. This development and the importance of state enterprises contributed to the development of powerful unions. During the 1940s, pro-labor governments also favored unions and established a legal system of collective and individual labor legislation. Only one union per economic sector is granted the right to bargain collective agreements and these are legally extended to all workers in that sector of the economy. Unions were later given the right to administrate the workers' health insurance system, which ('*obras sociales*') provided them with a considerable and enduring amount of power (Galiani and Gerchunoff, 2003).

A permanent distributive conflict broke out – between labor and capital, between urban and rural business, and between unions. The state became the arbiter of a conflictive society. This arbitration role was initially highly discretional. Thus, every sector tried to establish institutional arrangements to protect their own real incomes, introducing all sorts of rigidities in the economy (Mallon and Sourrouille, 1975; O'Donnell, 1977). Over time, these protected interests evolved into powerful interest groups that opposed any substantial change in the economic system. Even when this system led to severe economic inconsistencies, it was politically very hard to change. It took a long protracted economic decline and a number of crises, ending in a complete collapse of the currency, to generate the space for reform.

Import substitution led to rapid development of the industrial sector, but exports did not expand much, and over time this was at the core of the economic stagnation that marked the eventual collapse of that development model. The imports to GDP ratio contracted continuously until it reached a point at which further decline was not possible (see Figure 2.2). At this point, the country was extremely vulnerable to external shocks.

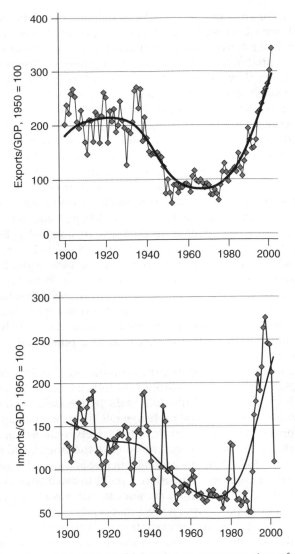

Figure 2.2 Exports and imports to GDP ratios at constant prices of 1986 indexes (1950 = 100)

Notes: GDP, exports and imports at constant prices of 1986. Index ratios equal 100 in 1950.

Source: Author's calculations based on data provided by ECLAC (Economic Commission for Latin America and the Caribbean).

After the dollar crisis in 1969, fundamental changes in the international context made the ISI–state-led strategy of development obsolete. In addition to the fast growth of international trade that started at the end of World War II, financial and productive globalization strengthened. However, no Latin American country showed much ability to adapt to this new reality.

A populist experiment (under President Perón and then his wife) in the early 1970s ended up in economic and political disorder. A top-down disciplinarian military experiment replaced it. The main objective of economic policy was to reduce inflation. This required eliminating the fiscal deficit (only partially accomplished) and getting rid of wage pressures. A market-oriented program with financial and trade liberalization was implemented. The government attempted to discipline unions (collective bargaining and other union rights were suppressed) and businessmen (through trade liberalization). Over time, both inflation inertia and prevalence of fiscal deficits made the exchange rate system (of pre-announced gradual devaluations) unsustainable. Between 1979 and 1981 capital flight amounted to around 20 per cent of GDP, leaving the government (which had absorbed private sector external debt) with a hefty external debt that has conditioned the country's economic performance ever since.

After taking over from the military government in 1983, President Alfonsín's constitutional government faced the triple threat of coping with mounting external debt arrears, confronting military upheavals related to human rights violations, and responding to the demands of a population that had just achieved political freedom.[2]

An important attempt to stabilize the economy was implemented in 1985, the Austral Plan. This was an attempt to combine an orthodox attack on the fundamentals (primarily the elimination of the budget deficit and its monetary financing) with a wage, price, and exchange-rate freeze (after an up-front devaluation). All prices, except those in flexible markets, were frozen at their pre-program levels. A new currency was introduced, the austral, and the currency was pegged to the dollar. Wages were set by decree at a level that gave compensation for the previous month's inflation. Finally, to avoid large wealth redistributions due to the fall of inflation, a currency reform was announced to correct the nominal value of pre-contracted payments.

Despite its initial success, the program faced several problems. Residual inflation triggered a rapid drift in wages. Just a year after its implementation, price controls were relaxed, unions were allowed to negotiate wages, and a crawling peg on the exchange rate and public-sector prices was reintroduced. More importantly, fiscal policies were not based on solid instruments and the fiscal correction proved to be transitory.

Yet another attempt to stabilize by pegging the currency to the dollar failed at the end of Alfonsín's government. This time, a massive portfolio shift toward the dollar brought about a devastating hyperinflationary process that caused the anticipated transfer of power from Alfonsín to the Peronist president-elect.[3] Throughout the 1980s the Argentine economy showed its worst performance in the post-World War II period (see Figure 2.3). Investment and savings collapsed. Per capita GDP decreased approximately 20 per cent between 1980 and 1989. Inflation was above 100 per cent every year except 1986. Both the external debt and the debt to exports ratio rose at an ominous pace (see Figure 2.3). The dollarization of the economy deepened, increasing the

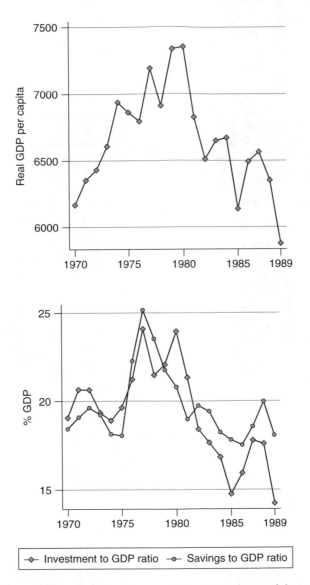

Figure 2.3   The performance of the economy before the reforms of the early 1990s
Source: Author's elaboration based on Gerchunoff and Llach (2003) and ECLAC.

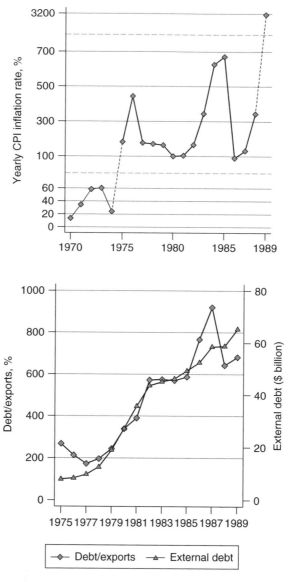

Figure 2.3   (*Continued*)

financial fragility of the economy. Finally, with maxi-devaluations and dispro-portionate increases in public prices, the high inflation regime moved towards hyperinflation.

Stabilization was imperative. When a society has reached this extreme, the alternatives become stark ('stabilize or else'), although not necessarily easy to decide, let alone instrument, as the rest of the chapter shows. Yet, it is true that the severity of the crises provided for a critical turning point. Contrary to the scenario faced by Alfonsín, Menem had more political breathing space but fewer degrees of freedom to define a course of action.

Thus, it was only after a brutal hyperinflation episode that a comprehensive response to the 'slow agony of Peronist Argentina' was formulated. This is how hyperinflation became the inflection point of a long period of deterioration of the old order, and stabilization was the cornerstone of the process of reform design (Palermo and Novaro, 1996).

2.2.2   Menem and the reforms

It was the Peronist government of President Menem which undertook a process of market-oriented reforms whose speed and breadth of process led Argentina to become the poster child of the Washington establishment throughout the 1990s. Menem himself and his party were seen at the time as unlikely charac-ters to undertake market-oriented reforms. In the words of Rodrik (1993: 356): '[i]t is ironic that these reforms were instituted under a Peronist president, Carlos Menem, since Peronism has been virtually synonymous with populism and protectionism. Within a year, Argentine reforms had already gone further than those adopted over a period of decades in the outward-oriented East Asian countries, which long served as the example of choice for countries like Argentina.' Menem's conversion was a surprise not only when measured against historical expectations but also when measured against his (vague but nonethe-less populist) campaign statements. Stokes (2001) provides a thorough analysis of the conditions leading to such a difference between campaign statements and policies. In a nutshell, Menem and his entourage had come to recognize that market-oriented reforms were the best bet against the ongoing economic disas-ter, yet they thought they would lose the election if they announced this during the campaign.[4]

On entering office in 1989, the government initiated ambitious programs of privatization and trade liberalization. Structural reforms were bundled with stabilization measures, and policy decisions on several fronts were taken with an eye to their impact on short-term fiscal needs. Additionally, due to the reputation of the Peronist party, the government had to send signals of com-mitment to the reformist course, which was attempted by undertaking a speedy and simultaneous pattern of reform on several fronts.[5]

Despite those efforts, stabilization during the initial period failed, resulting in renewed inflationary episodes in 1990, and the resignation of two ministers of the economy. The Convertibility Plan of 1991 marks the beginning of the most important stage of reform, which included monetary reform, fiscal reform (simplification of the tax system and strengthening of the tax collection agency), liberalization of domestic and external markets, and strengthening of the privatization program. The appointment of Domingo Cavallo (and his team) in the Ministry of the Economy brought renewed unity and coherence to the reform effort. Figure 2.4 presents our reading of the intensity of reform by area from 1988 to 1998.

Macroeconomic stability and economic growth were the immediate results of these measures. The hard peg-based stabilization, together with the reappearance of credit, led to a consumption boom, which was important in gaining popular approval of the new course. At the same time that the economy began to grow, traditional public funds manipulation for electoral purposes reappeared. The fragility of the reform efforts became evident in 1994 when the Tequila Crisis hit. At that point, a renewed sense of crisis gave room for the last bout of structural reforms of the Menem administration, which included some poorly-designed attempts to increase the flexibility of the labor market, as well as the privatization of some provincial banks and companies. Interestingly, fear of economic instability helped Menem to get re-elected in 1995; the notion being that the president and his team were the best pilots in stormy economic waters.[6]

The second Menem administration (1995–99) while maintaining the reform rhetoric did not make any substantial additional progress, as evidenced in Figure 2.4. We believe that this deceleration was due to the fact that the 'next frontier' required confronting the core of the coalition that enabled the previous

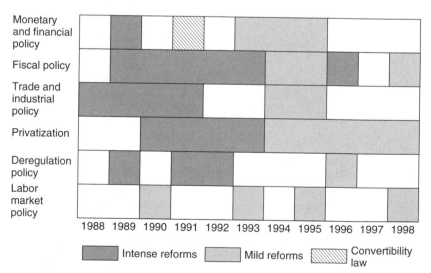

Figure 2.4   Intensity of reforms by area

set of reforms. The reforms put in place, even though implying a substantial achievement by Argentine standards, fell short of the Washington Consensus benchmark. The general picture was the co-existence of some important changes in economic incentives with the persistence of illiberal enclaves, scarce improvements at the provincial level, of fairly monopolistic and inefficient structures in some markets (such as health), and weak regulation of some of the privatized sectors.

2.2.3 The reform decision within the executive

A successful reform requires the emergence of a pro-reform actor within the government, who in turn needs to mobilize support (resolving collective action problems), and to neutralize opposition. All of these steps are conditioned by historical circumstances and by the institutional framework in which they take place.

The crisis experienced by Argentina towards the end of the 1980s forced the president to embark on actions leading to economic stabilization, a collective good whose relative importance rose in this context.[7] As the only political actor in the Argentine institutional framework elected by a nationwide constituency, the National Executive is the institutional actor with more encompassing interests, and hence the actor most likely to initiate such reforms. But why did Menem embark on such a reform process?

The literature on structural reforms has pointed out the relevance of socio-economic crisis in bringing about the conditions that in some polities might increase the feasibility of structural reform. The Argentine case seems to confirm this assumption. The Peronist leadership, an unlikely actor to lead pro-market structural reforms, concluded just before taking office that, given the nature and intensity of the Argentine socio-economic crisis at that time (1989), it had no choice but to embark on a deep pro-market process of reform (Acuña, 1995a; Palermo and Novaro, 1996).[8]

Structural reforms in Argentina appeared primarily as an instrument for the stabilization of an unwieldy macroeconomic situation. Before coming back to the politics of reform in Section 2.2.5, we devote the next section to discussing the economic logic of the decision to bundle a particular stabilization mechanism with a package of market-oriented reforms.[9]

2.2.4 Structural reforms as a stabilization device

From the outset, the Menem administration was eager to restore macro-economic stability. This required satisfying the perceived intertemporal budget constraint of the government without relying much, if at all, on the inflation tax. It was also critical to restore economic growth, which seemed to require the elimination of some of the severe inefficiencies in resource allocation. Most economists agreed that the widespread intervention of the ISI era needed to be reduced, and that the economy needed to be integrated into the world.

Stabilization was not an easy task. Argentina's history meant that a complete turnaround of expectation was called for. In order to build credibility, it was necessary to introduce, in a relatively binding way, a radical change in the strategy and politics regarding current and future deficits. Stabilization also required a policy package that would force a sudden change in the forms of behavior developed during the high-inflation era.

Economic agents faced deep uncertainty. Would the government be able to stabilize the economy? Would this stabilization be sustainable? Which reforms would eventually be implemented and at what cost? What would the short-run monetary and fiscal policies be? What would they be in the medium and long run? More deeply, what would the new rules of the game be? Many institutional arrangements in society exist in order to reduce this type of uncertainty and to provide reliability for social and economic interactions. For a variety of reasons, Argentina did not provide those certainties at the beginning of the reform period; in a sense, the overall reform strategy (with its cornerstone in convertibility) was an attempt to provide more certainty to economic planning.

On top of the technical complexity of the task, the new Menem administration entered government in 1989 lacking any credibility as to its ability to manage the economy well. In order to signal a credible shift in policy, the government adopted as its economic program a package including the entire list of first-generation reforms.

The consistency condition that the stream of revenues should finance the normal stream of spending does not dictate a particular composition of the flows. The government focused on improving tax collection, reducing subsidies and reducing the drag on fiscal accounts produced by public sector enterprises. It even used the proceeds from privatization in order to balance the budget. Public expenditures were seen as already quite low and rigid.

In order to enhance economic efficiency, the government also relied on trade and financial liberalization, deregulation of markets and privatization of public enterprises. In addition, in view of the fact that the government had entered a de facto moratorium of the services of its external debt in 1988, a debt renegotiation was needed to make clear what commitments the government would honor and what relief it would be able to obtain. The government made it plain that this was one of its policy priorities.

The literature on economic reforms is rich in discussions about the speed and sequencing of market liberalization (Tommasi and Velasco, 1996). Structural reforms in Argentina impressed the world because of their speed and scope. In a few years, the government substantially improved its fiscal performance, liberalized trade, opened up to foreign direct investment, reformed its pension system, privatized most state companies, liberalized the financial system and legislated a world-class bankruptcy law. All these reforms were bundled together and adopted at once. The structural reform package was also the stabilization program and vice versa. This was done not without haste. It is certainly different to privatize public firms with several objectives – for example, to finance the government, to signal the government type and to restore efficiency and investment – than it is to privatize just to enhance efficiency (Galiani and Petrecolla, 2000).

Although the government attempted to stabilize the economy by changing the expectations and behavior of economic agents by means of a wide program of structural reforms, economic performance was at first disappointing. In fact, the government reached the verge of hyperinflation twice before it adopted a new stabilization program based on the convertibility law. Convertibility tried to provide a framework for contractual and investment decisions by restricting monetary policies and validating the widespread use of the dollar as a unit of denomination for domestic transactions. The common view was that such measures were necessary to induce the emergence of credit markets. This, in turn, would make it possible to take advantage of large growth possibilities left unexploited in an unfavorable macroeconomic environment.

Reliability and predictability were built upon hard rules, which consequently lacked flexibility and ultimately broke down. The main institutional arrangement was the convertibility law (adopted in 1991).[10] Convertibility was, in the Argentina of the 1990s, much more than a monetary institution. It also shaped fiscal policies and provided the basis for an elaborate system of contracts, which clearly signified a break with the past in an economy where, say, private mortgage loans had been a rarity for decades. Over time the government became more and more committed to the fixed exchange rate in several ways. Since alternative mechanisms for gaining policy credibility did not arise, strict adherence to the existing monetary rule remained identified with stability (Galiani et al., 2003). Over time, the development of extremely high costs for exiting convertibility provided a self-sustaining system of shared beliefs about the salient way in which the game was repeatedly played.

Convertibility also served as a way of keeping political support for the structural reform process alive. One of the reasons why these reforms had usually been postponed during the 1980s was the belief that they would impose severe costs on society. However, in the favorable context of the emerging international financial markets of the 1990s, the framework created by convertibility allowed the emergence of credit, which enlarged the consumption and investment opportunities of many agents, including the government, and contributed to the growth in economic activity. Convertibility (like its predecessor the Austral Plan in 1985) rewarded the government in the legislative elections of 1991 and 1993 and led to the re-election of the president by a large margin in 1995. The consumption boom of 1992–93 was behind the excellent legislative election made by the Peronist party in 1993 when they even won for the first time in the always-adverse Federal district. The large number of people who had contracted dollar debts, and those who feared a return of high inflation if convertibility was abandoned created a very strong constituency against devaluation. Indeed, during the financial crisis of 1995, prior to the presidential elections, the authorities used as their main electoral argument that they had ended hyperinflation and that they constituted the only political force that would maintain convertibility (Starr, 1999).

2.2.5 Politico-institutional resources for reform[11]

In the Argentine case, its partisan distribution, the delegation of legislative faculties to the Executive, and its control over the Supreme Court, as well as the use of certain resources of doubtful constitutionality, enabled the Executive to concentrate political power. In this section we address the distribution of institutional power during the first (1989–95) and second (1995–99) Menem administrations and the delegation mechanisms present at the onset of his first mandate.

Distribution of institutional power

The electoral results throughout Menem's presidency were favorable to his party (Table 2.1a), conferring on Menem an ample mandate at the onset of his first administration, and further reinvigorating the reformist course later on. Favorable electoral results were mirrored in the resulting distribution of institutional power (Table 2.1b, c, and d). This power composition implied that several of the pivotal political negotiations were with actors within the Peronist Party (PJ), a point that we explore below.

The favorable partisan composition at key institutional nodes was furthered by a law that increased the number of Supreme Court Justices from five to nine. Through this device Menem was allowed to appoint four judges (with the agreement of the Senate). When one justice resigned in protest, Menem was granted the opportunity for a fifth appointment. In addition, Menem resorted to the use of two types of legislative instruments of (until the 1994 constitutional reform) dubious constitutionality – the decrees of 'necessity and urgency' (DNUs) and the line-item veto – in a way that far exceeded the historical record.

Delegation mechanisms

An additional effect of the economic crisis was to trigger a series of delegation patterns. In particular, there was a political agreement to move the presidential succession ahead in 1989, and two laws were enacted conferring on the Executive ample margins for defining the details of reform policies.

The economic crisis helped to forge a political agreement between the two major parties: the Radical Party (the outgoing administration) and the Peronist Party agreed to move the presidential succession forward in order to deal with the crisis. President Alfonsín (1983–89) resigned, Menem agreed to take office five months before originally scheduled, and in exchange the Radical Party committed itself to give legislative support to the new administration.

Soon after Menem became president (in July 1989), Congress delegated to the Executive vast legislative powers through *Ley 23.696 de Emergencia Económica* (Economic Emergency Law) and *Ley 23.697 de Reforma del Estado* (State Reform Law). The intent of the first of these laws was to dismantle most of

Table 2.1: Electoral results and partisan composition during Menem's government

(a) Electoral results, 1989–97 (%)

Political party	1989 (b)	1991 (a)	1993 (a)	1994 (c)	1995 (b)	1997 (a)
Peronist Party (PJ)	47	40	43	39	50	36
UCR	33	29	30	20	17	7
Center-right and provincial parties	12	16	18	12	1	9
Center-left parties	7	10	3	17	31	6
Alianza (UCR+Frepaso)	–	–	–	–	–	36
Others	2	4	6	12	2	–

Notes: (a) Legislative elections; (b) Legislative and presidential elections; (c) Elections for Constitutional Assembly.

(b) Partisan composition of the Chamber of Deputies, 1987–99 (%)

Political party	Deputy periods					
	1987–89	1989–91	1991–93	1993–95	1995–97	1997–99
Peronist Party (PJ)	43	50	50	50	52	47
Unión Cívica Radical	46	37	33	33	27	26
Center-right and provincial parties	6	7	9	9	8	11
Other parties	5	6	5	8	12	16

(c) Partisan composition of the Senate, 1986–98 (%)

Political party	Senate periods			
	1986–89	1989–92	1992–95	1995–98
Peronist Party (PJ)	47	54	62	56
Unión Cívica Radical	39	30	23	29
Provincial parties & others	15	16	15	15

(d) Partisan composition of Provincial Governorships, 1987–99

Political party	Gubernatorial periods		
	1987–91	1991–95	1995–97
Peronist Party (PJ)	77	61	61
Unión Cívica Radical	9	17	22
Provincial parties	14	22	17

the institutions related to the state-centered, inward-looking development model – subsidies, industrial promotion regimes, and so on. The second conferred vast powers on the Executive to define the details of the reform policies, including the privatization of state-owned enterprises.

In sum, the partisan distribution of institutional power coupled with these delegation patterns allowed the Executive to jump institutional hurdles for the initiation of structural reforms. Yet, this did not completely numb relevant political and institutional actors.

2.2.6   The political steering of the reforms: dealing with the relevant actors

Contrary to the assertions of much of the literature on the political economy of reforms in Argentina, the reform process was not carried out by an Executive power in isolation from other social, political, and institutional actors. Rather, reforms were the product of a series of transactions between the Executive and some key actors at every step of the process. In this subsection we present the relevant actors with whom the Executive dealt in order to advance the reformist course.

The reformist administration was clever in manipulating both electoral and policy coalition-making throughout the reforming period. Having been elected by a coalition of traditional Peronist sources with the center-left, it governed and was re-elected with a coalition of traditional Peronist sources (with changed weights within that coalition) with the center-right. The latter was taken into account not only as an electoral source but, mostly, because of its ties with business and international actors whose economic support was necessary.[12]

Menem made clever use of its institutional and fiscal resources to obtain the support of the politically important backward provinces; it gave selective benefits to some unions and union leaders while debilitating the overall labor movement; and it was able to gain the support of important business actors through a mix of general policies and particularistic deals. In the rest of this section we describe the strategy vis-à-vis each of the main actors. We start with several actors whose key roles are in the electoral/governmental arena (parties, provincial governments, voters), and then we refer to other (mostly corporate) actors who operate mainly in other arenas (conflict resolution, opinion-making, the economy).[13]

We implicitly use a theory in which an agenda-setting executive needs a given level of support for its reform package and insures it by 'buying' the necessary number of 'votes'. We can think of it as the Executive facing a price schedule for votes in favor of the policies that it is trying to implement. The spot price to be paid will depend, among other things, on the intertemporal political linkages between the president and each relevant actor. The cheapest votes (probably price zero, or even negative) will be those of actors who directly benefit from the reform package. From the actors who do not benefit from the package, the cheapest votes will come from those legislators with whom there are credible intertemporal reward mechanisms. These mechanisms will include future appointments in the Executive or in the party. Legislators from the same party will be first in line, legislators from small independent parties will come second, and legislators from the main opposition parties will be the most expensive. The spot currency used to buy votes might include outright bribery, policy benefits to the relevant constituency, or exemptions from reforms costly to the relevant constituency.

Which votes are actually purchased out of this schedule will depend on the rules of the game (for instance, what is the required majority), and on the actual composition of the legislature and other relevant institutional positions at the time of the reform. In the Argentine case under Menem, it turns out that the pivotal votes were some in the Peronist Party (from provincial blocs and from union-related actors) as well as some of the small provincial parties. We look at these actors in turn.

The Peronist Party

Due to the above-mentioned partisan distribution of institutional power, the Peronist Party had high leverage on the legislative process, becoming the fundamental veto player at the time of approving reforms (Corrales, 2000). When referring to the Peronist Party as a fundamental political actor, we are basically concerned with its two major historical constituencies – the provinces and trade unions, which we analyze in later subsections.

Menem's Peronist credentials allowed him, on the one hand, to achieve the acquiescence of popular sectors, a 'Nixon goes to China' effect analyzed in Cukierman and Tommasi (1998a and 1998b) (see discussion in the concluding section, though). On the other hand, there was major disruption in the party since the policies Menem was propounding constituted a dramatic break with the populist policies Peronism traditionally embodied. This break produced resistance and criticism inside the party, yet both the intellectual efforts devoted to 'rebuild' the Peronist identity as well as the concessions used to construct support, helped moderate these tensions.[14] Menem's conversion to neo-liberal policies created discrepancies between the government and official legislators which led to schisms in the Peronist bloc of the Deputy's Chamber. Pro-government deputies took part in arduous discussions prior to approving legislation regarding reform of the state. Eventually, under pressure from the Executive, the package was approved. Nevertheless, a dissident faction of Peronist deputies was formed, the so-called 'Group of Eight'.[15]

In contrast to the notion of an insulated all-powerful executive, between 1992 and 1994 Congress modified around 46 per cent of legislative initiatives of the president. The Executive managed to tackle these discrepancies through the extensive use of 'Decrees of Necessity and Urgency' and vetoes that strengthened its bargaining position in the legislature, through political transactions with provincial and small national parties, and through concessions in policy design.

Menem was also forced to engage in public arguments when other Peronist figures challenged him to return to the sources of Peronist doctrine. Menem countered the reaction within party ranks in several ways. He exploited the extreme crisis that prevailed when he entered office by deflecting criticism, which usually centered on the social costs of the policies adopted. He argued that alternatives did not exist, that the room for maneuver was limited. Finally, he filled party leadership positions with individuals close to the Executive.

Menem also displayed considerable pragmatism in choosing candidates for elections. Whenever non-Peronists were likely to win an election or support the government's economic course, the Executive did not hesitate to incorporate them. Even Peronists with little party experience were nominated as candidates. This occurred in Tucumán, Santa Fe, and the Federal Capital. Of course, the success of the economic policy strengthened this strategy. Moreover, resistance from his own party diminished with the progressive acquisition of new members, co-opted from center-right parties (especially the UCD).

Center-right parties

The government's resolute implementation of market-oriented reforms implied realignments within the party system. The convergence of the Peronists with the rightist UCD led to an important shift in the UCD electorate toward support for Menem's policies. Peronists and the UCD reached formal alliances in some districts, such as the Federal Capital. And UCD specialists and professionals held government positions, including secretariats in the Ministry of the Interior, provincial offices, and management of firms being privatized. (UCD, as had happened to most of its conservative predecessors, pretty much disappeared after this experiment.)

The opposition: the Radical Party

The Radical Party faced the Menem administration from a weak position, resulting from the disastrous economic performance of the Alfonsín government which led to the Executive taking office six months earlier than scheduled in 1989. The party agreed not to oppose any legislative initiatives originating in the Executive during the six months before the newly elected Congress was in place.

The initial success of Menem's economic and political strategy further weakened the potential for a strong opposition. The weakness of the main opposition party was reflected in the 1993 agreement ('Pacto de Olivos') between Menem and Alfonsín to launch the process of constitutional reform, giving Menem the chance to be re-elected for a second term (Acuña, 1995b). In a nutshell, even though the Radical Party did start reasserting itself after 1991, being ideologically divided and electorally weaker, it was a mild opposition.

The provinces

The Peronist machinery in the provinces constitutes one of the fundamental electoral pillars of the party. Argentine federalism confers a high degree of political and institutional power to the provinces, especially as veto players in the national arena (Spiller and Tommasi, 2003, and references therein). In this sense, it is possible to trace, throughout the reform period, a strong reformist impetus at the national level that contrasts with the scarce advances at provincial levels.

Gibson and Calvo (2001) show that the territorial organization of the electoral coalition – to the extent that poor and under-populated provinces received special treatment to generate legislative support to sustain the reformist agenda – was an important element in the successful implementation of reforms. Peronism historically encompassed two distinctive and regionally-based coalitions: a 'metropolitan' coalition, which gave support to the party's development strategies, and a 'peripheral' coalition, which carried the burden of generating electoral majorities. The metropolitan coalition is of very high economic importance, but carries less political weight in Congress given the notable malapportionment of seats. Under the Gibson and Calvo hypothesis, Menem decided to have the metropolitan coalition shoulder the full blow of adjustment costs, while he spared the peripheral coalition through several concessions in tax benefits and by allowing the subsidizing of interventionist and populist enclaves. Tommasi (2006) provides empirical evidence on the details of this strategy, supporting the Gibson-Calvo hypothesis. We provide below a very brief synthesis.

National legislators in Argentina tend to act as agents of provincial governments, rather than national policy-makers.[16] Small peripheral provinces have had special importance in general, and particularly within the Peronist coalition. The general importance of small provinces is the result of their over-representation in the National Congress.[17] These provinces have an institutional representation that far exceeds their population (and their economic importance).[18] In the period of market-oriented reforms, the peripheral regions held 83 per cent of Senate seats and 52 per cent of seats in the Chamber of Deputies.[19]

Independent provincial parties have also played an important role in lending presidents the support needed to pass legislation in Congress, as shown in Palanza and Sin (1997). In particular, during the Menem reform years the Peronist Party (PJ) had the majority of seats in the Senate, but not in the Lower Chamber. (The president chose to present his bills through the Senate.) Despite the general agreement attained with the main opposition UCR party – which guaranteed the PJ would always have the required quorum in Congress, Menem faced several obstacles when he tried to pass his reform projects. The way out of the gridlock was to buy in provincial party support. Palanza and Sin (1996) have documented the denial of support made by provincial party legislators during first rounds of negotiation, and how their positions changed to be aligned with the PJ when voting.[20]

This institutional over-representation, together with the 'subnational drag' on legislators' incentives, meant that no national legislative coalition could be put together without the support of the regional structures of power in the periphery. The need to buy this support affected the eventual outcome of the reform process in several ways. The burden of the costs of reform was shouldered predominantly by the metropolitan constituency. The reforms were timed and instrumented in a fashion that implied earlier and heavier hits on the central provinces, as well as differential benefits in favor of peripheral provinces.[21]

All provinces benefited from improved tax collection due to low inflation and from overall gains in tax bases, but there was a redistributive component favoring the provinces that are net recipients in the common pool of *coparticipación*. The main impact on provincial tax revenues in the reform process came from the increase in tax revenues due to the Olivera-Tanzi effect from the substantial drop in inflation, from tax reforms increasing and generalizing the value added tax, and from the consumption boom in the early years after convertibility. A very simple simulation of these effects (treating private sector and public sector as a unit) shows that the central provinces of Buenos Aires, Córdoba, and Santa Fe (and the capital city of Buenos Aires) were net losers, the province of Mendoza was about equal, and all the other (peripheral) provinces were net winners (Tommasi, 2006).

Similarly, the estimated 37 per cent reduction in public employment (both in the central administration and in privatized public enterprises) was concentrated in the metropolitan region. We do not have the exact figures of the territorial distribution of the reduction of national public employment, but even under the assumption that the reduction was uniform across the territory, 74 per cent would have taken place in the metropolitan region (Buenos Aires, Córdoba, Mendoza, Santa Fe, and the city of Buenos Aires), and 26 per cent in the periphery. However, the actual distribution of labor shedding was even more concentrated in the center. Even beyond labor shedding, other reform measures were also concentrated in national rather than subnational regulations.

In addition, peripheral provinces were given distortionary 'handouts', the most salient of which were:

- The subsidizing and increase of distortionary, expensive industrial promotion schemes that mainly benefit poorer provinces (Sawers and Massacane, 2001).
- The 1992 'Fondo de Desequilibrios Regionales' (Fund for Regional Imbalances), where money was distributed 2 per cent for metropolitan provinces and 98 per cent for peripheral provinces.
- The asymmetric reduction of labor taxes with special provisions for provinces farther from the capital: these rates in 1995, after the reduction, were 27 per cent in the city of Buenos Aires, 26 per cent in the province of Buenos Aires, 23 per cent in Córdoba, 22 percent in Santa Fe, and less than 20 per cent for almost all the peripheral provinces, reaching as low as 14 per cent for Chaco, Formosa, Santa Cruz, and Santiago del Estero.
- The distribution of contributions from the National Treasury (ATNs). This fund, 1 per cent of coparticipation revenues, has traditionally been

distributed independently of the fiscal situation of the province. In 1994, for instance, 20 per cent of ATN money went to the small province of La Rioja, followed by 2.4 per cent to San Luis and 2.3 per cent to Santiago del Estero.

The electorate

The way the electorate was handled in the strategy of the reformist government could be divided in two groups, following the Gibson-Calvo logic described above.

With regards to the electorate in the peripheral provinces, Menem built alliances with the (almost feudal) leaders of those provinces, through a series of handouts that they administered internally in order to maintain the traditional Peronist connection to the electorate in those provinces, in a way that was functional to the conformation of a government coalition cum electoral coalition in support of the government and of the reforms being implemented.

With regards to the metropolitan voters (irrelevant for the Senate, somewhat relevant for the Chamber of Deputies, crucial for presidential elections), the successful stabilizing effect of convertibility rendered popular support to the center-right governing coalition, fostering a solid electoral coalition that would start dismembering itself only in the last years of the decade.

The unions

The restructuring of the populist metropolitan coalition involved picking winners and losers within the business community (see next subsection) and the labor movement. In part the success of the reform process involved the division of the labor movement and the co-optation of certain sectors to prevent unified labor opposition to economic reform, as well as the more limited extent of reform of labor markets. Menem's credentials also proved to be an asset during the implementation of this strategy.

In 1989, Menem deepened divisions inside the unions, precipitating a fracture that diminished their bargaining power. The policy succeeded through the administration of 'carrots and sticks'. Unions opposing the reforms were punished; unions supporting the reforms were brought on board via 'new economic businesses', and through rewards to some leaders with government positions (Murillo, 1997). The carrot came in a variety of forms: several cooperative union leaders were appointed to government positions; Menem treated unions supporting him favorably when it came to wage negotiations and the transfer of welfare funds from the social security agency to individual union funds; the government provided some incentives like early retirement programs, re-training programs, and workers' ownership of stock (10 per cent of total) in privatizations of large public enterprises (telephones, petroleum, gas, and electricity). In several cases, privatization opened up new lucrative business opportunities for unions, as they were allowed to set up companies managing the shares transferred to workers.

The stick was used to break strikes by defiant unions by invoking the new legislation, enforced by decree in 1990, regulating the right to strike. The administration adopted massive lay-offs affecting employees who had participated in strikes regarded as illegal in the telephone, railway, and oil companies between 1990 and 1991. By 1992, many union leaders who had initially opposed Menem's state-shrinking policies understood that the process was irreversible and it was politically wise to jump on the president's bandwagon before it was too late.

The unions' new tolerant attitude to the reforms was evidenced by the decrease in their activism compared with the levels reached during the Alfonsín administration. In exchange for their non-conflictive behavior, the government allowed the unions to maintain their sources of power – the regulation of collective bargaining and 'Obras Sociales'[22] – in spite of the constant decrease in the unions' representation in the legislature.[23] The number of general strikes decreased from 13 during the Alfonsín administration to two in the first Menem term and five in the second. Furthermore, there was a reduction in the average number of people participating in each strike.[24]

Business sectors

Business actors at the most aggregate level – that is, as owners of capital – tend to be naturally supportive of measures that weaken trade unions, shrink the state, and privatize public services. At that level, the effort of the government was mainly to build credibility for those policies. At a more sectoral level, there were several business actors threatened by specific measures.

In the delicate fiscal situation of the 1989 economic crisis, reactions from business leaders could determine the success or failure of economic policy. Menem's political background generated distrust among most domestic and international businessmen and investors. This forced him to overreact in sending signals to give credibility to his reformist intentions. The initial signals of commitment to the new reform path were the privatization of firms such as the national airline and telecommunication companies; the invitation to influential economic groups – traditionally opposed to the Peronist Party – to take part in the government; and the alignment of foreign policy with the US. Menem included in his first cabinet as minister of finance a representative from a powerful holding of the business sector. The strategy consisted in establishing a close relationship with a particular holding, Bunge & Born (in Peronist imagery, a symbol of the oligarchy with interests incompatible with those of the 'people and the nation'), instead of dealing with representatives of business associations – as had been the Peronist tradition and as former Radical president Alfonsín had unsuccessfully attempted.

The administration faced some dilemmas in its relationship with specific business sectors. The industrial sector was reluctant to support trade liberalization policies, since such policies would generate competition from international products. Also, privatization policies implied a cost to many of the firms that were privileged suppliers of the state-owned companies, while also affecting business as a consumer of state-subsidized public services.

We could say that vis-à-vis different business sectors the government followed a strategy similar to the one dealing with partisan actors: ignore the weak, weaken those that you can, and buy the support of the strong.

Among 'the weak and weakened' we would include traditionally protected industries, such as textiles, electronics, and auto-parts that, even though hurt by reform, by that time had lost the capacity for collective action.[25] Furthermore, the government exacerbated their collective weaknesses by providing strong incentives to negotiate individual solutions to each particular sector.[26]

Intermediate cases were those industries, such as pharmaceuticals, which had more economic capacity to adapt to the new set of rules. In those cases, the government showed its determination to speed up and/or increase the opening of the economy, forcing them to acquiesce politically and adjust economically.

The (economically and politically) stronger business groups were the industrial conglomerates which were strengthened during the 1976–83 dictatorship and which saw their interests affected by the shrinkage of the state. Even though these groups were horizontally diversified and had export capacity, they depended heavily on their profits as (over-priced) state suppliers. These groups were a real threat, since they could shape an alliance with other sectors and build upon a 'nationalistic' discourse in defense of the state. The government strategy to neutralize the potential reaction of these conglomerates was to barter their loss of earnings as state suppliers by their appropriation via privatization of the state-owned companies which were placed in monopolistic or oligopolistic positions (especially providers of public services, made even more attractive by the peso–dollar parity). This strategy was very successful.[27] Although not all the large former suppliers of the state attained similar benefits in the process of privatization, those that ended up suffering absolute losses in the competition for the appropriation of state-owned firms did not constitute a sufficiently powerful group for their reaction to complicate the government strategy.

Politically, the government maintained a similar strategy as the one employed with some unions, namely, exchanging 'favors', accompanied by threats of sanctions in the event of not reaching a solution to the conflicts, with the business sectors that were affected by the plan as producers. The overall result of the reforms was a strong consolidation of the local industrial conglomerates to the detriment of the smaller, less horizontally diversified industrial companies that had to pay the costs of the liberalization of trade and the privatization of state-owned companies.

The process of privatizations did not benefit only these conglomerates. Banks (temporarily) and foreign firms were, as expected, important beneficiaries of the reforms. Beyond the urban sector and in the long run, agricultural producers also emerged as clear beneficiaries of trade liberalization.

To summarize, the government managed to build an alliance of the most powerful and diverse business interests, leaving little room for the reaction of those that were to pay the costs of the reforms.

International actors

The US government was a key international actor in assuring the right environment for the reforms. In order to include this government as one of the supporting actors for the reforms, Menem's strategy was to establish a close alliance with the US by radically shifting longstanding Argentine positions in the international arena. In this sense, Argentina did not condemn the US invasion of Panama, withdrew from the Non-aligned Movement, dismantled the Condor Missile project – a major interest of the US at that time (Acuña and Smith, 1994) – sent troops to the Gulf War, signed the Tlatelolco Treaty, and sustained voting behavior almost identical to that of the US in different international fora.

The consistent international support from the US government, EEC, IMF, IDB, and the World Bank was instrumental in boosting the credibility of the administration's reform program at home. For instance, in July 1997, the IMF decided to enhance Argentina's credit line because of the country's 'good governance' record. In addition, privatizations, for example, played a key role in Argentina's ability to enter the Brady Plan.[28] It was in seeking to achieve this goal that Menem pursued a foreign policy aimed closely at aligning Argentina with the US.

2.3   The effects of the reforms

After a decade of market-oriented reforms, what can be concluded in terms of their impact on economic outcomes? This is a very difficult, but important, question. First, it is always very hard to nail down the effect of macroeconomic policies. Confounding the impact of reforms with other secular trends and with other simultaneous interventions tends to be pervasive in these cases. Second, and in particular in the Argentine case, disentangling the aggregate effects of the 'reforms' from those of the stabilization based on convertibility is simply not possible. There is no way to assess the counterfactual of what would have happened if the reforms had been implemented without adopting convertibility. Thus, we will just provide a descriptive analysis of some key aggregate economic variables, whose ups and downs nevertheless were associated by all political actors with the reforms-cum-convertibility package.

Taking a broad and long perspective, and recognizing the starting point of the Argentine economy in the late 1980s, the 'reforms' seem to have been (in broad strokes) a movement in the right direction. Several overall outcomes were successful (if measured against reasonable counterfactuals).

In our view, the main achievement has been on the inflation front. After decades of high inflation, Argentina's inflation has been in single digits, with the exception of 2002 (in which the exchange rate multiplied by four after convertibility was abandoned). This substantial and so far permanent removal of inflation has had substantial microeconomic benefits.

The aggregate performance of the economy also improved substantially reverting a long declining trend (Figure 2.5), although this is somewhat obscured when the collapse of convertibility is taken into account. In addition, the economy recovered faster than expected. During the 1990s, GDP per capita grew at 3 per cent, twice the rate of growth of the world economy and 50 per cent more than that of Latin America as a whole. However, when the crisis period is incorporated, the economy only grew at 1.88 per cent per year, which is a substantially better performance than the one obtained during the 1980s, but it is similar to the one achieved in the 1970s (Table 2.2).

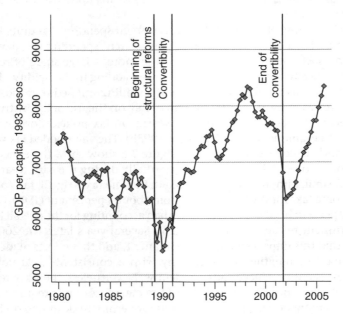

Figure 2.5   GDP per capita, 1980–2005

Table 2.2:   GDP per capita growth (Annualized rate, %)

	1970s	1980s	1990s	1990–2005
Argentina	1.73	−2.24	3.13	1.88
Latin America	1.60	−1.02	2.09	3.04
World	2.35	1.60	1.61	2.89

Source: Author's elaboration based on ECLAC, CIA World Factbook, Penn World Tables, Gerchunoff and Llach (2003) and INDEC.

Trade liberalization was also very successful. Starting in the early 1980s, and partially responding to the opening of the mid-1970s, exports to GDP almost tripled (Figure 2.2). This process continued in the aftermath of the convertibility crisis. The growth of exports was a necessary condition to re-instate economic growth in the country after the demise of the import substitution strategy adopted in the post-war period. During the 1990s, there were also significant gains in the productive efficiency of the economy – see Galiani et al. (2005b) for the privatized firms and Chudnovsky et al. (2004) for the manufacturing sector.

There were also substantial improvements on the fiscal front. Up until the end of the 1980s, the deficit (including inflationary tax revenue but not privatization income) was around 6 per cent of GDP. During the 1990s, the primary budget was balanced. Under convertibility, Argentina undeniably achieved the best fiscal results in 40 years.

At the beginning of convertibility, government spending was quite low and increasingly inelastic. A high share of government spending was devoted to wages and social security payments. Furthermore, a large share of resources was automatically transferred to the provinces, adding to the rigidity of the fiscal accounts. This rigidity in government spending implied that most of the action in terms of fiscal adjustment had to rely on the use of tax instruments.

Tax reform largely followed the consensus on tax policies for developing countries (see, among others, Harberger, 1993b). The value added tax was generalized and tax collection improved. Figure 2.6 shows how the effectiveness of the collection of VAT increased substantially during the early years of the reform. A similar improvement occurred in income taxes. In all, tax collection from income taxes and VAT increased from about 3 per cent of GDP in 1990 to about 10 per cent of GDP by 1998, more than accounting for the overall increase in government resources (see Figure 2.6). Several years later, the 2001 crisis showed that this improvement was permanent, and that efforts made during the decade to strengthen convertibility with a consistent fiscal policy are behind the stability achieved after its demise. Nevertheless, the fiscal retrenchment turned out insufficient in light of the macroeconomic requirements of a very rigid monetary regime.[29] Finally, the government defaulted on its debt.

Tax pressure in Argentina is still too low. It was below 22 per cent of GDP by the end of the 1990s, while it was above 30 per cent in Brazil and Uruguay, and between 35 and 40 per cent in most developed countries. Argentina still needs to broaden its tax base to improve the quality of her supply of public goods.

With respect to business, the overall result of the reforms shows clear benefits for mining, oil, and agricultural exporters with a strong consolidation of local industrial conglomerates to the detriment of smaller, less horizontally diversified industrial firms, which had to pay the full cost of trade liberalization and the privatization of state-owned companies. In the new context of liberalized trade and private ownership of public services, the economy in the long run also shows an increased weight of foreign capital and a novel (for Argentina)

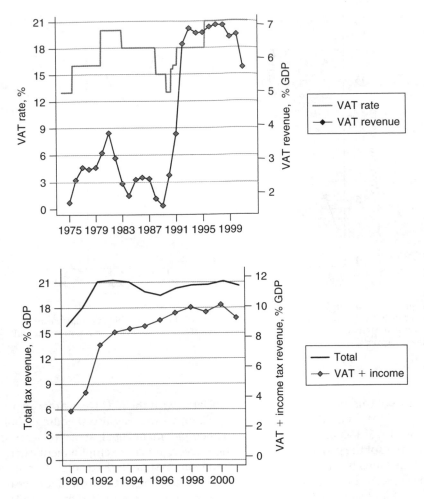

Figure 2.6 VAT, income, and total tax revenue
Source: Cetrángolo and Jiménez (2003).

tension between the producers of tradable and the (now private) producers of non-tradable goods and services.

One of the worst outcomes of the period was the substantial increase in unemployment (see Figure 2.7). However, and despite the fact that many commentators had blamed this on the structural reforms of the 1990s – privatization and trade liberalization – this trend seems in part related to a large secular increase in female labor supply, as well as to the rigidity of the monetary system adopted. Certainly, before 1995, unemployment increased substantially, reaching 12 per cent. However, only approximately 4 percentage

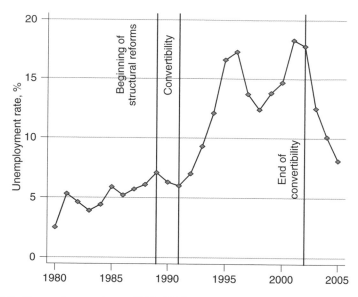

Figure 2.7   Unemployment rate, 1980–2005
Note: In 2003, the Argentine Statistical Agency changed the way in which unemployment was measured. We have adjusted unemployment figures since 2003 to make them comparable with the earlier ones.

points of this jump can be directly associated with the massive lay-offs by privatized firms and the manufacturing sector, which was also shedding labor. Since 1995, a series of severe shocks to unemployment kept it above 10 per cent for most of the period (Figure 2.7). These severe shocks to employment can be blamed mostly on the rigidity of the monetary system. Indeed, after the brutal decrease in real wages as a result of the demise of convertibility and four years of fast and sustained economic growth, unemployment has returned to the levels observed at the end of the 1980s (Figure 2.7).

Related to the increase in unemployment, there was a substantial increase in inequality and poverty (see Figure 2.8), particularly after 1995. Both poverty and inequality were at historical highs at the time convertibility collapsed. However, both indicators were growing fast well before the 1990s. Just as an example, note that the poverty index in 1998 was quite close to its value in 1988.[30] In any event, the most significant aspect of poverty is not whether it is higher or lower than in 1988, it is that now it has been above 20 per cent for almost 20 years, which makes poverty one of the most serious problems to be faced by Argentine society in the years to come. Income inequality has significantly increased since the 1970s. The Gini coefficient for the distribution of household income in Greater Buenos Aires climbed from 0.32 in 1974

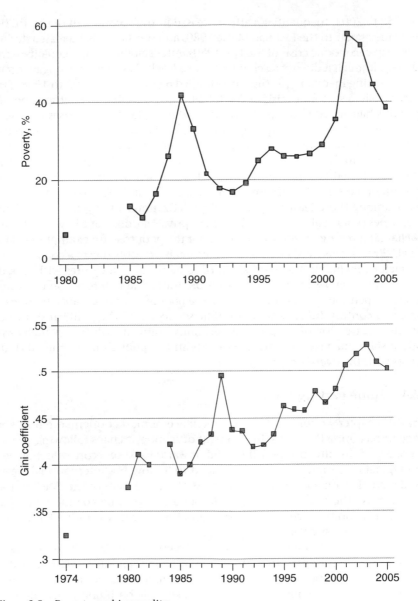

Figure 2.8   Poverty and inequality
Notes: Top panel, poverty head-count ratio. Bottom panel: Gini coefficient for household income per equivalent adult, with parameter of household economies of scale set at 0.5.
Source: Top panel: Gasparini (2003); bottom panel: authors' calculations from permanent household survey.

to 0.52 in 2003. Inequality greatly increased in the second half of the 1970s, remained stable in the first half of the 1980s and substantially increased during the macroeconomic crisis of the late 1980s. After stabilization, inequality went down, although it did not reach the pre-crisis levels. The 1990s were again times of increasing inequality, as the Gini climbed 6 points from 1992 to 1998. The recent macroeconomic crisis of 2001–02 pushed the Gini up another 4 points but this had already been partially reverted by 2005. The increases in unemployment, poverty and inequality, and the association of these events with the adopted economic model severely affected public support for the reforms.

To wrap up this section, we have a few words on public perception of the costs and benefits of the reforms. Overall, public sentiment towards the whole reform process is fairly negative. For instance, as of 2003, Argentine citizens rank among those least supportive of privatizations among Latin American countries (Lora et al., 2004), even though privatizations have in general been welfare improving, in some cases, even for the poor (see, for example, Galiani et al., 2005a). This overly negative impression is probably due to a combination of factors, including the association of some of these measures with lack of transparency and government corruption, the actual failure of some reforms (notably pensions) to meet their goals, the poor institutional capacity to regulate and control the provision of public services, and the political strategies in the construction of the post-convertibility political coalitions, which have successfully managed to further conflate in the public's mind the 2001–02 crisis with the overall reform package.

2.4   Some parting thoughts

In this chapter we summarize the experience of market-oriented reforms in Argentina during the 1990s. In a context of economic chaos following several decades of fiscally irresponsible and inward looking economic policies, a pragmatic incoming Executive decided to 'follow the international wave' and embarked on a broad reform process along the lines of the Washington Consensus. The Executive was able to build a governing coalition that put together economic sectors benefiting from the reforms with some of the traditional clientelistic Peronist networks.

One of the most salient features of the Argentine case was the bundling of measures such as privatization, trade liberalization, and deregulation, with a particular stabilization device, the monetary regime of convertibility. We argue in this chapter that convertibility played a key role both politically and economically, given the peculiar inflation history of Argentina and its impact on the contractual basis of the economy.

Argentina has made clear progress on some important fronts in the last decades. In 1983 it returned to democratic rule, and it has remained there ever since, even through deep crises like the one in 2001–02.[31] It also seems to be conventional wisdom even among political leaders nowadays that high inflation is not good politics, and that in order to avoid high inflation, care on the fiscal end seems necessary. The reform process also left behind a relatively modernized business sector, a more open economy, and some clear improvements in infrastructure.

The economy still has many unresolved problems, and the social situation has deteriorated throughout the reform decade. On the political and institutional end, Argentina is still a country that does not seem able to steer a clear direction, unlike some of its neighbors, such as Chile or Brazil.[32] Even though not the direct focus of this chapter, we believe that some of Argentina's unresolved problems relate to the inability of the polity to produce credible policies sustained by more cooperative political behavior.[33] Convertibility was an institutional shortcut towards the building of more adequate 'deep institutions' but in the end it did not work.

Even though in this chapter we seem to provide some evidence that crisis led to reform we believe that a narrow reading of that statement is misleading. Crises do not necessarily lead to better policies or even to policies in any particular direction. If anything, the 2001–02 crisis had the effect of pushing the discourse in the anti-reform direction. Crises are more likely to be necessary to trigger reforms in polities that have a poor capacity for (less costly) collective learning and to solve collective action problems. More importantly, a crisis does not seem the best time for the gradual and profound building of deep institutions that need time to develop, which are fundamental to deliver credible and adaptable policies over time. The type of solutions that tend to be adopted in some crisis situations, like the convertibility regime in Argentina, do not tend to provide the most adequate starting point for the building of good adaptive institutions.

Another common maxim in the reform folklore is that *left-wing governments are more likely to successfully implement reforms because they are more credible*. One of the authors of this chapter is one of those credited in the literature with the development of that hypothesis. We believe the hypothesis is theoretically relevant and practically relevant in some situations. Although some of that literature was partly motivated by examples such as that of Menem in Argentina, a deeper reading of the case suggests that it was only a small portion of the story in this particular case. The ability of Menem to maneuver the reforms with the traditional constituencies of Peronism is more related to the management of clientelistic political machineries than to the additional credibility lent to the necessity of reform by his Peronist credentials. The disastrous pre-existing situation was stronger evidence of the need for some change.

In this chapter we looked in a rather disaggregated manner at the way winners and losers were handled politically. This implicitly states that, contrary to some naive renderings of the political economy of reforms, the implementation (and sustainability) of market-oriented reforms does not depend on their Pareto-improving nature, but on political configurations in which losers do not have effective power to mobilize against implementation (or for reversal).

This brief chapter has focused on the broad aspects of the reform package and of the underlying politics. The more disaggregated analysis behind this project suggests the presence of important actors relevant for some specific reform areas. For instance, the military used to be an obstacle for privatization, but not so much for trade liberalization. Specific structural reforms are nested games; the logic of support and opposition by specific actors depends on the interplay among multiple reforms in multiple arenas. In the specific case of Argentina, the lack of intertemporal political credibility led to the bundling of multiple simultaneous reforms as a way of allowing exchanges to take place at a relatively low risk for the potential losers of some specific components of reform.

Finally, the impact of structural reforms cannot be assessed in narrow economic terms. The Argentine case shows that the weakness of its governmental institutions to sustain intertemporal exchanges in an efficient, effective, and legitimate way is at the core of the logic of reforms and, more broadly, at the core of its problems. In this context, the original promise of the Washington Decalogue that more market and less government would bring about better politics and economics was wrong. Economies cannot be understood or reformed independently of the political conditions and institutions in which they operate. Good governmental institutions allow bad policies to be redefined, while bad institutions cannot even assure that good policies will be maintained. Conceptually, the 'Washington' notion of first and second generation reforms got the order wrong.

Notes

We thank the valuable research assistance of Ignacio Franceschelli, Eugenia Garibotti, Germán Herrera, and Fernando Núñez, as well as the helpful comments of José Fanelli and Gary McMahon.

1. Our analysis focuses on the macroeconomic aspects of reform, not paying much attention at this point to other important questions such as the dynamics and impact of institutional changes (for example, decentralization) or to the microeconomic side of reform.
2. A good part of Alfonsín's energies were devoted to recuperating democratic politics in Argentina.
3. The shared beliefs that the economic agents had about Menem's prospective populist policies seem to have been at the core of the portfolio decisions they adopted.
4. See also Cukierman and Tommasi (1998a, 1998b) on the 'Nixon goes to China' paradox of populist presidents implementing right-wing policies. See, nonetheless, our further thoughts with regards to the 'Nixon hypothesis' in the concluding section.
5. An example of the multiple roles of some reforms is provided by privatization. They were an instrument to improve the efficiency of the economic system, yet they were also used to alleviate short-term fiscal needs; and the early and quick privatization of some national symbols (airlines, telephones) helped signal the government's commitment to the new policy direction.

6. The Argentine Constitution did not at the time allow the re-election of the president. Menem managed to get an agreement with the main opposition party to reform the Constitution.

7. This is consistent with Rodrik's notion (1994) that the likelihood of a reform is a function of the ratio of net social gain to net reallocation (redistribution). In times like those of Argentina in the early 1990s, efficiency gains from halting hyperinflation were large enough to swamp many distributive considerations (see also Mondino et al., 1996).

8. This does not mean that there is a one to one connection between crisis and reforms 'in the right direction', as explained in Tommasi (2004) and pointed out in Section 2.4 below.

9. We refer the readers to Galiani et al. (2003) for a more detailed analysis of the process of convertibility, and for a critique of the naive interpretations that see convertibility as 'the mistake' in the Argentine reform process (such as Williamson, 2003).

10. In a nutshell, the Argentine currency was made convertible to the US dollar by law, and the Central Bank was mandated to reduce its monetary policy to the management of a currency board. Thus, the monetary base had to be backed by assets denominated in foreign currencies, mainly issued abroad.

11. Several of the arguments of this and the next subsection are drawn from Acuña (1995a) and from Bambaci et al. (2002).

12. This strategy was also related to signaling to international financial actors, who provided crucial funding and opinion-making support for the reform process.

13. In earlier, and longer drafts of this chapter we also included actors such as the military. The military, which had opposed privatization while in government, was no longer an important actor by the time of reform partly because Menem's administration managed to subordinate this actor to constitutional rule. For a detailed account of these dynamics, see Acuña (2006).

14. Levitsky (2003) provides an insightful analysis of the internal process of Peronist adaptation to the new policies.

15. It is interesting to note that all the legislators leaving the Peronist bloc were from the two major districts (the city and the province of Buenos Aires). Some legislators from those districts tend to be the most ideological, the most visible, and the most focused on national policy. Legislators from the vast majority of peripheral provinces tend to respond mostly to provincial governments, and in general only need to be bought with provincial spoils in order to support whatever national policies the Executive might be pushing (Jones et al., forthcoming). It is also interesting to note that many of the legislators who supported pro-market reform under Menem applauded cheerfully when debt default was declared in late December 2001.

16. This is primarily a consequence of the electoral system (provinces are the electoral districts where party lists are drawn). See the details of the provincial nature of legislators' careers in Jones et al. (2002b and 2006).

17. Stepan (1999) utilizes three indicators of malapportionment across twelve modern federal democracies, and in all the indicators Argentina is the worst case.

18. The bulk of the Argentine economy is concentrated in a few districts: the city and the province of Buenos Aires, plus the provinces of Santa Fe, Cordoba, and Mendoza contain almost 80 per cent of economic activity and 70 per cent of the population.

19. Party politics do not seem to temper this influence: peripheral provinces have always been a central part of the Peronist coalition (Sawers, 1996: 199, and references therein).

20. Examples of legislation sanctioned thanks to the aid provided by provincial parties are, among others, law 23809 (Privatization of Altos Hornos Zapla), law 23871 (Fiscal Reform), law 23897 (Payment of Oil Royalties), 24154 (Transformation of YPF – the later privatized oil company).

21. It is worth noting that even though many peripheral provinces did suffer some economic costs from trade liberalization (and from some of the privatizations), provincial governors did not oppose those measures as long as there were some compensations in the form of resources that they themselves could distribute through their political machines (Spiller and Tommasi, forthcoming; Jones et al., 2002a).

22. 'Obras Sociales', union-administered welfare organizations (very important in the health market), are the main source of financing of unions. That is the reason why a profound health reform did not take place.

23. The number of deputies with ties to unions decreased from 35 in 1983–85 to 10 in 1993–95 and 14 in 1997–99. (They were concentrated mostly in the labor legislation committee.)

24. There was also a change in the main motivations behind strikes. During Alfonsín's presidency the protests were mainly related to wage levels and economic policy, whereas during Menem's presidency, they were related to labor policy and unemployment.

25. They used to group around the once powerful CGE (a corporatist business counterpart to CGT, the central trade union), which by the early 1990s was already weak and thus had no capacity for sustaining significant opposition to the government.

26. According to Viguera (1998), rather than isolating trade policy from political pressures (as was the case with monetary policy and the central bank) the government kept these decisions in the scope of the Ministry of Economy, where each sector, in a non-cooperative manner, lobbied for favorable treatment. The 'accommodating' response to these sectors is well encapsulated in a statement by the president of the Union Industrial Argentina, Israel Mahler: 'The level of deterioration of the productive sector showed by the fact that the production per capita in industry is now almost 40 per cent lower than in 1970, definitively influenced toward setting aside confrontational attitudes that would lead us nowhere' (our translation, *La Nación*, 1 September 1991, part 3ª, page 1; quoted by Acuña, 1995a: 356–7).

27. By way of illustration, Pérez-Companc participated in the privatizations of EnTel (telecommunications), SEGBA (electricity), YPF (oil), Gas del Estado (gas), and national roads; Techint participated in the privatizations of EnTel, YPF, SOMISA (steel), SEGBA, Gas del Estado, national railways and roads. Moreover, in the aftermath of privatizations, the energy market was concentrated in the hands of these few economic conglomerates.

28. Argentina's entry into the Brady Plan meant that the country received a discount of 35 per cent, or $10 billion, on its foreign debt and a rescheduling of the remaining outstanding debt. In addition, the IMF, World Bank, and IDB provided special loans exceeding $5 billion to finance the reforms.

29. To a large extent, the budget deficit in Menem's second term grew out of reductions in labor taxes and the privatization of social security.

30. Certainly, GDP per capita in 1998 was at a historical peak and, hence, one would have expected poverty to be lower than in 1988. But the increase in unemployment and inequality prevented poverty from decreasing in the second part of the 1990s.

31. According to some observers, the quality of Argentina's democracy deteriorated crisis after crisis from an incipient liberal democracy to a dangerous delegative democracy (O'Donnell, 1994). Also, the way in which political institutions work in Argentina does not facilitate consensus-building or high quality policy-making – see notes 32 and 33.

32. Compare for instance the volatility and quality of international policy-making in Argentina vis-à-vis its main neighbors (Spiller and Tommasi, forthcoming; Chapter 4).

33. Some of those issues are raised in Spiller and Tommasi (forthcoming), in Tommasi (2004), and in Acuña and Tommasi (2000).

Table A2.1: Reform chronology in Argentina, 1989–2000

Year	Monetary and financial policy	Fiscal policy	Trade and industrial policy	Privatization	Deregulation policy	Labor market policy
1989	Elimination of currency restrictions on transactions. Debt rescheduling program.	VAT generalized and rate reduced (15% to 13.5%). Reduction in income tax rates. Temporary tax on assets levied. Tax on financial operations.	Suspension of subsidies, industrial promotion, mining promotion. Increase in public utility prices. Promotional regimes in Tierra del Fuego were not affected. Import tariff reform. Reduction of maximum tariff to 30% by the end of the year. Quantitative restrictions were removed for more than half the goods in the quota list. Average tariff is reduced to 21%, and tariff dispersion falls. Temporary suspension of tax refunds for exports. Raise in export duties.	State companies audited. Legal framework for privatization of state-owned enterprises is established.	Price controls eliminated for goods and services. Economic Emergency Law removed prior approval requisite for foreign investment.	
1990	Bonex Plan. Banks' term deposits are repaid in external government bonds.	Tax on corporate assets is raised. Taxes on capital and net worth are repealed. VAT is raised to 15.6%, and its base is expanded.	Import tariffs were reduced. Reduced dispersion. Overall, the average tariff fell to 17%. Specific tariffs were gradually removed. Export refunds were reinstated. Initial Mercosur talks.	Telephones. Airlines. Petrochemicals. Air, oil and roads concessions.		

Integrated budget for state companies. Reduction in the number of areas of central administration.

1991   Convertibility Law. Reform of private companies securities law.

State debt law. VAT increased to 18%. Introduction of a tax on personal assets. Nation/Provinces Agreement: transfer of services.

Five different tariff levels, set according to the stage of the production process where the imported good was used. The average tariff was lowered to 12%, while tariff dispersion grew. A special regime for temporary inputs, which paid no tariff, was put in place. Most export taxes were eliminated, while refunds were lowered. A special regime for the automobile industry was created. Its main feature was a compensated trade regime for local manufacturers. Mercosur Treaty.

Telephone company's stock sale. Association deals and concessions for oil extraction. Railway concessions.

Deregulation of internal trade of goods and services. All restrictions on supply of goods and services not related to national defense, internal security or public utilities were abolished. Official wage schedules not present in collective bargaining agreements were also eliminated. Entry to professional activities was liberalized. State preferential policies for domestic suppliers were lifted.

Employment law introduced several fixed-term contracts and it constitutes the first attempt to flexibilize the Argentine labor market. Introduced fixed-term contracts and special training contracts for young workers. It also created the unemployment benefit system.

(Continued)

Table A2.1: (Continued)

Year	Monetary and financial policy	Fiscal policy	Trade and industrial policy	Privatization	Deregulation policy	Labor market policy
					Deregulated activities included the insurance market, medicine retail distribution and medicine imports. State regulatory entities were dissolved.	
1992	Central Bank Charter. Establishes central bank autarchy. Financial Regulation Law. Authorization to constitute reserve requirements in dollars. Deposit Insurance abolished in December. Basle Capital Requirements adopted.	Extended facilities agreement with IMF. Extension of VAT base. Increase in income tax rate. Nation/Provinces Agreement: tax sharing. Guaranteed minimum monthly transfers to provinces. Debt with pensioners is regularized.	Import reform. The maximum tariff was reduced to 20%. The statistics tax rate was raised, exempting capital goods and temporary imports. Quantitative restrictions were almost completely eliminated, with the exception of the automobile industry. Export refunds were increased. The tax on traditional exports was eliminated. A special regime, with higher refund rates, was in place in Tierra del Fuego. Advance in Mercosur preferential system.	Gas transport and distribution. Railway concessions. Passenger and freight lines. Water supply. Electricity supply. Iron and steel companies.	Ports Law. It authorized the creation of private ports, as well as the transfer to the provinces and privatization of existing national ports. Deregulation of medium and long-distance bus services.	

(Continued)

| 1993 | Brady Plan. Prohibition of deposits for periods shorter than 30 days. Mutual Funds Law. New securitization rules. | Nation/Provinces Agreement: tax structure coordination. Income tax modifications. New scale for rates on individual earnings. Tax on corporate assets repealed. Reform of social security system is sanctioned. | Industrial promotion regimes were hardened, imposing greater accountability and more severe punishments. Reduced restrictions on investment in mining projects. The ban on foreign investment in frontier areas, where most mineral deposits are located, is lifted. So is the prior approval requirement for all mining investments on both foreign and domestic projects. Finally, it removed transport restrictions and taxes on mineral exports. | Placement of anti-dumping measures. Specific import tariffs (mainly those on textiles and steel) were raised. Tax-free zones regime. | YPF (oil and energy company). Hydroelectric and thermal plants. Electricity transmission. Railway and subway concessions. | Foreign investment further liberalized – treated on a par with domestic investment. |

Table A2.1: (*Continued*)

Year	Monetary and financial policy	Fiscal policy	Trade and industrial policy	Privatization	Deregulation policy	Labor market policy
		Creates a private savings funds system to coexist with a public 'pay as you go' system.				
1994	Financial Entities Law: equal treatment for domestic and foreign capital. Capital requirements raised in December.	Reduction in employer payroll taxes. New social security system in place.	Agreement for the Mercosur Common External Tariff.	Power plants. Electricity distribution. Gas transport and distribution stock sale.		
1995	Central Bank charter is modified: grants the central bank greater authority over banks. Bank capitalization fiduciary fund to aid financial institutions with liquidity problems. Provisioning requirements are raised. Introduction of liquidity requirements.	Increase in VAT rate to 21%. Personal assets tax lowered. Income and personal assets tax bases extended. Partial and transitory elimination of the reduction in employer payroll taxes.	Mercosur operational. Common External Tariff is enacted. Export refunds were redefined for exports outside Mercosur, and gradually reduced for intra-Mercosur trades. Raise in import tariffs.	Power plants. Bahia Blanca petrochemical.		Flexibilization law generalized the set of fixed-term contracts regulated in 1991 by law 24.013. It also introduced a trial period of up to six months.

	Deposits insurance (limited, fully funded).					
1996	Financial Entities Law: sets forth the legal framework applicable to assets and liabilities of liquidated financial institutions. Market risk capital requirements.	Expansion of income tax base. Rise in tax on liquid fuels and gas. Modification of family allowances regime. Reduction of employer payroll taxes. Customs authority (DGA) and the federal tax collection agency (DGI) were merged.	Suspension of refunds on the production of capital goods. Mercosur-Bolivia and Mercosur-Chile treaties.	Provincial banks.	*Obras Sociales* deregulation: employees could choose a service provider other than their labor union.	Modifications to the Accidents and Professional Sickness regime. Establishment of an insurance system.
1997	Liquidity requirements for banks were raised, as well as capital requirements. Reserves for risky credits are raised. BASIC criteria introduced.			National Post Office.		

(Continued)

Table A2.1: (*Continued*)

Year	Monetary and financial policy	Fiscal policy	Trade and industrial policy	Privatization	Deregulation policy	Labor market policy
1998	Mercosur: rules for the operation of banks from one country in the market in another.	Tax reform: reduction in social security taxes, reduction of VAT rate to half (from 21% to 10.5%) for basic foodstuffs, VAT exemptions eliminated, rise in internal taxes, income tax rate raised to 35%. Creation of tax on interest payments by firms.	Tariffs and statistics tax unified.	Airports. Transfer mechanism for nuclear power plants. Congressional approval to sell Banco Hipotecario Nacional.		Elimination of promoted contracts. Substantial reduction of severance payment for short tenure employment relationships. Increase in the degree of centralization prevalent in collective bargaining.
1999	Introduction of capital requirements for exposure to interest rate risk.					
2000						Decentralization of collective bargaining.

Source: Author's elaboration based on Berlinski (1998), Calomiris and Powell (2000), Chudnovsky and López (2001), Galiani and Gerchunoff (2003), Heymann (2000), Rojo and Hoberman (1994), and relevant laws and decrees.

3
Pragmatism and Market Reforms in Brazil

Armando Castelar Pinheiro, Regis Bonelli, and
Ben Ross Schneider

3.1   Introduction

In comparison with reform processes in the other major countries of Latin America – especially Chile, Mexico, and Argentina – market reforms in Brazil came later and were implemented more gradually and flexibly.[1] In both trade liberalization and privatization, for instance, Brazil lagged behind the regional average until 1994 and 1999, respectively, although eventually catching up and even surpassing it in the case of privatization. Indeed, in 1999 Brazil's overall index of structural reform matched Chile's, a regional benchmark with respect to market reforms (Lora, 2001).

However, what stands out in Brazil's reform process is less the depth and direction of reform or the main contextual factors encouraging it, than the 'why' and 'how' of reform. In contrast to other reform experiences, especially in Latin America, reforms in Brazil were usually more gradual, contested, piecemeal, and pragmatic, in the sense of being largely targeted at solving specific problems. Ideology and partisan politics played a lesser role in fostering market reforms in Brazil than in other countries. Although reforms were often bundled together with other urgent or popular policies to facilitate their approval, they were not enacted as a coherent, overall change in development strategy, but rather as an incomplete, flexible, mostly disconnected reform process. That they reduced state intervention in the economy was more the result of a pragmatic reaction to economic constraints, internal and external, and a lack of alternatives than the outcome of 'a newfound ideological conviction in the virtues of the market' (Fishlow, 1990: 62).

This chapter argues that to understand the peculiarities of reform implementation, and post-reform economic performance, we need to look back to the motivations of the policy-makers who started the reforms and shepherded them through implementation. This focus on motivations and implementation is a sharp departure from the bulk of the literature on the domestic politics of market reform, considered further in the next section, which assumes motivations and concentrates instead on the structural and institutional factors affecting the initial adoption of reforms. Among the few studies that do consider motives, most focus exclusively on ideology, partisanship, clientelism, and rent-seeking, and neglect the sort of pragmatic and problem solving approaches that we highlight.

This chapter analyzes the gradual, pragmatic process of partial state retrenchment in Brazil that spans the last twenty years. Section 3.2 defines pragmatism in reform politics and compares it to other motivations such as ideology and partisan politics. Section 3.3 examines the reform process in Brazil and focuses primarily on three crucial areas in the 1990s – privatization, trade liberalization, and regulatory reform. Section 3.4 considers the uneven economic consequences of these reforms and contrasts the positive impact in particular areas, such as telecommunications and some manufacturing sectors, with their weak aggregate effects on growth. The conclusion raises some further issues on the sources and consequences of pragmatism in policy-making in Brazil.

3.2   Varieties of reform politics and the political economy of pragmatism

The now large literature on reforms offers several competing theoretical approaches to explaining why so many developing countries adopted market-oriented reforms after 1980. Globalization or convergence theories, for instance, privilege either international finance and capital mobility (Mahon, 1996), ideas (Weyland, 2004b), or pressure from international financial institutions through the so-called Washington Consensus. However, these approaches all emphasize fairly uniform international pressures on developing countries and are thus less helpful in explaining the wide cross-national variations in the timing, motivation, and implementation of reform.

A number of alternative approaches have turned to domestic politics to identify the sources of variation in reform processes. Some analyses privileged domestic coalitions, especially opposing coalitions of economic winners and losers in the reform process (see Schneider, 2004b for a review). The expectation was that, other things being equal, the coalition of potential losers from market reforms would prevail over the coalition of potential winners. Attention therefore shifted to institutions and especially the kinds of institutional configurations that allowed reformers in some countries to prevail over coalitions of potential losers. Factors like party fragmentation, relations between executive and legislative branches, and institutional veto points were central to these institutional analyses (Haggard and Kaufman, 1995). These institutional analyses helped identify obstacles that slowed reform in later reforming countries, but, like much coalitional and institutional analysis, they were sometimes fairly mechanical, and privileged structure over agency. Corrective explanations often turned to agents and analyzed the roles of political entrepreneurs (Haggard, 2000) and leadership (Corrales, 2002; Gibson, 1997) in promoting reform. These analyses illuminated instances where particularly adept reformers overcame unfavorable institutional obstacles.

Even in these agent-centered accounts, what is often missing (as in most institutional arguments as well) is motivation: Why is it that reformers want to reform in the first place? In some ways this brings us full circle to international convergence and economic coalitions where motivations were clearer, either externally imposed or simple self-interest. Self-interest and ideas are useful starting points for assessing the orientations of key policy actors, but they hardly do justice to the complexities of motivation in policy-making. Many early analyses considered market reforms as public goods (hence the pessimism on coalitional grounds). But policy-makers in Latin America quickly discovered that neutral looking market-oriented policies could in fact, like most redistributive policies, be used to further a variety of goals, regardless of whether the end result was a public good or not. One line of analysis emphasizes how reform politics, especially privatization, create massive, divisible, private goods that politicians therefore have incentives to distribute in particularistic ways to generate political support (Schamis, 2002; Murillo, 2002). Other perspectives take a broader, less venial view of political self-interest and consider the kinds of general partisan beliefs and party interests that infuse policy options in implementing reforms (Murillo, 2004; Boix, 1997).

Although more nuanced, this partisan perspective is still an over-simplification that does not capture the wider range of goals which empirically have motivated reformers. This chapter proposes a more inclusive typology which encompasses a fuller range of motivations – ideological, partisan, or pragmatic – that inspired market reform and better explains the comparative diversity of reform processes.[2]

In the *ideological* approach policy-makers are guided by coherent, longer-term strategies to create new development models and societies to fit them. In terms of recent market reforms, policy-makers were sometimes inspired by radical neo-liberalism. Ideologically-motivated policy implementation comprises a comprehensive, interconnected, unidirectional set of deep reforms that are implemented inflexibly even if they entail high upfront economic and political costs. The classic example is Chile in the 1970s where the economic team had a complete neo-liberal blueprint of the new economic model to be put in place.

Reform implementation inspired primarily by *partisan* goals is designed to hurt political groups opposed to the government and favor those who support (or who could be induced to support) the government (see especially Murillo, 2002 and 2004, and Schamis, 2002). For example, selling a particular government firm might weaken an opposition union and curry favor with the new buyers. Many logistical details of selling any particular SOE – sale price, debt, output pricing, or post-privatization restrictions on entry – can be structured by partisan reformers to provide major benefits to supporters who want to buy the firms.

The concept of *pragmatism* in policy-making and reform is more complicated. Posner (2003: 24) laments that pragmatism 'is a devil to define'. Most definitions characterize pragmatism in primarily negative terms, in the absence of other kinds of motivation. In practice negative definitions are useful in identifying non-pragmatic behavior, but an exclusive focus on negative aspects, such as the absence of ideology, creates an overly large and diverse residual category. To infuse pragmatism with more positive connotations, we understand pragmatic policy processes to be characterized by: (1) more specific, *measurable* goals, such as increased exports or investment in energy; (2) close, simple connections between *means and ends* (also known as instrumental policies, usually de-linked from other policy goals or packages); (3) *flexible* implementation to adjust to exogenous shocks and problems in initial policies (sensitive to feedback); and (4) greater *gradualism and continuity* in discrete policy areas, that is, adjusting policy (learning from experience) rather than wholesale policy shifts.[3]

Fiscal and monetary policy-making tend naturally to be pragmatic, in part because they have ongoing targets of budget deficits, borrowing, inflation, and interest rates that are easily measured and less open, especially by the 1990s, to ideological and partisan uses. The analytic challenge grows in instances where reforms can serve multiple policy goals, as with privatization, which can both reduce budget deficits and promote sectoral investment, or trade liberalization, which can help hold prices down and simultaneously foster productivity growth. However, when macro goals trump micro concerns, then the process may be pragmatic in macro terms, and yet reduce pragmatic features of micro reforms. For example, privatizing firms as monopolies enhances their sale price, allowing for a larger reduction in the public debt, but the monopoly structure may undermine post-privatization performance.

Thus, pragmatic reforms are not driven by an overarching ideological model, but by the effort to solve specific problems. For some pragmatists, market-friendly policies may not even be viewed as inherently superior to a state-led alternative. Thus, pragmatic privatization is not motivated by a liberal view about restricting the role of the state but more often by fiscal constraints which limit public investment and encourage policy-makers to look for ways to attract private investment. Or, pragmatists may lower tariffs to maximize the longer-term efficiency of firms and promote export-oriented sectors, but they may later increase tariffs temporarily or partially to reduce short-term trade deficits or temporarily relieve import pressure on sectors that are deemed to be competitive over the longer run. What is distinctive about the two other approaches – ideological and partisan – is that they favor more rigid policies and tolerate higher economic costs in order to maximize other political or economic goals. In pragmatic reforms, policy-makers know which variables to monitor to gauge success, and generally adjust policy instruments flexibly in the face of changing performance and conditions in the target area of the economy. Moreover, they are comfortable mixing policies that reduce state intervention with others that do not.

A mixture of approaches, reflecting the multiple goals motivating governments, often marked country reform experiences and even individual policies.

Moreover, some policies provided happy coincidence among multiple goals, although that was not the norm. Still, it is usually possible to weigh the mix of approaches and goals and compare them across policies, across countries, and across governments within individual countries. A full comparative analysis is beyond the scope of this chapter, but among the large countries of Latin America, market reforms in Brazil in the 1990s were more pragmatic than in Chile in the 1970s – where ideological and partisan motives predominated – or in Argentina and Mexico in the 1990s – where a mix of ideological and partisan goals tended to prevail. Or, to take policy change over time in one country, most observers draw a sharp distinction in Chile between ideologically-motivated reforms in the 1970s and a more pragmatic reform approach in the 1980s (Silva, 1996). The gradual reform process in Colombia may most closely resemble the pragmatism of Brazilian reform. In what follows we justify our preference for the pragmatic view of Brazil's recent reform process, but we concede that sometimes pragmatism was combined with alternative approaches (that is, ideological) in pushing specific reforms.

Brazil is generally classified as a case of later and incomplete, yet relatively successful market reform (Lora, 2001). Applied to Brazil, many of the analytic perspectives presented at the beginning of this section seem to illuminate at least part of the story. From a globalization perspective, Brazil was relatively insulated from international pressures because it lacked the sorts of strong transnational networks (Teichman, 2001) from US universities that were major conduits in other countries for the diffusion of the Washington Consensus, and initially the capital privation of the debt crisis was not as severe in Brazil as elsewhere in the region. Institutional perspectives on Brazil highlighted the major impediments created by the electoral and party systems, which generated fragmentation and centrifugal electoral and legislative incentives inimical to coherent market reform.

Yet, reformers in Brazil, especially Presidents Collor (1990–92) and Cardoso (1995–2002), exercised leadership and political entrepreneurship that helped them overcome institutional obstacles. However, the record of their actions does not provide a full explanation of Brazilian reform. In fact, the reform trajectory in Brazil begins at the end of the term of one of Brazil's least effective Presidents, José Sarney (1985–89), and continues through another place-holder president, Itamar Franco (1992–94). Moreover, reform continued across presidential administrations of right (Collor), center (Cardoso), and left (Lula), which reduces the explanatory potential of ideology and partisanship. If one looks in greater depth at the policy-making involving mid-level reformers in the executive branch, a brand of pragmatism is revealed that had a strong and lasting influence on market reform, though its impact varied over time and across policy areas.

We now turn to a closer examination of the reform process in Brazil, first with a brief overview and then a more in-depth analysis of trade liberalization, privatization, and regulatory reform. This empirical analysis highlights

pragmatic features of the reform process, especially in the adaptive implementation of major reforms, and includes where possible direct evidence on
the motives of policy-makers.

3.3   The process of market reform in Brazil

A full list of major reform initiatives in Brazil after the mid-1980s would encom-
pass most of the 10 areas of the first Washington Consensus as well as second-
and third-generation reforms in other major policy areas. Among the most
far-reaching reforms were decentralization, trade liberalization, privatization,
and fiscal and regulatory reforms. In addition, governments since the 1990s
have attempted important reforms in capital account liberalization, health
care, public administration, education, social security, and banking. After a
brief overview of the overall progress of market reform, we move to a closer
examination of trade liberalization, privatization, and regulatory reform.
Reforms in these three areas have had the greatest impact overall in terms of
shifting allocative decisions from the state to the market, and in shifting
operational control from government to business.

For the most part, major reform processes in Brazil in trade, privatization,
and regulation were pragmatic. Occasionally reforms were bundled with macro
policies, and in some more isolated instances partisan motives were also part
of the mix. The overall reform process in Brazil followed a wave-like pattern
common in other countries, with intense periods of reform activity in the
first years of the Collor, Cardoso, and, to a lesser extent, Lula governments
(1990, 1994–95, and 2003), when reforms were bundled with efforts to restore
macro stability and investor confidence. Coming off electoral victories, governments initially enjoyed a honeymoon period during which Congress was
most inclined to approve the government's legislative initiatives. This was
particularly true with Collor in 1990, his first year in office, but the last year
for all deputies and a third of the senators. In subsequent years, as macro
policies either failed or succeeded, the bundling connection weakened.
However, significant reforms continued, pushed largely by state and business elites with narrower, more pragmatic goals.

Unlike many countries in Latin America, market reforms in Brazil were not
associated primarily with any single president or party coalition in democratic contexts, or with the rise of a new dominant technocracy in the executive branch in authoritarian settings (Chile in the 1970s or the neo-liberal
technocracy in Mexico in the 1980s and 1990s). In Brazil, a series of presidents from different parties pushed reforms, and top bureaucrats who implemented these reforms resembled in most respects those who preceded them
in the military regime. The initial impetus for reform generally came from small
groups of top economic policy-makers – 'change teams' in Waterbury's (1989)
term – who usually counted on support from key allies in big business. As such,
these change teams resembled the public–private networks that predominated

in economic policy-making during military rule.[4] Among top policy-makers after 1985 there was a relatively consistent mix of career bureaucrats, domestically trained economists, foreign trained economists, occasionally elected politicians, and appointees drawn from business. These policy-making elites were the primary proponents of pragmatic approaches to market reform.

The low growth rates of the 1980s pressured policy-makers to shift from a strategy focused on industrial diversification to one more concerned with productivity growth and competitiveness. Although of little practical significance, the reforms of the 1980s were important in launching a domestic debate over market-oriented reforms, and paving the way for their acceleration in the 1990s. The reforms of the 1980s also revealed and strengthened a new generation of reform-oriented officials who would later be important actors in the broader reform process. Indeed, many of the reform proposals came from inside the state bureaucracy, including calls for furthering privatization, which some SOE managers considered the only way out for their companies (Schneider, 1990). Also, officials in the Ministry of Finance who managed the elimination of redundant tariffs in the late 1980s would later be responsible for implementing the more significant opening of the early 1990s.

Some idiosyncratic and conjunctural factors also influenced Brazil's reform trajectory. For example, prospects for reform were greatly enhanced in 1989, when Fernando Collor de Mello, a previously little known political outsider, won the presidential election with a platform of ideological sounding neo-liberalism (see Kingstone, 1999). Collor had little political support among Brazil's main parties, as was later evident in his impeachment in 1992, but his lack of ties to the existing political elite also facilitated his decision to break from the gradualist approach that had characterized the controlled policy transition in the 1980s. He was also successful in bundling market-oriented reforms – in particular, privatization, trade and regulatory reform – with his stabilization plan, all launched and approved together by Congress (and the judiciary) in his first months in office. The hyperinflation of 1988–89 helped to legitimize the draconian stabilization plan and, indirectly, market reforms. Had the Collor government lasted longer and succeeded in implementing its reform agenda, it might have been remembered as an ideologically inspired reform process. However, even the partial reforms Collor did manage to set in motion were less radical than they initially appeared. For example, the Collor government announced a radical, sweeping privatization program, yet in fact the implementation started gradually, with state enterprises in manufacturing (such as petrochemicals, steel, and fertilizers), where opinion among state and private elites already favored privatization (IDESP, 1990). Collor did have, though, a more lasting impact by legitimizing neo-liberalism in policy debates and in mobilizing a loose coalition of reform supporters.

In 1990, Collor adopted a big-bang reform package, tied initially to a radical stabilization program, which among other things started serious trade liberalization, promised to privatize major state enterprises, and deregulated a number of sectors. However, the bundling was loose because both privatization and trade liberalization were designed to be gradual and would not have a major impact on macro stabilization in the short term. Moreover, Collor's stabilization plan relied centrally on a freeze of private banking assets, which proved to be excessively harsh in its beginnings. Over the course of 1991, a number of reform proposals stalled in Congress, where Collor lacked a legislative support coalition. Nonetheless, privatization and trade liberalization proceeded, to a large extent because their implementation had been delegated to relatively autonomous agencies (see Bonelli et al., 1997).

In 1992 Collor was impeached on corruption charges and replaced by his vice-president Itamar Franco. Policies in the Franco government returned to the patterns observed in the late 1980s: inconsistent, piecemeal reforms that were generally overshadowed by short-term macroeconomic and political issues. Franco personally was no fan of privatization, but he did not block the sale of firms already slated for privatization. Moreover, the gradual schedule of tariff reductions announced in 1990 continued and even accelerated in late 1994.

With the Real Plan and Cardoso's election in late 1994, the reform process was again bundled, this time more directly and consequentially to the stabilization plan. By 1994, tariffs were low enough that import competition, especially with an overvalued exchange rate from the second semester onwards, was a significant constraint on price increases. The Cardoso government also contracted enormous additional debt, both foreign and domestic, thereby increasing the importance of maintaining investor confidence. Moreover, privatization attracted FDI inflows and generated resources used to redeem public debt securities. In this way privatization was instrumental in relaxing the foreign exchange and fiscal constraints that threatened the sustainability of the policy mix adopted in Cardoso's first administration (1995–98).

To the surprise of most observers, the Lula government that took office in 2003 made a renewed drive for reform its top priority, starting with (public sector) pension reform, as it attempted to restore investor confidence and contain inflation. While reforms in pensions and taxation were not strictly speaking market reforms, they were indispensable to fiscal management. In other areas of market reform the Lula government froze ongoing reform initiatives, but did not backtrack on them, as many observers feared. In its first year, the PT government severely criticized the regulatory framework for recently privatized public utilities. However, the legislation the PT government ultimately proposed to reform the regulatory framework was intended more to standardize regulatory practices across sectors than as a radical redesign. This legislation, nonetheless, subsequently stalled in Congress.

The next sections examine in greater depth the reform process in three core policy areas. These detailed narratives highlight different aspects of pragmatism in action. The analysis of trade liberalization follows its uneven implementation over time and across sectors to illuminate both flexibility in adjusting to changing circumstances and occasional subordination to macro policy.

The examination of the privatization process reveals the impetus provided by fairly autonomous mid-level officials working to solve specific problems of low investment. Lastly, the section on regulation provides a telling comparison between the pragmatism in telecommunications versus more partisan politicking in electricity.

3.3.1 Trade liberalization

Starting in 1988, Brazil liberalized import policies to foster allocative efficiency via external competition. Three rounds of tariff reductions took place – 1988–89, 1991–93, and 1994 (Kume et al., 2003). In the late 1980s, pressure from multilateral institutions, spontaneous initiatives from bureaucratic elites, and the easing of foreign exchange constraints fostered a cut on the average tariff on imports from 51 to 35 per cent. The main goal was to modernize the industrial sector, while reinstating some sector differentiation in protection. Because they focused essentially on reducing tariff redundancies, these reductions faced little opposition. The second round was more radical and has had by far the deepest and most lasting effects on the economy. According to the original schedule, the median tariff was to fall gradually from 30 to 10 per cent, with the maximum tariff declining from 105 to 20 per cent. The post-1990 liberalization also eliminated many non-tariff barriers.

Underlying the option for gradual tariff reductions was the concern with raising public support for the liberalization program. Thus, the way the tariff reduction schedule was organized was supposed to gradually increase access to imported consumer goods, without pushing the trade balance into a deficit or swamping domestic markets with imports, which would quickly stimulate resistance to trade liberalization from domestic producers. Moreover, imports of industrial inputs and capital goods were liberalized first, to allow domestic producers to become more competitive before foreign competition increased in the final stages of the process. By then, it would be important to have a clear perception of advantages stemming from liberalization to guarantee support for the program's continuity (Kume et al., 2003). This staggered opening, designed to help firms adjust, distinguishes the reform process in Brazil from other countries where trade liberalization was more uniform and less concerned with assisting micro adjustment. In Brazil, the linking of the implementation of trade liberalization to medium-term performance by Brazilian firms is a good illustration of pragmatism in the way reformers conceived of a close means–end connection (opening and firm competitiveness) and adjusted implementation flexibly.

The 1990 schedule was modified several times, mostly in order to anticipate tariff cuts. In 1992, when it became likely that Collor would be impeached, the outgoing government decided to speed up the process to pre-empt pressures for a suspension of the original schedule by the less liberal Itamar Franco government. The widening of trade liberalization at the end of 1994 illustrates the kind of macro bundling that permeated most reform processes at the time.

Import tariffs were reduced to check domestic price increases, when doubts about the sustainability of the new stabilization plan were high and producers threatened to raise prices under domestic demand pressures and low idle capacity. An opposite trend was observed after 1994, when tariffs were increased on a number of consumer goods, some of which had received tariff reductions only a few months before, reflecting the pressure from interest groups, worries over 'excessive' import penetration in bellwether sectors like autos, and fears that rising trade deficits could threaten the sustainability of the stabilization plan. Then, as in the following years, the fear was that an exchange rate depreciation, to check the deficit in the external accounts, would bring high inflation back. This was the case, in November 1997, when authorities raised tariffs by three percentage points in reaction to increasing current account deficits and the shortage of external finance in the wake of the Asian crisis. At the same time, from 1995 onwards, tariffs on a selected set of food products, chemicals, textiles, and metallurgical products were reduced to check (so-called abusive) price increases. The pragmatic, flexible character of trade liberalization was clear in this selective tinkering with tariffs, which also encompassed frequent alterations of import duties of goods on the 'exception list' of Mercosur's common external tariffs (CET), so as to keep duties on certain products well above those accorded among Mercosur partners (Baumann et al., 1997).

Opposition grew stronger in the 1990s when imports were de facto liberalized. Companies that had invested in Brazil as part of the import substitution process, notably those of foreign capital, and the associated labor unions, were the main opponents of trade liberalization in the early 1990s. These were sectors in which domestic competition was low or nonexistent, allowing for the extraction of rents that were partly shared with organized labor. Four different factors were instrumental in dealing with those pressures and keeping the economy relatively open. First, the impact of trade liberalization on import flows was delayed by the 1990–92 recession, the still high average tariffs prevailing up to 1993, and the lack of distribution channels to commercialize imported goods. The protracted reaction of import volumes helped to allay the resistance of domestic manufacturers and nationalist groups to trade liberalization. Second, there was greater support in public opinion as consumers benefited from the opportunity to buy imported goods they had been denied for decades. Firms also benefited from newly imported raw materials, parts, components, and machinery and equipment of superior quality, which helped to boost productivity and competitiveness. Moreover, the firms established to commercialize imports, as in the automobile sector, formed a new constituency in favor of low tariffs. Third, the fixing of import tariffs in Brazil is a prerogative of the Executive, with little influence from Congress and the judiciary. Fourth, pressures from politically powerful sectors were accommodated selectively, increasing the dispersion of tariffs, but not affecting the average tariff as much.[5] This reaction was facilitated by the flexibility afforded by Mercosur's exception list. Protectionist interests were particularly strong in the automotive sector, among many interest groups, ranging from the industry itself to powerful labor unions, auto dealers, and politicians and government officials who frequently called attention to the income and employment-generating effects associated with the industry's performance.

Overall, by regional standards Brazil's trade opening was late, gradual, flexibly and unevenly implemented, and, by the end of the 1990s, still lagged somewhat behind the regional average (Lora, 2001). Nonetheless, liberalization constituted one of the most important shifts in post-war development strategy. Total trade more than doubled in the 1990s and liberalization promoted significant increases in productivity (as discussed in Section 3.4).

3.3.2 Privatization

Spanning two decades, with total revenues of close to US$83 billion and almost 170 SOEs sold, privatization substantially changed Brazil's economic and political landscape. Yet, privatization in Brazil was above all a pragmatic response to the public sector's inability to carry out needed investments in key sectors of the economy. It also had secondary bundling motivations, stemming from short-term macroeconomic problems, related mostly to curbing the growth of the public debt (Pinheiro and Giambiagi, 2000).

Privatization entered the economic policy agenda in 1981 with the creation of the Special Privatization Commission (*Comissão Especial de Desestatização*). Overall, 38 companies were privatized in 1981–89, grossing US$0.7 billion in revenues. A number of other small SOEs were closed down or transferred to local governments. Most of the sales in the 1980s were carried out by BNDES, whose motivation for privatizing owed more to the need to free itself of these problematic, loss-making companies than to a favorable perception of privatization on the part of the government. Márcio Fortes, the president of the BNDES in the late 1980s and a central figure in this early phase of Brazilian privatization, put the issue this way:

> Privatization, in reality, was not such a central policy. It was the need which the BNDES had, primarily, to generate funds from within its own equity holdings; secondly, to obtain liquidity for its normal activities; and, thirdly, because its own internal management was greatly weakened by the build-up of necessary management activities in its day-to-day routine. It was, after all, owner or controlling stockholder of more than 25 highly complex companies.
>
> (Fortes, 1994)

In 1990, the Collor administration launched the Brazilian Privatization Program (PND) which significantly widened the scope of privatization. The government initially bundled privatization together with the stabilization program launched at the same time, which froze public debt securities at the Central Bank for 18 months. One of the few things the holders of government debt could do with their frozen assets was to buy shares in SOEs. The idea was to encourage a swap between frozen securities and SOE shares with the goal of simultaneously reducing public indebtedness and creating a captive demand for the privatization program. However, this synergy between stabilization and privatization failed due to problems in both programs. Privatization began with overly optimistic targets regarding revenue and speed, which turned out to be unrealistic due to the bad financial situation of the SOEs and the complexity of their stockholders' agreements. It was in fact only at the end of 1991 that the first company was sold under the PND. By that time the Central Bank had already begun to return frozen assets to firms and individuals, and their use as a privatization 'currency' was negligible in the end.[6]

Also important was the autonomy of the BNDES within the government and the commitment with which it pursued privatization. The freedom BNDES enjoyed in managing the PND stemmed from a number of factors, including the way the privatization law was set up, the fact that the same person presided over the bank and the privatization commission that had to approve its actions and decisions, the BNDES' control over sizable resources (as Brazil's largest development bank), and support from others in government. Its history as leader of the privatization drive in the 1980s, the know-how thus obtained, and a board of executive directors composed mostly of young liberal economists generated an autonomous bond between BNDES and the PND, which kept the program going even after corruption charges against Collor nearly paralyzed the government.

Although representing a substantial expansion with respect to the 1980s, the scope of privatization in the early 1990s was limited by rising inflation and low growth, which reduced the already compressed levels of domestic and foreign investment. In all, 33 companies were privatized during the Collor and Franco governments (1990–94). Total revenues reached US$8.6 billion (Table 3.1). Almost all companies were in manufacturing, with revenues concentrated in the steel, petrochemicals, and fertilizer sectors. The companies selected for sale had in common the fact that they belonged to relatively competitive sectors. The privatization of the state monopolies was not even considered at the time because it required major political mobilization and coalition-building beyond the capacity of the weak Collor and Franco governments. Nonetheless, by the end of the Franco government the PND had managed to sell off all SOEs not protected by constitutional provisions.

Brazilian privatization peaked during Cardoso's first term (1995–98), when 80 companies were sold, grossing more than US$60 billion in total proceeds. In only five years (1996–2000), the state greatly reduced its participation in telecommunications, electricity, railways, ports, roads, and water and sanitation. The telecommunication and railroad sectors and most port terminals were completely privatized. In the electricity industry, the private sector became dominant in distribution and acquired a large stake in generation.

Table 3.1: Privatization proceeds and number of SOEs sold, 1991–2002

Year	Proceeds (US$ million)[a]					Number of SOEs		
	Federal level	State level	Total	% of GDP	Privatization related FDI	Federal level	State level	Total
1991	1,614		1,614	0.4	*	4		4
1992	2,401		2,401	0.6	*	14		14
1993	2,627		2,627	0.6	*	6		6
1994	1,966		1,966	0.4	*	9		9
1995	1,004		1,004	0.1	*	8		8
1996	4,080	1,406	5,486	0.7	2,645	16	2	18
1997	8,999	13,617	22,616	2.8	5,249	21	15	36
1998	23,478	7,497	30,975	3.9	6,121	7	11	18
1999	554	2,648	3,202	0.6	8,766	6	5	11
2000	7,670	2,752	10,422	1.7	7,051	1	5	6
2001	2,905	27	2,935	0.6	1,079	1	1	2
2002	2,233		2,233	0.5	280	1		1
Total	59,531	27,949	87,480		31,191	94	39	133

Notes: Data on proceeds is distributed according to year of sale, that for privatization related FDI according to year in which resources actually entered the country. (*) Information not available prior to 1996; foreign participation in the privatization program prior to 1996 was, though, close to nil.
[a] Includes sales of minority shareholdings.
Source: BNDES and Central Bank.

Private participation remains less significant in roads and water and sanitation, but there too it expanded (see Pinheiro and Fukasaku, 2000).

In the Cardoso government, privatization was largely a 'creature' of the government's inner circle, including the president, the economic team, relatively autonomous institutions such as BNDES, and some occasional allies, such as the Minister of Communications in Cardoso's first term. In the new government's initial honeymoon years, they were able to amend the constitution and greatly enlarge the scope of the privatization program. Later, when the government's popularity dropped in the wake of the 1999 devaluation and the alleged improprieties in the sale of Telebrás, the privatization program stalled. The main motivation of the 'change team' in the Cardoso government was the perception that the poor situation of the fiscal accounts blocked a rise in much needed SOE investment, which was expected to occur under private ownership. Only a fraction of those in this inner circle or in the larger group that helped to push privatization forward did this in pursuit of an ideological neo-liberal agenda (Velasco, 1997a and 1997b).

Overall, Brazil took its privatization program further than the regional average, and was surpassed only by Bolivia and Peru (Lora, 2001). In total, the program generated revenues of almost 13 per cent of one year's average GDP from

1991–2002, with the bulk coming after 1995, and attracted large inflows of FDI. Post-privatization regulatory reform also reached impressive results in breadth and depth. New regulatory agencies in several sectors gained institutional foundations and helped promote positive outcomes in newly privatized areas, though the outcomes varied greatly across sectors, as we discuss in the next section.

3.3.3   Regulatory reform

Privatization and free entry were deemed necessary but not sufficient measures to increase investment in infrastructure; the very poor regulatory framework also needed to be revamped in order to attract sufficient private capital. Traditionally, regulation and supervision had been entrusted to departments in the sector ministries that controlled the corresponding SOEs. These departments often lacked independence from the government or were captured by SOEs, and they did not control prices – which were set by the Ministry of Finance, mostly in accordance with macroeconomic objectives. Price structures carried a number of cross-subsidies across consumer groups and companies, leading to allocative and technical inefficiency. Lack of proper regulation also meant that SOEs were left unaccountable regarding the quality of services offered to consumers, not least because they faced no competition.

Infrastructure regulation started to change in the early 1990s, but the first critical steps were taken in 1995, when Congress approved a Concessions Law. Overall, regulatory reform followed a similar blueprint in all sectors, although the final result varied with respect to timing, emphasis, and success, reflecting the specific motivations of reform supporters and opponents in each sector, as well as different degrees of institutional and technical complexity (Pinheiro, 2005; Oliveira and Fujiwara, 2005).

The reform process separated the policy, regulatory, and business activities in each sector, while introducing a greater degree of competition among regulated companies. Policy responsibilities were ascribed to the sector ministry, regulation entrusted to an independent agency, and business activities left with sector SOEs (slated for eventual privatization). Private ownership and competition were expected to raise efficiency and, together with adequate prices and the higher creditworthiness of the new private owners, facilitate access to finance and raise investment. Regulatory agencies were to enjoy administrative and financial independence and to control prices in segments where firms had significant market power – subject to the rules set out in the concession contracts and the general principle of financial and economic equilibrium of the concession established in the Concessions Law. The agencies were to play the dual role of fostering investment and efficiency while protecting private investors from the risk of administrative expropriation. As a rule, the concern to introduce competition was reflected in the setting up of non-monopolistic industry structures with several SOEs being separated horizontally (railroads, electricity, and telecommunications) and vertically (telecommunications and electricity) before privatization. In addition, new regulations limited the participation of individual investors in different markets, regional and national, and even on the ownership structure of some companies (such as the railroads).

The most successful case of privatization cum regulatory reform was telecommunications. The process began with the approval of the so-called 'Minimum Law', which authorized auctions of B-Band cellular concessions.[7] When privatization took place, the entire regulatory structure was already established and the regulatory agency responsible for the sector, Anatel, was fully operational. Implementation of regulatory reform in the electricity sector was much less successful. Aneel, the sector regulator, was created only in 1997, two years after privatization in the sector had begun. The order of events tended to limit the capacity of the regulatory agency to operate and, as a result, limited its prestige in the eyes of the public at large. Moreover, electricity regulation lacked a clear separation between the functions of the various agencies involved, reducing their accountability. In 2001, a severe power shortage revealed several flaws in the sector's regulatory framework and virtually paralyzed the reform process.

Much of the difference in the processes of regulatory reform in telecommunications and electricity resulted from differences in political contention among major stakeholders within the government, especially in the federal executive branch.[8] The Minister of Communications, a close ally of Cardoso and a core member of Cardoso's party (PSDB), had full freedom to appoint his staff and worked with SOE and ministry officials to devise a program of privatization and regulation without much interference from other stakeholders. In electricity, in contrast, the Minister of Mines and Energy came from an allied party (PFL), did not appoint all of his staff, and could not control contention among numerous stakeholders, which included ministry staff (DNAEE), Eletrobrás, state governments, and BNDES. Intra-government conflicts thus slowed privatization and regulatory reform in electricity.

This contrast between the reform processes in telecommunications and electricity illuminates well the role of pragmatism in the former, and politics, partly partisan, in the latter. In the former case the change team focused on an instrumental reform plan with close connections between means (privatization and regulation) and ends (efficiency and investment in the sector). Ideological motivations were not apparent in reform planning, and protection against interference from both partisan politicians and macroeconomic policy-makers was assured.[9] The reform process in electricity was less pragmatic and more subject to partisan and bureaucratic politics. Given that the minister's appointment was intended first to balance the government's legislative coalition, and compounded by the minister's lack of control within the ministry, the reform process was likely to be vulnerable to partisan pressures. In addition, the sector involved numerous public stakeholders and reform therefore had to navigate contentious turf battles and their partisan underpinnings.

The congressional focus after 1999 on rebuilding fiscal and monetary institutions, in turn, crowded out further reforms in water, sanitation, and electricity (in this case also due to the distractions of the 2001 energy shortage).[10] Moreover, as a coalition government, the Cardoso administration had ministers who were eagerly pursuing market-oriented reform, sitting next to others who made little effort in that direction, either because they were more skeptical about the benefits or because it would reduce their ability to make political appointments to influential positions. These ministers tended to support insiders who opposed reform and were able in that way to delay the whole process. So, while discussions about changing the regulation of the electricity sector started in 1992 and were still incomplete 12 years later, in telecoms the whole regulatory apparatus was completely changed in three years.

Sequencing problems in the reform of infrastructure regulation stemmed in part from this intra-government heterogeneity and from the fact that different agencies were in charge of privatization (BNDES) and regulatory reform (sector ministries). Fiscal objectives and bundling were also more powerful in pushing privatization forward (both at the regional and at the federal level) than in encouraging the establishment of new regulation. Finally, some of the SOEs are so powerful that they were able to stall or simply weaken the new regulation. Thus, some of the federal power generators never signed concession contracts with the sector's regulatory agency (Aneel), reducing its ability to supervise them, whereas Petrobrás, the country's (de facto) oil monopoly has a sector regulator whose mandate does not include fighting anti-competitive practices.

Overall, the 1990s was a watershed for the deregulation and re-regulation of the Brazilian economy. The process of institutionalizing the new, and still evolving, regulatory framework will take many more years. The process to date reveals some of the limits of pragmatism as well as a different set of stakeholders from other reform processes. The exceptional process in telecommunications helps illuminate the more normal political problems encountered in other sectors. In telecoms the Minister of Communications had power within the Cardoso administration, which he used to insulate the reform process from interference by outside stakeholders while at the same time building-in participation by internal stakeholders in the ministry and telecom SOEs. He also used his privileged position to get regulatory reform enacted prior to privatization (now universally considered to be the best sequence) and maximize competition between privatized parts of the telecommunications system. In other sectors, especially public utilities in electricity, water, and transportation, the political conditions were quite different. The ministers often did not remain long in the cabinet and sometimes came from parties less central to the governing coalition. Reassigning policy attributes in these other public utilities also involved much more contention and negotiation with other levels of government, especially the powerful and often obstructionist state governments.

3.4   Performance: the impact of reforms

Individual reforms had profound impacts on their respective areas. For example, trade liberalization greatly expanded imports as a percentage of GDP – from 4 per cent in 1990 to 10 per cent in 2002 – while total trade rose from 10 to nearly 24 per cent of GDP. But, not surprisingly, Brazil's piecemeal, gradual, pragmatic reform process had a disappointing impact on economy-wide performance. Overall, reforms were able to accelerate growth in the short term but failed to put the economy back on a path of sustained growth similar to rates in the previous five decades (Moreira, 2003; Pinheiro, 2004). Thus, after a contraction of GDP in 1990–92 associated with Collor's stabilization package, the economy expanded vigorously in 1993–97, at 4.2 per cent per year, but then stalled at growth of only 1.4 per cent per year in 1998–2003. Furthermore, the rise in GDP growth stemmed exclusively from an acceleration in productivity change, as reforms failed to raise investment levels.

Most studies at sector and firm level agree that productivity grew substantially in many manufacturing industries and public utilities in the 1990s, especially compared with the poor record of the 1980s (Bonelli, 2002). The underlying model is one in which firms faced with the threat of increasing imports and the easier entry of competitors react by raising productivity. Trade liberalization also spurred productivity growth by allowing access to better (imported) inputs and equipment and by forcing the least productive firms out of business. Despite large increases in productivity, the expansion of output capacity was often small, and hence the reduction of manufacturing employment was substantial (Bonelli, 1999).

Four leading sectors in terms of productivity growth in the 1990s were communications, steel, public utilities, and chemicals (petrochemicals), all sectors with substantial asset privatization in the 1990s (Bonelli, 2002). Pinheiro (1996) shows that privatization in Brazil substantially improved the performance of the former SOEs. Efficiency practically doubled when measured in terms of sales per employee. Profitability went from negative to positive, stockholders' equity increased by a factor of almost five, while debt diminished and liquidity increased. The median investment also increased almost by a factor of five, rising more than four times as a proportion of sales and more than doubling in relation to fixed assets.

In infrastructure in particular, privatization and regulatory reform succeeded in increasing productivity and investment, but most investment was geared to modernization rather than expansion. In the second half of the 1990s, infrastructure output capacity expanded even more slowly than in the previous decade. The telecom sector was the exception, with its output capacity increasing annually at double-digit rates after reform began (Pinheiro, 2005).

Two main factors explain this weak reaction of private investors. One was the continued macro instability that characterized the economy even after inflation was brought under control. The other was the only partial implementation of some of the reforms and the lack of complementary, second-generation reforms. In infrastructure, for instance, only in telecom was regulatory reform carried out with proper sequencing and to its full extent. In other sectors, such as electricity and sanitation, the new regulatory model was never completely spelled out, let alone implemented. Several general factors discouraged investment, including the lack of deep complementary reforms in financial and labor markets; the poor performance of the judiciary, characterized by slow and highly-politicized decisions; and the uncertainty surrounding the extent and timing of the reform process. Thus, as should be expected given its instrumental focus, pragmatic reform produced positive results regarding the productivity of individual sectors, but failed to generate the kind of overall environment that would stimulate a large aggregate rise in investment.

3.5 Conclusion: probable consequences and sources of pragmatism

In principle, pragmatic reform has distinctive advantages and disadvantages compared to other sorts of reform processes. Pragmatic reform tends to be piecemeal and disconnected. In the sectors or areas targeted, pragmatic policy-making tends to have better economic results, but without, as noted above, having decisive overall impact. Of course pragmatic policy, like any policy, can be wrong, either in basic premises or design, or be overwhelmed by exogenous shocks. Flexibility and gradualism in a pragmatic reform process mean that policy-makers are more likely to have opportunities to adjust implementation to redress errors and accommodate unforeseen shocks, although flexibility in implementation also opens up opportunities for rent-seeking and lobbying, as was suspected in several episodes of tariff readjustments. Vulnerability to rent-seeking and capture are exacerbated by the narrowness and disconnectedness of many pragmatic policies. Moreover, in most pragmatic processes reformers lack extensive political backing, precisely because their policies lack ideology, partisan appeal, or integration into an overall economic plan. Flexibility and gradualism also have the disadvantage of delaying private sector responses to policies, generating overall uncertainty, and creating a wait-and-see disposition among private businesses.

Although a full treatment is not possible here, it is worth noting briefly some of the likely sources of pragmatism in the Brazilian political economy. Five possible sources seem especially important: (1) the relative autonomy of policy-makers from legislatures and politicians (clientelist, partisan, or ideological); (2) the close contact of policy-makers with the objects of policy (such as consultation with private sector, or circulation between public and private sectors); (3) the eclectic training of top policy-makers; (4) a coalitional government with multiple veto points; and (5) slow or late reformers who then have the opportunity to learn from mistakes in other countries (and better specify ex ante policy goals and means–end connections). Let us elaborate briefly on each of these sources, and by way of summary note where they were prominent in the reform politics we examined.

In Brazil, policy-makers have usually enjoyed both formal and informal autonomy and insulation. For example, the significant agenda-setting power of the Brazilian president and the executive branch reduced the potential influence from Congress and political parties (Figueiredo and Limongi, 1999). Some of the reforms – especially privatization and trade liberalization – proceeded most rapidly in policy areas where the executive branch could act without prior approval from Congress. In addition, so-called 'pockets of efficiency' or institutionally insulated, non-partisan bureaucrats in scattered agencies and state enterprises pushed policy change in particular sectors (Evans, 1995). The best example of this traditional autonomy was the BNDES. As they had throughout the second half of the twentieth century, BNDES *técnicos* took the lead in designing and implementing new policies. Almost by coincidence, the BNDES pioneered privatization in rearranging its own hodge-podge portfolio and thus was well positioned to lead the first phase of privatization in the early 1990s.

On the dimension of contact, or what Evans (1995) called 'embeddedness', relations were more informal than formal. Policy-making was generally open to influence, especially during implementation, by big business (Schneider, 2004a). The channels of influence varied from formal business associations to informal networks to appointments of prominent businessmen as heads of key economic ministries. Such influence sometimes meant only capture and rent-seeking, but in other cases it added another element of practicality, as business could contribute views on what kinds of reforms would fly. In Brazil, business influence was minor in macro policy, largely because business lacked encompassing associations, but often close and collaborative on narrower policy areas where pragmatism tended to thrive.

As elsewhere in Latin America, the members of reform change teams in Brazil in the 1990s were largely economists by training. Most Brazilian economists studied in Brazil where there has long been a sustained debate among monetarists, structuralists, liberals, and developmentalists, without clear hegemony of any one doctrine. This heterogeneity and domestic training contrasts sharply with the foreign (US) training and greater homogeneity among reform teams in Chile and Mexico.

Brazil also differed from other countries in terms of coalition politics. Unlike stronger parties in Argentina, Venezuela, or Mexico, Brazilian parties were too weak to impose lasting partisan or ideological influences on policy-making. The Brazilian party system is highly fragmented and is classified as having seven or more effective parties since the late 1980s. Most presidents consequently build multi-party coalitions, which precludes radical majoritarian shifts in government similar to Menem in Argentina or Pérez in Venezuela. Fragmentation alone did not guarantee that policy-making would be pragmatic, but it did mean that most policies took time, were negotiated, and had to go through multiple veto points, so that the policy result was unlikely to be extreme (Tavares, 2004). Within this context, centrist, non-ideological parties like the PFL and PMDB were usually willing coalition partners for presidents elected from other parties, and these parties generally pushed centrist policies and restrained efforts at more radical policy departures. It is telling that the period of most dramatic neo-liberal reform and policy experimentation came during the first year of Collor's short-lived government when Collor tried to govern without a coalition government. Of course, coalitional government also sometimes introduced partisan and clientelist interference that undermined the autonomy of more pragmatic officials, as was the case with the stunted evolution of Aneel.

Party fragmentation, negotiation, and multiple veto points all mean that changes in policy and in overall development strategies are likely to be delayed, as was clearly the case in market reform in Brazil. These delays, however, open up opportunities for more pragmatically minded reformers to learn from the mistakes of other reform pioneers and generally better specify the means–ends connections that they expect to underpin reform.

Notes

The following were interviewed in the preparation for this chapter:
André Franco Montoro Filho (Director of the National Program of Privatization, 1992–94); Alejandra Herrera (Adviser, Ministry of Communications, 1995–98, ANATEL 1998–2000); Dione Craveiro (career official, through 2000, in Ministry of Communication and Telebrás); José Tavares de Araújo Jr (Secretaria de Acompanhamento Econômico, SEAE, Ministério da Fazenda); Marcus Vinicius Pó (Consultant, Instituto de Defesa do Consumidor (IDEC)); Marcilio Marques Moreira (Minister of Economics, 1991–92); Omar Alves Abbud (Chefe de Gabinete do Presidente, ANEEL); Pedro Sampaio Malan (Minister of Finance, 1994–2002); Peter Greiner (Secretary of Energy, Ministry of Mines and Energy, 1994–99).

1. For comparative overviews, see Murillo (2001 and 2002), Schamis (2002), Stallings and Peres (2000), Teichman (2001), and Weyland (2004a).
2. Schneider (1990) classified reform approaches as systemic, partisan, or pragmatic. Systemic corresponds roughly to our category of ideological. Feigenbaum et al. (1999) make similar distinctions. See also Santiso (2005).
3. In our usage, we sometimes refer to particular policies or individuals as pragmatic, but pragmatism characterizes primarily the overall policy process. In the abstract, policy-making can be broken down into separate stages: recognition of problems to be solved; decisions on policy instruments to address the problems; adoption of a plan; implementation; and adjustment of implementation over time. More or less pragmatism can be identified at each stage. Government or country reform experiences can be characterized in aggregate as more or less pragmatic, but only by summing up reform processes across main policy areas.
4. The end of the military regime removed, though, one kind of active participant from these policy networks, namely mid-level military officers who were commonly appointed to top-level positions in economic ministries and state enterprises (Schneider, 1991). The exclusion of the military removed one source of ideological influence – usually nationalist and developmentalist – on policy-making.

5. Ferreira and Facchini (2004) show that more concentrated sectors were able to obtain higher protection from imports, whereas more atomized sectors ended up with lower protection, revealing the sensitivity of trade liberalization to industrial lobbies.

6. As the failure of the government's stabilization plan became evident, the administration started to rely more on the PND to signal its commitment to structural change. To a large extent, this responded to international pressures from multilateral organizations – then the leading source of external finance – and foreign investors in general. An illuminating instance of this linkage came in late 1991 when a street demonstration succeeded in blocking the sale of Usiminas, a major steel firm. The government feared a speculative attack on the currency and moved quickly to insist on selling Usiminas, along with other measures to bolster the currency, in order to signal the government's resolve (interview with Marcilio Marques Moreira).

7. The B-band companies are private sector firms operating in a range of the spectrum different from the one used by former SOE operators, which is called the A-band.

8. This summary draws on accounts from interviewees who were in government at the time, Alejandra Herrera in telecoms and Peter Greiner in electricity. See also Prata et al. (1999) on telecommunications. Non-state stakeholders in business and labor did not have much impact on the course of regulatory reform.

9. Indeed, the initial plan was not to sell the former telecom monopolist (Telebrás). Its sale was decided only once the government realized Telebrás would be unable to compete against more efficient private operators once entry was allowed.

10. In transportation, regulatory reform was slow and uneven (Castro, 2000). In highways, toll road concessions were to be granted to private bidders with subsequent oversight by a federal regulatory agency, but most of the road network remains in state hands because political problems have delayed transfer to private operators. The regulation of railways also experienced problems, with several operators failing to meet contractual targets, without penalty. In both cases, problems partly stem from the long lag between the moment concessions were awarded (mostly in 1996–98) and the date the sector agency was established (2001). Water and sewage are the sectors where progress in regulatory reform has been slowest. The main hindrance has been the dispute between state and municipal governments about which of them has the power to award concessions in these areas, an issue on which the constitution has conflicting provisions. Regulatory reform has also been extensive in banking, corporate governance (CVM, Comissão de Valores Mobiliários), health care (ANS, the National Health Agency), and sanitation (ANVISA, the National Sanitary Vigilance Agency).

4
Understanding Chilean Reforms

Rómulo Chumacero, Rodrigo Fuentes,
Rolf Lüders, and Joaquín Vial

4.1 Introduction

Chile's economic performance in the last 20 years has been outstanding and it is the only country in the region that can claim significant progress in reducing income gaps with the developed world. However, in the 1960s and 1970s Chile's per capita GDP growth was way below the average of East Asia, OECD countries, and the world economy. When compared with the other Latin American countries, the Chilean economy grew at about average rates in the 1960s, below average rates in the 1970s and only outperformed them in the 1980s and 1990s.

As Chumacero and Fuentes (2002) point out, Chile was extremely vulnerable to major international crises (the Great Depression, the oil shock crisis, and the debt crisis). Despite this vulnerability, Chile recovered faster than other countries in the region. After the debt crisis, Chile exhibited not only the highest growth rates of the region, but also a level of volatility that is not statistically different from the average of the region. Something happened with Chile, transforming it from an 'average' Latin American country to a dynamic economy that now exhibits accelerated growth rates and decreased volatility.

The market-oriented reforms put in place in the 1970s and 1980s and deepened in the 1990s are prime candidates to explain this transformation. This chapter describes the nature of the process leading to the reforms, with emphasis on the political economy and incentives behind the two main political regimes that undertook them. Our goal is to address questions such as:

- Why did Chile start its reform process fifteen years prior to the Washington Consensus?
- Why were the reforms so profound?
- What role did the political regimes play in implementing the reforms?
- Why were the reforms maintained with the advent of democracy?

The Chilean experience during the implementation and consolidation of the reforms was unique. The early reforms were conducted under an authoritarian government, and, contrary to experiences elsewhere in the region, the return to democracy did not entail reform reversals but brought their consolidation.

We concentrate our analysis on how political institutions affected the processes of implementation and consolidation. We argue that, under the authoritarian regime, the initial conditions and the intertemporal linkage of policies allowed policy-makers to follow something close to a first-best policy. During the 1990s and early 2000s, the prevalence of common views on matters of economic policy between government officials and the opposition reduced 'transaction costs' and permitted the economic reform to continue at a reasonable pace. We will discuss how the electoral system and the constitutional powers of the president and Congress configured a setup that made reform reversal difficult. We also argue that success was a determinant factor in preventing reform reversal in the early 1990s.

We follow the transactional theory to policy decision-making in which public policies are the result of a political transaction game that is conditioned by the functioning of political institutions and historical circumstances (Spiller and Tommasi, 2003). Under this approach the first-best policy is reachable only when conditions favor political cooperation. Spiller and Tommasi (2003) consider six elements that determine how the political game is played. They argue that a Pareto-optimal solution is more likely to be attained:

(1) The smaller the number of key political actors (reducing transaction costs).
(2) If there are strong intertemporal linkages among the political actors (under a repeated game scheme, players have incentives to cooperate).
(3) The easier it is to observe the moves of different players (reducing monitoring cost and increasing cooperation).
(4) When effective enforcement technologies are available.
(5) If the field where the exchange among the political actors takes place facilitates the enforcement of cooperation (depending on the type of legislation available).
(6) The lower are the short-run pay-offs to deviate from non-cooperative solutions.

We also follow Aninat et al. (2004), who argue that the prevalence of common views as opposed to widely divergent proposals can play a significant role, especially in the presence of strong veto players, as is the case in Chile in the post-reform period.

We use these frameworks and evaluate these elements during the military and democratic governments. The rest of the chapter is organized as follows: Section 4.2 describes the situation prior to the first wave of reforms and lists the reforms conducted since then. Section 4.3 analyzes the political economy of the reform process under the military and democratic regimes. It describes their political structure, identifying the key players and how the reform process took place. Section 4.4 provides a closer look at some reforms. Section 4.5 concludes.

4.2 The Chilean economy: a historical description

As Fanelli and Popov (2005) point out, initial conditions are crucial for understanding the timing and shape of reforms. This section briefly describes the historical background that led the Chilean economy to the situation prior to the reforms and presents a brief summary of the reforms themselves.

The Chilean economy is relatively small (16 million people in 2005). Since its independence in 1810, its economic record has been mixed. After an initial setback, the income gap with the US closed in the nineteenth century, but, until the 1980s, it continuously deteriorated during the twentieth century, particularly during the import substitution period (between 1940 and 1973).

4.2.1 The import substitution period[1]

After the Great Depression, the internationally prevailing notions about ideal development policies heavily influenced the Chilean elite's economic thinking. In the 1940s, under the Popular Front governments,[2] a new development ideology emerged.[3] It was heavily influenced by the circumstances of the time, the breakdown of trade as a result of the Great Depression and later World War II, and by new beliefs about the role of government,[4] not only for short-term macroeconomic stabilization, but also as an engine of growth.[5] Along with higher inflation rates, the main effects of these policies were:

1. *Growing macroeconomic imbalances.* The economic ideas that prevailed after the Great Depression generated pressures to increase fiscal expenditures destined to finance industrial infrastructure (steel mills, energy supplies, transport facilities, and so on) and social expenditures (education, health, housing, and so on). As a consequence, from the early 1940s governments began to run deficits.[6] In the absence of functioning capital markets and with no access to international loans,[7] they were financed by a central bank that gradually lost its independence.[8] Keynesian ideas and the widespread belief that supply was bound to react to expanding demand heavily influenced macroeconomic thinking. On the other hand, inflation was seen mostly as a 'structural problem' due to low agricultural productivity, monopoly power by industries, and redistributive conflicts. Growing imbalances led to rising inflation rates and chronic foreign exchange crises and massive devaluations. Consumer prices rose on average by 16.6, 34.5, and 23.7 per cent annually during the 1940s, 1950s, and 1960s, respectively. By 1956, successive governments initiated anti-inflationary programs that ended in failure after a few years of transitory success.[9] This process reached

a climax in 1971–73 during Salvador Allende's government, when the inflation rate reached over 600 per cent in the last year.

2. *A more active role of government in the economy.* After the Great Depression, the government started taking over activities previously conducted by the private sector. The symbol of the 'entrepreneurial state' was CORFO (created in 1939), a state-owned and managed development corporation commissioned to promote industrialization, either directly (creating new SOEs), or with preferential loans to the private sector that invested in high priority industries. Over time, it took over failed large private firms that the government did not want to close down. In 1970, 64 of the largest firms in the country were either CORFO subsidiaries or other SOEs. Government intervention is attested by the activities in which it was involved.[10] During Allende's government, 500 additional medium- and large-sized firms were either nationalized or taken over by the government.[11] The value added by SOEs, which was negligible in 1940, rose to 14 per cent of GDP in 1965 and 39 per cent in 1973.[12]

3. *Protectionism.* Besides supplying the private sector with the infrastructure for industrial development, the government provided protection to local producers. Protection took many forms, of which import licenses and quotas, differential custom duties, multiple exchange rates, and low and often negative real interest rates were the most important. During Allende's regime, extremely high previous import deposits were added and eventually, the government directly carried out all foreign trade operations. As a result, trade to GDP ratios fell from 29.2 per cent in 1929 to 16.7 per cent in 1970.

4. *The welfare system.* The industrialization process and increased population growth rates early in the twentieth century induced large migrations from the rural sector to the main cities. As migrants could not always find employment, large and evident differences in living standards gave rise to the so-called 'social problem'. The official reaction was to increase government expenditures on education, public housing, health and pensions, as well as the development of a mandatory and onerous social insurance system. Governments yielded to the many demands, more often than not financing them through monetary emission. As inflation rates picked up, governments relied on stop-gap measures, like price controls and subsidies. These new distortions reduced growth rates even further, compounding the social problem. By 1970, 42.5 per cent of central government expenses were already 'social' expenditures, most of them, merit goods. They accounted for 10.5 per cent of GDP. However, social expenditures largely missed the poor and in large part were captured by emerging pressure groups in the middle and upper classes (Arellano, 1985).

Allende's government represents the cusp of previous trends, imposing the highest restrictions on international trade and finance ever experienced. Practically all prices in the economy – including wages, interest rates, and exchange rates – were not only fixed but also micro-managed by government decrees. Most of the large- and medium-sized firms were taken over by the government and managed by it. Rent-seeking reached its peak. Although freedom of expression existed and most democratic institutions were in place, the economy began to resemble a Central European centralized economy. Massive expropriations, dramatic economic failure reflected in runaway inflation and widespread shortages of all kinds of goods, as well as an extremely confrontational political climate, were major sources of social turmoil.

After the military coup of 1973, major economic reforms were enacted to reintroduce free markets and free trade, restore the solvency of public finances, stabilize the economy, and reduce the role of the government. All these reforms began 15 years ahead of the Washington Consensus and were met with widespread skepticism, nationally and abroad.

4.2.2   The reforms of the 1974–89 period

By September 1973, socio-economic conditions had deteriorated to the extent that deep reforms were possible.[13] Relative to the US, Latin America, or any other region except Africa, Chile's GDP per capita had been losing position since the early 1900s and the country had fallen into socio-political chaos.

After an initial period of hesitation and disorganization, the military government adopted a socio-economic reform agenda proposed by a group of liberal economists early in 1975, partly forced by a severe deterioration of the international economic environment.[14] These economists – the so-called 'Chicago Boys' – had similar academic backgrounds and most of them had no active political experience, although their sympathies tended to lie with the center-right.[15]

Principles behind the reforms

The guiding principles for the implementation of a modern market economy in Chile were:

- *Secure property rights*, which had been severely undermined, especially during the Allende regime when many companies in all sectors of the economy and of almost every size were nationalized or put under state management with little or no compensation.
- *A subsidiary role of the state*, which limited state interventions to cases of clear market failures. Exceptions were made on the basis of political considerations, with the preservation of state-owned firms in the mining sector being the most flagrant.
- *Freedom of choice*, reflected in the elimination of trade permits and prohibitions, as well as rationing procedures and price controls, which pervaded every activity by the end of Allende's government.
- *Fiscal consolidation and orthodox management of monetary and foreign exchange policies*, which were a necessary condition for a well functioning market economy and an area in which governments had failed in the past.

- *Systematic reduction of the spaces for public discretion and potential arbitrariness, introducing impersonal rules whenever possible.* Rent-seeking was seen as a major source of inefficiency and corruption, with a significant impact on overall factor productivity and growth.
- *Trade and financial openness*, which would provide the impulse for growth that the limited size of the domestic economy could not provide, as well as creating competition in the local economy.
- *Social policies were focused on poverty reduction, with means testing and expenditure targeting as main instruments.* This approach was in stark contrast with prevailing views in the 1960s and early 1970s that put a very strong emphasis on income redistribution.
- *Institutionalization of the 'rules of the game' in such a way that it would not be easy to change them,* with the purpose of granting stability of those rules under different governments.

Most of these principles can still be recognized in today's economic policies, even though in many cases they are qualified in recognition of the increasing complexities of the policy issues.

The political environment surrounding the initial reforms was unique. After the military coup, political parties were outlawed and political opposition was strongly repressed. However, when the economic crisis of 1982–83 severely weakened the regime, an organized political opposition emerged de facto. This opposition took advantage of the fact that the regime allowed public discussion of the socio-economic management of the country and their criticism of economic policies was publicly circulated. The weakened state of the political parties and the repression of normal political activities did not mean that policy-making processes were simple. There were dissenting views within the armed forces and there was always a nationalistic faction, sharing many of the old views about state intervention and in favor of protection of traditional agriculture against foreign competition, that was trying to block many reforms. The strong backing by Pinochet was essential for their implementation and survival through economic crises. However, the power of Pinochet was limited by his need to preserve the unity of the armed forces.

Chronology of the reforms

The economic reforms between 1973 and 1989 were not continuous. The following reform periods can be distinguished:

1. *Basic Structural reforms.*   Between late 1973 and 1981, the structure of the economy was drastically changed:

(a) Prices, interest rates and wages were left to be determined by market forces.[16]
(b) Customs duties, which reached up to 200 per cent, were drastically reduced and non-custom barriers were virtually eliminated.

(c) Fiscal and monetary responsibilities, which had been exceptionally weak for several decades, were restored and the tax system reformed, including the introduction of a VAT.

(d) The foreign investment code was changed to make it attractive to investors. The exchange rate system was significantly liberalized.

(e) Except for the traditional SOEs, over 500 large- and medium-sized firms managed by the government were privatized.

(f) Labor market regulations were changed. Collective bargaining was limited to the firm level, and firms could dismiss workers and negotiate wages.

(g) Social security legislation was 'revolutionized' by the replacement of a pay-as-you-go system with a fully funded system based on individual retirement accounts privately managed.

(h) Competition regulation was introduced.

(i) Public utilities were regulated in a market-friendly manner.

2. *The 'debt crisis' and reform reversals.*   During 1982 and 1983, the country experienced a deep economic and financial recession, which had political consequences. Discontent and social unrest were expressed in large public demonstrations, organized by union leaders with the backing of the political opposition. This led the military regime to some partial reform reversals. The tipping point was the realization by the government that traditional supporters among farmers, small business owners in commerce and transportation were leaning against it. Yielding to pressures from unions and the entrepreneurial leadership, custom duties were raised from a uniform 10 per cent to 35 per cent and loans were granted with preferential interest rates. As a consequence of the bankruptcy of a relatively high proportion of commercial banks, the government 'intervened' in them, replacing their boards of directors and managers by public sector appointed teams. It also instructed the latter to declare the bankruptcy of the holding companies that were not in a position to serve their loans regularly. As a result, the management of many large firms, among them a good number of those which had been privatized by the military regime a few years before were again indirectly managed by the government. This was made possible because capital shares of those holdings were used as collateral for commercial bank loans.[17]

3. *Policy reforms.*   Between 1985 and 1989, once the economy had recovered from the recession and the government had regained some of its political power, the regime went back to its pre-recession track. The cabinet was changed and a new generation of economists took over. Custom duties were reduced to a uniform 15 per cent. Firms that had fallen under public sector management were re-privatized. Most of the large, traditional SOEs were also privatized, spreading share ownership as widely as possible. Most significantly, important policy changes intended to increase savings and exports were implemented.

(a) The main instrument used to increase private savings was a reduction in government taxes, made possible by lower government expenditures, which included the granting of special tax incentives on savings.

(b) The export promotion tool was the maintenance of a high real exchange rate, made possible by an aggressive foreign debt repayment policy, which also increased savings.

Compared with the pre-recession period, in which structural changes clearly dominated economic policy-making and an effort was made to maintain a 'neutral' economic policy stance, the post-recession period was characterized by an active role of the government intended to increase exports and savings.[18]

4.2.3 Reforms after the return of democracy

After the defeat of Pinochet in the October 1988 referendum, it was clear that a transition towards democracy had started and, in all likelihood, the new president would come from the ranks of the political opposition.

Early stage

When elected, the first democratic government did not have an agenda for structural reforms. Its first priority was to secure a stable macroeconomic environment and to build the necessary support to pass through Congress a tax increase to roll back part of the tax cuts introduced in the late 1980s. The latter was essential to get the social programs of the new government in place. The only exception had to do with reforms of the labor codes, which were bound to appear as a key issue in any social dialogue initiative (a priority of the new government). The social dialogue was a forum for negotiation between labor and business leaders to revise the labor code while maintaining key provisions intact.[19]

Despite the fact that the government did not have an explicit reform agenda, it took advantage of specific circumstances to introduce reforms in several areas:

- *International trade.* There was a unilateral reduction of import duties from a uniform tariff of 15 per cent to 11 per cent. An agenda to negotiate an FTA with the US was placed, taking advantage of an invitation from President Bush (senior) to create a Free Trade Area of the Americas.
- *Regulation of capital flows.* Changes were in different, and sometimes opposite, directions. On the one hand, the Central Bank lifted restrictions on capital movements, gradually allowing private companies to issue bonds and stocks in international markets. On the other hand, a controversial reserve requirement to foreign loans (linked to the duration of the loan) was introduced.
- *Capital markets reform.* When the government took power it was clear that a reform of domestic financial and capital markets was needed to

adapt them to the emerging reality of huge long-term savings accumulated in the pension system.

- *Privatization.* The political coalition supporting the government had been very critical of privatizations made during the military regime. The very special nature of the political transition in Chile forced a tacit understanding not to reopen previous privatization processes, but nobody was expecting the new government actually to privatize state companies. The decision to sell a majority fraction of the last major hydroelectric power generator in the hands of the state was a major shift in the *Concertación*. The privatization was conducted in such a way as to strengthen competition in the electric sector.

- *The start of concessions of public works.*   An aggressive program to give concessions of public infrastructure to the private sector took off in full in the second half of the 1990s, and totally revamped the Chilean infrastructure in less than a decade.

Second-generation reforms

The second government of the *Concertación* led by Eduardo Frei started in 1994 with a broad program and little sense of actual priorities. As the government consolidated the internal decision-making process, a clearer agenda began to emerge, with an emphasis on what would later be classified as 'second-generation' reforms:

- *Expanding the role of the private sector.*   The main pillar of this program was the highway concessions program that had started in the previous administration and allowed the accumulation of expertise leading to a revision of the law (Marcel, 2000, 2002). The other privatizations were: operation of ports,[20] and the water and sewage utilities.[21]

- *Educational reform.*   Even though Chile enjoyed better education indicators than most of the region, they were still quite low when compared to developed countries or emerging market economies in Asia (Fuentes and Mies, 2005). The government decided to push ahead with an ambitious (and expensive) educational reform including major changes in two areas: the number of hours of classroom work in primary and secondary education, and a major revision of the curriculum. The results of this reform have not been as expected as educational attainment tests have shown no major improvements.[22] During President Lagos's administration secondary school education was made mandatory, with the goal to reach universal coverage.[23]

- *The penal system reform.*   This involved a major change in the way penal justice was administered. Instead of a judge conducting the investigation and sentencing in a written process, the new system involved separating the investigation process from the judging and sentencing in an oral process. A public prosecution service had to be created from scratch, to take care of the investigation process, and another to provide public defenders for those who could not afford private lawyers.[24]

- *Macroeconomic policy reform.* The fiscal policy processes (examined in detail below), starting with the Central Bank Independence Law of 1989 (at the end of the military government), resulted in continuous budget surpluses for more than a decade, leading to a substantial reduction in public sector debt. This outcome would have been unlikely in an environment with a weaker Ministry of Finance, or stronger powers of Congress in fiscal matters. The last stage in this process was the introduction in 2001 of the Structural Balance Rule for the Central Government. An efficient management of monetary policy by the Central Bank of Chile has complemented the fiscal policy.

4.3 The political economy of the reforms

In this section we discuss the political economy of the reforms implemented in the 1970s through the 1980s and 1990s. Prior to that, we briefly describe the political system existing before the 1973 military coup. We also discuss how the military government modified the rules of the political game for the democratic government that followed.

4.3.1 Before 1973

The political system in place was based on a presidential system, while political parties in Congress were elected on a proportional basis. Since the number of deputies varied from one district to the other roughly in proportion to the size of the electoral registry, this led to a very fragmented congressional representation.

The party system was consolidated in the first half of the nineteenth century, within a competitive environment among atomized parties. At the same time, this was the most unstable period of Chilean political history, with several military coups taking place (Scully, 1995). The consolidation of the party system was reflected in the parliamentary elections of 1932 where 27 parties competed and 19 obtained representation. During most of the post-war period, governments did not have a majority in Congress and had limited powers to rein in political pressures and to pass corrective legislation.

Political alliances were needed to govern. Over the twentieth century the parties grouped in three loose – and shifting – coalitions (right, center, and left). As a result, absolute majority was difficult to attain.[25] With opposition from two fronts, governments could not set their agendas. One of the most extreme cases was the presidential election of Salvador Allende in 1970, who won with 36.6 per cent of the votes.

The proportional system encouraged competition between parties, increased the transactions costs required to govern, increased the number of negotiating agents, and reduced the retaliatory powers of the executive branch. Naturally, center parties – first the Radical Party and, starting in the 1960s, the Christian Democrats – tried to arbitrate opportunities between the right and the left, making short-term agreements to approve certain laws.

On the other hand, policy-making institutions were weak. The Ministry of Finance had limited control on public finances, while Congress had almost unlimited powers to legislate benefits for key constituencies (pension benefits being a prominent instrument). Finally, monetary policies were subordinated to fiscal financial requirements.

4.3.2   1974–89

Why was Chile able to carry out such drastic, far-reaching, and successful reforms? The simple – but wrong – answer is that Chile was under a military government. Dictatorships in other developing countries provide countless counter-examples.[26] Either they did not try to improve the existing institutions or if they did, they failed.

While the critical economic situation faced in 1973 played a role in the type of policies considered, other countries in the region had been in similar circumstances and were not able to find a way out of their problems.

What happened in Chile is a fortunate conjunction of a number of factors that contributed to the positive outcome of an extremely ambitious reform project. Fewer actors and a concentration of power in the hands of the president resulted in less frequent political transactions, facilitating the implementation of effective economic policies. The following are some of the factors that contributed to reform:

(1) The deep socio-political and economic crisis of 1971–73, which was the culmination of about 15 years during which the country experienced a wide variety of regimes – from conservative to a mild reform and finally to a full-blown socialist government – that did not produce the desired results. The climate was propitious for the introduction of deep market-oriented reforms, since most citizens were willing to postpone their short-term private interests in favor of a reform that promised prosperous medium- and long-run prospects.

(2) A strategically competent military leadership. Contrary to what happened elsewhere, the military was not as involved in civil matters after 1930. Although they were aware that the experiments of the previous decades had failed, they had no expertise in economic matters and were willing to take the advice of professional economists. They also believed that a viable democracy required a rapidly growing economy. To achieve that end they were willing to withstand the initial political cost of the structural changes.

(3) The existence of a relatively large group of internationally trained economists who shared a common view – liberal, in the European sense of the

word – of what a successful economy should look like. The largest group of these economists had followed graduate studies at the University of Chicago, but many others had studied at other top economic institutions in the US and Europe.

(4) A large cadre of business graduates who had been influenced by the ideas of those economists and who understood the workings of such an economy.

(5) The ability to conduct several reforms in a big-bang way. The importance of policy complementarities (that is, how some policies require others to enhance economic growth and to avoid reform reversals) has been recognized in the literature.[27] This was reinforced by macroeconomic stability, a priority objective of all Chilean governments since 1973.[28]

(6) The way the military government was organized and managed its affairs. The military Junta, formed by the chief commanders of the army, navy, air force, and police, had advisers on different economic matters. Although the first finance minister was a member of the armed forces, the Junta soon realized that it lacked a coherent plan to effectively conduct economic policy. The availability of '*El Ladrillo*', a blueprint for an economic plan for the government following Allende's regime, and the strikingly different policies it proposed, helps us to understand the path taken. After 1974, the military government delegated the definition and management of economic matters almost exclusively to professional economists. This may be one of the reasons why the government allowed some debate on economic – as opposed to political – matters. At the beginning, the members of the military Junta shared power and Pinochet's control of the army was limited. Several key projects, such as pension reform, for instance, were blocked by the Chief Commander of the Air Force, General Leigh, who was the most prominent supporter of the nationalist forces. By the end of the 1970s, Leigh had been dismissed and Pinochet had consolidated his power over the army. At the same time a constitution had been drafted and enacted, setting a clear path for a transfer of power to civilians in the long run. This also allowed the unblocking of the pension reform.

The structure of the government was simple. The president of the Junta and later president of the country, General Pinochet, exercised executive power, while the Junta was the legislative body. Under such a setting, political transactions to decide economic policies took place among a small group of actors. The most important transactions were of an intertemporal nature. In general, reforms are expected to have important effects in the long run, while the pay-off tends to be small in the short run. The military government – given the initial support it enjoyed – thought it would have enough time to receive the benefits of the reforms. After the approval of the new constitution in the plebiscite of 1980, the government knew that it would remain in power for a long period of time.[29] Furthermore, as the economy had experienced rapid growth after both the 1975 and 1982 crises, the government stressed the idea that the reforms underlay the economic success.

Among other things, the constitution fixed the presidential term of Pinochet and it established that after eight years of that presidency, the Junta would nominate a presidential candidate for another six-year term, to be approved in a plebiscite. If the name was not approved – as happened – one year later, Pinochet was to call open elections, which he did in 1989. Part of the political uncertainty was eliminated when the constitution was approved, since Pinochet and the population knew that he would remain in power for at least nine more years.

Criticism and political unrest followed the debt crisis of 1982–83, but with a monolithic government and a set path for the transfer of power, the government was able to weather the storm. Transitory political and economic concessions were made but there was very little room for maneuver, since the country had become critically dependent on the financial support of the IMF and the World Bank. The so-called Structural Adjustment Loans (SAL) became a source of much needed foreign financing and an instrument to support economic reforms at a moment in which the government's political and economic teams were inclined to undo some of them.

In terms of political transactions, the implementation of the reforms was not necessarily efficient, but it was effective. The military regime used a number of instruments adapted from their own institutions. A coordinator, with the rank of minister, would receive the reform proposals, approve or reject them, and decide when to send them to 'Congress' (the Junta).[30] This office was (and still is) housed at the Moneda, the presidential palace, and had easy access to the president. In addition, every year, the ministries prepared a list of the main reforms that they wanted to have approved. After a reform was analyzed, modified, and approved by the minister, the ministry adopted it as its own. Each minister was evaluated on a yearly basis in large part on how effective he was on implementing such programs.

(7) A strong technocracy that provided good enforcement. The military government replaced the existing bureaucracy with a strong technocracy, which had a clear focus. They were housed mainly at ODEPLAN (the planning office), the budget office at the Ministry of Finance and the Central Bank. Special teams were assembled in key areas of reform, such as pensions, comprising economists and lawyers from the different institutions involved. In most cases these teams were recruited by the leader of the economic reform in the government, Sergio de Castro and later on, Hernán Büchi (ministers of finance) and Miguel Kast (ODEPLAN). The technocrats behind the reforms made special efforts to avoid rent-seeking behavior and activities. Examples of this principle were the pricing of all public utilities at marginal cost of production as well as uniform import

tariffs for all goods. Pinochet was very supportive of this, as he disliked a dynastic type of society, where family name was an important asset that perpetuated economic and political power.

The economic reform process was far from even and linear. Reforms of the institutions came in waves, as political and economic conditions permitted. It was not uncommon for economic measures approved by the government to be reversed as the result of political pressures. In fact, the military regime was relatively sensitive to public opinion and gradually allowed more public discussion of economic matters. The best known and most significant reversals took place during the debt crisis (approximately a year and a half after the constitutional referendum). Management of commercial banks handling a high proportion of the financial assets and liabilities of the country was transferred to the public sector (due to the financial crisis) and later custom duties were raised. Those were only tactical moves, since as soon as conditions permitted the banks were re-privatized and custom duties were again lowered.

The electoral reform put in place during the military government has been crucial. By the end of the 1980s there was a clear sense of economic success and the military felt that economic reforms and the constitution were their main legacy. The existing political structure, inherited from the military government, is strongly presidential and has a binominal system for electing the members of parliament, replacing the proportional system. As a result of this and the conditions prevailing at the time, two large coalitions were formed, one center-right and the other center-left.

Given the new electoral system, negotiation within the coalitions for the definition of the ballots is the key factor to get elected, so that the power of the party leaders over members of Congress has been enhanced. This reduces the number of players and gives strong retaliatory powers to party leaders. The constitution also allowed the president to designate two senators directly and four indirectly, out of a total of 48 senators. Pinochet nominated the first group of designated senators, independently of the result of the 1988 plebiscite. This structure gave the military a de facto veto power that was used to block political reform until Pinochet became discredited by corruption scandals, after his temporary imprisonment in London. This meant that veto powers built into Congress were also used to shield economic reforms from attempts to reverse them.[31]

4.3.3 The 1990s

One concern at the end of the military regime was the possibility that major economic reforms could be reversed, or populism could stall the economic recovery as well as reaccelerate inflation. Another was the diversity of the coalition (*Concertación*) that finally won the election, comprising a wide range of political parties from the centrist Christian Democrats to the Socialist Party of the late President Allende, still professing Marxist ideals. Last, but far from least, was the concern that after 17 years of a military regime, economic and social demands from organized labor and other groups would overwhelm the government, breaking fiscal and monetary discipline and dismantling key reforms, even against the will of the political leadership.

The return to democracy brought a deepening and not a reversal of the reforms. Some of the factors that can explain this surprising outcome are:

- *The economic success of the late 1980s.*   From 1985 on, the economy had high and sustained growth, employment recovered, and new export activities flourished. Doubts about the wisdom of having low import tariffs and complaints about the social costs of economic reforms were disappearing. A genuine appreciation of the market economy was evident in the middle class. The continuity of market reforms and the ability to keep the economy working were the main themes in the political campaign to ratify Pinochet in 1988, as well as in the ensuing presidential campaign in 1989. The presidential candidate of the supporters of the military regime was Hernán Büchi. The prevailing mood, even among the opposition to Pinochet, was that Chile had paid dearly to build an economic system that was delivering results, and was not willing to risk it. This forced the *Concertación* to take a moderate stance on economic issues.

- *The collapse of the socialist system in Europe.*   At the time of the transition, the economic failure of the socialist regimes in Europe was evident. Many leaders of the Chilean socialist and communist parties were involuntary front-row witnesses of that failure during the years of exile that preceded their return to Chilean politics. This was an important factor shaping the views of those who led the ideological renovation of the Socialist Party, who were also influenced by the experience of Felipe González in Spain.

- *The economic failure of the democratic transition in Argentina.*   President Alfonsín of Argentina was greatly respected and admired in Chile for his management of the democratic transition in Argentina. The utter failure of his government to bring inflation under control and resume economic growth left a deep mark in the mind of the leaders of the *Concertación*. His resignation before the legal end of his tenure was a clear demonstration that a decent government could not count just on the reconstruction of the democratic system: to be successful it also had to deliver economic order and prosperity.

- *The revaluation of continuity.*   A reappraisal of the economic reforms had taken hold in academic circles close to the *Concertación*. This was most evident at CIEPLAN, a group of economists and social scientists created under the leadership of Alejandro Foxley in the mid-1970s, after they were expelled or resigned from major universities, which at that time were under military rule. They were critical of the economic policies being implemented at the time. By the end of the 1980s they realized that macroeconomic orthodoxy, continuity of some key elements of the existing open free-market economy, and a commitment to social equity, could be combined with some hope of success.[32] At the same time, the old-political leadership of the *Concertación*, more inclined towards state intervention, had been severely traumatized by the economic and social consequences of the chaotic Allende period in the early 1970s and was also shocked by the failure of Alfonsín in Argentina. This made it receptive to the views emerging from intellectuals like those at CIEPLAN and other academic centers.

• *The presence of strong veto players.* Because of the senators designated by Pinochet, the Senate was controlled by the opposition. As this was enough to block any government initiative, it was evident that a confrontational approach would lead nowhere. This forced the *Concertación* to take a pragmatic approach, which gave the upper hand to the moderates, led by Foxley, who wanted to preserve some basic continuity in economic reform and stick to macroeconomic orthodoxy.

Thus, it was not just luck that brought to the forefront of the political and economic team of the *Concertación* the otherwise very unlikely combination of socialists like Correa (Minister General Secretariat of Government) and Ominami (Economy Minister), with Christian Democrats like Foxley (Finance Minister), Boeninger (Minister of the Presidential Staff) and Cortázar (Labor Minister), under the leadership of Patricio Aylwin, a severe critic of Allende, lawyer by profession, and, to this day, a very reluctant supporter of a free-market economy.

A necessary, but not sufficient, condition to prevent a policy reversal during the first democratic government was the fact that the leaders of the economic area agreed to continue with the same economic system. After ten years of criticism of the market economy, there were many actors expecting changes. The role of the state in the economy, trade policy, industrial policy, and labor regulations were among the important issues expected to be changed.

The new democratic system was completely different from the one prevailing until 1973. The Executive now has the exclusive right to set the legislative agenda in several areas and the president has veto power at different stages of the legislative process.

According to the binominal electoral system two representatives for each district are elected. Each district has competing lists (formed by parties or coalitions). The candidates of the two most voted lists are both elected, unless the winning list obtains twice the votes of the second list, in which case candidates of the winning list fill both vacancies. This system encourages the formation of coalitions and enhances the national leadership of parties (Aninat et al., 2004). There are six parties with congressional representation grouped into two large coalitions: *Concertación de Partidos por la Democracia* (center-left wing which has supported the four presidents since democracy came back to the country) and the *Alianza por Chile* (center-right wing). Given the difficulties for any list to double the other, the composition of Congress is approximately 50 per cent for each coalition.

The parties that comprise the two coalitions have different views on moral, social, and economic issues. Transactions often take place within each coalition. Negotiations also take place at the time of elections, when candidates have to be nominated for Congress or the presidency. Competition is important within each coalition, since it is likely that only one candidate from each will win.

Nine of the original 48 senators were not elected by popular vote, the so-called institutional senators. The Executive nominated two of them every eight years. The Supreme Court appointed three and the National Security Council (COSENA) the other four.[33] The members of this council are split between representatives of civil society (the president, the president of the Senate, the president of the Supreme Court, and the Republic General Comptroller) and the military (the heads of the army, navy, air force, and the police). Thus, the constitution of 1980 gave the armed forces some influence upon the political system and restricted the way in which the president nominated the head of the armed forces. One final ingredient in the composition of the Senate was that all former presidents who served for at least six years had the right to become lifetime senators.

Unless a broad consensus is formed, this structure deters changes. A constitutional reform enacted in May 2005 eliminated all non-elected members of Congress, but the electoral system was not reformed.

Given their heterogeneity, the institutional senators could not be considered as a bloc. However, they played a key role in the first presidential period. Although Pinochet nominated the first institutional senators, they decided to support the majority in all major legislative initiatives, once a clear majority had been set. Therefore, they forced the center-left coalition to negotiate with the center-right coalition and helped to reach cooperative solutions.

The binominal system provided an 'insurance' against abrupt changes. Depending on the initial conditions, this may be a blessing or a curse. As the reforms implemented prior to the return to democracy were successful, the binominal system provided a defense against reversals. But, as the binominal system does not foster competition between coalitions, competition is manifested inside each coalition. The outcome has been that the most radical elements of each coalition are gaining the internal battles and the center parties of both coalitions are losing ground. It is not inconceivable then that this system may end up producing a third coalition (between the two).

Next, we consider whether the elements necessary to achieve first-best policies were present in the period:

(1) *Small number of key players.*   The electoral system has produced an equilibrium outcome of two strong coalitions that must negotiate.[34]

(2) *Actors must have strong intertemporal linkages.*   The members of the Senate are appointed for eight years and the members of the Chamber of Deputies

for four years. Both can be re-elected, while the president is appointed for six years with no immediate re-election.[35]

(3) *Policy and political moves have to be widely observable.* According to most international comparisons, Chile shows a high level of transparency and good quality of its institutions (Fuentes and Mies, 2005). As the Executive heavily dictates the legislative agenda, congressmen tend to follow the dictates of the leaders of the coalitions.

(4) *Good enforcement technologies have to be available.* Even though the Executive has more power than Congress, the intertemporal linkages and the political system create strong incentives to cooperate and build long-term relations. In addition, three politically independent enforcement institutions check upon the Executive: the Judiciary Power, the Constitutional Tribunal, and the General Comptroller.

(5) *The key political exchanges take place in arenas where conditions (1) to (4) are likely to be satisfied.* This is the case of Congress (see point (3) above).

(6) *The short-run pay-offs from non-cooperation are not too high.* As Congress is split between the coalitions; a non-cooperative strategy would paralyze the legislative agenda without changing the prevailing rules.

Thus, reform reversals were very difficult in the prevailing legal and institutional framework. On the one hand, the *Concertación* required the cooperation of the *Alianza*, either to roll back previous reforms or to push new ones through Congress. This condition, which was absent in many other countries when democracy returned, can help explain the orderly transition in Chile. On the other hand, the *Concertación* was able to contain social and political pressures and to deepen some reforms.[36]

The democratic system provided an important validation of the reforms introduced under the military regime. The institutional structure helped to achieve political stability after the return to democracy. As it is not prone to changes, it generates stability. Deep structural reforms are possible only with consensus. If trapped in a bad equilibrium, the system would make it difficult to move away from it.

4.4   A further look at the reforms

Over the past 30 years, the Chilean economy, polity, and society have been significantly reformed. This section analyzes the characteristics of some of the reforms.

4.4.1   Trade integration

Perhaps the most drastic and deepest reform conducted under the military government had to do with international trade. This meant a big shift in the development strategy followed since the 1940s. The reforms of the military regime have been deepened by all the elected governments since 1990, using both unilateral tariff reductions and free trade agreements with several trade partners.[37]

In 1973 import tariffs ranged from zero to 750 per cent, with an average nominal tariff of 105 per cent and a mode of 90 per cent. Half the tariffs were above 80 per cent and only 4 per cent of the goods had rates below 25 per cent (Corbo, 1985). There were import prohibitions for 187 tariff positions, a 90-day import deposit requirement of 10,000 per cent of CIF (cost, insurance, freight) value, plus some other discretionary actions that could be taken by the Central Bank.[38]

The reforms

Trade policy reform was an important project for the group that conducted economic policy under the military regime. It was repeatedly mentioned in *'El Ladrillo'* and the idea of openness was present from the very beginning in the discourse of the new government (Méndez, 1979). However, the government had not defined the extent of reform until Chile pulled out of the Andean Pact (Table 4.1). The non-discrimination principle and the idea of avoiding rent-seeking were the driving forces.

Table 4.1: Trade reform

Period	Reform
1974	Maximum tariff was cut down from 700% to 220%, and tariffs in the range of 50% to 220% were reduced by 10%. The effects on imports were negligible.
1975	Further reduction in trade distortions. The government announced that by 1978 tariffs would be in the range of 25% to 35%.
1976	All the quantitative restrictions were eliminated and it was announced that a range of 10% to 35% for import tariffs was adequate (Méndez, 1979).
1977	Chile retreated from the Andean Pact and further tariff reductions towards a uniform 10% level were announced.
1979–82	Tariffs reached the uniform level of 10% in June 1979 and a fixed exchange rate regime was set. The low speed of convergence between domestic and international inflation rates (due in part to wage indexation based on past inflation) and a surge of capital inflows (as a result of the external financial liberalization) led to a large real appreciation of the peso.[a]
1982–85	The fixed exchange rate was abandoned in 1982 and, after several devaluations and a short episode of flexible exchange rate, Chile adopted a crawling peg system. The government decided to increase tariffs from 10% to 20% in 1983 and to 35% in 1984. Additional tariffs were imposed for electronic goods and automobiles, and a price band for certain crops (wheat, sugar, and oil seed) was implemented.
1986–88	Tariffs were reduced from 35% to 20% in 1986 and to 15% in 1988.

Note: [a] See Edwards (1989) and Le Fort (1988) for empirical evidence on the behavior of the real exchange rate.

Trade liberalization was conducted quickly. It introduced a large change in relative prices and resources allocations. Abolishing all non-tariff barriers (NTB) complemented the process of tariff reduction. Table 4.2 shows the evolution of the effective rate of protection (ERP) during that period. In 1974 the manufacturing sector was highly protected, while other tradable sectors, such as agriculture and mining, were subject to high, but negative rates of protection. Among those sectors, textile and apparel enjoyed the highest protection, which is typical of most countries with non-uniform tariffs. At the end of the process, in 1979, the ERP was similar across sectors.[39]

In 1991, the new democratic government reduced tariffs further to 11 per cent and changed the trade strategy from unilateral reductions to bilateral trade agreements, criticizing unilateralism on the ground that it did not obtain additional market access in exchange for lower tariffs.[40] Aylwin's administration signed agreements with Mexico, Colombia, Venezuela, Mercosur, and Canada. Between 1998 and 2002 tariffs were reduced from 11 per cent to 6 per cent uniformly for all goods.[41] By the end of 2003, Chile had signed agreements with the United States, the European Union and Korea, and by

Table 4.2: Effective protection rates, 1974–79 (%)

Sector	1974	1975	1976	1977	1978	1979
Food	161	105	48	28	16	12
Beverages	203	119	47	32	19	13
Tobacco	114	68	29	19	11	11
Textile	239	138	74	49	28	14
Apparel and footwear	264	164	71	48	27	14
Leather	181	98	46	36	21	13
Wood products	157	93	45	28	16	15
Furniture, except metal	95	58	28	17	11	11
Paper and pulp	184	114	62	37	22	17
Printing	140	75	40	32	20	12
Chemical products	80	53	45	24	16	13
Plastic	80	53	45	24	16	13
Petroleum and coal	265	101	17	0	12	13
Glass, pottery and non-metallic minerals	128	87	55	32	20	14
Basic metals	127	86	64	38	25	17
Metallic products	147	101	77	52	27	15
Electrical and non-electrical machinery	96	72	58	35	19	13
Manufacturing industry (average ERP)	157	93	50	31	19	14
Agriculture	30	27	19	11	10	10
Mining	7	18	24	17	13	14
Non-tradable	−30	−19	−11	−7	−4	−3

Source: Aedo and Lagos (1984).

2005 with China. Thus, tariff differences were again introduced according to origin and type of good, but now at a much lower level.

Political economy of the reform

Trade liberalization in the 1970s was coherent with the basic principles of the reform process. Non-discrimination across sectors and a market economy as the mechanism for resource allocation guided the process. Several groups lobbied against the abrupt trade liberalization.

Two factors help to explain why trade liberalization was possible. First, the Minister of Finance was in charge of trade policy and was not vulnerable to pressures from different groups. Second, the minister's decisions were technically supported and were easier to defend when confronted by protectionists. The Minister of Finance was advised by a highly regarded technical group called *Comité Asesor de Política Arancelaria* (Advisory Committee for Trade Policy).

Detractors of the policy inside the government were not absent. At the beginning, CORFO, the official development corporation, opposed this process, since its main objective was to promote industrialization. The representative of the *Junta de Gobierno* on the advisory committee was against the speed at which the reforms were taking place. Regional governors (who were members of the armed forces) also opposed the reform and actively lobbied the Junta to delay it.

However, representatives of the private sector in the advisory committee did not oppose the reforms. The representative of the agricultural sector was in favor of the reform because until 1973 the sector had been subject to a negative effective protection rate. The industrial sector did not block trade liberalization because almost all medium-sized and large industries had fallen under state control in 1970–73, and management of many of them had only recently been returned to their legitimate owners. Gratitude and the fear of a backlash certainly prevented many industrialists from playing a more active role in opposing trade liberalization.

The brief reversal during the debt crisis lasted until 1986, when a new liberalization process was launched. Support from the private sector remained because of the traumatic memories of the protectionist policies of 1940–73. Furthermore, the lower tariff pushed the real exchange rate further up, giving an additional boost to the exportable sector. The economic authority also introduced compensation for small exporters through indirect tax rebates.

When the *Concertación* took office, most of its member parties had been critical of the process. According to them, Chile gave away protection without negotiating any privileges, for example, market access. Nevertheless, in 1991 Foxley decided to present to Congress a project for an additional unilateral tariff reduction. In a historical vote, the law was unanimously approved.[42] This unprecedented support may have been due to the fact that lower tariffs were needed to avoid potential trade diversion coming from the preferential trade agreements, but there was something more than that. Workers and entrepreneurs of some sectors expected tariff differentiation across sectors and higher protection.

Among the members of the coalition were two groups. One pushed for regionalism and Latin American integration. The idea was that after the consolidation of a Latin American bloc, Chile would be in a better position to negotiate jointly with large blocs such as the European Union and the US. The second group, led by the Minister of Finance and the Minister of Presidential Staff, took advantage of a visit by President Bush to launch the idea of a free trade agreement with the US. This was seen as a way to escape from regionalism, as in Mercosur, and to consolidate the openness of the economy. The idea received strong support from the private sector, as groups that were negatively affected by the unilateral openness saw the agreement with the US as beneficial for them. Nobody would have thought at that time that the agreement would take 12 years to be signed because the US presidents had difficulties in getting the necessary approval from Congress.

In the early 1990s, the law fixed a uniform tariff level, helping the government to resist pressures for higher tariffs, which emerged from time to time. In particular, some sectors asked for higher protection as an anti-dumping policy. However, these sectors were small (traditional agriculture and textiles). Unions were also asking for more protection, but good political management and the need for changes in the law, helped to keep the reform on track. The other key element is that, under the 1980 constitution, economic matters can only be initiated by the Executive. Remarkably enough, in all these years of discussion about constitutional reform, the issue of who has the initiative in economic matters has never been raised, suggesting that it enjoys legitimacy.

4.4.2   Fiscal policy and macroeconomic stability

Fiscal reform is at the core of the transformation of macroeconomic policies and outcomes. A major economic and fiscal crisis provided the necessary momentum to produce institutional changes and shifts in political attitudes.

In the 1950s and 1960s governments had severe difficulties in carrying out a fiscal policy consistent with the general objectives of macroeconomic policy and much was written in the structuralist tradition about inflexibilities in public expenditures, fiscal gaps, and so on. Political leaders recognized some of these problems and proposed constitutional changes to give more fiscal powers to the Executive and expand the authority of the ministry of finance in budgetary matters. However, most of these reforms did not prosper. The economic policies of *Unidad Popular* (1970–73) exacerbated fiscal problems and the size of the deficit reached catastrophic proportions. The military coup in 1973 put an end to those policies but the task of major fiscal adjustments remained.

The founding of the modern fiscal institutions and tax system

The efforts to balance the fiscal accounts hinged on three important policies: budget cuts, tax hikes, and devolution and privatization of companies. The fast economic recovery of the late 1970s helped to fortify government revenues, which in turn helped finance the shortfalls produced by the reduction in import duties.

At the beginning of the military government most of the effort was devoted to public expenditure control, with major cuts in government employment as well as reductions in public sector investment and real wages in the public sector.[43] The latter was made possible by the expedient of allowing a partial adjustment to past inflation.[44]

In 1975 three major reforms were introduced.

(1) The tax system was deeply reformed with the introduction of VAT (with an ample base and an initial rate of 20%), the introduction of automatic indexation, and the elimination of all special preferences. As a result, tax collection rose by 3 per cent of GDP, mostly thanks to the introduction of VAT.

(2) Control of public finances was unified (for both central government and public enterprises) under the Ministry of Finance and more specifically, the budget office (DIPRES by its Spanish acronym).[45] The government defined and combined the accounting and budgetary framework, expanding the budget's coverage to include all income and expenses of public entities. The responsibility for state management, which falls to the Executive branch, would be backed by attributions regarding the formulation of laws with an economic impact and, especially, definition of the spending ceiling and composition at the time of formulating the budget. The Executive branch was also given a margin of flexibility to manage the budget during the year. All of this was supported and reinforced by the 1980 constitution and confirmed by the 1997 constitutional court decision regarding the constitutionality of the norms on flexibility in budgetary administration. This general framework is contained in the State Financial Administration Law (DL 1263 from 1975), which was complemented by the norms of the 1980 constitution relative to legislation initiative and the budgetary process.

(3) SOEs that were running high deficits inherited from the previous government were privatized. An aggressive program to return companies under government management to their legal owners was carried out, but very little was done with the rest.[46] Since deficits persisted, DIPRES received a lot of power to control and enforce fiscal discipline in SOEs. Only after 1975 was privatization of the companies purchased by CORFO carried out, and the proceeds of the sales helped shore up public finances.

By the end of the 1970s the government began to run significant fiscal surpluses. With a new constitution in place, the time was ripe to introduce another major reform: the replacement of the old pension system, based on a pay-as-you-go scheme and different contributions and benefits for groups with similar characteristics, but different affiliations, to a fully funded system based on individual capitalization accounts (see Section 4.4.4). The new system started in 1980, and while affiliation to the new system by new entrants to the labor force was mandatory, existing workers could opt to remain in the old system or move into the new one. The rate of contribution was such as to give a rise in net salaries to those who moved into the new system. After the reform, the government was left with three major fiscal commitments:

(1) Pay retirement benefits to those who remained in the old system.
(2) A bond was issued to compensate the migrants to the new system for the contributions already made to the old one (recognition bonds).
(3) A guaranteed minimum pension was defined so that all of those who had 20 or more years of contributions could have that minimum pension, regardless of their accumulated savings by the end of their working life.

The size of the first two commitments was determined by the number of migrants to the new system, which was rather high, producing a pension revenues shortfall of 4.7 per cent of GDP at its peak in 1984, and which even now stands at about 3 per cent of GDP. Recognition bonds began to rise and became a significant expense in the mid-1990s, reaching 1 per cent of GDP at the end of the decade. These will peak at about 2.5 per cent of GDP in the coming decades, disappearing around 2025. The minimum pension guarantee has had a low impact so far (0.05 per cent of GDP in 2000), but it is expected to grow once the system reaches full maturity (Arenas and Marcel, 1999).[47]

The economic crisis in 1982 induced additional fiscal pressure. Tax revenues fell as a result of the deep recession. The government decided to bail out the banks, but not their owners, and subsidized debtors with dollar-denominated liabilities. Increased public debt made these transfers feasible. The debt was documented as public debt from the government to the Central Bank and still has considerable impact in the Central Bank balance sheet, representing a high proportion of the public debt today (Dirección de Presupuestos, 2003).

After the economy began to recover, fiscal discipline enabled a quick restoration of surpluses in the central government accounts. This process was helped by the second wave of privatizations that this time fell on more traditional public sector companies. During the 1980s the government sold the main telecommunications state monopolies, electric utilities, airlines, nitrate mines, iron and steel complexes, and so on. In 1984 the main goal of a new tax reform was to induce private savings by mimicking several characteristics of an expenditure-tax system. To achieve this goal, the system was consolidated at the personal level, so that income tax rates were applied in the same manner to all sources of income, and corporate taxes gave origin to credits in the personal income tax of the owners. Corporate and personal tax rates were reduced. In 1988, during the pre-plebiscite period, the rate of VAT was lowered to 16 per cent.

At the end of the military regime, a new tax change was enacted, replacing the tax base for the corporate tax. This change meant that the actual tax revenues for 1990, the first year of the newly elected government, were far lower than budgeted, since the fiscal impact of that reform was severely underestimated by the outgoing fiscal authorities.

Fiscal responsibility: the economic keystone of the democratic transition

The 1990s began with an orderly transfer of power from the outgoing military regime to the newly elected one. During the early stages of the campaign, the economic and political leaders of the *Concertación* knew that the first priority was to secure macroeconomic stability. Before any new expenses were introduced, a tax reform had to be implemented to help cool down the economy and provide funds for social programs. The value added tax rose from 16 per cent to 18 per cent and corporate taxes went from 10 per cent to 15 per cent. These changes required congressional approval and government authorities were quick to negotiate these changes as a package with the main opposition party. The tax changes fell short of the initial goals, but were enough to maintain public finances on a solid footing, while increasing social expenditures. The opposition was willing to back these reforms because they felt that after the solid mandate gained by the *Concertación*, it would have been suicidal to block these initiatives and the whole political and economic system might have been jeopardized. On the other hand, there was a broad consensus on the need to have a successful consolidation of the democratic regime and the opposition was keen to prove that the institutions of the 1980 constitution could produce an effective democracy.

In 1991, with the peso under pressure to appreciate after foreign capital began to flow into the country, the government reached an agreement to lower the import duty tariff from 15 per cent to 11 per cent, compensating the lost revenues with increases in specific indirect taxes, so as not to change the overall tax burden.

Fiscal policy remained unchanged after Aylwin was replaced by Frei in 1994, with the fiscal accounts in surplus and a systematic reduction in public debt (Marfán, 1998). At the end of this presidential period, and taking advantage of the Asian Crisis, a further gradual reduction in tariffs from 11 per cent to 6 per cent was enacted, compensating the revenue losses with some indirect taxes (Vial, 2001).

The recession of 1999 caused a small deficit but by 2000 the fiscal accounts were back in the blue when the new administration led by President Lagos implemented a fiscal rule based on the structural balance of the government.[48] The structural balance, as defined in Chile, has two major corrections from the traditional balance: the standard one to fiscal revenues taking into account departures from potential GDP (and normal tax collection), and the special adjustment to copper revenues, based on a long-term projection of the price of copper. To improve transparency in the computation of the two corrections, these parameters are set after public consultation with committees of outside experts.

The political economy of this reform

Under the leadership of Jorge Cauas, Sergio de Castro, and Juan Carlos Méndez, the first fiscal reform of the military government was designed by a team of economists and policy-makers from different sides of the political spectrum. Learning from the experience of the 1960s and 1970s, the norms instituted gave strong powers to the president and the minister of finance in all fiscal matters. The opportunity for change came with a major shock in 1975, after copper prices fell precipitously during the economic slowdown that followed the first oil crisis. The need for a major fiscal adjustment, on top of that of 1973, to compensate the revenue shortfall at a moment in which the government had little access to foreign credit, gave rise to budget cuts, privatization and tax hikes. The military government strengthened the influence of the minister of finance, who prepared the budget and presented it to the Junta for approval.

The new constitution in 1980 deepened the changes. It concentrated responsibilities for running the state in the Executive Branch and granted it clear primacy in all matters concerning public finances. This is reflected in the way the budget bill is processed in Chile:

- Congress has a fixed 60-day period for dispatching the bill. Failure to do so results in its automatic approval.[49]
- The income calculation is made known to Congress but is not voted on. Unlike other countries, particularly those with a parliamentary system, tax legislation is understood as having a 'permanent' nature, and cannot be altered by the (annual) budget law.
- Congress does not have the ability to increase spending or introduce new items. It can only approve or reduce the amounts the Executive proposed but, in a strict interpretation of the constitution, cannot eliminate them or reduce them so far that they impede the exercise of the functions that the Executive wants to perform. Congress cannot cut the proposed amounts of spending items allocated to cover commitments derived from permanent laws (pension payments, salaries to tenured public personnel, debt service, etc.).[50]

The fact that the constitution grants such 'advantages' to the Executive in the budget debate goes along with the full responsibility for macroeconomic management that also resides in the Executive Branch, particularly with the finance minister, who initiates the budget debate with a speech on the 'Public Finances Account'. During the military government these norms were less relevant since ad hoc committees headed by the members of the Junta carried out the legislative action. However, they became very important after the transfer of power to civilian rule. The political composition of Congress, differing interpretations of key aspects of the constitution, and the fact that the Executive needs congressional collaboration to approve other laws makes the legislative negotiation far more balanced in practice, but still limits the initiative of Congress to set the fiscal agenda.

After 1990 the political leadership was willing to go ahead with fiscal austerity for three reasons. First, the new leaders were aware of the political consequences of economic mismanagement, since all of them had gone through the economic chaos of the Allende period. Second, the military regime left power on a very high note, with the economy growing and the inflation rate coming down. Even though unemployment was still high, it had fallen from the heights of the crisis years, so there was a perception that economic failure would have caused a return of the pro-Pinochet opposition to power in the future. This was an important incentive for the *Concertación* to contain the social pressures. Finally, the economic failure of President Alfonsín in Argentina made a big impression on Chilean politicians. It made clear that restoration of political freedom, respect for human rights, and some punishment for previous abuses were not enough for political survival.

The diagnostic permeated even the presidential campaign, when candidate Aylwin took pains to explain to supporters that social demands had to be moderated and coherent with the available resources. After the election, the new team started negotiations with the opposition leaders even before being sworn in, and reached an agreement to raise VAT, roll back the change in the base of corporate tax, and increase personal income tax. The new law entered into effect in June 1990 at a time when the government was cutting down expenses within the budget left from the previous administration in order to balance public finances, which they did. Only in 1991 were they able to start increasing some social programs (Foxley, 1996).

Several studies concur that the concentration of budgetary power in the hands of the Ministry of Finance is of crucial importance for conducting a consistent fiscal policy (Alesina et al., 1996; Stein et al., 1998). However, the institutional framework cannot be the only explanation for good fiscal outcomes.

The most outstanding aspect is perhaps that the improvement in public finances has been maintained despite the institutional and political changes that have occurred since 1975. The legal framework for fiscal policy has remained stable with very few changes and the tax burden as a percentage of the GDP fell from around 20 per cent at the end of the 1970s and first half of the 1980s to between 18 per cent and 19 per cent in the 1990s (Table 4.3). The experience of previous decades and a strong conviction that the serious economic crisis at the beginning of the 1970s was largely caused by acute imbalances in fiscal policy have been essential factors in attaining agreement around a responsible fiscal policy.[51] It is no accident that the countries that went through the worst economic and political crises in the 1970s and 1980s

Table 4.3: Central government income, expenditures, and surplus (% of GDP)

Period	Total revenue	Total expenses	Overall balance	Copper and oil stabilization fund
1970–74	28.1	37.3	−9.2	0.0
1975–79	37.5	35.1	2.5	0.0
1980–84	36.2	36.2	0.0	0.0
1985–89	27.6	27.2	0.4	1.5
1990–94	21.9	20.3	1.6	1.5
1995–99	21.5	20.4	1.1	0.1
2000–03	22.2	22.7	−0.4	−0.6

Sources: 1970–80: Larraín (1991); 1980–86: built from rates of change of figures published by the Contraloría General de la República; 1987–2003: Dirección de Presupuestos. Estadísticas de las Finanzas Públicas.

have shown the greatest progress in consolidating a low and stable inflation rate, as well as greater fiscal discipline for the most part.

The Structural Balance Rule introduced in 2000 was in a way a culmination of a process initiated earlier. That process helped build the necessary credibility to gain access to international financial markets at reasonable costs, a prerequisite for such a rule.

4.4.3 Financial market reforms

There were two main reforms of the financial system. The first started in 1974 and deregulated the financial sector. The second, resulting from a deep macroeconomic and financial crisis, took place in the early 1980s and established a new institutional framework.

Financial liberalization in the 1970s

Low levels of intermediation and a long history of financial repression characterized the financial sector by 1974 (Edwards and Edwards, 1987). Interest rate controls yielded negative real interest rates for several years. Under Allende, the banking sector was nationalized and severe restrictions were imposed on the allocation of credit.

The deregulation of the financial sector involved releasing credit controls (credit limits, interest rate controls, reserve requirements and restrictions on foreign borrowing, and so on). Reserve requirements were reduced over the 1975–80 period. In 1975 interest rates paid and charged by commercial banks were liberalized. The minister of finance and the Central Bank led this reform, which initially required little new legislation, as interest rates were set free and regulations eliminated. It only became evident after the financial crisis of 1983 that the old banking laws were inadequate for the operation of a modern financial market. Major sources of controversy were the extremely high level of interest rates and the slow convergence towards normal levels.

Another important piece of the reform was the privatization of banks controlled by the government. The legislation restricted individuals from acquiring more than 3 per cent of a bank's property, while the limit for private firms was set at 5 per cent of a bank's stock. However, economic groups found a way to get around this rule (through the creation of investment companies) and the property of banks became highly concentrated. According to Edwards and Edwards (1987) a few economic groups controlled more than 80 per cent of the equity of private banks. These groups participated in the privatization of productive firms. As these firms needed to be capitalized, the groups used the banks to intermediate financial resources toward them.

At the beginning, firms owned by the groups borrowed from the banking sector competitively (not necessarily from the bank owned by the group). As the government fixed the exchange rate and indexed wage contracts, abrupt real appreciations of the peso followed. Moreover a slowdown of the non-oil exporting economies and a sudden fall in the terms of trade severely affected real incomes. The firms owned by the groups were mainly involved in the tradable sector and suffered the consequences. Banks stopped lending them money, which made firms borrow from related banks. The additional credits were used to pay past loans, rolling over bad credits.

This situation created what Harberger (1985) called a 'false demand' on top of the 'true demand' for credit. This false demand was used to refinance loans that could not be paid. Due to the lack of risk classification, losses did not appear in financial statements.

The crisis of 1982 and the reforms of the financial sector

Despite the commitment to a fixed exchange rate after June 1979, the peso was devalued in June 1982. Many banks and private companies were highly leveraged in dollars and their capacity for serving the debt was damaged. As interest rates never converged to international rates, between 1976 and 1982 companies ended up paying real interest rates on 30-day loans ranging from 11 per cent to 57 per cent.

The financial sector was not ready to face the fast reforms, and inadequate financial practices aggravated the macroeconomic crisis (Larraín, 1989). These practices were the consequence of an implicit insurance on deposits, a moral hazard problem, the absence of prudential supervision, the propagation of highly leveraged conglomerates, and the inexperience of domestic bankers in operating in an unregulated environment. Groups owned banks and related companies that went bankrupt when conditions deteriorated and external financial resources became scarce.

De la Cuadra and Valdés (1992) state that the banks made no effort to take the collateral before the crisis worsened because they had no control over the borrowers; the judicial system was very inefficient; and the banks and the conglomerates were related – the owners of the banks would not execute collateral that also belonged to them.

Two extreme solutions were at hand: let the banks go bankrupt or bail out the banking system (Larraín, 1989). The first had no direct cost for the government but was considered to have huge negative effects for the real sector. The second was considered too costly and against the market-oriented principles that guided the government. An intermediate solution was finally implemented: banks' shareholders and future generations of taxpayers would have to pay the losses. This triggered the second stage of the reforms.

During 1980–83, 11 banks and six financial companies were subject to intervention and some of them were liquidated. Between 1983 and 1984 an intense debt rescheduling process took place, and interest rates and conditions for debtors were changed. The banks that had been subject to intervention were 're-privatized' during 1985–86, through the so-called system of 'popular capitalism', whereby the banks were sold to small stockholders who had access to governmental credit under special conditions.

A new banking law was enacted in 1986. It was intended to prevent a banking crisis and to provide more transparency.[52] The law required a more active role of the superintendent in evaluating banks' risk, according to loan classifications, more disclosure of information, and a strict enforcement of restrictions on how to conduct business with parties related to a bank. The government also restricted the insurance to depositors, as a way of inducing depositors to seek more information on bank risk.

Fuentes and Maquieira (2001) argue that the introduction of prudential regulation and supervision explains a good deal of the differences between the development of the financial market and the low level of arrears in the banking system. This type of regulation induced banks to introduce better screening techniques and to share information on the indebtedness levels of individuals and firms.

The political economy of the reforms

As with other reforms, the prevailing idea was that the market should allocate resources. The principles behind the first stage of financial liberalization were established in 1974. Undurraga (1974) states that the policies intended to make the financial system more competitive and efficient were based on:

- Non-discrimination among financial institutions and instruments of similar characteristics. Similar institutions and instruments should face the same legal and tax constraints.
- Broadening the scope of business for financial institutions and provision of more flexibility to their operations to facilitate innovation and adaptation to market requirements.
- Elimination of preferential treatment to priority sectors, especially through interest rate subsidies. The Central Bank was forbidden to give credit to non-financial companies.

Economic authorities were considering the non-discrimination principle and a movement towards universal banking as early as 1974. The idea was that commercial banks should be the exclusive providers of lending services, unifying the role of commercial banks, development banks, and financial companies (De la Cuadra and Valdés, 1992). Competition in the financial market was seen as a way of imposing market discipline (Barandarian and Hernández, 1999).

The bail out of Banco Osorno in early 1977 contradicted this view. A year before, several small financial intermediaries (*financieras*), some of them unregistered, went bankrupt and the government did not bail them out. In the case of Banco Osorno the principle of 'too big to fail' was applied. The authority needed to build a reputation to gain access to the international credit market. Furthermore, the reforms were just starting and the bankruptcy of an important bank was seen as an element that could negatively affect them.

On a bigger scale, a similar dilemma was faced in the banking crisis of 1981–83. The ratio of non-performing loans to banks' total equity increased from 22.4 per cent to 158.1 per cent between 1981 and 1983. The competing groups in the economic team that advised the government proposed three solutions. De la Cuadra and Valdés (1992) call these groups the financial market repression school, the free-banking school, and the state supervision school.

The financial repression school believed that the government should bail out the banks by absorbing their losses and taking over bank ownership. The central argument was that banks cannot be controlled and that they should be administered by the state. This was equivalent to a return to the situation prevalent before 1975 and was discarded because of the disastrous past experiences of state-owned banks.

The free-banking group considered that insolvent financial institutions should go bankrupt. Shareholders and depositors would have to absorb the losses. This alternative carried a political cost, not considered crucial at that time. The problem with it was that two-thirds of the system would have to file for bankruptcy, providing a negative externality to the whole economy. In addition, there was concern that such losses would abort the pension reform, as a large fraction of the funds were invested in the banking sector.

The third alternative was an intermediate solution, in which government should intervene, and losses should be absorbed by shareholders and the government (taxpayers), and to a small extent by depositors. The group supporting this solution proposed establishing prudential regulation and a close supervision of the financial institutions. Several practices were proposed which were later formally established in a new banking law. The new rules gave more power to the superintendence of banks and financial institutions to supervise the banks. A more transparent and efficient credit system was implemented from 1980. As a first step, loans were rated in four categories (A, B, C and D).[53] This empowered the regulatory agency to obtain information on the 300 most important debtors of each bank. It also required banks to classify the loans (consumer loans, mortgage loans, and so on).

This happened at a time when the government was under severe political pressure and the nationalistic faction had taken the upper hand in a cabinet reshuffle. After intense debates, the third alternative was applied with the political support of the Ministry of Internal Affairs. The resources needed for the bail-out convinced the authorities to enact the new bank regulation.

As the owners of the banks were also the owners of the borrowing firms, the intervention meant that shareholders lost the property of the banks and the firms that were not able to pay their loans. The owners of the economic groups (banks and borrowing firms) lost their capital and their personal assets. The National Security Council investigated the responsibility of the shareholders in the crisis. As a result long judicial processes started.[54]

In summary, this reform started as a consequence of a deep economic crisis. The new banking law was the initial step in the revamping of the banking system. As the savings accumulated in pension funds became too big for the limited size of the domestic market, new laws were enacted in the 1990s to open up new investment opportunities, first in local equity and to a lesser extent in variable and fixed income abroad. In later years, the laws have been relaxed and regulation has been adjusted in conformity with new international standards.

The subordinated debt that other banks owed to the Central Bank as a consequence of their bail-out became a major contentious issue in the 1990s. It was solved in the mid-1990s with a change in the law that required a difficult political negotiation with the banks and Congress.

4.4.4 The new pension system[55]

In the late 1970s the military regime initiated several 'modernizations', as they were called, most of them in the social area. The best known is the pension reform, because it represented a drastic departure from international practice, as well as from Chilean tradition.

Social security was introduced relatively early in Chile, before the mid-1920s. Pensions were based on a 'pay-as-you-go' (PAYG) scheme, a system that was eventually adopted by all countries with a market economy. Under PAYG, contributions are pooled to pay for defined benefits, and are financed by mandatory contributions by workers. When a country is in the initial stages of the demographic transition, the system should be accumulating a sizable surplus. Adequately invested, they should help finance pensions once the system reaches maturity. Because of this feature, the system is vulnerable to political pressure by well-connected groups.

Chile represents an extreme case of capture by interest groups. The system quickly degenerated into a constellation of pension institutions; each designed for a special constituency, with special norms concerning contributions, value of pensions, retirement age, and so on. About 80 per cent of the working population depended on the *Servicio de Seguro Social* (SSS) run by the state, with the lowest benefits and without protection of pensions against inflation. By contrast, some *'cajas'* catered to the need of a few thousand affiliates, allowing for early retirement after 20 years of work and with pensions equivalent to salaries at the time of retirement. By the end of the 1970s the government was contributing 7 to 8 per cent of GDP to make up the financial shortfall of the system.[56] Financial projections made at the budget office showed an explosive growth of fiscal outlays originating in the deficit of the pension system (Hepp, 1980).

The problems were evident well before the late 1970s. Many studies had been made about the subject and reforms were proposed. The best known of these studies, a monumental piece of work, had been carried out during the presidency of Jorge Alessandri in the late 1950s and early 1960s, under the leadership of Jorge Prat, a respected politician. As with previous and subsequent attempts, this effort did not lead anywhere, because of political opposition.

When the Chicago Boys entered the military government in the mid-1970s, they set out, among other objectives, to restore a lasting equilibrium to government finances and to reform the pension system.[57] One key step in the achievement of both objectives was a proposal – approved by the legislative power in 1978 as Decree Law No. 2488, but for political reasons only implemented in 1979 – to fix a mandatory minimum age of retirement, valid for all social security institutions, except the military. This minimum was set at 65 years for men and 60 years for women.

The importance of this reform cannot be understated. Fixing uniform minimum retirement ages eliminated one of the most important sources of discrimination and privilege in the PAYG system. It also increased the number of years workers had to contribute in most social security institutions, thereby improving their finances, as well as those of the whole system. This allowed a very significant reduction in contribution rates, which boosted employment.

Curiously, but not surprisingly given the substantial loss of special privileges, the reform did not affect the institution that was in power (the armed forces). It also meant no losses for most blue-collar workers who were in the SSS and who already retired after 65 (60 for women) years of age. However, the government was aware of the negative political impact this reform had on some powerful and privileged groups of workers. This reform was finally approved in 1979, after General Leigh had been dismissed and General Pinochet had consolidated his power over the army, and at a time when the government could afford some of its political costs as it had a high approval rating and the economy was booming.

The principles of the new mandatory, individual account, defined contribution, and privately managed pension system

'El Ladrillo' (CEP, 1994) had a chapter on the need to replace the PAYG scheme with a fully funded, mandatory defined contribution, and privately managed pension system. The main characteristics of the system were embodied in the legislation.[58]

The system is based on the principles of individual freedom, individual responsibility, and social responsibility with respect to the needy. The three pillars of the system are: (1) low income assistance and minimum pensions are available for the poor, irrespective of their contributions; (2) pensions should be directly proportional to contributions made;[59] and (3) the management of the pension funds should be private and competitive.[60]

The new system has a completely different base from that of the old one. It has solidarity, but is paid for by all taxpayers, not only workers. Except for the poor, pensions are directly related to contributions, which minimizes the intra- and inter-generational transfers, and significantly diminishes the incentive to evade pension contributions. Competition between pension fund managers as well as a careful institutional design assures that it is in the best interest of financial managers to achieve the highest rate of return for the pension funds, at limited levels of risk, defined by regulations on the investment portfolio. There was free entry to the system and provisions were made in order to facilitate voluntary affiliation and changes between pension fund managers (AFPs).

The new pension system is coherent with respect to the general principles on which the model was built. There is a reasonable degree of choice with respect to (1) the amount of total contributions to be made,[61] (2) the provider, (3) the amount and form of the pension payments, and (4) the age of retirement.[62] The counterpart of this choice is the responsibility which each individual has in deciding the quality of the pension. The system is highly regulated, but authorities have almost no discretionary power – that is, rules dominate over discretion. Furthermore, the state plays a subsidiary role, because it (1) created the legal framework of the system, which otherwise would certainly not exist at this time, (2) monitors its proper functioning, and (3) finances part or total pensions, but only for those who otherwise could not even reach a minimum pension level. However, the state does not operate the pension fund administrators, which are private firms. Finally, for obvious reasons, the pension system requires strict respect for property rights and, given the proportion of the population that participates and has an interest in it, indirectly contributes to the strengthening of those rights.[63]

The political economy of the pension reform

José Piñera, the Minister of Labor, was responsible for the detailed design of the new system and its approval by the Junta.[64] The economic team, especially the Ministry of Finance, headed by Sergio de Castro and the Budget Director Juan Carlos Méndez, and ODEPLAN, led by Miguel Kast, supported the reform, and had a key role in the special committee set up to reform the pension system, led by Alfonso Serrano, Undersecretary in the Ministry of Labor, that included, among others, Hernán Büchi, who later on became a very influential minister of finance and presidential candidate, and Martín Costabal, who later became budget director.

Pinochet and the members of the Junta approved the social security reform project at a meeting in April 1980. Piñera had previously presented the idea and basic principles of the reform to Pinochet, who endorsed it, but was not willing to force workers to transfer from the old to the new system. Therefore, the project allowed workers to choose, during the initial five years, the system they wanted to belong to. In so doing, workers were to have the last word about which system would prevail. If few workers had chosen to transfer, a counter-reform would in all likelihood have taken place.

The reform was announced on 1 May 1980. According to Piñera, the opponents of the reforms included people from the right and left, civilians and military, people in and outside government. Some opposed it in principle and others because of vested interests in the old system. First, those who received special privileges under the old system were, of course, opposed to the reform. Second, opposition also came from the so-called 'social security specialists', who only knew about PAYG systems. They could not conceive a system based on different principles. Third, managers of the social security management institutions, generally retired military personnel, who could not understand why the government was going to relinquish the power they believed it had over vast pension fund resources. Fourth, opposition came from labor leaders, who had recently suffered a defeat over the new labor law that was approved only shortly before the new social security system and ended their monopoly. Fifth, the political opposition to the military regime was also against the reform. Although not allowed to express itself openly as such, this opposition was very active and did have a voice in the press and influence on government decisions in socio-economic matters. Sixth, some opposition came from the economic right, which in general approved the market economy, but did not understand the benefits of several of the 'modernizations', including that of social security, because they were born and raised under a system where social matters were taken care of exclusively by the state.

The final and perhaps most powerful opposition came from the military advisers to the president and the generals who ran the pension system of the armed forces. The latter did not agree to join the new system. The former saw the discussion about the pension reform as an opportunity to achieve a reorientation of all economic and social policy, which they felt was too liberal and would cause the disintegration of society. However, some generals in the advisory committee to the president either changed their minds, as they learned more about the project, from opposition to neutrality or abstained from active opposition. Among these, Piñera mentions General Alejandro Medina, Fernando Lyon, and especially important, Chief of Staff, Santiago Sinclair. This proved decisive, and once the political field cleared, after the promulgation of the new constitution in 1980, President Pinochet gave the final go ahead to the reform.

The reform was a decisive success with most of the labor force switching into the new system in about a year, albeit they were encouraged by gains in take-home pay in the range of 12 per cent, as a result of the reduced rate of contributions in the new system. The next test came as a result of the banking crisis in 1982–83, but as was mentioned above, precautions were taken to shield the system from financial losses.

By the end of the 1980s the system was consolidating. It showed very high rates of return and legislation was passed to open them up for investment in local equity, and in a very limited manner for investments abroad.

The final test came after the transfer of power to democratically elected authorities that chose not to reverse the reforms. This was not only the result of political calculation, but also the belief that the pension system was working, as reflected in subsequent reforms to introduce more flexibility for investment by the pension funds. In later years further changes have been made to improve the system, by allowing wider limits for investments abroad, the creation of multiple funds (five) in each AFP, based on different limits for investments in equity, to give affiliates options based on their risk aversion and age. New incentives have also been given to promote voluntary contributions with generous tax breaks.

Currently there is an important debate about future adjustments to the system to improve coverage, provide better protection to the poor and improve competition among AFPs, but there are no proposals to revert to a PAYG system.

4.5   Concluding remarks

Few countries have faced such dramatic changes in such a relatively brief period of time as Chile. From being an economy that was in tune with the meager performance of other Latin American economies, Chile became a pioneer in the implementation of bold and innovative reforms.

Unquestionably, some of the main reforms conducted in the first years of the military regime would have been difficult to implement with the same speed and depth under a democratic government. Nevertheless, countless experiences of frustrated reforms in similar situations prove that this type of government provides neither necessary nor sufficient conditions for conducting reforms. There are also cases in which major economic crises provided conditions to introduce sweeping reforms in democratic countries, even under very weak governance conditions.

Why did Chile make reforms fifteen years earlier than the Washington Consensus? The disastrous shape of the economy after the Allende government provided fertile ground for profound reforms. But more instrumental was the existence of sufficient critical mass in terms of the human capital necessary to lead the reforms. The ideas for reform and the team to make them happen incubated during the crisis and the military regime provided the means to bring them forward.

Why did the reforms go so deep? The military government delegated the conduct of the reforms to the technocrats. In addition, the government knew that it would stay in power for a long period of time, which created strong intertemporal linkages.

Why, rather than reversing the reforms, did the change in the political system deepen them? The return to democracy shows something atypical in Chile. The economic success of the late 1980s, the memory of Allende's economic crisis, the collapse of the communist regimes, and the experience of Argentina and other democratic governments in the region, played a critical role in shaping a political climate that favored continuity. The polity showed signs of maturity by not changing the spirit of the reforms and in some cases advancing them. The new democratic government knew that the economic situation was key to making the democratic system last and did not cave in to pressures from different agents. In addition, some key institutions of the 1980 constitution played a major role: veto players had a deterrent effect on counter-reform proposals, and, most important of all, limited the power of Congress to set the legislative agenda. The electoral system also played a role, both by securing a balance of power in Congress and by strengthening the powers of party leaders, increasing their capacity to enforce party discipline among Congress members.

As the analyses of some of the most important reforms show, building institutions with special emphasis on empowering the ministry of finance and the technocracy installed there helps to explain why some of the many pressures for reversal could be avoided. Equally important was the creation of laws that made it costly and difficult to modify the reforms. The rules of the game, based on a strong presidential system that acts as the main veto player, and the binominal system induced the need for broad consensus.

Can this political institution be exported? The binominal system generates a balance in the Congress and therefore facilitates the status quo. If the country has reached a good equilibrium, this political structure helps to maintain it. If the country were in a bad equilibrium, it would not help it to move. The stability brought about by the binominal system comes at the cost of reduced political competition, to a point that it would be deemed unacceptable for almost any country to adopt it voluntarily. A strong presidential system is also positive when the country is capable of building state capacity to sustain and deepen the reform (Rius and van de Walle, 2005). Of course, strong presidential powers are only as good as the president. If he or she were in favor of reversing reforms, it would certainly be a major weakness. What is interesting in the case of Chile is that political leaders such as Aylwin, Frei, Lagos, and Bachelet, coming from very different backgrounds, were willing to adopt a favorable view of the reforms and work to deepen them.

Notes

We thank José M. Fanelli and Gary McMahon for their comments and suggestions, and Andrés Allamand, Patricia Arancibia, Camilo Carrasco, Mauricio Larraín Garcés, Patricio Navia, and Ricardo Vicuña for helpful discussions. The usual disclaimer applies.

1. See Harberger (1959), Davis (1967), Cruzat (1969), Lüders (1970, 1990), Ffrench-Davis (1973), Heskia (1973), Butelman et al. (1981), Larraín and Meller (1990), Barahona et al. (1993), and Borner et al. (1993).
2. A coalition led by the Radical Party (center-left) that included the socialist and, initially, the communist parties.
3. See Lüders and Wagner (2003).
4. The successes of Germany and Russia during the 1930s, in which governments instead of markets played a key role in the allocation of resources, had a decided influence. So did some economic ideas, especially those of Keynes. Contrary to popular belief, the ECLAC import substitution doctrine was not articulated until after the new model had begun to be implemented. ECLAC began its operations in 1947 and its doctrine can be considered as one way to rationalize the economic policies already adopted in several Latin American countries, after the breakdown of international trade during the Great Depression.
5. Critics of the liberal development model always existed (Encina, 1911). They only gathered support after the Great Depression.
6. The average fiscal deficit to GDP ratio was 1.2.
7. Chile suspended service of its foreign debt early during the Great Depression and only resumed servicing it in the 1950s.
8. The Central Bank of Chile was created in 1925 and had a governing board in which government-appointed directors were a minority, while those representing commercial banks, the private sector, and labor were a majority. The composition of the board gradually changed and in the second half of the 1960s the government appointed all board members.
9. See Lüders (1970) and Ffrench-Davis (1973).
10. These included the post office, electricity generation and distribution, the water and sewage company, the national petroleum company, the national steel mill, 50 per cent of the largest copper producers, the national port company, the national airline, the national railroad, a state bank, and even a national bus company.
11. The firms included in this process were public utilities, commercial banks and other financial institutions, the large wholesale trading firms, and 100 per cent of the large copper producers.
12. See Hachette and Lüders (1993).
13. There is no evidence that a crisis always fosters reforms as it may actually destroy institutions (Fanelli and Popov, 2005).
14. Documented in what is popularly referred to as '*El Ladrillo*' (CEP, 1994).
15. The origins of the 'Chicago Boys' and their role in the military government are discussed in Valdés (1995) and Fontaine (1988).
16. Mandatory indexation to past inflation (preserved until the 1982 crisis) limited wage movements. This may have been one factor contributing to generating and intensifying the crisis.
17. These companies, which were managed by 'intervened' commercial banks, and banks themselves, constituted what has been called the 'odd sector', because legally those companies and banks had private owners, but were managed by the government.
18. This difference between the pre- and post-recession periods reflects the different preferences of the two major economic policy-makers of the time. Sergio de Castro, the leader of the economic reforms, favored a 'hands-off' policy, while Hernán Büchi, the most influential economic policy-maker of the post-recession period, favored more active government policies.

19. The provisions that had to remain were free and voluntary affiliation to unions, decentralized negotiations at the firm level, and the freedom for firms to hire and lay-off employees without the consent of the government authorities or the unions.
20. As a result of their lobby, workers in the state conglomerate managing the ports received very generous concessions in a specially legislated severance package.
21. The actual privatization proceeded smoothly and quickly, under the leadership of CORFO. By the end of Frei's term all major companies were privatized or in the final stages of the process. See Aninat et al. (2004) for a discussion of the main aspects of the policy-making process in this case.
22. After two weeks of strikes and school takeovers by some high-school students, President Bachelet has recently appointed a commission comprising a cross-section of participants of the educational sector to propose yet another educational reform.
23. Universal coverage of secondary education has been reached in most of the major urban areas.
24. Although it is too early to judge the results of this reform, preliminary evidence suggests a significant shortening of the process time and clear signs of improvement in terms of accountability of those involved in the investigation, judgment and sentencing.
25. The exception was the first half of Eduardo Frei Montalva's presidency (1965–70).
26. Rius and van de Walle (2005) point out that there is not enough evidence to support the claim that an autocratic regime has a higher propensity to reform than a democratic regime. They argue that the main opposition to reforms is clientelism, where the political power provides some benefits to key constituencies to remain in power. Clientelism can be present either in autocracies or democracies.
27. Calderón and Fuentes (2005) provide cross-country evidence of the importance of policy complementarity for economic growth. Gallego and Loayza (2002) and Fuentes et al. (2004) do so for Chile.
28. The effect of macroeconomic policies on reform reversals is highlighted in Fanelli and McMahon (2005b) and Liew et al. (2005).
29. The new constitution that replaced that of 1925 had been drafted by a special commission and approved, after difficult negotiations, by it, the Junta, and the State Council, the latter headed by former President Jorge Alessandri. One outstanding feature of the constitution is that it put a time limit on the military government at a moment at which the government was under no pressure to relinquish power.
30. In Spanish this is the Ministro Secretario General de Gobierno.
31. Constitutional changes which eliminated the designation of senators were recently approved. In June 2006, Pinochet was under house arrest under charges of tax evasion.
32. The views of this group can be found in the many publications by CIEPLAN (Foxley, 1983). The main political and economic elements of the strategy of the Aylwin government can be found in the proceedings of a seminar held at CIEPLAN in early 1990, just before the inauguration. They contain brief presentations by Correa, Boeninger, Cortázar, and Foxley, all of whom held key cabinet positions during the Aylwin administration (Muñoz, 1990).
33. COSENA has as its primary objective to serve as a formal meeting place of the top authorities of the country to air sensitive policy issues, as well as to enforce the law. It was created as a device aimed at avoiding an institutional breakdown like the one that took place in 1973.

34. This element is also emphasized in Rius and van de Walle (2005), where they discuss how a small number of veto players increases the probability of reforms.
35. The 2005 constitutional reform reduced the term of the president to four years, with no possibility for re-election, making presidential and congressional elections simultaneous.
36. Sometimes it may be easier for the party that is (ideologically) less likely to implement a successful reform (Cukierman and Tommasi, 1998a).
37. The trade reform and its effects has been the object of numerous studies (Edwards and Edwards, 1987; Cauas and De la Cuadra, 1981; and Ffrench-Davis, 1981).
38. Chile had one of the highest trade distortions in the world (Edwards, 1995).
39. Fuentes (1995) analyzes the changes in productivity and resource allocations due to the trade reform.
40. Saez et al. (1995) analyze the trade policy of the Aylwin administration.
41. Tariffs are lower or nonexistent for goods imported from countries that have preferential trade agreements with Chile.
42. It is ironic that two decades before, during Allende's government, a freely elected Congress approved, also by unanimity, the nationalization without compensation of the copper mines. These two votes reflect, perhaps better then anything else, the change in the mood of the country brought about by the economic reforms.
43. See Larraín and Vergara (2000).
44. The computation of the CPI in 1974 severely underestimated actual inflation that year, facilitating the process.
45. For more background, see Dirección de Presupuestos (1974).
46. For more details, see Hachette (2000) and Arellano and Marfán (1987).
47. The proponents of the reform were aware of this fiscal shortfall and took steps to generate the necessary resources to finance it (Hepp, 1980). The Chilean pension reform has been accompanied by overall fiscal surpluses over the whole period (except during the debt crisis) and helps to explain the significant rise in domestic savings after the 1980s.
48. The rule is a policy decision, without a formal backing in any law, and states that the central government will maintain a 1 per cent surplus in the structural balance.
49. Constitutional experts do not agree on what 'dispatching of the law' means. Some even hold that there are doubts regarding which budget should go into effect if a bill has been approved in the first round by the Chamber of Deputies.
50. In the Budget Law of 2000, the fixed expenses derived from permanent laws reached 66 per cent of the total. These laws force the Executive to provide the resources to make the payments, which means that there is no discretionary space for either the executive or legislative branches in these matters.
51. See Méndez (1979) and the annual presentations of the public treasury statement by the respective finance ministers during the 1990–99 period.
52. See Ramírez and Rosende (1992) for a summary of the changes in the banking legislation.
53. Category A: normal loans, with high probability of recovery; Category B: loans with some weakness in the conditions under which they were granted; Category C: loans with uncertain recovery; Category D: defaulted loans, that is, loans not paid.
54. The most important one, concerning the BHC group led by Javier Vial, finished in 2005, with a complete clearance of all charges. Vial died in 2004 when the matter was still unresolved, 20 years after the start of the judicial process.
55. This part of the chapter draws from World Bank (1994), Piñera (1991), and Corbo et al. (1997).

56. Superintendencia de Seguridad Social (1992).
57. The existence of this team – which in the broader acceptance of the name, was comprised mainly of graduates from the University of Chicago, from other US universities, and also many from the Pontifical Catholic University of Chile – is believed to have been one of the key elements of the successful reforms of 1974 and following years (Piñera, 1991). Others were (1) the existence of true leadership; (2) an element of surprise to avoid the organization of resistance to a particular reform; and (3) the appropriate use of the media to relay the benefits of a given reform.
58. Decree Law 3500, which went into effect in May 1981.
59. This reduces the tax element of the contribution and the negative effects of social security on labor supply.
60. At the time of retirement, retirees can choose to invest the accumulated funds in an insurance annuity or a system of 'programmed or phased withdrawal'. Under the latter, the retiree receives an actuarially determined amount each year, enjoying a higher pension in the initial years after retirement, but potentially receiving a lower pension income than under the insurance scheme.
61. Tax-exempt voluntary contributions can be made. The limit of these is almost four times the mandatory contributions.
62. Early retirement is possible if accumulated funds can finance the minimum pension level.
63. For a detailed description of the system see Corbo et al. (1997).
64. Piñera (1991) describes the characteristics of the process that led to the approval.

5
A Common Thread? Democratic Façades, Institutional Governance, and Economic Reform Outcomes in Mexico and Peru

José Alberto Garibaldi

5.1 Introduction

This chapter presents a structural reform process as an attempt to change the institutional setting in which the economy operates; a transaction between agents within a central policy and organizational domain intended to alter the pattern of interaction between political and economic rules, with the purpose of improving the performance of the economy. Reform is not the change in formal rules, but rather of the actual interaction pattern. Strategies devised to overcome opposition affect which reforms advance and which do not. This is key to understanding the sequence, pace, and timing of reforms.

The chapter argues that the institutional environment provides the setting and means to reject, abort, or enforce the proposed deals in the process of reform – the introduction of new formal rules, regulatory commissions, agents within the state, and so on. Institutions also help create the mental models agents employ to make sense of – or seek to modify – the arrangements under which they live. As institutions result from human agency and simultaneously constrain it, they help show not only how agents respond to policy and reform initiatives, but also how they negotiate strategies to advance reform, as the evolving institutional conditions open or close windows of opportunities.

Peru and Mexico are taken as contrasting, polar, examples. Both suffered informal undemocratic regimes which operated quite differently from what was prescribed by their formal rules. However, this case study argues that if the interaction between the institutional environment and implementation strategy is analyzed institutionally, it becomes clear that they shared similarities in the mechanisms used to implement reforms, which plays a crucial role in explaining differences in reform strategy, pace, sequence, and depth, as well as in their political processes. Obviously economic size, political regime, technical capacity, and resource endowment differences make the implementation similarities more striking.

The chapter is divided into four main sections and a conclusion. Section 5.2 presents a theoretical framework to be employed in the reform cases. Section 5.3 presents an analytical narrative of the reform processes undertaken in Mexico and Peru, analyzing the logic and sequence of the reforms and the external characteristics of the policies which moved them forward, with a particular emphasis on the policy networks and informal institutional settings through which reforms were advanced. Section 5.4 compares the two countries. The conclusions in Section 5.5 summarize the argument and outline the main points. While in neither country has the reform process totally stopped, it has lasted longer in Mexico than in Peru because of the more gradual approach in Mexico. Thus the reform period covered is 1982–2000 in the case of Mexico, and 1990–2000 in the case of Peru.

5.2 Structure and agents: endogenous institutional change as a theoretical framework

The Latin American developmental states of the late 1970s were the basis for the reforms of the 1990s. Stylized models usually include a large public sector, with an important share of GDP in state-owned companies, operating within protected internal markets and employing macroeconomic policy to redistribute income among fragmented groups, while suffering frequent external and fiscal sector imbalances and reduced competitiveness. Abundant literature has examined the political economy behind the 1990s' reforms, but seldom delved into their institutional background. We will argue that any regime's economic institutional foundations are the result of the strategic interaction between agents, but also have a stable existence outside of the choices of any agent, buttressed by organizations and mental models.

Analyzing institutions formed by interactions between agents in specific domains is the first step to examining how these evolve. Institutions can be taken as the endogenous rules of the game, a decentralized, self-organizing system of social constructs that represent objective conditions of equilibrium between strategies followed by agents, providing them with expectations about others' reactions, while simultaneously constraining their own.[1] From this point of view, the term institution ought to refer only to the substantive characteristics of an equilibrium within the rules employed, robust enough to the mildly changing environments of the domain in which it operates.[2] While formal rules can on occasion represent the actual equilibrium across domains, this need not be the case; these can also be just an attempt by a set of agents to secure a new one.

Institutions, domains, and reforms

We define a domain as the feasible set of strategies formed by all relevant agents to enforce equilibrium of interactions over a period of time. Agents are relevant within a domain when others cannot ignore their possible reactions to any action of their own. We argue that (i) a domain can have various over-lapping arenas where agents from the same domain interact, (ii) several key domains can be isolated for analysis, and (iii) the articulation of these key domains creates a characteristic overall institutional architecture within the polity and the economy. Aoki (2001: 378–9) argues that an economy can be characterized by institutional equilibria within the financial, industrial organization, supply, labor, corporate governance, and formal enforcement domains, each with its own set of agents and strategies.

To allow a more precise examination of political as well as economic issues, we will focus on two additional but central domains. The first we will call the organizational domain, comprising the higher level (meta-constitutional, constitutional, and legal) rules defining who has access to the power vested in state organs.[3] Parties, executives, and high-level civil servants (including the military in the case of Peru) are its main institutional agents. It comprises three arenas: (i) the formal or informal constitutional rules regulating political power within groups; (ii) electoral systems and intra-party relations; and (iii) the internal organization of the executive, including the formal (or informal, as in Mexico) institutions within the central administration of the state. The organizational domain provides a coordinating role across domains. Coordination across a number of domains can be achieved from a policy nexus (economic, political, or security) within the domain. From there, institutional equilibria within the financial, industrial organization, labor, supply, and enforcement domains cascade down. We will argue throughout that agents having a dominant role in any of the latter can carve a role for themselves within the organizational domain, and that while the executive can be particularly effective at providing coordination within this domain, it is by no means the only player, nor necessarily the dominant one.

The second additional domain we will focus on is the social domain, formed by three other interrelated arenas: public opinion (including the mass media), social norms (including society-wide inter-subjective norms), and the embedded mental models agents form of a specific game (including the societal consensus over the overall institutional arrangement of the polity and the economy). While as noted above, the judiciary can be a domain of its own (formed by courts, congress, and/or other formal judicial and quasi-judicial institutions), enforcement is an element of all domains (agents must rely on some force of enforcement, formal or otherwise, to ensure the stability of the equilibrium within their own domain).

Last but not least, we would like to note that these – as most other – domains can frequently be linked and in certain cases made complementary across the polity and the economy by agents who can see gains in bundling them together to overcome constraints. Linked domains include domains bundled together or institutions linked across domains by third-party intermediaries. Complementary domains involve all those whose institutional viability was made possible by non-related institutions in other domains, in which the latter supported the former. In both, we will argue that bundling or linking agents can benefit from rents arising from linkages or complementarities. The interrelated character of the different domains, coupled with the mechanisms employed to enforce equilibrium provide the main indication of the overall institutional arrangements across domains (corporatist, oligarchic, market driven, and so on).

In this context, each set of interactions within domain(s) in a period can open or close windows for reform previously unavailable. A strategy to advance successive alliances between agents in domains to be linked or complemented can provide means to help enforce the transactions at the root of the process, as reform moves from changes that are easier to win to more complex changes, and/or to preventing other parties from mounting an effective opposition. Furthermore, this control provides access to sets of public goods delivery mechanisms to gain support from bundling agents and/or from groups outside the organizational domain. As Tanaka (1998) argues, this capacity, together with the strength, level of organization, and self-identity of the groups serving as bundling and support agents (political parties, unions, NGOs, and/or other social organizations) within civil society and, we may add, the strength of the mental models and embedded social norms they employ to define their collective identity, can help define the character of negotiation for support, and/or the degree of clientelism that will take place. Table 5.1 characterizes the relations between organized social groups and the state based on the variables already mentioned.

Table 5.1 helps define terms which will be employed through this study. The term 'public goods' is well known, and its provision constitutes a crucial bargaining chip for the dominant agent or coalition within the organizational domain. 'Support groups' are agents serving as independent bundling agents for the social groups operating within the social domain, while 'collective identities' refer to the strength of the mental model these groups form about themselves. Their interaction creates categories defined in italics: in the first

Table 5.1:   Relations between organized groups and the state

	Greater state capacity to deliver public goods	Lower state capacity to deliver public goods
Strong support groups	Strong collective identities: *Participative democracies* Weak popular collective identities: *Elitist democracy*	Strong collective identities: *Movements* Weak collective identities: *Negotiation*
Weak support groups	Strong collective identities: *Corporatism* Weak collective identities: *Neo-clientelism*	Strong collective identities: *Social movements* Weak collective identities: *Pragmatism*

column, with strong public goods, *participative democracy* refers to the political participation of organized popular groups with strong collective identities within government, while *elitist democracy* refers to the same but without the strong identities, having more of an oligarchic character. *Corporatism* and *neo-clientelism* suppose a similar relation between public goods and collective identities, but with weaker independent bundling (support) groups. An analogous group of relations applies to the second column, characterized by a lower state capacity to deliver public goods: *movements* – also employed here as social movement logic – refers to groups with strong bundling agents and collective identities. As the strength of parties or other bundling agents collapse, *social movements* and *pragmatism* emerge, depending on the strength of the mental model employed.

The length of the temporal policy horizon allows stable patterns of interaction to emerge and can help categorize institutional arrangements. A longer policy horizon within the organizational domain would allow a larger or smaller number of successive interactions through policy cycles within it. Successive interactions lead to patterns of interaction (informal institutions), 'rules' for group organization, and eventually to the creation of a formal institutional set-up based upon them. If long-term horizons are unavailable, agents can seek to improve their chances of success: (a) by trying nevertheless to extend their own temporal horizon by modifying the formal institutional environment that controls their presence within the organizational domain; (b) by engaging in simultaneous transactions in related domains (countering the threat of non-compliance in one domain with a related non-compliance in another); and/or (c) by developing linkages and/or complementarities across domains to create a new institutional architecture that enhances their own survival chances. Hegemonic positions within the organizational domain facilitate dealing with those refusing to cooperate by breaking the established rules of interaction among groups established in the constitution, or in the extreme case through more or less stringent repression – physical or institutional.[4] Hierarchical control of bundled (linked or complementary) policy domains through the organizational domain means formal enforcement mechanisms can be employed in impeding other parties from effectively opposing reform attempts.

The net result of the status quo could be an informal but stable and effective network of institutional domains, composed of various layers of hierarchical relations, more or less well structured, and in which certain political and or economic domains provide support to others through linked or complementary institutions – something which resembles a formal organization, but which need not be one.

Regime breakdown, institutional creation, and policy horizons

Winiecki (1996) would argue that the breakdown of a regime (a domain equilibrium) and/or the conditions for reform can be brought about by: (i) breakdown of internal consensus (that is, the collapse of the shared mental model agents employ); (ii) the drag of accumulated losses due to the inefficiencies of the system; or (iii) the entry of new agents or external shocks and constraints (or a combination of any of these). In Latin America, the latter are represented by the debt crisis and the recurrent external and related fiscal sector crises of the 1980s, as this diminished the resources available externally to finance the status quo. As North (1979, 1990) would argue, resistance can be expected as existing rents might be dissipated through change. Furthermore, crisis can potentially break down cooperation patterns between groups formerly operating together, or open opportunities for new agents to engage in domains in which they were previously absent. As change takes place, further opportunities arise: old or new agents can see opportunities for new institutional development as linked or complementary institutions evolve; organizations that include some of the agents themselves are modified; or momentum from a new combination of these increases.[5] In this context, a group of agents can seek to rearrange the existing institutions within policy domains in a manner that benefits a new coalition of agents within the polity and the economy.

This endogenous view means reform cannot be enacted by fiat: it would just be another move by an agent with privileged attributions, but nevertheless potentially contested by support groups from organized civil society or any key player in the relevant domain(s). Consequently, to overcome a potential veto from any player, the reformer needs to devise measures which can either compensate or repress losers across domains, develop reform sequences that can help build support coalitions and/or link institutions across them, or develop complementarities that can help advance his or her agenda until a new arrangement is established and new mental models develop. Social policy and the means to sustainable finance become key considerations. Policy coordination and enforcement mechanisms that can operate across institutional domains provide strategic advantages, as they enhance the creation of complementarities or linkages, and in turn, develop momentum: as more domains or institutions are linked, new rents start to flow and information and other externalities arise.[6]

Reform consolidation and (unintended) effects

Institutional reforms become consolidated when the introduction of proposed new rules cannot be contested by other players. Provided it is economically and politically sustainable, this new institutional arrangement will most likely develop endurance mechanisms: constitutional amendments or a new constitution; congressional legislation (which has a similar, albeit less strenuous, effect); or international agreements (the NAFTA case, for instance), to create commitments that cannot be easily reversed.

However, policy can also seek to move equilibrium in a specific direction, instead providing unexpected results: bundling gives policy leverage to an unexpected agent; poorly trained human resources fail to coordinate policies or make results negligible; reforms fail to produce complementarities, resulting instead in one policy undermining another. Likewise, the lack of verifiability can help foster corrupt transactions, as the use of informal institutions allows agents to engage in corrupt transactions, which, even when they do not leave obvious traces, can undermine formal institutional performance. Whilst strong formal public administrative institutions can be effective bulwarks against employing public service as a source of rents, they are not always available. Their nonexistence can translate into corrupt structures operating within the context of an otherwise formal hierarchical structure.

Institutional reform is thus a rather plastic process: as windows for change open, only minor changes can appear (the existing institutions, either beneficial or harmful, remain operating as they had been); or new equilibria develop, blending elements from the previous institutional environment with the new one, with the dual possibility of achieving the desired results or a set of unintended consequences.[7]

5.3   An analytical narrative of two case studies

The case studies focus not on the specifics of different reform attempts, but rather on the underlying logic that propelled them. Following the discussion outlined above, the objective is to follow the reform process through the means devised to advance the new institutional inter-domain equilibria that constituted the reform themselves.

In each case, the analysis will move in four stages. First, the analysis will examine the institutional foundations of the pre-reform regime: its principal agents, its economic and political bases and enforcement mechanisms across domains. Starting conditions will be presented next: the cause(s) for institutional equilibrium disruption, and, where possible, the consequences, and the reform windows that opened. The third stage will outline reform initiation, including the reformers' characters, origins, and strategies. The analysis will focus on the opportunities, incentives, and risks they faced, as well as the content, sequence, and extent of reform. Finally, reform consequences will be examined, including both unexpected consequences and the possibility (or lack of) for further reforms along similar lines.

In both studies, the analysis will place the organizational domain at center stage, as it was from here that coordination and implementation of policy across various domains could be implemented. Reforms are described by their policy content (fiscal, trade, energy, and so on), by the coordination and strategy deployed by the reforming group, and by the means devised to enforce policy deals, create momentum, and prevent other agents from blocking the reform process. The analysis will show how the interaction between the implementation resulted in new sets of institutional equilibria appearing, or failing to do so: not only how reforms were implemented, but also which reforms were advanced and which not, and how conditions for reform opened and closed.

Mexico

Institutional background

In the early 1950s Mexico had an overall institutional arrangement in which political control and corporatist manipulation of most economic domains operated together with a coordinated control of the economy. Economic policy followed an import substitution strategy combining orthodox deficit control with fiscal exemptions, subsidies through price fixing and built-in commercial barriers through particularly high import tariffs and compulsory import permits. This created a protected internal market and nascent domestic industrial base, as well as an alliance between the main industrial groups, the financial sector, and the Executive.

The Partido Revolucionario Institucional (PRI) was until the late 1990s the hegemonic party serving as the overall domain bundling mechanism within the organizational domain. In such a system, the central administration was the central player in the policy games in which other groups also participated. The president served as an arbiter between agents and the ultimate enforcer of agreements within the groups represented in the administration, and provided the overall political guidance. PRI's revolutionary rhetoric was not an obstacle for a mutually beneficial relation among groups, which was based on the common interest of maintaining economic and political stability.

Regional control relied on governors, in theory elected, in practice appointed by the president from PRI grandees. Large-scale migration to the cities and rural control was handled by the 'worker' and 'peasant' sectors of PRI respectively, which in turn controlled unions and other social organizations though corporatist enforcement. Presidential control over PRI obscured the relatively small powers the constitution gave the president, if contrasted with other Latin American constitutions. As written, Congress represented the different groups within the revolutionary 'family'; the president would operate as a check to initiatives coming from those quarters. Unlike most Latin American countries, the Mexican president cannot issue emergency or legislative decrees. Formally speaking, in Mexico the president is the source of constraint and Congress of innovation. Under PRI presidents, control over the party reversed this: the president would become the key policy-maker. The constitutional reform of 1933, prohibiting successive re-election, had precisely this purpose of strengthening the president vis-à-vis Congress.

The electoral regime provided easy party entry rules, a single election round, and voluntary voting. In practice, it gave electoral control to PRI (and through it, to the president), while allowing the minor – and frequently satellite parties – to operate within a strongly centralized state. (Figure 5.1 shows PRI's performance between 1946 and 1991.) Electoral institutions would only provide the results already agreed through intra-party PRI control mechanisms. The strong capacity of the Mexican state to provide public goods, patronage, and other resources to allies – and to repress opposition – coupled with the strong identity

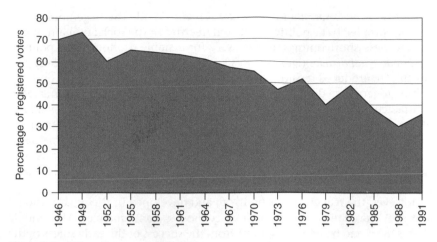

Figure 5.1   PRI performance, 1946–91
Source: Molinar Horcasitas (1991).

of the groups coming from the revolution and their weak autonomous support, translated into corporatist social and organizational domains. In the latter, the Mexican administration operated in an environment that allowed it to design and execute policies without the need for domestic external approval.

Three distinct groups of agents had replaced the revolution's original military by the early 1950s: politicians closely related to the Interior Ministry (the *Secretaría de Gobernación* or Secretary for the Interior); technicians, mostly engineers, and closely related to the development of large-scale infrastructure and development projects; and those from which the future technocrats would evolve, related to finance and planning (Centeno, 1996). Patronage and patrimonialism existed in all three, although they seemed greater among politicians and technicians. Nevertheless, key economic agencies boasted high technical competence standards, from the Bank of Mexico to the ministries of finance and planning, as well as those which would later evolve into commerce and industrial promotion.

Institutional bundling took place at two distinct nodes. The Secretary for the Interior was probably the key player in the organizational domain, negotiating with the other organized groups – including, if needed, labor – within the corporatist state, as well as its key electoral authority. The planning and technical secretaries with the development bank directors (with the finance secretary as their head) were key players in the supply, finance, and corporate governance domains. They would ensure the technical viability of the measures proposed. Complementarities were sought by making each institutional bundling agent a veto player on the other's proposals. The president was required to consult them on key public policy issues before implementing them.

The crisis of the Desarrollo Estabilizador period.   While the hegemonic party regime curtailed basic political and civil liberties in the social domain, it presented these shortcomings as necessary for a stable economy and polity, a *Desarrollo Estabilizador* (DE) as it was known. While macroeconomically successful, DE produced tensions in the industrial organization, supply and corporate governance domains, as the microeconomic incentives agents faced contradicted the macroeconomic stability necessary for growth. The small size of the domestic market prevented scale economies and alternative markets from developing; the high level of protection forced agents within the industrial domain to operate with relatively low levels of quality, high costs, and small profit margins; and all of these resulted in stagnant entrepreneurship and industries becoming obsolete relatively quickly.

However, the real crisis was political, and developed in the organizational and social domains, with disastrous economic consequences. The middle classes, who had benefited the most from the success of the early stages of the DE policies, saw its political contradictions more clearly. The bloody repression of student uprisings in 1968 during the Diaz Ordaz government undermined the regime's legitimacy and the internal consensus it had so far relatively enjoyed. When Luis Echeverría, the *Secretario de Gobernación* behind the massacres, attained the presidency, he used an expansion of public sector expenditures and aggregate demand management to regain legitimacy, while sidelining attempts to open internal markets to external competition. Instead, microeconomic intervention and a radical social rhetoric increased, as the teams who managed DE were replaced.

Nevertheless, as oil prices collapsed, serious imbalances hidden by massive increases in the country's external debt were impossible to hide through newly found oil deposits. Figure 5.2 shows the evolution of the public sector deficit, and its mounting numbers in the 1980s. Echeverría's successor, Jose Lopez

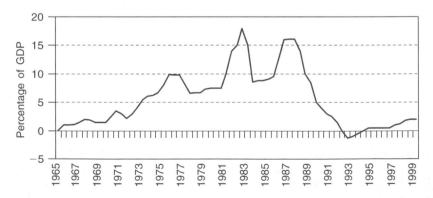

Figure 5.2   Public sector fiscal deficit, 1965–99

Portillo's decision to nationalize banks not only broke previously fundamental rules within the financial and industrial organization domains but destroyed private sector trust, providing the final blow to the DE period. Economic adjustment, with a previously unheard of leverage from external financial agents within the financial domain, was now to play a key role within the Mexican state.

Starting conditions

Economic adjustment under crisis (Miguel de la Madrid, 1982–88).   De la Madrid himself, and his senior staff, came from the budgetary control area. Their adjustment would start from a weak position. Changes had to be attempted without previous key allies: those benefiting from rents developed during the government's fiscal expansion as well as those controlling most local governments. The SOEs (state-owned enterprises) were to be privatized. This placed agents working within them in opposition to the central government, as privatization policy was likely to leave many of them unemployed under the new private owners. Thus, while previously SOEs and the central government had been partners in most domains, they were now adversaries (and remain so in most existing SOEs in Mexico). Likewise, after Lopez Portillo's nationalization of the banking sector, the private sector mistrusted the government; consequently, in spite of de la Madrid's declarations (which were taken as similar tricks to those used by Lopez Portillo to gain business sector confidence, only to be betrayed later through expropriation), the private sector was also in opposition. Thus, the incoming government was starting without a key ally (agents within the SOE), and with another agent as antagonist – the private sector, which had been in a non-adversarial position throughout the *Desarrollo Estabilizador* period. Reform implied rearranging industrial organization, finance, supply, and even labor relations via agents based mostly in the organizational domains, while lacking previously effective enforcement mechanisms across domains.

Externally, the financial autonomy of the Mexican state had significantly deteriorated. The view of most creditor groups was that adjustment was timid and a stronger fiscal effort and push towards trade liberalization and privatization were needed. As Kaufman et al. (1994) argue, within the Mexican government views would crystallize around three points: previous stabilization had not been backed sufficiently by external financing, government should carry adjustment at its own pace, and shock treatment was not seen as politically viable.

The consensus required was achieved through increasingly expansive pacts (from industrial organization and labor domains) made possible by the administration's dominant role within the organizational domain. Relative prices, public expenditure and public salaries were adjusted one way or another by these social pacts. This same process served as a check to those supporting the faster pace of multilateral initiatives. Simultaneously, institutional bundling was implemented where possible through intersecretarial committees,[8] but also by changing career patterns within the upper levels of the administration: rather than advancing within the same organization, higher civil servants from the same policy network (the ministries of finance and planning) would be sent to key positions in the areas which were going to be reformed.[9] This would allow for a closer coordination of economic reform activities from the center, and in relative cooperation between technocrats and politicians, with the technicians in an increasingly minor position. Additionally, a 'Moral Renewal' campaign for state modernization was initiated to try and garner support for the adjustment agenda from the underlying nascent social movements.

This resulted in an arrangement with a certain degree of complementarity between the economy and *gobernación* nexus, with civil servants with economic training taking the technical lead, while those with a political background provided coverage. This combination sought step by step to overcome opposition from both mid-level managers and bureaucrats remaining from the Echeverría–López Portillo era, who constituted most of the patrimonialist agents still in power.

The government's economic response was packaged in a *Programa Inmediato de Reordenación Económica*, starting in 1982, but extending until 1987. A massive privatization program translated into an important retreat of the state from the industrial organization domain and a change in corporate governance. This also had the effect of diminishing the rents previously available to government agents operating in the industrial organization, corporate governance and, to a lesser extent, the finance domains. Additional measures reduced aggregate demand by reducing expenditures while liberalizing relative prices. These were managed through 'leader' prices, employing nominal wages and exchange rates as anti-inflationary anchors. Relative prices of tradable goods were corrected through a peso depreciation. In 1985 commercial liberalization was accelerated as Mexico entered the General Agreement on Tariffs and Trade (GATT), which forced the country to change tariff rates, setting the highest at 50 per cent. The program achieved a successful external debt stabilization, reducing debt service to 3 from 8 per cent of GDP, and introducing a restrictive credit policy to eliminate sharp exchange rate movements.

While these measures corrected balance of payments disequilibria and excess demand in the goods market, they also produced a strong recession, with no visible effects on inflation. This further exacerbated social policy and public good shortcomings, both impacting the government's overall popularity (and increasing negotiation needs with social domain agents) and undermining business sector trust, a problem left over from the Echeverría–López Portillo era. Likewise, it meant abandoning any pretense of a return to the DE developmental cooperation bias. The labor domain was left basically untouched, with the same people remaining in its leadership since the 1940s, in exchange for its support of the social pacts. However, social movements got an unexpected, although unfortunate boost from the 1984 earthquake, when effective horizontal cooperation underlined the extent of coordination possible in civil society, while changing the existing socially-embedded mental models of PRI's supposedly indispensable role. A now increasingly independent and active mass media contributed to the erosion of PRI's legitimacy. Social movements could not be ignored thereafter.

In fact, de la Madrid's government had stabilized the economy, but major problems remained. The business sector remained alienated, significant internal opposition remained in the administration, and there were barely any resources to allow for an aggressive social and poverty control policy. The state lacked resources to finance basic infrastructure and domestic resources for investment had almost dried up.

Last but not least, the Mexican state continued depending on oil: in the 1990s PEMEX produced around 40 per cent of state revenue. Without a secure source of independent fiscal revenue, fiscal autonomy continued to be precarious. Figures 5.3 and 5.4 show federal revenue both as a share of GDP and a share of the total from 1977–2002.

Amidst fraud accusations from splinter groups to the left of PRI, the much debated 1988 elections put the group that had engineered the 1985–88 adjustment into power, although in a precarious position.

Initiation of reforms

The rise of technocracy and the struggle for a new equilibrium (1988–94).   In this context, the Salinas administration implemented a set of reform initiatives that would dramatically change the face of Mexico. These would closely align Mexico to the US market, employing a major free-trade treaty with the US

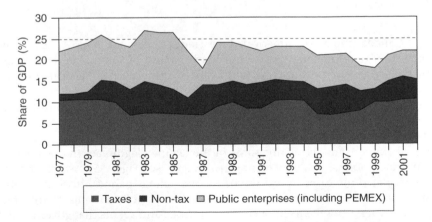

Figure 5.3   Federal and public enterprise revenues, 1977–2002 (share of GDP)
Source: Salinas (2003).

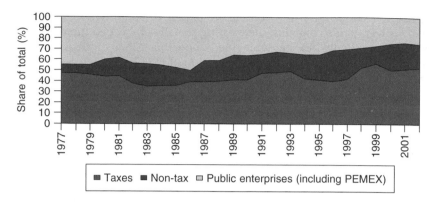

Figure 5.4   Federal and public enterprise revenues, 1977–2002 (share of total)
Source: Salinas (2003).

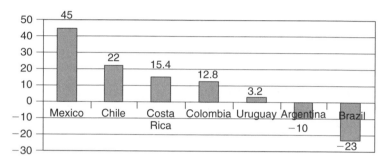

Figure 5.5   Accumulated increases in real wages, 1989–94 (%)
Source: Salinas (2003).

and Canada (the North American Free Trade Agreement, NAFTA) as a new pattern of development, based on a liberalization of internal and external markets, extensive privatization, significant diversification of Mexican foreign relations, and heavy reliance on foreign investment. Improved economic performance, increased efficiency, and partial electoral reform contributed to gaining business sector support in the corporate and industrial organization domains, consolidating the position of technocratic groups in the organizational domain, and recovering some of the regime's legitimacy in the socially embedded norms, while increasing real wages (see Figure 5.5 which shows accumulated increases in real wages for the Salinas period). Institutionally speaking, these were the reverse of Echeverría's populist attempt to run the economy ignoring the technocratic institutions and agents that governed it. From this base, an attack could be launched on the most traditional patrimonialist agents within PRI still resisting reform.

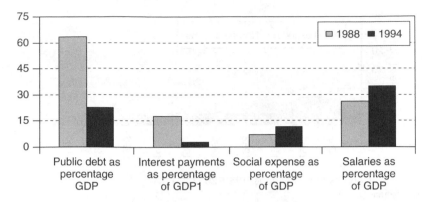

Figure 5.6 Public debt, social expenses, and salaries, 1988–94
Source: Salinas (2003).

The NAFTA agreement was built upon the external sector liberalization and economic adjustment accomplished during the de la Madrid period. Complementarities between the external sector in trade and finance and social policy were the keystone. In policy terms, cutting the external debt (by US$7 billion) was the first item on the new government's agenda; this in turn reduced interest rates and net external transfers. This was followed by internal debt reductions, allowing for the financing of social policy. Figure 5.6 illustrates the evolution between debt and social expenses and salary expenditures between 1988 and 1994.

This negotiation was a complex process which took place at a delicate time as ratification passed through US elections. Solving economic asymmetries through generalized exceptions would have diluted the treaty's objective. Mexico solved the problem by linking the GATT and the NAFTA negotiation forums. The Mexican party wanted to start at Mexico's average tariff level (20 per cent) within GATT's generalized system of preferences. At the Uruguay Round, Mexico called at the start of negotiations for a 50 per cent minimum tariff level. The Americans suggested the existing level (20 per cent) and asked that this should be the basis for negotiation (both at GATT and NAFTA), precisely what Mexico was expecting on the NAFTA front.[10] Further along, it was agreed that sensitive sectors (certain agricultural products, textiles, automobiles) were subject to specific provisions or could be opened only after a 10 to 15 year period. Others (energy, for instance) were rejected out of hand.[11]

The treaty negotiation turned into the central policy linkage, advanced through additional complementarities in the organizational, financial, industrial organization, and supply domains, while offering promises of additional domestic momentum as it was deployed. Complementarities within the US

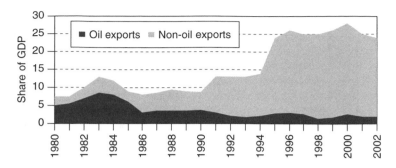

Figure 5.7   Composition of exports, 1980–2002 (%)
Source: Salinas (2003).

and Mexico resulted in Mexico providing labor-intensive activities, as well as *maquila* production while the US provided capital. Subsequently, other exports increased by more than *maquila* production.[12] As a result, Mexico's non-oil exports increased massively (see Figure 5.7). Additionally, the treaty developed a set of organizations (the dispute resolution and tripartite commissions on environment and labor, as well as a North American Bank), to regulate trade between Mexico and the US, which in turn served as lock-in mechanisms for a number of institutional arrangements within the industrial organization, supply, and labor domains.

The treaty needed congressional approval, and had been publicly debated in Mexico and the US; this continuous discussion contributed to the progressive formation of a social mental model within Mexico which placed the country on the verge of entering the developed world. Mexico's entrance into the OECD reinforced this view. While providing a mechanism to support reforms, a social base (*Solidaridad*) which could operate out of the traditional PRI channels, enhanced the president's position within the key organizational domain.

The struggle with the still powerful enclaves of high and mid-level agents from the populist Echeverría–López Portillo era started almost immediately. Leaving aside honest ideological opponents, the sectors with the most to lose came from those suffering dissipation of rents developed in the DE and populist periods.[13] The government sent a powerful message by accusing the most powerful union leader at the time, Joaquín Hernández, 'La Quina' (the PEMEX union head), of illegal arms possession and murder.[14] Support from the possible replacement was agreed in advance. The relatively weak showing of PRI at the 1988 elections ironically eased the president's agenda, as it diminished the standing of traditional PRI politicians (and related electoral alchemists) and their links with the presidency.

Nevertheless, the president continued using all the traditional levers of power. He maintained the same pact structure, including business, worker and peasant representatives. The 'Pacto de Solidaridad Económica' was designed to 'sustain the compromise to permanently correct the public finances, to apply a restrictive monetary policy, to correct wage inertia, and to define agreements over prices on leader sectors' (Aspe, 1993: 29–30).

Strategic control could be maintained by appointing trusted and qualified personnel in key government and economic positions as bundling agents.[15] The upper administrative levels were characterized by groups of politicians and technocrats with different, albeit clearly defined, characteristics. Additionally, the same intersecretarial commissions employed during the de la Madrid term were maintained to insure fiscal and monetary policy coherence.[16] While some prices were increased through the pact mechanism, the increases did not exceed the inflation goal. While the business sector was forced to accept some of the costs of the pact's implementation, it was also offered deregulation and improved conditions for private sector competitiveness.

Fiscal policy linkages allowed increases in real salaries and employment, gaining labor domain leverage in the aftermath of conflict with the unions. Likewise, social spending was increased, while the tax rate went down. The public sector deficit went from 12.5 per cent in 1988 to 0.1 per cent surplus in 1994. The key to these developments was increasing the tax base while reducing internal sector debt.[17] The number of taxpayers was increased, as were the sanctions on those who did not pay taxes. This increased fiscal revenue by 30 per cent in real terms; additionally, payments on internal and external interest rates, representing 18 per cent of GDP by 1988, were reduced to only 2.8 per cent by 1994 as a consequence of SOEs privatization and external debt renegotiation.[18] Social spending could now grow: it rose from 6 per cent of GDP in 1988 to more than 10 per cent in 1994.[19] This in turn reinforced the president's political standing, and that of the government's pet project, *Solidaridad*.

The industrial organization domain continued to be modified through deregulation and privatization. Deregulation sought a minimum government supervision of the activities of the economic agents, while quitting activities in productive activities. Principal among those affected were Telmex, and state-owned TV companies, but also companies in the siderurgical, mining, and sugar sectors. The steel mills in particular, had turned into a major economic disaster (accumulating almost US$10 billion in losses),[20] with major ecological damage to the areas involved and significant inefficiencies in production. Finally, a system of new regulatory commissions served as lock-in mechanisms, providing long-term support to initiatives advanced in the industrial organization, supply, and labor domains through different presidential terms.[21]

These proposals were presented as attempts to improve service delivery, rather than as a radical change in the role of the state, to avoid further opposition from agents suffering rent disenfranchisement. However, in 1982, when the process started, there were 1150 SOEs; by 1994, there were only 70.[22] The Salinas government would sell 261 SOEs, with most of the proceeds going to pay public debt: out of the almost US$23 billion resulting from privatization, nearly 94 per cent went to pay internal public debt, which fell from 19 to 6 per cent of GDP.[23] Salinas (2003: 412) claims most of the remaining companies were considered 'strategical' for national development; it could be argued that this was opportunistic behavior, as these were also those which had the strongest unions, closely related to PRI and with significant backing in Congress.

Instead, attention was given to areas where potential support could be garnered at minor cost. The banks could not operate without subsidies.[24] Privatizing them increased support in the industrial organization and financial domains, while increasing economic efficiency and reducing fiscal pressure, with opposition only from groups already against the reforms anyway. Those taking them over – relatively inexperienced, albeit carefully screened – would increase the number of business sector allies. Meanwhile, civil society continued developing. The capacity of the state to deliver public goods increased, while strong collective identities, support groups, and active opposition political parties continued to develop during the de la Madrid period. Salinas's initial attacks were devoted mostly to Cardenas's leftist PRD and to the 'Quina's' group. The latter, together with active deregulation and privatization, provided him with domestic intellectual support. NAFTA also increased foreign interest and attention in internal electoral affairs in Mexico.

An unexpected consequence of this new economic external sector opening was that the state-level electoral wizardry – systematically modifying voting results by manipulating votes after they had been cast – could result in a significant impact on foreign investment in Mexico. Its international consequences, together with the increased strength of civil society and Congress's opposition after the 1988 elections, all helped explain the reduced traditional PRI electoral alchemy of transmuting voting defeat into official 'victory' through electoral corruption. It was making virtue of necessity: after the 1988 election, the right wing PAN had more than 100 federal representatives, forcing PRI to engage them in any negotiation required to reform the constitution. The creation of a new Instituto Federal Electoral (IFE) in 1990[25] took elections out of the realm of the *Secretaría de Gobernación*, and contributed to diminishing the contested domestic legitimacy of Salinas's first months.[26] As with the rising technocracy, resistance from traditional politicians was overcome through political operatives chosen due to their capacity to make deals. These believed it was better to include the opposition in the reform negotiations than have it outside sabotaging the process. Thus, a double pincer strategy, including both the economy and politics, was followed.[27]

The combination of the economic reforms with this inclusive approach seems to have been successful. By 1991 PRI had more than two-thirds of the votes in Congress (allowing it to reform the constitution at its will). While two opposition state governments were recognized before the 1991 elections, a similar strategy was maintained even after the recomposition of the PRI, and the 1992 PAN triumph in Chihuahua was also recognized. The resisting of electoral triumphs would have created significant resistance and under-mined the legitimacy for minor political gain. Instead, the strategy provided support for the overall policy arrangement, without implying prohibitive costs to those advancing it within PRI.

Success and the seeds of revolt. The Salinas term would finish with a 70 per cent approval rate, with public calls for his re-election (unheard of since the late 1940s). Most of the population perceived a fundamental shift in the overall institutional arrangement: not only had significant legal and organizational changes taken place across most domains, but these had eventually been accepted by most relevant agents. While the left had staged a fiery opposition (particularly PRD), the president seemed to have won the argument on the facts, passing, domestically and internationally, an agenda crafted on his own terms. The perceptions of agents regarding the character of the changes had muted into a new model of the operation of the Mexican system, which crys-tallized around the approval of the NAFTA agreement in 1993 by the three countries involved. Mexico was perceived by most of the population to be on the verge of entering into the developed world.

However, this approval rating hid a number of problems. The peso crisis (examined below) was probably the biggest; others were no less salient. The emphasis on trade, the economic arena and the urban sector at the expense of the politicians, the rural area and the peasants would translate into unex-pected reactions from (until then) marginal actors. On 1 January 1994, a pre-viously unknown player in the social domain emerged, with the Zapatista uprising in Chiapas, protesting against NAFTA.[28] Negotiation for a solution pitted Manuel Camacho Solís, the former Mexico City regent and presiden-tial contender, against Luis Donaldo Colosio, *Solidaridad's* head and Salinas's designated heir. The latter was considered weak and too close to the presi-dent, and as such was perceived – particularly among PRI's populist groups which had opposed the reforms – as violating the unwritten rule of not seek-ing re-election through a third party. Colosio's still unsolved assassination in March 1994 started the succession battle anew, with groups from the former Echeverría government suggesting a candidate. Salinas nominated instead Ernesto Zedillo, former budgeting and planning and education minister as PRI's presidential candidate.[29] The election, while effectively contested, was legitimately won by Zedillo with the biggest vote in Mexican history.

The closure of the reform window

Zedillo and the peso crisis (1994–97). Ernest Zedillo's campaign slogan – *Bienestar para tu familia* (well-being for your family) – was carefully built upon the idea that a substantive economic and institutional shift was at hand after the Salinas reforms. This of course, would in a sense restore PRI's legitimacy. In spite of Zedillo's electoral support, his outsider status, coupled with the eco-nomic context he inherited, translated into massive problems almost as soon as he took office. His responses effectively addressed those problems, but they created others by increasing internal debt and diminishing available expenditures, thus exacerbating dependency on oil revenues. His attempt to reform the energy sector was unsuccessful. Finally, he tried to replace the informal institutional arrangements, which had allowed policy coordination and implementation during the PRI regime, with more formal institutions. These proved to be insufficient. However, Zedillo managed to transfer power to the opposition without major upheavals or revolts or coup attempts from PRI hardliners. This smooth transfer was a major feat and could not have been achieved had Zedillo governed as a typical PRI president.

The decision to delay control of a high current account deficit resulted in the 1994 peso crisis. This delay originally caused an exchange rate overvaluation (which had reached almost 9 per cent of GDP) at electoral time. The exchange rate rule employed a band, which neither the exiting nor the incoming administrations had changed. To top it off, the economy had witnessed a significant growth of monetary supply, through a massive expansion of short-term, dollar indexed, financial instruments (Tesobonos), which reached US$29 billion by the end of 1994 (Figure 5.8 compares Tesobonos and international reserves in 1994). This would become the main cause of the peso crisis.

In the midst of financial turmoil, the assassination of Colosio, and the Chiapas uprising, the impending crisis was compounded by short-term economic management problems: investors had been retiring deposits since the final months of 1994 as the US Federal Reserve increased interest rates, attracting capital to the US. Meanwhile, the incoming Zedillo administration announced the removal of Salinas's finance minister, Pedro Aspe, and replaced him with Jaime Serra, who had been at SECOFI. Aspe had already faced several devaluatory attacks, and had gained the markets' trust. His removal not only obliterated this trust, but also deprived the incoming government of valuable experience. Once effective, this change was accompanied by the subsequent removal of most of the career teams at Hacienda.[30]

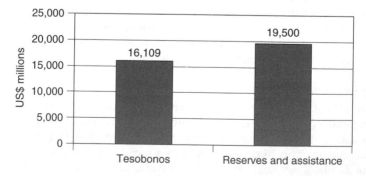

Figure 5.8   Tesobonos and international resources

The massive retrieval of short-term Tesobonos, caught the incoming Serra team by surprise; it responded slowly, almost a month after the crisis had set in. After various failed stabilization attempts,[31] a second stabilization package (*Programa de Acción para Reforzar el Acuerdo de Unidad para Superar la Emergencia Económica*) was implemented in March. This pegged the dollar at 7.5 pesos, a 100 per cent increase in the exchange rate in little more than two months. Foreign reserves dropped more than US$6.3 billion to US$5.8 billion.

The consequences were massive. During 1995, GDP fell 6.9 per cent, GDP per capita 8.7 per cent, and real wages more than 13 per cent. Fixed capital formation reached a historical minimum of 16.1 per cent of GDP, a reduction of 39 per cent on the previous year, while external debt increased more than US$25 billion. Consumption was reduced by 11.6 per cent, aggregate demand by 10.9 per cent, and internal demand by 20.3 per cent.

Zedillo responded to mounting public criticism by arguing that the crisis had been the result of imbalances left by the previous administration. A massive rescue package arranged by the Clinton Administration helped stabilize the peso, employing Mexico's oil wells as collateral. The collapsed financial domain was rescued through a financial rescue fund (*Fondo para la protección del ahorro, Fobaproa*, created with revenues from the Salinas privatization program) which absorbed banking sector losses. Furthermore, the banking sector was open for foreign investment. Mexico returned to growth by 1997. While it is true that there were imbalances as the transition from the Salinas to the Zedillo era took place, it can also be argued that the rapid recovery was in part due to the resilience of the basic architecture left by the previous administration, particularly if the growth in exports derived from the NAFTA treaty is considered, which allowed Mexico to recover in a shorter time span than in previous governments.

Shifting the policy initiative. While Zedillo eventually conquered the peso crisis, it left behind a number of consequences that affected the underlying logic of the Salinas reforms, and undermined the political foundations of the architecture that had so far allowed their implementation. First, it not only undermined confidence in the incoming PRI government, but also the relative standing of those who had implemented reforms under Salinas vis-à-vis the traditional politicians and the opposing populists: technocrats could also fail, and big time.[32] This, together with the string of corruption accusations against Salinas's brother Raul, destroyed the social mental model of Mexico as an 'almost developed country', and Salinas's previous high standing and reputation. Moreover, as Salinas and Zedillo went their separate ways over who was to blame for the crisis, the position of those opposing Salinas – and his reform legacy – was enhanced, as now they could be on the side of the president and still blame Salinas and his agenda. Second, the money available for social policy, the major argument of the first phase of reforms, was gone, as the payment of the debt once again displaced the social policy agenda. Third, the decision of President Zedillo to continue and complete the democratic agenda which was implicit in the structural reforms – both in word and deed – undermined presidential powers within the informal power structure.

Notwithstanding the president's weakened position after the 1994 crisis, Zedillo continued reform in several areas, and opened some new fronts. Tax administration, labor, and pension reforms were only partial successes; several state reform attempts – and energy reform in particular – were failures. A fiscal reform was attempted in 1997, which however, was limited in scope:[33] an increase in the overall tax rate was achieved; although this was not enough, as state revenues continued to depend on oil revenues. Pension reform was completed by 1997, with a privatized and individualized structure substituting the earlier bankrupt system based on revolving funds administered by state agencies. Labor reform was also advanced, although only partially.

The shifting center of policy control explained the partial character of these initiatives. Unlike in the previous PRI term, formal economic control levers were being changed;[34] not by the Executive elite, but by the voters. For the first time in PRI's tenure, in 1996 the opposition took control of the lower chamber of Congress (although PRI retained control of the Senate). This shifted the reform initiative from the informal policy networks under the Mexican presidentialist regime to the formal constitutional rules of the opposition-controlled Congress. The chamber's increased independence showed in the new scheme to transfer funds for education and infrastructure to the states. This reduced the control of federal funding for social and infrastructure policy, but also its overall amount. While a sign of a renewed federalism, it also decreased central government control over social spending. Traditional PRI governance was now divided, and the president's capacity to direct change limited.

Growing tensions and stalemate (1997–2003).   However, the true sign of the times was Zedillo's failure to pass a complete fiscal reform and a new energy sector framework, which called for electricity privatization and a gas market liberalization, essential to developing new private electricity markets. Fiscal and energy reform are linked, as the energy sector's crucial fiscal role secures a source of independent fiscal revenue. Without fiscal reform, liberalizing the energy sector would be fiscally dangerous. The fiscal reform failure notwithstanding, an energy sector reform bill was introduced, with parallel proposals calling for a new oil regulation redefining regulatory roles within the administration, and calling for the privatization of an important share of the petrochemical industry. The proposal failed to gain the confidence of the ministry of finance, as it would have limited its power by taking from its purview some of its attributions, and was rejected – a previously unheard of event – by the opposition-controlled chamber of deputies. Meanwhile, the petrochemical proposal failed to win the hearts of investors in the industrial organization domain, as it included only 49 per cent of the shares, leaving ultimate control in state hands. The power sector reform, while less contentious than the oil sector reform, faced severe opposition from the energy sector unions, coming mostly from PRI, and also failed to pass.

What is more striking still was Zedillo's behavior as a PRI president. Either because his actions were constrained, or because he truly thought it was the appropriate thing to do, the president deliberately undermined a number of meta-constitutional presidential rights which remained from the PRI era by not exercising them.[35] His political reforms would greatly change the incentives existing within the informal system within the administration, increasing difficulties for renewing its members.[36] Furthermore, it undermined his key arbiter position within PRI, central to its role within the organizational domain. It is likely that the president realized that after the peso crisis, the subsequent banking rescue, and the electoral reform, his best option was actually to stage an open and transparent election, with no designated successor and no wizardry whatsoever: if PRI won, he would have achieved what was originally proposed by the technocratic elite to the rest of PRI and to the country; if PRI failed, he could count on his successor not to start a prosecution against him for PRI's past actions: it would have been politically unfair to the architect of Mexican democracy.

The government of Vicente Fox played the part that was expected in Zedillo's strategy for the key organizational domain. Under Fox, the institutional dilemmas that Zedillo had managed to navigate successfully would become more acute. Fox was the first president actually to operate only under formal Mexican constitutional rules, which called for a strong Congress and a president who (without PRI) actually had limited powers. Furthermore, his election had created for the first time a division between political and policy positions within the administration,[37] significantly altering incentives within it: reduced career horizons increased uncertainty within the administration and weakened the informal rules of the informal civil service.[38] This denied Fox a key coordination instrument for advancing institutional linkages and complementarities, until then the bread and butter of Mexican reform. Finally, he was the first president of a democracy with not only a fully involved and participatory civil society, but also parties that had little incentive for compromise in the post-PRI era.

While Fox came from the business sector, he failed to translate this into an effective policy coalition across the institutional domains, and developed little if any of the complementarities and linkages that had proved crucial to reform attempts during the Salinas era. He advanced multiple initiatives to improve the overall transparency and formal coherence of the Mexican administration, but failed to develop institutional complementarities and linkages in his substantive policy initiatives. In neither of two attempts to pass an energy reform bill did Fox reach the level of votes that Zedillo reached; the same happened with the fiscal reform attempts.

While a policy reversal seems unlikely (as these would involve constitutional, treaty, and legal changes, which any other party would find as difficult as Fox to advance) it is not impossible. In any case, the reform initiative had definitively shifted: it seems now to be with the opposition parties, not with the president. The window of opportunity for structural reform seems to have closed for the time being in Mexico.

Peru

Institutional background

Peru's overall institutional architecture in the 1950 could best be described as an elitist democracy or an 'Aristocratic Republic', with an organizational domain in which a small government was controlled by an alliance between business groups from the export sector including both urban and rural (sugar cane and cotton) industries, large-scale landholders in the rural areas, and implicitly, the army.[39] The economy's reliance on relatively abundant primary exports, the favorable external environment, and Peru's export-led policies of the late 1950s led to opportunities to take advantage of new technological development, with spectacular growth in some industries, particularly in fishing. The social domain included a relatively small, mostly urban population of European descent (around 30 per cent of the overall population in the mid-1940s), together with a relatively large rural indigenous population. Meanwhile, in 1950 the upper 10 per cent of the population earned 65 per cent of the income.[40]

While in Mexico control over the rural area was handled by PRI's 'peasant sector', in Peru the landed classes had a similar function, albeit with a different mental model. Shared common social norms were uncommon; rather, Peru had two sets, one for the European minority and another for the larger Indian population.[41] Furthermore, there was no political consensus: an increasingly radical assault from APRA (*Alianza Popular Revolucionaria Americana*), the populist and oldest Peruvian party, as well as the organized Peruvian left, challenged the institutional equilibrium.

By the early 1960s most of the resources in the supply domain which could be used for export had already been identified and were being exploited.[42] The drop in stocks of exportable primary products resulted in a private sector confidence shock, and a slow withdrawal of the most active Peruvian business groups from the export sector. A bitter conflict between government and foreign export companies for production expansion ensued, further undermining the basis of equilibrium.

As in Mexico, income disparities between the cities and rural areas had led to large-scale migration to the cities. However, in Peru fiscal revenue did not grow quickly enough to support the service improvements required to sustain migrant populations, and the traditional rural intermediary role of the landed classes used within the organizational domain would be destroyed by the 1970s' military government. APRA and the left increased pressure to access the hegemonic position within the organizational domain by organizing these migrant groups. Their combined impact translated into a perception across social mental models that an overall institutional equilibrium change was needed. Both civilian and military attempts to counter APRA's claims by dealing with the substantive issues failed to deliver a solution within the existing equilibrium, albeit for different reasons. Fernando Belaúnde's first Accion Popular – a center-left party – government between 1963 and 1968 failed to deliver its oil and agrarian reforms, while its fiscal expansion was minor. The subsequent armed forces' institutional seizure of power – the army took all positions within government – destroyed the control of the landed classes over rural areas through agrarian reform, but failed to consolidate the relatively weak participatory democracy. When its demand expansion and import substitution strategy collapsed, the military called for a constitutional assembly in 1979 and a transfer of power in 1980.

The 1980s' equilibrium: a larger, but weaker, state to lead development. Nevertheless, these changes had already translated into a consensus around a stronger administration within the organizational domain. The right sought to curtail executive economic prerogatives, while promoting strong government to prevent further nationalizations; the organized left was also supportive of a strong administration, albeit for different reasons. APRA – now not only an insider but an electoral majority in the constitutional assembly – argued against its historical position for a strong executive, to implement its own agenda. This coincidence of outlook would translate into the 1979 constitutional arrangement, which suggested a stable organizational domain equilibrium could be reached by easing party access and then increasing powers to whoever gained government control.

New voting rules translated into a massive (150 per cent) increase in the voting population. While party entry was eased, political movements, rather than parties were the focus of the constitution, and Congress was now elected under proportional representation, from a single national district. Once elected (under obligatory voting), the president had significant powers.[43] However, in this equilibrium, the newly enfranchised voters (mostly rural poor, recent urban migrants, poor women, and young adults) could shift allegiances relatively easily; while weak political parties could easily fail to represent these recently created and large groups of voters.

These changes would eventually foster the already significant party fragmentation from which Peru had always suffered. While state capacity for public goods provision was still limited, civil society was characterized by strong support groups with strong collective identities, particularly on the left, which sought to articulate and organize social movements to bolster their electoral chances after the late 1970s.[44] Simultaneously, the preferential double vote scheme created strategic voting incentives: in the first round, citizens could vote for a candidate likely to undermine the rival of a preferred candidate, bolstering their candidate's chances to enter the second tally. This could also result in the appearance of 'dark horses' in the presidential election, as these 'strategic' choices – coming from any of the small parties – gained votes in the first round. Little if any incentive remained for long-lasting political alliances between these small political parties. The strength of the inter-party agreement was the implied, albeit unwritten, check on the presidential powers.

APRA's social organization expected to reap the fruits of its electoral majority; instead Fernando Belaúnde was elected for five years in 1980. He would spend most of them stabilizing the economy. His main problem was the huge external debt. Unlike Mexico, neither size nor oil revenues could help dampen its impact. Its growth undermined social policy and translated into significant problems in industry and labor. A very short expansion was followed by three long years of recession. While the economy stabilized, radical terrorist groups (Shining Path, SP, among others) outside the 1979 pact expanded – as would later be the case in Mexico, but with a cruelty unheard of in the Zapatistas uprising – while strike activity in the labor domain increased and the left strengthened in the public opinion arena. In spite of this, he managed to increase reserves, lower the fiscal deficit, and stabilize inflation. This nevertheless took its political toll: his party obtained only 4 per cent in the 1985 elections, and APRA gained a hegemonic position within the organizational domain after more than 50 years in opposition.

Starting conditions: the collapse of APRA's populism

APRA's external reserves and unemployed internal capacity provided the basis for a two-year demand expansion. The new APRA president's (Alan García) claim for countries to serve debt with only 10 per cent of exports – unsuccessful abroad, and heard but not followed in de la Madrid's Mexico – liberated domestic resources to advance a social and macroeconomic policy agenda, with spectacular gains in the public opinion arena. However, although Peru saw an impressive 20 per cent GDP growth in the first two years, this was not accompanied by private sector investments, there was little growth in the tax rate and no increase in exports (although drug exports would grow significantly, albeit for other reasons), resulting in the repetition of a traditional populist political economy cycle, with a short-lived demand expansion followed by dangerous imbalances on the fiscal and external fronts.

The collapse of the populist project: the García government. As Gonzáles de Olarte (1994) notes, by early 1987 Peru was heading towards a reserve crisis: banking sector net reserves diminished to US$198 million, with those in the Central Bank diminishing to US$138 million (Figure 5.9 shows the evolution of the balance of payments). Negotiations with key business leaders to expand supply and counter losses failed, while price controls were replaced with direct quantity controls and long queues. In 1987 the president decided on an ultimately botched takeover of the banking sector within the financial domain to consolidate its wobbling organizational domain control. While his standing in the public opinion arena would remain at 40 per cent during this

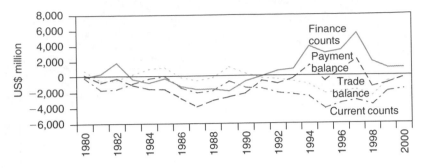

Figure 5.9   Balance of payments, 1980–2002
Source: Based on IMF, EFI Yearbook.

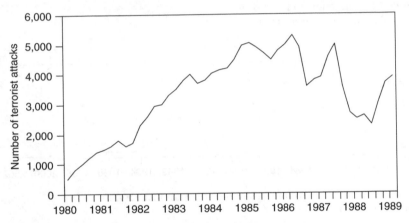

Figure 5.10   Dynamics of political violence, 1980–94

period, its failure severely weakened him: he lost APRA support in Congress, miscalculated the organized resistance of the private sector and the right – galvanized by Mario Vargas Llosa's (MVLL) spirited defiance – and witnessed the collapse of confidence in his economic program. Meanwhile, as Figure 5.10 shows, terrorist attacks increased significantly during his tenure, and as Figure 5.11 indicates, the increased inflation in his term seemed to fuel terrorist acts.

In September 1988 García was forced to undertake a large and severe stabilization package, as reserves turned negative. His government ended with the worst economic crisis in Peru's republican history. Figure 5.12 shows graphically the extent of the crisis, by considering inflation's evolution in terms of its annual variation between 1980 and 2002. Between 1988 and 1989, GDP decreased 16.1 per cent, tax collection fell to 3.5 per cent of GDP, and the deficit was 4.5 per cent of GDP. His government caused the total collapse of

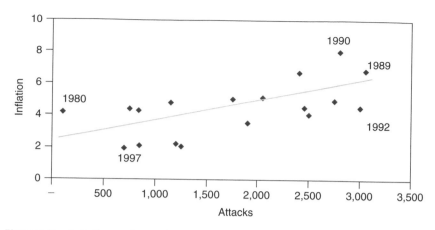

Figure 5.11   Inflation and terrorism
Source: BCRP and Department of State.

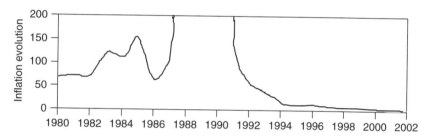

Figure 5.12   Inflation evolution, 1980–2002 (% annual variation)
Source: Data from INEI, Peru.

private sector confidence, with inflation running into four figures, private investment almost nonexistent, massive infrastructure destruction through terrorist activity, and the country financially isolated. Bundling agents within the social domain turned increasingly weak and social agents increasingly pragmatic as they struggled to survive. Consequences were dramatic: if 1979 is taken as a basis (100), salaries in 1988–89, went down to 39.7 and 32.1, the lowest since 1979. Likewise, between 1985 and 1991, poverty increased from 43 to 59 per cent, with an increase from 36 to 53 per cent in urban areas, and from 55 to 80 per cent in rural sectors. Infant mortality grew 27 per cent, from 25.1 to 30.3 per 1000, with perinatal mortality doubling.[45]

The once lean Peruvian public sector had become large and centralized but inefficient. In 1990, SOEs controlled between 15 to 20 per cent of GDP, while the state monopolized 28 per cent of exports and 26 per cent of imports, and enjoyed monopoly power over electricity, oil, and telecommunications. It also controlled 35 per cent of mining and 60 per cent of the financial system, which had turned into a repressed and fragile sector. The supply domains were extensively regulated, while the industrial domain remained overprotected and oligopolic. Within the organizational domain, the central administration was severely weakened: fiscal revenue was only 7.9 per cent of GDP. Of the already small universe of 100,000 possible taxpayers, only 13,482 paid taxes.[46]

Barbarians at the gates: the 1990 elections and the undermining of the 1979 party regime. In spite of such a catastrophic collapse, the 1979 organizational domain equilibrium seemed to hold fast. As McClintock (1999) argues, it benefited from a confluence of views: an interest in avoiding civil war, an acknowledgement by the armed forces that they could no longer take power on their own, and a mobilized middle class interested in maintaining democracy (socially interpreted as freely-held elections).

However, crucial changes were starting to take place in the intra-party arena, which together with the 1989 crisis, would lead to the downfall of the 1979 equilibrium. Internecine and inter-party struggles within FREDEMO – the right-wing front organized by MVLL to counter APRA and IU – in the midst of economic crisis and of the Shining Path's offensive reduced their public opinion standing. APRA and IU had little if no support due to its government performance. The population perceived parties as illegitimate agents, preferring short-term interests to those for society at large. Parties' control over social movements slid while the collective identities of the coalitions of social movements formed under them weakened. Simultaneously, the crisis destroyed the administration's capacity to provide public goods and undermined support groups. The successful 1999 mayoral bid of Ricardo Belmont, an independent, to the Lima municipal government was a first warning. The presidential candidacy of Alberto Fujimori, a similar independent, and a TV personality, was the second.

As the two-round 1990 election progressed, Fujimori's strategic role become increasingly clear to voters, and led him to gain financial and logistic support from García, who additionally ordered the intelligence service to help.[47] These newly available resources provided a surge in electoral surveys and a further increase in strategic voting. As he came second in the first round, and MVLL failed to win a decisive victory in the presidential debate, Fujimori consolidated his position. In a hotly contested second round, Alberto Fujimori won the 1990 election as a party system outsider, without party backing and with gradual stabilization his main pledge.

The initiation of reforms: towards a market-based new equilibrium under Fujimori

Fujimori gained the presidency seemingly against all odds. His choices seemed limited: he had no economic team, no Congress majority, a weak party supporting him, no possibility for re-election, and faced parties with more tradition, resources, and discipline. Furthermore, he was facing the worst economic crisis in Peru's history and threats from ruthless and powerful terrorist movements. Figure 5.13 shows both reported terrorist actions and victims of police violence from 1980–94. Additionally, although an anti-party discourse heralded his arrival to the presidency, he needed to build a multiparty 'national interest' first cabinet, with ministers from many different parties. Governance was difficult: no party held a majority in Congress, although FREDEMO, Cambio 90 – Fujimori's electoral vehicle – and APRA were the three largest blocs, with the left fragmented. Cambio 90's internal weaknesses and lack of support in the intra-party arena, and the president's poor control over the executive, was somehow countered by his support in the public opinion arena, and by his extraordinary showing in the electoral arena.

The election resulted in a major shift in the mental model agents had regarding the strength of the 1979 regime. The critical moment of his election, coupled with the makeshift nature of his nevertheless successful party, seemed to mark an end to the traditional roles parties had played since the 1979 regime. Social movements, so far central elements of the party's political articulation strategies, were increasingly weak. As Cameron (1994) argues, the reduction in industrial employment, the extension of the informal economy, and the tenuous associative life resulting from both the crisis and the war all contributed to their decreased strength. Furthermore, the election had used preferential voting in Congress for the first time, diminishing parties' control over representatives.

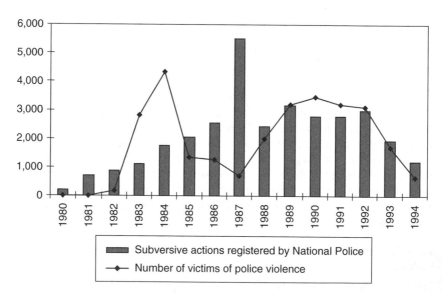

Figure 5.13   Terrorist acts and victims of police violence, 1980–94
Source: Webb and Fernández Baca (1995).

Economic adjustment and security issues: the building blocks. The economic program and the anti-subversive strategy would be key for Fujimori's success and his Achilles heel: a failure in either would make him vulnerable in the key public opinion arena; losing his legitimacy, he would then be fair game for the opposition-controlled Congress, a potential lame-duck in a conflict with Congress and/or the army. He was in a similar position as Salinas, relying on effective governance as a way to ensure legitimacy. He would follow an alternative path: rather than making democratic concessions, he would minimize them, protecting his electoral legitimacy through a continuing party system critique. Finally, he decided – as will be examined below – that the shock economic stabilization program advocated by MVLL would be easy to manage, had the best chances of success, and eventually the best chances of gaining external support towards an end of Peru's financial isolation.

An ad hoc 'Peru supporting group of countries' provided resources to pay arrears, allowing Peruvian reinsertion into financial markets.[48] Domestically, Fujimori met with the business leaders' organizations, and received support from the largest and its president, Jorge Camet Dickmann (to become Fujimori's longest serving economy minister), in exchange for his proposed adoption of FREDEMO's plan. Fujimori lacked a significant amount of technical personnel on whom to rely, and distrusted the civil service he inherited, but he received significant technical support from multilateral agencies after his election.[49] Following Mexico's example, he had originally planned a gradual approach which called for the complete 'dollarization' of the economy before fixing the exchange rate. However, he quickly discovered that Peru lacked the resources which had allowed Mexico a gradual economic adjustment. Consequently, he made a radical volte-face: on 8 August 1990, his cabinet head and minister of economy, FREDEMO's Juan Carlos Hurtado Miller, introduced a shock stabilization program.

The logic of Fujimori's new found program also followed a double pincer strategy. Economically, it suggested that price stability, coupled with the use of an exchange rate anchor would create expectations of stability among economic agents. The subsequent expansion of previously nonexistent consumer credit coupled with a significant decrease in interest rates, and last but by no means least, inflation control, might create a significant consumption boost. A radical fiscal reform would provide the means to expand the tax base to finance social policy without a deficit. A set of structural reforms and a privatization process would provide the resources required to correct external sector imbalances and renew growth. Politically, popularity should help sway the public opinion arena, while support from the business sector in the corporate and supply domains developed, as did support from international financial institutions within the financial domain. Moreover, the fragmentation of the strong centralized union greatly reduced the possibility of labor unrest. Responding to the armed forces' security concerns would gain their support.

The program advanced through three successive stages. Initially, a large stabilization package was introduced in August 1990, creating conditions for major institutional reforms between February and December 1992 (including Fujimori's army-supported April 1992 self-coup). A second reform package locked these changes in through a new constitution (after the April 1992 self-coup), allowing presidential re-election. Finally, consolidation followed through complementary institutional creation.

Key considerations were macro disequilibria and credibility gaps. Fiscal control was achieved through extraordinary taxes and public prices realignment (including a 34-time increase in fuel prices), as well as the creation of an expenses committee. Monetary policy included a short-term loan to cover public salaries together with a promise not to request additional loans. Additionally, 34 import tariffs (ranging from zero to 108 per cent) were compacted into three: 50, 25, and 15 per cent (eventually to be followed by an additional 10 per cent tariff). Salaries were raised 400 per cent, and public sector rises forbidden until December 1990.

Fiscal and monetary policy were the main macroeconomic policy tools, followed soon by a structural reform process (Figure 5.14 shows the evolution of public finance between 1987 and 2001). In the first two years, the policy objective was not only to control inflation, but to create a fiscal surplus to pay off debt and eliminate the international financial blockage, employing increases in public prices to heal public finances. Room for maneuver could be facilitated by staging the debt renegotiation so some debt relief could be achieved during the first two years of the stabilization programs.

A hybrid approach was used with regard to the exchange rate, which unified the various existing rates, and provided for a 50 per cent devaluation, plus an equilibrium exchange rate to be achieved through an unannounced trajectory. Monetary control was maintained through a relatively flexible, unannounced anchor.[50] This would allow certain flexibility to support the announced exchange rate goal, as well as degrees of freedom to resist pressures to finance the national development bank's deficits through Central Bank

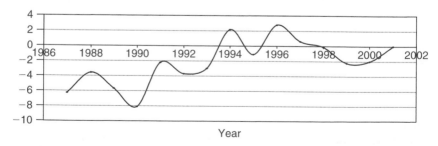

Figure 5.14 Public finance, 1987–2001 (% of GDP)
Source: Own elaboration based on IMF, EFI Yearbook.

credits. The Central Bank had to estimate money demand and the exchange rate at a level that would not unduly affect exports.

Initial results were not unsatisfactory, but not spectacular. Prices initially increased, and later descended to clear inventories, while salaries were set over the inflation rate, with indexes for private salaries still operating. Shock readjustment of public prices was effective, although the overall adjustment was relatively long (almost 37 months to stabilize the economy, from August 1990 to September 1993).[51] The adjustment process through public prices resulted in the state maintaining the inflationary effect through its continuous readjustments of public prices, and the distorted – albeit by then, relatively stable – relative prices would only translate into serious distortions later. Inflation was still significant: in August 1990 it was at 397 per cent *monthly*, but then fell to 13.8 per cent in September, 9.6 per cent in October, and 5.9 per cent in November. The decrease in the monetary stock triggered the ensuing recession, with overall GDP growth in September 25 per cent below the level in July. However, some GDP growth was achieved in the next months. Devaluation was 40 per cent between August and September, while interest rates fell from an average of 59.9 per cent monthly in June to 10.9 per cent in September.

While in the past this sort of adjustment would have created significant upheaval in unions and other organized entities, the preceding crisis had undermined the organizations that could oppose the government, while simultaneously fragmenting the population into informal settlements which could be reached through a targeted social policy which only sought to cover bare survival necessities. As Fujimori was weaving into his reforms proposals that originated from FREDEMO, a flow of support came from the right. The package's success also made the military take notice. Since García's government their thinking had been moving towards the need to combine market-oriented reforms with a radical counter-insurgency strategy. Finally, the population at large, while acknowledging that the program could in fact diminish their welfare in the short term, also felt it could help them in the long run: between July and September 1990, Fujimori maintained a 55 per cent approval rating, in spite of the severity of the adjustment.

Governance basis: the 1992 structural reforms and the underlying organization. Structural reforms were launched employing the ability to use legislative decrees granted under the 1979 constitution. Economic reform decrees were drafted by the groups that had originally supported FREDEMO; security decrees were negotiated with the army by Fujimori's new security agent, Vladimiro Montesinos, an army captain who would derive significant power from this role. There were 923 legal decrees issued between March 1991 and December 1992, more than 44 decrees a month on average.[52] On this basis, sectoral reforms defined a new role for the state (through the privatization of most of the major state enterprises). As in Mexico, these created a wide array of new regulatory frameworks for the main production sectors of the economy (fisheries, mining, and oil), the public sector (tax administration, regulatory commissions, social spending), and the economy in general (new labor and competition laws, anti-monopoly legislation, environmental regulations). A number of commissions were established with responsibilities for handling the new regulatory framework. These were staffed by personnel drawn mostly from the private sector, particularly from policy groups linked to FREDEMO.

The fragmented parties in Congress did not oppose the structural reforms embodied in the 1992 decrees, but were relatively liberal in granting extraordinary legislative capacity to the president. None of the emergency decrees was rejected, and legislative decrees passed without revision. As a result, the economic and security agendas would create a bundling nexus in the economic policy and security arenas within a newly arranged organizational domain from which to handle reforms. Support from achievements of the economic program would help sustain activities on the national security front. Agents within the embedded policy games resulting from these decrees would receive a common advantage in coordination through a small inner circle at the palace of government and information collected by the intelligence services. A complex set of alliances orchestrated within the president's inner circle combined support from the business community and the economic arena with that from the military on the security front; bundling them allowed the Fujimori government to take advantage of complementarities that provided further momentum to the president's strategy.

The economic team.   The economic team was relatively stable, and was a vital component of the early years of Fujimori's first term. Two key groups of agents in the economic policy nexus were controlled by the minister of the presidency and by Santiago Fujimori, the president's brother. The first handled most of the issues related to the functioning of the state, including the restructuring of key public entities and services, and the privatization process. The second was crucial to the operation of the newly created regulatory commissions, as well as in increasing state efficiency. Both functioned as gates of access to the president, and picked candidates for upper-level positions in ministries and other high-ranking positions, as well as (after 1993) candidates to Congress and local government. Most other high-ranking offices were staffed by personnel directly hired by multilateral agencies but reporting to the government.

The security reforms.   In the crucial relations with the military, the president tended to rely on the security services, and particularly on Vladimiro Montesinos (the former army captain and, unbeknownst at the time, very effective drug trafficker attorney) as a reliable bundling agent with the various army groups. Opposition came from the army leadership at the time of the Fujimori accession, mostly from generals supporting existing army arrangements and against the coup,[53] while support came from the then smaller group of politically minded generals. Montesinos's presidential access gave him control over higher-ranking army officers, and, based on the power such closeness provided, allowed for reform of the promotion system.[54] By 1997, all regional commanders came from either Montesinos's own 1966 generation, or were political kin. Additionally, the president claimed the power to name the Head of the Combined Armed Forces Staff, rejecting the traditional autonomous chain of command. The designation of loyalist General Nicolas Hermoza as head ensured that control would not shift in the next few years. Finally, Montesinos achieved control of the police. This concentrated control of intelligence and security in the president – and through him, in Montesinos. In exchange, a fast-track processing of terrorist crimes by the military was granted through presidential decrees. As a result, control of a key aspect of the organizational domain was significantly enhanced.

Coordination and implementation. While cabinets were quite fluid, a group of ministers remained (mostly in MEF, agriculture and the president's ministry MINPRE, which handled social policy), providing a core from which to coordinate policy.[55] As in Mexico, key policies were handed to specially appointed teams; however, unlike in Mexico, these operated in parallel to the formal official hierarchies, around the second- and third-tier positions, not within direct control of the minister, but reporting directly to the cliques surrounding the president. Thus, the president had a parallel chain of command and control. The intelligence services were used to monitor ministers. Simultaneously, most of the traditional planning and control mechanisms became superfluous and were dismantled, including the National Planning Institute (INP) and the planning and coordination entities in the ministries.

These policy arrangements also provided enforcement mechanisms in the economic and security nexus, as well as within social arenas. While in the past there had been significant divisions within the business community as policy shifted from support to either exports or industrial development, all had suffered under the crisis of the past years. While the economic program supported exports more than industrial development, the private sector's inclination towards the privatization program and state retrenchment components of the reforms tended to unify them behind the measures passed through the decrees. Furthermore, the relative success of the stabilization program showed there was more to gain by maintaining support for the president. Business sector allegiance could be taken for granted as the economic success continued. In the social arena, a timid state publicity and promotion campaign began, using the support of media dependent on government advertising revenues. The combined impact of these arrangements provided the president with related coordination and enforcement mechanisms, used to coordinate policy within the administration and promote allegiance from the business and social policy communities and from the military over the overall strategy.

Lock-in mechanisms: the 1992 self-coup and constitutional change. Parties kept their distance from Fujimori as his anti-party discourse developed, by recalling most of the ministers who served in cabinet. However, two years later they seemed still not to have enough leverage to contain the coalition behind Fujimori. While in 1991 a self-coup against the formal institutional framework that got him elected might have resulted in his being ousted (which happened almost at the same time with President Serrano in Guatemala), by 1992 such a self-coup had all the elements of a potential success: it had popular, military, and business community support, and even enjoyed a degree of legitimacy. The party system's weaknesses, Fujimori's successes, and the degree of support and coordination achieved would provide a platform for the Executive's closure of Congress and the judiciary in April 1992, claiming they represented a regime that prevented decisive action in both the economic and security nexus. The Constitutional Court was also closed, to prevent formal pronouncements against Fujimori's unconstitutionality. If unchallenged, these measures would effectively change the overall equilibrium of the 1979 institutional architecture, providing the president with a meta-constitutional facility to control Congress and the courts.

While domestic views were mixed, foreign reaction was significantly opposed to the self-coup. However, Fujimori's management of the event reinforced the new equilibrium: elections were called, but international sanctions avoided. The containment strategy called for the election of a new constitutional Congress and a judiciary where Fujimori had absolute majority. They drafted – although the true work was done by the business sector and think tanks[56] – a new constitution that gave constitutional rank to the contents of legislative decrees.[57] Other modifications diminished the power of other state powers while increasing those of the president: Congress's two chambers were combined, the Executive increasingly controlled the judiciary, party creation and election entry rules were eased, and the capacity of electoral organs was restricted. Presidential legislative attributions were maintained: Fujimori could still issue legislative and urgency decrees, now under even easier conditions.

Relaxed party entry rules translated into further fragmentation of the already weak opposition parties. Last but not least, the president's new re-election capacity not only potentially extended the temporal horizon of the group in power, but also provided a relatively long-term incentive for the development of policy groups within the Fujimori administration.[58] This was bolstered by Fujimori's claim that the 1993 constitution allowed him an additional re-election opportunity. He argued that after the 1995 election (under the 1993 constitution rules), he was only in the *first* of the two terms that the constitution allowed him. Furthermore, the ease with which political parties could be registered would even allow the president (as the PRI did in Mexico) to create his own 'loyal opposition' and support groups, and register them as parties. This, coupled with the weakness of the electoral institutions allowed, as in Mexico, for a significant rigging of the elections, which translated into Fujimori planning to maintain his administration through almost 15 years.[59]

The reform agenda and its policy development. Several other conditions needed to be met to ensure structural adjustment success. Avoiding fiscal deficits and maintaining tight momentary supply were key to controlling inflation. The new private pension regime, strengthening the tax base, and improving the expenditure capacity of the state would help to increase savings and expenditure, while the harsh conditions the adjustment imposed on the population at large called for an emergency social support program. The Dirección General de Contribuciones (DGC) – a nest of tax corruption and inefficiency – was replaced by a new Superintendencia (Superintendencia Nacional de Administración Tributaria, SUNAT) whose employees were hired under private sector rules, and which could charge a percentage of the amounts it collected. Another Superintendencia, SAFP (Superintendencia de Administración de Fondos de Pensiones) controlled the percentage each of the private retirement fund administrators could charge to those who put their funds into private AFPs.

As in Mexico, privatization was handled by special commissions. A private investment promotion commission (COPRI) coordinated, while specific privatizations were handled by special units within a privatization committee (CEPRI). In 1996, an additional commission to promote private investment in infrastructure (PROMCEPRI) was also created.[60] The process employed overall a methodology that included future investment promises as a pre-qualification and the participation of individual citizens through public stock offers. Market mechanisms were employed to evaluate company value, and private control was achieved either by contractual means or through majority stock sales.

Privatization generated US$7250 million. This allowed external sector strengthening and some social policy finance, while generating 360,000 new positions, with a net gain of 266,000 jobs.[61] The privatization process was accompanied by both a new fiscal policy law, which gave legal protection to fiscal stability,[62] and a significant process of institutional creation. This was directed to enhance areas that were key to the structural reform agenda, including taxation, privatization, and poverty and social policy. After several experiments, the president's office (through MINPRE) would control the resources for the last two areas.

Most of the first-term sectoral reforms were linked (for example, the case of ports, which otherwise would have become a major bottleneck for the external trade reform) or increased the return to the state, and included those assets which could fetch the largest investments for the Peruvian economy, such as telecommunications (privatized with expansion and investment promises), and energy. Additionally, commissions to control areas transferred to the private sector were created. These included telecommunications (OSIPTEL), electricity (OSINERG), and a regulatory body for the previously state-held oil sector (Peru-Petro). A transversal body, with rights to intervene in general market operation and competition INDECOPI (Instituto Nacional de la Competencia y de la Propiedad Intelectual), was also created, led by councils with state and interested stakeholders as representatives. However, there were delays in creating these commissions, thus creating an interim regulatory vacuum.

A new banking law liberalized interest rates and the foreign currency market, and modified the way credits were assigned by the Central Bank. While most of the previous aspects were deregulated, the already existing Superintendencia de Banca y Seguros (SBS) was reinforced to increase control capacity. Additionally, a large-scale effort was made to create a new titling system, to allow for the people living in shantytowns around Lima and some other cities to make formal property claims on their properties, providing them with an additional source of capital through new banking sector mortgages.

The labor domain had been one of the most rigid in the region, with significant worker protection in both individual and collective labor law. Figure 5.15 compares the flexibility indices between 1985 and 1995 for Peru and other Latin American countries. As Saavedra (2003) emphasizes, the costs were transferred to consumers and to the informal sector of the economy. Regulatory liberalization eliminated employment stability (providing instead for reduced compensation) and scrapped judicial job reinstallation as well as most benefits. Additionally, it allowed for more flexible collective labor negotiations, more than one union in a company, and union competition. These reforms radically reformed labor law between 1990 and 1995.

The combination of macroeconomic stabilization and structural reforms resulted in a major inflow of foreign investment between 1993 and 1997. While in 1992 external investment barely reached US$200 million, it was already US$3838 million by 1994 (US$2214 million from privatizations), and US$4080 million in 1996, although it decreased as a consequence of the 1997 crisis to US$2736 million. The Central Bank tried to dampen overvaluation of the national currency by increasing the banks' Central Bank deposits in foreign currency, the use of open market operations, and the central

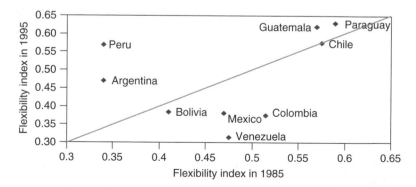

Figure 5.15   Flexibility indices for selected Latin American countries, 1985–95
Source: Saavedra (2000).

government foreign currency deposits in the Central Bank (Figure 5.16 shows international reserves between 1988 and 2001). In addition to optimistic expectations, there was consumption credit expansion, which reinforced increases in fiscal and private expenditures. An expansion in investment and imports added to the previous effects, leading to significant import and GDP growth (its evolution is shown in Figure 5.17).

The contribution of exports was limited, and took place in the mid-1990s. Imports grew significantly, as a consequence of the trade reforms and the increasing economic activities, and began to exert pressure on the balance of payments. They were financed by the surplus in the balance of capital resulting from privatizations, which led to the growth of reserves. Growth was greater in the extractive sectors (in particular, mining, fisheries, and agriculture), while transportation and industry declined after the mid-1990s. (Figure 5.18 shows the evolution of sectoral output between 1991 and 2002.) Growth

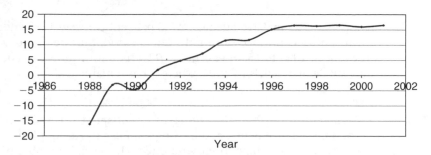

Figure 5.16 International reserves, Central Bank, 1988–2001 (% of GDP)
Source: Own elaboration with base to the IMF, EFI Yearbook.

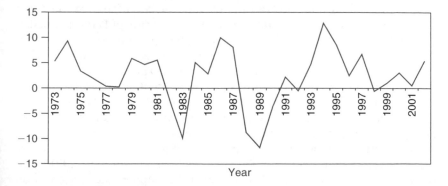

Figure 5.17 Real GDP, 1973–2002 (annual percentage)
Source: Own elaboration based on IMF, EFI Yearbook.

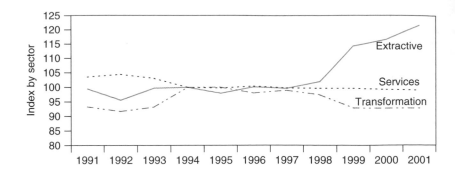

Figure 5.18   Evolution of sectoral output, 1991–2002
Note: Base 1994 = 100.
Source: Own elaboration based on INEI: INEI data: http://www.inei.gob.pe/.

reached an impressive annual average rate of 7.3 per cent between 1993 and 1994. Inflation control continued during the same period; the rate dropped from 39.5 per cent in 1993 to 15.4 per cent in 1994. It continued its descent later, reaching single digit levels in 1997, where it has remained.

Reform closure

Fujimori's re-election and the 1996 crisis: the economy entrapped.   These were impressive economic achievements, and the original logic of Fujimori's program and strategy seemed to have been vindicated. However, a number of latent problems became increasingly clear in the late 1990s. These came to the fore immediately after the 1995 elections that pitted Fujimori against Javier Perez de Cuellar. Fujimori's pre-electoral expenditure expansion, the national sense of urgency to rally behind the president in the unexpected 1995 Peru–Ecuador war, and last but not least, the lack of resolve and organization from the opposition, translated into the routing of Perez de Cuellar's electoral bid. However, the elections caused an important expansion of public expenditures, which generated a deficit of 1.9 per cent of GDP. By 1995, the external trade deficit reached US$2.9 billion (50 per cent of exports), and the deficit in the current account reached 7.2 per cent of GDP. After the 1995 election was won, the perception that the balance of payments deficit would be difficult to finance led to an increasingly restrictive fiscal and monetary policy, with a negative impact on internal demand.

This adjustment brought some unresolved difficulties within the structural adjustment program to the fore. The economy's dollarization meant the Central Bank controlled only one-third of the money supply. The limited autonomy and impact of fiscal and monetary policies meant that they needed to be very tight to balance the external sector and reduce the current account deficit, with serious effects on economic activity. In 1996, a 15 per cent reduction in current expenditures resulted in GDP growing only 0.2 per cent per capita, with real income diminishing 4 per cent. However, the current account deficit was reduced to only US$2.5 billion, passing from 7.2 per cent of GDP to 5.8 per cent. A fiscal surplus was the means for achieving this adjustment. The reduction in the public sector size and capacity, however, meant the administration lacked policy leverage and could apply only a limited number of measures. Likewise, the exit of most of the original economic policy team after 1996 affected the government's economic policy dexterity.

The adjustment process had also produced a set of relative prices in the supply and industrial organization domains that neither promoted an export economy nor facilitated an internal market-based economy. In fact, the economic program became increasingly entrapped: macroeconomic imbalances derived from the initial stabilization package proved difficult to correct. Subsidy elimination and increased taxes from public prices, indispensable in the stabilization, translated into higher public prices. Once set, these were maintained to attract investors for the subsequent privatization process. Public prices could not be reduced without increasing the tax base, which had proved elusive. Capital inflows from the privatization process (coupled with inflows from the burgeoning coca leaf trade) propelled an exchange rate overvaluation, while the commercial banks' risk avoidance and debt portfolio from the 1980s' crisis, combined with their high operation costs, produced high interest rates.

The external debt was also an increasingly important burden. Interest payments almost doubled between 1990 and 1996, from US$20 billion to US$33.6 billion, while its subsequent renegotiation reduced it to US$28.3 billion. This meant Peru would have to pay US$1.8 billion per month beginning in 1997, equivalent to a quarter of exports, a sixth of internal savings or a fifth of public savings. Privatization had resulted in major inflows – US$6.3 billion by December 1996 – but these could hardly be spent at all without contributing to a further exchange rate appreciation or risking a further increase in inflation. Privatization resources were employed as a security device against external sector shocks instead.

However, the most severe problem facing the hastily assembled economic team was the difficulty in increasing employment and income. The collapse of the unions in the early 1990s saved a labor domain defeat. In fact, adequate employment had not followed GDP growth since 1990. Salaries rose from 1990 until 1994, but decreased in real terms after that. Gonzáles de Olarte (1998) argues that labor and commercial liberalization, coupled with the increase in public prices and exchange rate appreciation after the 1990 adjustment resulted in salaries having relatively small domestic purchasing power; ironically, the high exchange rate also made export businesses in Peru internationally uncompetitive due to the relatively high cost of salaries.

To top it off, three significant external negative shocks were experienced in 1998. The appearance of the 'El Niño' current off Peru's northern coasts caused climatic impacts with significant economic and infrastructure losses. Then, the terms of trade seriously deteriorated in the second half of 1997, with a negative impact on the balance of accounts. Finally, external credit interruptions appeared as a consequence of the 1997 Asian and Brazilian crises, starting an internal credit default reaction, to which the government responded slowly, compounding the problem.

Policy retrenchment and reform capture.   Meanwhile, the increased relevance of the security nexus and the relative neglect of the economy made effective overall coordination and economic and social policy capacity suffer. Within the central government, most of the policy groups which had designed the reforms had been set against further legal and/or constitutional modifications for a third term. None of the other leaders (and particularly Fujimori's minister of the presidency, Yoshiyama) had been effective electorally, or had any future as an eventual successor to Fujimori. As has happened in the past, the increasingly weak economic reform nexus ended up headless. This opened opportunities for agents within the security arena to take a more active role. Control over designation of key positions within the central administration and other key organizational domain positions, activities previously handled by Santiago Fujimori, now came under the purview of the security services, as did coordination with other state powers already within the influence of the security services. These received additional, non-budgetary rents from the central administration.

The economic ministry position continued to control business sector relations (up to Fujimori's third minister of the economy, Jaime Camet). Business pressure groups remained weak, and relations between big business and the government tended to concentrate on direct bilateral talks between economy or security nexus agents within the organizational domain and major business groups. Social policy was mostly controlled from the Ministry of Agriculture and the presidency.[63] However, these, as well as the areas of economy and finance, would become increasingly vulnerable to the expansion of power of the intelligence services.

These acted as an agent to the president, while simultaneously increasing the capacity to engage and control other groups.[64] The president increasingly required cooperation from the resulting organization to co-opt and handle relations across groups, including business sector relations and electoral control. The relative closeness of this group's head to the president, the related opportunity to appoint congressmen and high-ranking officers (including the cabinet),[65] and its control over the judiciary provided an informal (that is, not legally regulated) but crucial coordination position within government. Hostage relations[66] provided means from which to enter advantageously into transactions with agents from within the industrial organization, corporate governance, and financial domains, and the opportunity to increase the strength and scope of the leverage of this informal organization within those domains by using both formal and informal means to enforce cooperation.

The president's favour led to the expanded organization taking direct control of most of the parallel structures created to manage the reform process and the other state organs.[67] By 1998, Montesinos was publicly considered the second most powerful person in government, and *the* most powerful by 1999.[68] By 1997, his agents had already engaged with Congress, the Tribunal de Garantías Constitucionales, and the judiciary to change the existing equilibria once again. From a rule of law perspective, this amounted to taking control of organs involved in making, enforcing, and administering law, namely, Congress, the judiciary, and the security forces.

Poor growth and rigidity as policy problems. While the economic team lost government clout and economic program leadership vis-à-vis the security nexus, the growth failure of the late 1990s continued. Gonzáles de Olarte (1998) argues that, as Peru had started from an under-accumulated capital situation, most of the growth had been capital intensive. The high (overvalued) exchange rate, which led to relatively high wages compared to international competitors, contributed to a small number of available positions and a decreased salary base, and annual growth of less than 6 to 7 per cent was insufficient to overcome distributional growth problems and ensure real income expansion. However, most of the growth depended by now on foreign direct investment, as public investment turned increasingly marginal as debt payments increased. Furthermore, most of the high revenue investments through privatization were gone by 1997, while internal demand did not grow as salaries remained stagnant, and some initial signals of reform and (eventually) legal retrenchment were already starting to appear. While some investment could also be expected from Peruvian capital, this faced less attractive conditions than those for foreign investors.

Changing the direction of the structural reform program would require altering the financial and industrial organization domain equilibrium, where IFIs and multilateral institutions played a leading role, and whose agents were in turn crucial for the coalition Fujimori had assembled within the organizational domain. The weakness of unions and other organized labor agents meant that no organized opposition could play a major role in developing a new equilibrium there. Furthermore, these would face the potential veto from agents within the security arena, who had the upper hand in policy. As a result, a policy stalemate developed over the next two years. Privatization problems brewed between 1998 and 1999, as attempts were made to privatize electricity and water companies in the south. Recession followed in 1998, and was not countered until the first half of 1999, when a coherent countercyclical fiscal policy was applied.

By the end of Fujimori's second term, poverty had lessened with regard to 1991, but not with regard to 1986, before Alan García's botched nationalization

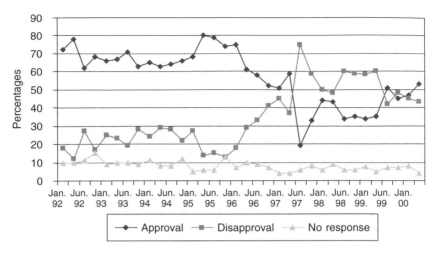

Figure 5.19   Evolution of Fujimori's presidential approval
Source: Degregori (2000).

attempt. By 1996, 49 per cent of the population was still below the poverty line, with 16 per cent extremely poor. The urban population was increasingly impoverished, and the middle classes suffered: employees (public and private) had their incomes reduced, even while GDP was growing (as Figure 5.19 shows, Fujimori's popularity declined after 1997). These developments created unease about the long-term viability of Fujimori's economic program among the population at large.

The third term and the dismissal of the Fujimori government.   Fujimori's transition into his strikingly short third term was marked by economic crisis and the consequences of his bid for a second (or first, according to his counting) re-election, including a major debate as to its constitutionality. Attempts to formalize Montesinos's responsibilities backfired,[69] resulting in his informal position being weakened. The simultaneous weakness of the opposition parties had increased the relevance of the press and the mass media. However, the reliance of the mass media on government advertising for commercial subsistence provided the government with a powerful weapon.[70] Control of the judiciary was achieved through the same structures which had originally been deployed to increase efficiency in court and case handling during Fujimori's first term.[71] Attempts to control the armed forces had created an armed focus of resistance (in the southern parts of the country), while control over mass media undermined government credibility (and as such, much of its utility). While the door for a third term seemed opened, it was clear that the coalition behind Fujimori's government had suffered major casualties.

Corruption had become increasingly evident: crucial congressional votes were tainted by vote-buying accusations, while signatures required for Fujimori's candidacy were proved to have been falsified by his support movements – ad hoc organizations prepared as electoral vehicles – with intelligence service support. However, none of the several independent opposition candidates enjoyed coordinated support, a consequence of acute party fragmentation.

In this context, the Peruvian electoral system produced another dark horse candidate in Alejandro Toledo, then leader of a minor opposition party. A timely scandal produced by the opposition obtaining and airing a video showing Montesinos buying a crucial re-election congressional vote forced the president to turn against his erstwhile head spy. A month later, amidst a severe popularity decline, Fujimori resigned. Congress elected its leader as president and elections were called a year later, this time won by Toledo.

Transition and policymaking under the 1993 constitution. While Toledo achieved what had seemed almost impossible in the first months of 2000, his government has lacked gravitas and capacity to continue the reforms. His party support base lacks an organized platform, while his main opponent, APRA's Alan García, employed APRA's original structure to re-build the party as a viable alternative to Toledo, who nonetheless won a second term in July 2006. While no reversal has yet taken place, the lack of credible counterweights to the power of the presidency makes the transition to another government problematic. Additionally, and unlike in Mexico, there is less external constraint for a major policy change. Thus, while the window of opportunity for reform in Peru has for now been closed, some additional change could happen in the near future, although not necessarily in the same direction in which the original 1990s reforms were advanced.

5.4   An analytical comparison

The reforms in both Mexico and Peru, while of relatively similar scope and intent, differ if the process and context of the reforms are taken into account. Both sought to transform the role of the state, expand the operation of markets, and modify the institutional framework. Seen from this perspective, they differ in scope and depth, with Peru probably more radical. Their origin is similar in that they were triggered by accumulated losses, external sector shocks and legitimacy crises, with a more or less acute security issue:[72] in Mexico, due to the DE period decay and the subsequent 1970 populist imbalances; in Peru, due to the catastrophic García period and terrorist expansion. Institutional differences are marked, from the difference in political regimes to the stability of the underlying equilibria. If the starting conditions and the processes followed are considered, differences seem to increase: Mexican reforms were based on a thorough gradualism, while the Peruvian reforms demonstrated an extreme big-bang approach. The first case gradually molded the existing institutions into something different, while the second created a totally new set of institutions. Peru was experiencing an almost terminal crisis as reforms started, while Mexico's situation was not as acute.

However, a striking similarity emerges if the means employed to advance the reforms are considered. On the surface, there is similarity in that the authoritarian character of the regimes involved was concealed behind a façade of formal democratic institutions whose formal remit differed significantly from their actual informal operations. If one scratches the surface, a further similitude appears. This includes the character of the agents involved (including the role of those coming from the external sector) and the means through which deals that constituted the reform were enforced. This in turn affected the relative hierarchical level of the reformed institutions, the sequence followed, and, last but not least, the strength of the institutional legacy of the reform process. To better examine these issues, this section will examine similarities arising from implementation in the two cases. This can in turn allow for a review of the differences under a new light in the following section, and the drawing of some conclusions and common lessons.

The underlying similitude

The most obvious is probably the already mentioned use made of formal democratic institutions to hide a gamut of informal policy-making and informal mechanisms and agents unaccountable and unanswerable to the public at large. However, a deeper view shows an underlying similitude encompassing the overall transactions at the root of the reform process, and particularly the strategy the groups leading reform followed to take control of the organizational domain and coordinate policy to extend it to other domains. Reformers used formal institutions strategically to support the proposed changes, as well as bundled agents and developed complementarities and linkages to garner momentum for their bid. In neither was their role an explicit part of the bargain. Formal institutions served mostly to confirm deals already made.

Success would have placed them in a central position within a reorganized organizational domain; however, in Peru as in Mexico, the reforms generated unintended consequences that made the initial institutional arrangement unsustainable as the reforms were advanced. Summing up this argument, following the thread of implementation strategies and means through the maze of reform may lead to the conclusion that different reform outcomes can be attributed to a set of common causes.

The basic transaction and strategy

Mexico and Peru share a certain resemblance in the way that new proposals for the articulation of the overall institutional architecture were proposed by the leadership of the reformist groups to other agents within the social domain. In Peru, reformist agents proposed a trade between improved economic performance and enhanced security and the political reform process; while in Mexico, economic performance and democratic opening were the aims. In

Mexico, the structural reforms implied a dual political bargain. The first was proposed by the technocratic elite to the political operatives who had so far ruled key institutional domains within the economy and the polity. These reforms would allow PRI legitimately to retain power through transparent elections, because of the effective performance of the economy. The second was proposed to key agents within the remaining domains in what was by then more of an elitist democracy: this same effective performance would continue ensuring the welfare of the population at large, providing a sensible reason to vote for PRI in open and transparent elections within a more participative democracy. If these two deals could be completed, then a democratic transition would be in place without having to transfer power to the opposition. This assumed that economic policy control by a technocratic elite could be retained in spite of increased political competitiveness and social mobilization, something only guaranteed within the previous, corporatist structure. The technocratic elite saw an opportunity to access the presidency in a set of policies proposed after the failure of the populist experiments, a set in which they were likely to play a leading role. Once the process had started, their own survival as a group within the PRI regime depended on their capacity to deliver the promised results.

In Peru, Fujimori followed a confrontational strategy, proposing to agents within the social and organizational domains effectively to trade security and economic governance (which he represented) against political representation (represented by the 1979 pact and the allied opposition parties). Representation, he argued, would lead to the ultimate collapse of predictable interaction in all domains, given the extreme conditions Peru was facing.[73] This emphasis played well with the pragmatism which the sheer necessity for survival in the preceding crisis had inspired within social domain agents. It also provided grounds for the modification – and eventual scrapping – of the 1979 pact (in which the president was at a disadvantage within the organizational domain because of his lack of party support); and provided a basis for expanding the policy horizon of the president and his most immediate group of policy supporters. His reform programs not only provided means to centrally manage the most pressing problems of Peru, but also to bypass parties and gain support from the business sector and the armed forces. Given the fragmentation of social support groups and opposition, this strategy helped destroy sources for potential reaction to government measures within the organizational domain, while insuring support from the finance, industrial organization, and corporate governance domains. As in Mexico, the president would be placed in a central position within the newly changed organizational domain.

Coordinating and enforcing reform deals

Access and coordination capacity within the organizational domain and across others were crucial to sustaining presidential position, advancing the reform agenda and, eventually, imposing a new institutional architecture. Policy changes were advanced within the organizational domain – by introducing policies across domains previously not linked or bundled – and within the social domain, by enhancing public goods, social policy resources and, to a different degree in Mexico than in Peru, through press and media control across the social domain arenas.

This need to gain support from allies in key policy domains would also translate to a policy mix that sought to increase government leverage where it was most needed. In Peru and Mexico these included securing success for the economic program and the support of private domestic (Mexico) and international (Peru) investors. In Peru it also meant gaining army support in its counter-terrorism program. In both, privatization provided resources to balance the external sector while tax reform helped balance the fiscal deficit.

Advancing policy transactions across policy domains was closely related to the groups formed by agents engaged in them, and the means these employed to enforce policies and reform deals. Gaining control of the policy levers required combining careful management of political relations within the organizational domain with detailed knowledge regarding the more technical character of the reforms. In both Mexico and Peru reformers built political coalitions with groups which could help enforce the changes they proposed. Filling policy positions with allies to push the reform through was a well-trodden strategy: in Mexico, by sending personnel from the top positions in the financial and economic ministries to other ministries, while retaining personnel in the more political ministries to ensure policy deals; in Peru, by linking the economic and the security policy arenas in a powerful tandem, which could then be deployed against the opposition in other, originally not linked domains.[74] In Mexico, the informal institutions included alliances between reform minded technocrats and the political operatives of a corporatist and rather pragmatic hegemonic party (as argued by Garibaldi, 2000; Zaid, 1995), while in Peru, informal policy networks included not only the same technocrats, but also the security agency and the upper levels of the army (Rospigliosi, 2000; Degregori, 2000).

Shaping the reform agenda

Political support across specific domains and the expertise required to advance each reform contributed to shaping the reform agenda. The areas where the traditional politicians had their support were spared reform. Thus, for instance, in Mexico, the energy sector – where the powerful PEMEX and SME (power sector unions) were located – was left as an illiberal enclave. Likewise, the need to enhance social support made social policy a source of key initiatives. Thus, in Mexico this was done by increasing democratic concessions and expanding social programs, including the *Solidaridad* program, also following the strategy of placing reformers in key positions (Hernández Rodrigues, 1993). Something similar was done in the case of Peru, starting with the timid arrangements under various social agencies leading to their concentration within MINPRE. These created situations where political control and corporatist manipulation (in Mexico) or pragmatism and neoclientelism (in Peru) were exercised side by side in ways that allowed coordinated control of the economy.

This resulted in reform implementation sequences which strengthened the reformers' position. As policy wins translated into enhanced hierarchical control from the organizational domain through others, these wins could be used to increase policy momentum and to prevent effective opposition.[75] The president's position served throughout as source of political guidance (albeit more in Mexico than in Peru) and arbiter between groups. Moreover, through this position and its immediate entourage, agents shared a stake in the process and in the policy spoils, and gained an enforcement role in key agreements. Checks and balances operated within each domain, and, in particular, within the administration itself, while other state organs were frequently in a subservient position. Finally, commissions, institutional development through decrees, and other lock-in mechanisms allowed equilibrium conditions to be extended through government terms. In such a centralized system, the central administration was a key player in policy games where other groups also participated.

The process sustainability and outcome

Reform implementation conditions were unsustainable in both countries. In Peru, as the first reforms were implemented, Fujimori was re-elected, and the impossibility of appointing a successor became clear, the priority of structural reform diminished vis-à-vis the institutional maneuvers required within the organizational domain to preserve the regime status quo. The balance of power among the agents who engineered the pacts with the army and the business groups seemed to have been lost by 1996. As the technical teams departed, capacity and incentives for further reform decreased. The economic program compounded the problem as its unintended entrapments could not be corrected without modifying the coalition underlying Fujimori's inter-domain control. The reformers loss in the internecine struggle and the absence of checks on the national security groups would combine to create a coordination framework which, while initially effective, turned significantly self-serving, eventually hijacking the reform agenda and devoting most of its policy to supporting its own control of the organizational domain amidst an increasingly serious economic crisis, until the government fell.

In Mexico, the democratic concessions made to secure reform advance would translate into PRI losing some of its traditional policy levers. The collapse of the informal structures employed within the central administration to advance reforms within the regime, the failure of their formal replacement to take hold, and the increased political competitiveness and enhanced role of the opposition parties, would make conditions for further reform untenable. This increased the chances of reform stalemate, and opened the door for a democratic transition, as witnessed under the government of Vicente Fox. The result was the shell of a structure, which could no longer deliver what it was intended for. Reforms would not only change institutions, but would end up changing the reformers themselves.

5.5   As a conclusion: differences reviewed and common lessons

It is within this common pattern that some of the implementation differences – the different coordination mechanisms, pace, sequence, and depth of the reforms outlined at the beginning of the above section – can be better understood. The different entry point, character, coordination capacity, and length of the policy horizon of the reform teams within government, and the different responses employed by Mexican and Peruvian governments to deal with the opposition help explain some of those differences.

The different entry point and location of these networks would have important consequences and explain differences in reform implementation and outcome. In Mexico these groups rose through the ranks to reach the highest levels of government, while in Peru they were outsiders coming in after an unexpected electoral win. Furthermore, they developed by employing the higher levels of the formal administration in the first country, while in the second they were positioned within the administration, but creating parallel channels of access to the president. The Mexican networks could use the strength of formal organization to support their decisions; the Peruvian had to devise parallel means. The slow rise through the bureaucracy helps to explain the more detailed knowledge the Mexican teams had with regard to the administration, as well as the pattern of change from policies to mid-level institutions to high level (constitutional) changes in Mexico; this is not true for Peru.

However, what is more significant is that, as Winiecki (1996) suggested for the case of Russia, achieving control of these parallel channels resulted in Peru in the hijacking of the reform agenda. The lack of strong and operative formal institutions and the collateral corruption seems to be another of the reforms' unintended consequences. The serious crisis in Peru in late 2000, as the extent of corruption in the Fujimori government started to come to light, was only the latest in a long string of scandals with similar (albeit not as extreme) circumstances in other structural reformers; as in Salinas's Mexico (or for that matter, in Menem's Argentina and Collor de Mello's and Cardoso's Brazil).[76] In Mexico, their more formal character insured most teams would be transferred as PRI exited power; however, the lack of a formal civil service and the shifting pattern of incentives would eventually decimate this group through their dismissal and exodus as President Fox's term advanced, with the subsequent decay in policy quality.

As was outlined before, the length of the policy horizon provided grounds for agent interaction, and, if sufficiently long, contributed to a basis for informal organization. While different in extent, it played a similar role in both countries: weak formal rules to regulate relations between political powers and formal control institutions contributed to informal arrangements. Teams evolved in which mutual trust developed, and loyalty to the superior was rewarded, even at the cost of weak formal control and corruption. In fact, the repeated games created a structure of mutual hostages, in which non-compliance in one iteration could lead to non-compliance in the next one, resulting in a net loss for both parties, provided the horizon was long enough. PRI's long tenure within Mexico's organizational domain provided such a long horizon and coordination capacity in Mexico; Peruvian reformist agents had to create them. Thus the insistence, particularly of the national security nexus, in extending their policy horizon through successive re-elections: it made policy promises and threats credible. This also helps explain why the Peruvian case exhibited more bribery at all levels of the administration than in Mexico, where payment could be honored through future promotions, influence peddling and/or 'exchange of promises' for future compensation (all of which require time to gain credibility), which would not always ring true in the case of Peru. Furthermore, long-term horizons provided incentives for academic training and human capital formation within the administration, as they suggested there would be enough time to recover the costs incurred. This also helped explain the relative strength of the Mexican teams versus the Peruvian ones.

Probably what was most important is the contribution the different policy horizon and coordination capacity in both countries made to the pace of reform they experienced. It is usually argued that the strength of the preceding crisis is central to explaining the consequent reform pace. Macroeconomic constraints are also a frequent explanation. However, it is equally true that if agents have a long horizon with secure informal enforcement mechanisms to ensure policy delivery across domains, a gradual reform process seems more credible and viable, as specific transactions can be advanced gradually, and momentum built as reforms slowly advance from domains where control is stronger to others where it was originally weaker. As the case analysis showed, Mexico certainly followed this pattern. However, if the policy horizon is short, and the government has only weak coordination mechanisms across domains and nascent informal enforcement controls, a shock adjustment seems to be a more viable option. If successful, it creates enough credibility to force further changes across other domains.

These were more resilient than might appear at first sight to be the case. In spite of their apparent precariousness, Mexico was capable of maintaining a similar strategy through three different PRI governments (the conflict between Salinas and Zedillo being more an implementation problem than a dispute about the overall character of the reform process), while Vicente Fox's PAN has basically followed a similar reform route. Peru managed to transform its economy and polity within the short span of ten years, even with a central administration significantly weaker than its Mexican counterpart. In fact, in the Peruvian case cooperation between security and economic agents provided complementarities that would prove central to ensuring enough momentum to change the highest formal institutional rules.

While these institutional arrangements were not part of the proposed overall deal underlying the reforms, they were nonetheless crucial in determining the economic and political bargains at its roots. The strategy to implement the proposed institutional architecture would entail significant consequences later, as the actions leading to the newly implemented institutional equilibrium left turbulence in their wake. In Mexico, successive presidents insisted it was better to include PRI's opposition in the reform negotiations than to have it outside opposing them. Political operatives ensured deals by following a double-pincer strategy including both the economy and politics. The net result was strengthening of the rules to engage the opposition and their parties, as well as the credibility of PRI's project. In this context, the central public administration was the means to deliver the PRI presidents' promises. In contrast, the Peruvian president's rejection of the previous constitutional framework, his deliberate destruction of any opposition, and the overall weakening and fragmentation of intermediate groups created a vacuum in which only the presidency seemed to count. However, the hijacking of the alliances that the president made to move his reform agenda forward by bundling agents eventually made him incapable of advancing any further reform. At the end, the reform agenda was a hostage of the groups who implemented a large part of it, particularly in the security area.

While agents cannot ensure the end results of their strategies, they are certainly responsible for the responses they choose within an interaction pattern. Salinas and his predecessors decided to include rather than exclude the opposition while implementing their reforms. In addition, Zedillo decided to abandon some crucial powers – for example, handpicking governors and the next PRI electoral candidate. Fujimori decided instead to sideline democratic openings and undermine the formal institutional framework he inherited. Some of the unintended effects were the transfer of power to an opposition party and the effective initiation of a rule of law democracy in Mexico. In Peru, the end result was a significantly weakened presidency and an undermined formal institutional background. This chapter has striven to show other differences as well as similarities across and within outcomes. However, as Amartya Sen (2000) argues, in development, freedom is not only the ends, but also the means. In a deeper sense, probably in Mexico and Peru the divergence on this point is more than rhetorical, and reformers are indeed responsible for the choices they made: it is from this peculiar stuff that reforms – and their legacies – are made.

Notes

This chapter builds upon previous papers written with insights and cooperation from Jonathan Molinet, and his encouragement made it possible. I am also grateful for original conversations with Joe Foweraker at the University of Essex, as well as for comments at the Understanding Reform Seminars in Cairo (2002) and Delhi (2003), made there and subsequently by José María Fanelli and by other participants in the Latin American workshops within those seminars, and by the insightful editorial comments Barbara Stallings made to earlier versions of this document. Valuable comments and support were made by German Alarco, Patricia del Hierro (Universidad Panamericana, Mexico City), and David Mejia (Pontificia Universidad Católica del Perú), who provided guidance and research results which were particularly useful. The usual disclaimer applies.

1. This endogenous equilibrium approach to the rules of the game was pioneered in papers produced by Schotter (1981) and has been developed by Greiff (1994, 2002), Kreps et al. (1982), Greiff et al. (1994), Weingast (1997), Young (1998), and Aoki (1999, 2001), among others.

2. This equilibrium refers not only to the existing formal institutions, but the effective rules of the game. Thus, if bribing is prohibited in procurement, but no contract can be obtained without the previous payment of a bribe, then the institutional equilibrium solution corresponds to the domain of the bribing game between contracts and company officers.

3. We define meta-constitutional rules as those rules and attributions which are effectively followed and enjoyed by agents within the organizational domain but that do not have a written character. See Carpizo (1978) for an application to Mexico.

4. This, however, would affect the legitimacy of the mental agents emerging from the institutional equilibrium, while affecting its external financing and support.

5. In this context, the introduction of a new set of formal rules and regulatory agencies by the state can be viewed as nothing more than new data within the existing game – an exogenous variable affecting the game's equilibrium as the agents perceive it.

6. Coordination instances, however, can also provide an arena for corrupt practices: as Huntington (2006) would argue, in a transition period they are bound by neither the old set of rules, which is being replaced, nor by the new one, which is still being implemented.

7. Asking for the conditions upon which reforms can be started only partially answers this issue, as it focuses the question only on the subset of cases where reforms effectively induced the institutional change the reformers sought; the cases where outcomes other than those expected resulted would be regarded as failures. However, both are actually institutional changes if the whole institutional framework (formal and informal) is considered; the qualification of success or failure is only a further consideration.

8. The matching of the pact's agreements with fiscal policy, and its coordination with monetary policy were controlled from the Intersecretarial Committee on Income and Expenses. This was a commission created in the late 1970s to ensure expenditures matched revenues. It included the secretaries for finance, planning, and commerce, the Comptroller General and the Central Bank's president. This same commission had to approve specific privatizations, and provided input to the economic cabinet for the implementation of specific programs.

9. Among these were Jesus Silva Herzog and Gustavo Petricioli (SHCP), Carlos Salinas de Gortari (SPP), Alfredo del Mazo and Francisco Labastida Ochoa (SEMIP), Hector Hernández Cervantes (SECOFI), Daniel Diaz Diaz (SCT), Manuel Bartlett Diaz (SG), and Miguel Mancera Aguayo (BANXICO; who would remain there until the administration of Ernesto Zedillo). Close personnel were also placed in secretariats that were of importance for the reforms, such as Manuel Camacho Solis (SEDUE), Francisco Rojas Gutierrez and Ignacio Pichardo Pagaza (SECOGEF), see Garibaldi (2000).

10. Salinas (2003: 135). For a general view of the negotiation, see J. García Diego et al. (1994).
11. For a description of the most difficult negotiations, see Rubio (1992).
12. See Weintraub (1997).
13. These were (and remain) particularly strong in the state-owned enterprises' unions, which would combine in a single entity representation within the party, Congress, and the companies in which they worked. Due to its access to significant resources and political connections, opposition from the energy industry had proved a particular headache for the previous government.
14. At the time, Riding (1984) claimed Hernández had accumulated enough power to threaten and hijack the agenda of the three previous governments. After a trial for illegal weapons possession, he was sent to jail. While this action was condemned from the left, it drew significant approval from intellectuals and policy analysts.
15. These included monetary policy (with Banxico Mexico's Central Bank), banking (CNBV), communications (Cofetel), industrial property (IMPI), fiscal collection (SAT), retirement funds (Consar), energy (CRE), water (CNA), security (PFP), and other strategic areas such as the protection of savings (FOBAPROA).
16. Additionally, three other separate cabinets used to meet regularly: economic, social, and security.
17. The fiscal reform developed between 1989 and 1991 was enacted in three parts: the first was focused on the income tax regime, where the tax rates were lowered for firms and individuals. Additionally, the base income tax for individuals was indexed to the national consumer price index, whereas the income tax base for firms was adjusted to the national producer price index. Finally, fiscal administration was reformed and partially decentralized, with the objective of increasing the level of fiscal revenues, and there were changes in the audit and fiscal crimes prosecution areas, to avoid fiscal evasion. However, these latter modifications were not totally effective, and fiscal evasion remains a complex problem in today's Mexico.
18. See Statistical Annex, Ernesto Zedillo Ponce de León; 1er Informe de Gobierno (Zedillo, 1995: 45).
19. See Carlos Salinas de Gortari: Sexto Informe de Gobierno, Statistical Annex (Salinas, 2003: 63).
20. See World Bank (1996).
21. If the institutional framework of the decentralized agencies with technical and operational autonomy is reviewed, it can be seen that in their committees and decision boards it is clearly stated that decisions are binding for their successors; that new commission officers and even the president (of another force or party, for example) cannot change previous decisions as the rules only allow for the president to appoint a commissioner. However, in some of these commissions, the limit of appointment in these positions is not stipulated, thus limiting the possibility of removal. For a more detailed analysis of these commissions, see Molinet (2000).
22. In fact, 261 entities remained at the end of the Salinas period; however, only 70 were properly enterprises, while the others were public entities with no major productive activities.
23. See Secretary of Finance (SHCP) (1995: 43).
24. Eighteen banks were sold by public privatization, with the results (almost US$13 billion) going to the internal debt fund. Interest rates were liberalized, while two constitutional reforms were passed to increase Central Bank autonomy and increase social participation in the banking system.

25. This resulted from a dialogue between PRI and PAN (with the leftist Partido de la Revolución Democrática, PRD, finally declining to enter into an agreement). For these electoral reforms, see Woldenberg et al. (2000) and Nuñez (1994).
26. IFE included an executive council where PRI did not have the majority, and would later open new national electoral registries and electoral photo identifications as well as new rules for party financing.
27. As Salinas himself would put it: 'It was a double pincers tactic: in the political area, I formed a cabinet with politicians coming from different groups, from different geographical areas and different professions; in the economic area, I invited a coherent group of excellent professionals, with similar ideas and projects, and great political negotiation capacity' (Salinas, 2003: 1029).
28. While the real military threat posed by this revolt was negligible, its impact on the international image of Mexico was significant. Furthermore, it came at the time when the succession battle had already started, pitching (as the public saw it) Luis Donaldo Colosio against the officer that Salinas had nominated as the Chiapas negotiator, the former mayor of Mexico City and Colosio's rival, Manuel Camacho Solís.
29. While Colosio had a fluid relation with Pedro Aspe, the finance minister, Zedillo was his rival. Without support from the Colosio team (he was on his way out as campaign coordinator), he would also be bitterly opposed initially by Salinas's own opposition within PRI. This situation would have momentous consequences later, as we will see.
30. The three undersecretaries, as well as the *Procurador Fiscal* and the treasurer were removed. While massive second-tier changes occasionally happened, they rarely reached the third tier, that of the *Directores Generales*, 90 per cent of whom were also removed. In fact, the changes seemed to have continued up to the fifth level: in the aftermath of the removal, 70 directors and 179 subdirectors were also removed. So were directors at key positions in decentralized entities.
31. Initially, the incoming administration pretended to maintain the exchange rate band. However, as the ongoing attack on the peso made it obvious that this would be impossible, the usual consultations with the business sector backfired: the information obtained was employed to change pesos into dollars beforehand. Whatever the case, the peso moved immediately to the higher level of the band: it was effectively a devaluation. By January, the government announced a first and failed initial response, including a package (*Acuerdo de Unidad para Superar la Emergencia Económica*) with an exchange rate at 4.5 pesos on average and a US$14 billion commercial balance deficit, which would be followed by the announcement in February of US support for the peso, and a subsequent further stock exchange fall.
32. In fact, it was almost the reversal of the political crisis faced by Salinas at the beginning of his term, when political operatives were diminished: now, it was the turn for the technocrats.
33. The general sales tax did not become universal (it left food and medicines out of its coverage), although a new *Sistema de Administración Tributaria* (SAT) was introduced in 1995 (starting operations in 1997).
34. As this chamber had budgetary and fiscal functions, this change allowed opposition parties to demand budgetary and fiscal responsibilities that used to be in the hands of the administration. While the independence of the regulatory commissions assured long-term policy in key areas of the economy would remain along the lines advanced by the reforms, short-term fiscal policy required participation of groups not previously included in the technocratic and political mix which had developed since the late 1980s.

35. These included a reduced participation in the appointments of candidates to Congress, a judicial reform that enhanced the independence of the judicial system, a minimization of the presidential interventions in the appointments of governors, and above all the declining of the right to name a successor, which he announced years in advance.

36. This not only reduced the number of positions that the president could freely designate, but also changed the flows of circulation of personnel who were implicit in the system. The consequences of these changes were compounded by the officials' selection pattern in the Zedillo administration. During the terms of de la Madrid and Salinas, homogeneous teams with relatively short administrative careers had assured cohesion in the cabinet and sub-cabinet, but limited the fluidity and mobility in the rest of the levels of the federal public administration.

37. Fox's first cabinet included a majority of personnel that came not from the administration but from Congress, the academy, or the private sector. Unlike previous six-year terms, reaching the higher levels of government – the secretary and undersecretary positions – no longer depended on the careers followed within the administration; furthermore, the president was no longer chosen from within the cabinet, but from any of the political parties. This in practice eliminated the single access track to the presidency. This, coupled with Zedillo's disregard for one of the central rules of the system – the naming of his successor – meant that the secretaries were not second in the line of succession, and so on with the positions below.

38. This not only affected long-term incentives for human capital formation, but also reduced the number of possible games between the agents themselves, making the informal mechanisms of political coordination within the administration less effective.

39. For an overall view of the period, see Thorpe and Bertram (1978).

40. Income distribution and differential growth rates strained the existing institutional equilibrium. By the late 1960s, the lower 20 per cent received only 3.5 per cent of income (Webb, 1972); the modern–traditional division in the economy had been reinforced (Fitzgerald, 1976); the first sector produced in the late 1960s around 60 per cent of aggregate income, while employing 25 per cent of the working age population (ibid.: Appendix II). Finally, the population growth of the traditional sector was greater, thus contributing to the difference.

41. See Mallon (1995) and Thurner (1997).

42. In the mining sector, no new large mining sites had been discovered, and the exploration strategy depended mostly on foreign firms which had shown little interest in new exploration. Overfishing risks appeared (which would eventually materialize in 1972, as anchovy, the raw material for fish flour, was wiped out of the Peruvian sea), while the external markets for sugar and cotton entered into a dump. See Thorpe and Bertram (1978: Chapter 4, II section).

43. His cabinet could only be censured twice, and he enjoyed significant legislative authority; he could not only veto laws, but also under specific conditions issue emergency decrees with legal status, as well as legislative decrees, also with legal status, both subject to different degrees of authorization by Congress.

44. In fact, bundling agents within each of the major parties during the late 1970s and early 1980s (M.A. Mufarech in PPC, Andrés Townsend in APRA, and Hugo Blanco within IU) would become key in the intra-party and electoral arenas, as they could help broker the alliances across party (and group) lines needed to advance policies.

45. These data come from the National Income–Expenses Surveys conducted between 1985 and 1986 (ENNIV1986) and in 1990 (ENNIV1990).

46. As will be seen below, the tax administration faced significant corruption and morale problems, with extremely low salaries, a lax tax code, and a relatively large number of taxes, which however were collected only very partially.
47. García was not completely supportive of the presidential campaign of his rival within APRA, and possibly saw Fujimori as someone who could detract from FREDEMO and, if he won, act as an ally or even a possible puppet. See Tanaka (1998).
48. As Peru had ceased repaying debt in 1987, only paying arrears could provide fresh credit. This was impossible without external financial assistance. Furthermore, Fujimori lacked the leverage (and the experience) that allowed a Mexican president to manage pressure groups within the country. In his initial trip as a candidate-elect, he did not find any support for creation of a financial backing group, which could sustain a gradual adjustment, and was encouraged instead to follow a shock treatment.
49. The crisis left by Alan García had failed to pay public salaries, and diminished significantly the quality of the Peruvian administration. Additionally, one of Alan García's last actions had been to significantly increase the number of public employees and to protect these positions through a legal decree. Naturally, Fujimori distrusted the civil service he inherited.
50. While on the previous issues there was consensus, there was a significant debate with regard to the exchange rate. The debate centered on two options: employing the exchange rate as an anchor, or fixing a monetary target with a floating exchange rate. However, as credibility was low, employing a fixed exchange rate would have required significant overshooting, as well as the capacity to effectively sustain the rate over time.
51. As Dancourt (1999) notes, while a restrictive monetary policy sought to control inflation, fiscal policy counteracted these same effects. This is long if compared with other processes. In two similar cases, those of Argentina and Bolivia, the first one took only 4 months (April 1991 to September 1991), while the second one took 13 (August 1985 to September 1986). See Dancourt (1999: 49–70).
52. While most were developed at the Ministry of Economy, there were several which were drafted at the Instituto Libertad y Democracia, led by Hernando de Soto, from where Carlos Boloña had come.
53. These included Generals Fernández Dávila, Palomino, and Salinas Sedó, who would have taken control of the army as years went by if Fujimori had not taken action. Montesinos arranged for them to be removed or retired, together with all of the navy leadership as soon as Fujimori came into the presidency. Later on, a significant number of army cadres would, under the leadership of (the now retired) General Jaime Salinas Sedó stage a coup attempt in late 1992, which however was deactivated by the army's intelligence as the coup was taking place. See Rospigliosi (2000) for a more comprehensive view of military relations.
54. Those originally supportive of Fujimori's overall action plan, would become increasingly critical – and eventually lose power – after the rough treatment given to General Salinas Sedó and his group in the aftermath of the 1992 coup attempt, and after they lost the fight against Montesinos regarding the promotion procedures.
55. While Fujimori had 13 cabinets and 112 ministers – one cabinet approximately every 10 months on average – such fluidity hides some underlying patterns as to how power was handled. In fact, out of those 112 ministers, eight would stay more than five years in power, while around 20 would stay more than four years; out of these, 12 would serve in two or more positions. In the related military

arena, the head of the armed forces would remain in his position for eight years, something unheard of in Peru, where the position traditionally lasted only one year. See Mejia (2003) for more details.

56. See Tanaka (1998: Chapter 5).
57. These provided protection for economic competition, gave priority to monetary stability, emphasized consumer rather than productive activities, provided additional protection to foreign investment (and particularly, to international financial transactions), and scrapped the previous constitution's 'programmatic' guarantees on full employment, housing, and health, calling for the state only to orient developments in these areas.
58. But not within its party system: Fujimori's original basis of support (Cambio 90), was to lose any power it might have had on its own after the coup.
59. This resulted from the first five years under the 1979 constitution (which he claimed he completed in 1995), his *first* term under the 1993 constitution (to which terms he argued he was elected under the 1995 elections), and his *second* term under the 1993 constitution (which he claimed started after the initially successful 2000 re-election). For a complete view of this argument, see Bustamante Belaúnde (2003: 10–21).
60. Private participation in infrastructure was also enhanced. Legislative decree no. 758 (with a further Law on Infrastructure and Public Services following in 1996) allowed the state (at any level) to provide concessions in infrastructure to the private sector.
61. Muñoz in Abusada (2003).
62. Fujimori presented a Fiscal Transparency Law, which sought to force the Executive to maintain fiscal equilibrium, restricting deficits to no more than 1 per cent after 2002, as well as a budget framework, which established how the annual budget would be managed. Additionally, a fiscal stabilization fund was created with the resources coming from the privatization process. This was however, only implemented partially (Abusada, 2003: 115).
63. This was particularly so by Absalon Vasquez, Fujimori's most influential agriculture minister, in charge of extreme poverty groups and government proselytizing. See Mejia (2003).
64. This included a major reorientation of the Peruvian state's intelligence apparatus: while previously it had been deployed mostly to intercept calls and gather intelligence on the opposition parties and (marginally) on the armed forces, now it was used almost exclusively to spy on the Executive's operation itself as well as key media, army, and political party members. Additionally, a major increase in funding, scope, and technological capacity was achieved, with a massive telephone interception capacity, which was used basically to bolster both Fujimori's re-election chances and to ensure Montesinos's control over his parallel network. For a detailed analysis of the expansion of the intelligence services within the armed forces, see Rospigliosi (2000).
65. See the memoirs of the two last prime minister's during Fujimori's second term, which show how they had to visit Montesinos to negotiate both appointments for their cabinets and policy measures, the practice of which was forbidden by law but nevertheless real. See Salas (2001) and Bustamante Belaúnde (2003).
66. Continuous video recording of all policy transactions created hostage relationships with other groups, while other agents had little if any way of checking their power.
67. After the success of the Japanese Embassy takeover (1998), Montesinos was successful in forcing the separation of General Nicolas de Bari Hermoza, the head of the joint chiefs of staff, from the armed forces joint command. General Hermoza

had controlled promotions, career advancements, and his own power base expansion within the army; he had resisted becoming an intelligence service group agent; his retirement removed threats to the emerging pattern of authority within the armed forces.

68. See Apoyo Surveys, El Poder en el Peru, 1998, 1999, Lima.

69. These included a meeting Montesinos forced upon the US antidrug czar, Barry MacCaffrey, photographs of which were later released to the press, and a press conference on Montesinos's efforts to derail an arms trade negotiation with Colombian guerillas. However, MacCaffrey publicly complained a few days later about the meeting and the arrangement of an unprepared and unwelcome meeting with Montesinos; and the Peruvian press later showed that Montesinos himself had been involved in the Colombian arms deal.

70. The intelligence service's reliance on video recordings later provided evidence of the extent of its media control – all open signal TV, most of the established national newspapers, and all newly created newspapers. Almost ten new newspapers were created with the sole purpose of influencing elections. For a complete analysis of the videos, see the Proceedings of the Congress Investigative Commission on Corruption, Peruvian Congress, 2001.

71. See Gonzáles Arica (2001) and Dammert (2002). It should also be noted that the constitutional court had been closed since 1992, with its members being forced into silence.

72. In both cases, these derived from the debt crisis, while the rise (or collapse) of central primary export commodity prices hid the potential for significant losses. Finally, there were losses derived from the accumulated inefficiencies of a closed market.

73. Fujimori sought to take the means provided to the president by the 1979 constitution to both advance his policies and increase his legitimacy. In particular, as Tanaka (1998) notes, he seems to have focused on (i) using Supreme Emergency decrees and legislative delegation to advance key policies – concerted opposition would only prove Fujimori's point on the 'obstructionist' nature of party politics, and enhance the overall legitimacy of his argument; (ii) avoiding an opposition block by engaging in alliances with parties upon different topics, and (iii) bypassing FREDEMO parties to directly contact their support groups, key for his economic strategy.

74. In both countries, the organized groups of 'winners' arising from the loosely regulated or 'informal' situation did not destroy losing groups, but rather offered them integration under the winner's leadership in the future (a strategy followed by Salinas in Mexico and by Montesinos in Peru). For an analysis of this sort of strategy, see Charap and Harm (1999).

75. Thus, lower level formal institutions were embedded in higher level institutional arrangements; these in turn tended to reflect the relative ranks of the policy games played within each arena and their use of the last resort enforcement mechanism, access to the president and/or ultimate arbiter in each domain. For an analysis of this sort of strategy, see López Presa and Garibaldi (1998) or Garibaldi (1999a).

76. For Peru, see Rospigliosi (2000) and Degregori (2000). For Mexico, see López Presa and Garibaldi (1999), Zaid (1995), and Garibaldi (1999a).

6
The Predatory State and Economic Reform: an Examination of Paraguay's Political Economic Transition

Donald G. Richards and Dionisio Borda

6.1   Introduction

The central proposition of this study is that successful policy reform in Paraguay has been impeded by a lack of necessary institutional prerequisites. When the reform process started at the beginning of the 1990s existing institutions could neither protect the property rights of actual and potential investors, provide political stability nor ensure that political elites faced effective, formal constraints on their behavior. Neither could these same institutions promote the participation of a broad cross-section of society in either the formal economy or in the political life of the nation.

The puzzle is why Paraguay operated with a set of mostly dysfunctional institutions. A satisfactory solution to this puzzle requires a brief analysis of Paraguay's political history to show how key events contributed to the failure to build appropriate institutions to facilitate successful policy reforms.[1] Our argument is that Paraguay's institutions reflect a combination of factors that are part and parcel of its historical inheritance. This inheritance is marked by authoritarian personalities, two bloody wars, and a political culture where interpersonal relations based on familial ties, friendship, and partisan allegiances prevailed regularly over impersonal relationships, rules, and obligations. We further argue that the Stroessner dictatorship (1954–89) is an exemplary model of what social scientists recently have described as a *predatory state* (PS). We shall see that the PS is largely responsible for the failure of the country to grow and to establish development-promoting institutions. The reform process initiated in the 1990s was a failure largely because it never properly took account of the institutional inheritance of the Stroessner era. Moreover, it overestimated the technical capabilities and commitment of the Paraguayan bureaucracy as well as the ability of civil society to hold the state accountable for the manner in which the reforms were implemented and carried out. In other words, the reform process undertaken in the 1990s presupposed the kinds of institutions characteristic of a development state rather than a predatory one.

After establishing the character and operation of the PS in Paraguay, we shall examine how it limited the effectiveness of several market reform initiatives including those associated with international trade, monetary and exchange rate policies, public finance, and state-owned enterprises (SOEs). At the root of these policy failures, it is shown, are similarly limited reforms of the nation's key state policy institutions as well as its stunted civil society.

6.2 The predatory state

Theory of the predatory state

A predatory state (PS) is understood as one that sets policy and exercises power not in the interests of promoting the social welfare of its broad citizenry, but rather in serving the interests of those who wield direct power, that is, the ruler himself and those closest to him.

It needs to be emphasized that there is no necessary contradiction between the exercise of power by a predatory state and the possibility of economic growth and (limited) development. Much depends on the circumstances under which official predation takes place. At the same time, however, it is generally recognized that the chances for growth and development are substantially reduced in the presence of a PS. In the specific case of Paraguay, we shall see that the PS is largely responsible for the failure of the country to grow and to establish development-promoting institutions. The thirty-five year rule of Stroessner established a definite path-dependency for Paraguay's subsequent political economy that continues to account for its relative economic stagnation and its continuing fragility as a democracy.

Theories of the PS have been developed from distinct social science perspectives. One strain of the theory sees the PS as a rational, calculating actor that makes decisions aimed at maximizing its own utility function. Much the same, of course, could be claimed about any state, depending on how one defines its utility function and the constraints that bind it. What distinguishes the PS from other types of state is the narrowness of its welfare function. Specifically the utility function of the typical PS is confined to the consumption of the elites in whose service the state operates, as well as the desire of the state to maintain power.[2]

An alternative view of the PS derives from Peter Evans (1989, 1995) who contrasts the predatory state to the developmental state. Evans does not necessarily reject the insights into the character of some aspects of PS behavior provided by the rational choice school. Accounts that rely exclusively on the alleged utility maximizing behavior of individual state agents, however, are inadequate in his estimation. Evans (1989) argues instead that under the appropriate historical circumstances a state may emerge wherein individual behavior is constrained by collective goals.

Central to the positive developmental function of the capitalist state is the role played by a professional bureaucracy that is committed to a corporatist, rather than an individualistic, vision of its mission. This mission is seen as complementary and supportive of the private accumulative activities of capital, without being capable of capture by capitalist interests in particular, or by the capitalist class as a whole. There is no presumption made by Evans that a fixed recipe exists to guide the developmental state. The examples he offers of existing developmental states include the so-called 'newly industrializing countries' (NICs), defined broadly enough to include Brazil and India as well as the East Asian states (1995: 11).

We might enquire here as to the nature of the set of social ties that binds the state to society referred to by Evans. Certainly the presence or absence of these social ties is key to the characterization of a state at the extremes of the developmental-predatory continuum. The predatory state, argues Evans, is precisely characterized by the absence of such ties. In their place exist only personal ties that link the predatory dictator, or elite, to other individuals or groups who seek some advantage by the relationship. Particularly lacking is anything akin to the Weberian bureaucracy.

Some working hypotheses

The following hypotheses (H1–H4) regarding the predatory state can be proposed as a guide to our study of the historical and contemporary experience of Paraguay.

The predatory state is more likely to emerge under the following particular historical static conditions (H1):

- There is a high concentration in the loci of power (S1).
- There exists an abundance of opportunities for the exploitation of rent havens (S2).
- Civil society institutions are weak (S3).
- The costs of monitoring opponents and enforcing regime rules are low (S4).
- The emerging PS operates under conditions of relative international autarky (S5).

Condition (S1) is useful insofar as the instruments of coercion and co-optation are most efficiently employed when they are concentrated in the hands of a tight-knit elite. This reduces the risk that they could be used at cross-purposes. Coordination problems in general are reduced when power is narrowly held. Finally, the risks of cheating are reduced when power is concentrated.

Condition (S2) increases the chances that a PS will emerge, inasmuch as predation of available rents is the sine qua non of such a state.

Condition (S3) advances the historical likelihood of a PS insofar as it suggests the absence of a counterweight to the exercise of the state's power. The existence of strong civil society institutions may act to challenge the continued viability of a state dedicated to predation. Weak civil society institutions then enhance the risks of predatory state behavior.

Condition (S4) is connected to conditions (S1) and (S3). The rational choice perspective suggests that predatory state behavior will be preferred to other models insofar as it yields larger expected returns. There is a strong emphasis, therefore, on reducing as far as possible the costs associated with state maintenance and defending its ability to collect rents. Monitoring opponents is important since it reduces the probability of regime change. Enforcing regime rules provides the regime order and stability. Low costs of enforcement allow for efficient capture and distribution of rents. If the potential opposition from civil society is weak and easily controlled, and if the state's powers of coercion and co-optation are strong and well organized, then the associated transaction costs will be low.

Relative international autarky, static condition (S5), reduces or eliminates the likelihood that a challenge to the PS will emanate from abroad. Limited external (political and economic) linkages reduce the impact of the state's predatory behavior on its geographical neighbors. If the state's predatory actions can be ignored at a small cost by its neighbors, then the chances of intervention by the latter are reduced.

Likewise, a condition of relative autarky in the financial sense is supportive to the emergence and functioning of the PS. Insofar as a country is independent of external sources of capital, or international financial institutions, it will have much more latitude in its operations and a correspondingly stronger ability to hold off challenges to its authority.

The stability of the predatory state depends on the continued maintenance of the five conditions described above (H2).

This requires that the following several dynamic conditions also be met:

- As new actors and organizations emerge who represent a potential threat to the organizational effectiveness of the PS and its continued ability to generate rewards, they must be co-opted or repressed. New actors and organizations are likely to emerge as a result of underlying structural changes in the political economy such as demographic shifts or technical change (D1).
- Opportunities for the exploitation of existing rent havens must not be exhausted, or they must be replaced by new opportunities. In this regard, a PS based on the exploitation of finite, non-renewable natural resources, for example, faces definite limits to its ability to continue to function. Rent opportunities, however, are not limited to natural resources. As economic theory has amply demonstrated, they may exist on the basis of other structural conditions of the political economy including a variety of market imperfections. Structural change can obviously destroy given rent havens, but it also may create the basis for others. The continued viability of the PS

will depend on its ability to respond to new opportunities for the generation of rents as well its ability to distribute them in a manner that ensures the integrity of the institutional coalition on which its power is based (D2).

- Structural change also provides the opportunity for the emergence of new civil society institutions. Urbanization, for example, provides greater opportunities for popular organizations to grow and develop that seek to challenge the prerogatives of the PS. They may present a variety of economic and political demands that call into question both the ability of the PS to accumulate and distribute rents and the state's political legitimacy. The inability of the PS to meet these demands, and to control the organizations, may result in a crisis that undermines its continued ability to function and a political transition to a post-PS regime. It becomes clear then that crisis presents both challenge as well as opportunity for effective policy reform. The effectiveness of policy, however, will require the emergence of new institutions that promote and sustain pro-development reforms (D3).

The predatory state operates as an obstacle to the emergence of the development state when (H3):

- It prevents the development of a (Weberian) bureaucracy (R1).
- It constrains the development of civil society institutions (R2).
- It slows the accumulation of social capital (R3).

As the predatory state relies on tight control over both resources and decision-making authority, it is inimical to the development of a relatively autonomous, professional bureaucracy. The absence of such a bureaucracy constrains development by distorting the state's resource allocation choices as well as denying it the opportunity to accumulate and use technical expertise. As North (1990: 78) has argued, the institutional framework of a society, of which the state is an essential part, will shape the direction of acquisition of knowledge and skills. That direction will be the decisive factor for the long-run development of society. The predatory state, and the institutional structure of which it is a part and which it promotes, operates against the acquisition of knowledge and skills typical of a society that seeks to promote production-based maximization strategies. Rather it promotes the acquisition of knowledge and skills that promote maximization strategies based on the exploitation of rent opportunities.

In constraining the development of civil society institutions the PS limits the development of potential sources of opposition to its own functioning. It limits, therefore, the development of sources of political balance that serve to counteract the abuse of the state's political power. It also limits the development of sources of entrepreneurial imagination and risk-taking that are the essence of capitalist development.

Finally, in serving as a model of predation, the PS inhibits the development of social capital that, along with the rule of law, provides the integrating material of social life. Predatory behavior may become diffuse at all levels of society when it is the basis of official behavior. Ordinary citizens may eschew production in favor of non-productive activities. Tax avoidance and evasion may come to be seen as acceptable. Political participation will be limited to those who derive direct benefits from such involvement. Cynicism and skepticism will become the dominant attitudes towards the public realm in general. Individuals of talent will avoid careers in public service, placing additional obstacles in the way of creating either an effective political leadership or a professional bureaucracy.

When the above-described conditions for the maintenance of the predatory state are not met, there is likely to occur a state of crisis leading to political transition. The fact of political transition itself, however, is not necessarily sufficient for the success of policy reforms that economists often cite as the keys to economic growth and development. This then lead us to a fourth hypothesis to apply to our analysis of reform in Paraguay.

Successful policy reform requires appropriate institutions, including those associated with the state itself (H4).

Such appropriate institutions are characteristic of the development state. The lack of these institutions, on the other hand, provides a definite brake on the pace and depth of economic reform possibilities. At a minimum, successful policy reform in a nation seeking to make a transition from a PS must seek to promote: (1) greater diversity in the loci of power; (2) greater support for the development of civil society institutions; and (3) greater and more diversified exposure to the external political economy. Each of these elements will be recognized as mechanisms that challenge the monopoly position held by the PS, or its lingering institutional elements, over the instruments of power. Each can also be understood as a potential source of new energy and ideas directed at a new wealth-generating orientation for the economy in place of the traditional emphasis on the generation and distribution of rents. Only with such an orientation for the economy can we expect traditional policy reform measures such as tax reform, exchange rate reform, and financial sector reform to be effective in achieving their desired ends.

6.3 The predatory state in Paraguay

The five (static) conditions underlying the emergence of Paraguay's PS can be traced to its post-colonial history, which established a political culture of strong patrimonial rule.

The legacy of nationalist pride and integrity associated with the dictatorships of Dr Rodriguez de Francia (1814–40), Carlos Antonio Lopez (1841–62), and Francisco Solano Lopez (1862–70) was brought to an end after the devastating and brutal defeat of Paraguay in the war of the Triple Alliance against Argentina,

Brazil, and Uruguay (1865–70).[3] The result of the defeat included an abandonment of the process of political and economic institutionalization that might have transformed Paraguay into a modern state. From 1870 onwards, the country experienced continuous political instability and *'caudillismo'*, led by the two traditional parties (Colorados and Liberals) that alternated in power until 1954.

Between 1932 and 1935 Paraguay fought another devastating war, the Chaco War against Bolivia (1932–35) for control over the Chaco region bordering the two countries. This time Paraguay was more successful in defending its territorial integrity, but again at the cost of a substantial portion of its population, especially males. The Liberal era came to end in 1947 as a result of civil war that once again took its toll on the nation's population, either in the form of casualties or forced exile from the country.

As a result of the wars of the Triple Alliance and Chaco, the revolution of 1947 and the opportunistic behavior of politicians, the basis for a predatory state was developed (H1). The sense of national vulnerability resulting from the two wars, a small population heavily concentrated in the central zone of the country around the capital (Asunción), and a sharp imbalance in the geographical distribution of cultural and natural resources caused the country to develop a strong centralist tradition without regional tiers of government and with a very weak system of local government. The traditions of authoritarianism (*mbareté*) and submission (*ñembotavy*) characteristic of patron–client relationships facilitated rent-seeking behavior among politicians and established deeply ingrained habits of corruption in public administration. Moreover, as result of the revolution of 1947, a new vertically integrated, tripartite power bloc emerged in Paraguay. This bloc consisted of the executive, the armed forces, and the Colorado Party. At the head of this bloc sat an army officer by the name of Alfredo Stroessner, who would prove adept enough at politico-administrative manipulation eventually to assume near total control of the governing apparatus. In May 1954 Stroessner initiated his reign as the longest dictatorship in Paraguay's history.

The Stroessner dictatorship constitutes a near perfect case study of the predatory state. The dictator wielded near monopoly control over the nation's economic, political, and coercive resources during his long tenure (S1). The central government, for example, was a monopolist distributor of large tracts of land along the thinly settled border areas with Brazil (S2). While the distribution of these lands was used to generate revenues for the state, it played an equally important role in solidifying political relationships among and between the triad of institutions that provided the dictatorship with its stabilizing base – the Colorado Party, the military, and the presidency.

The Colorado Party was controlled by purging major political rivals within the party, repressing and discriminating against opposition members, and by managing a system of pay-offs to ensure loyalty to the regime. This system reached its highest expression in the late 1960s and 1970s, a period in which

Stroessner was able to invest in infrastructure, for example, highways and dams, which enabled the elites of these key institutions, mainly party members, to derive large fortunes.

The Colorado Party was instrumental in the management of potential conflict within the PS. The party was a vertically organized political machine particularly efficient at managing Paraguay's countryside. Local government organizations were invariably controlled by party officers and supported by the police and military. These party personnel were themselves in the service of state-level bosses functioning under the Colorado umbrella who, in turn, answered up the line to party leaders at the national level. At the top of the party pyramid sat Alfredo Stroessner dispensing patronage and terror throughout the network. In the language of neoclassical economics, the Colorado Party functioned as an efficient mechanism by which to reduce the transaction costs associated with the predatory state (S4). All state employees, including members of the armed forces, and even workers in private companies belonging to the regime's supporters, were forced to be party members. Hence, the Colorado Party developed into a powerful instrument of repression, civil control, and immobilization of the population.

The stability of the PS under the dictatorship must also be understood in relation to the larger regional context of which it was a part. As noted earlier, Paraguay historically pursued a policy of autonomy relative to its Southern Cone neighbors (S5). Its conservative leaders, going back to Francia, never had large development ambitions. The country did not pursue either industrial or urban development projects in the same manner as its neighboring states. Correspondingly, growth in Paraguayan civil society had been constrained. Independent labor unions and peasant organizations failed to develop either to defend the civil and economic interests of the masses or to present a source of popular opposition to the dictator (S3).

It is important to recognize the extremely favorable constraints under which the Stroessner regime operated. The nation's population had been sufficiently reduced by wars and emigration as to endow the nation with a comparatively high land to man ratio, especially by Latin American standards. These same factors also mitigated potential pressure for either industrialization and/or urbanization. Such conditions operated very favorably to provide the nation with a long period of apparent political calm which it desperately sought in the aftermath of the turbulence of the preceding several decades.

External circumstances also played an important role in accounting for the relative tranquility enjoyed by the Paraguayan dictatorship between the years 1954 and 1989. Argentina and Brazil, the dominant and often competing economies in the Southern Cone region, enjoyed robust economic growth until the early 1980s, fueled in part by import substitution industrialization drives. Argentina in the 1960s provided an outlet not only for Paraguayan political dissidents, but also served as a safety valve to release the pressure created by Paraguayan landlessness and/or unemployment. Despite a minifundia/latifundia (small holdings/large holdings) structure of land distribution to rival any other in Latin America, Paraguay did not face corresponding political opposition based on contracting employment opportunities. Rather, land ownership decisions could be more strategically settled by the dictatorship in ways that cemented the patron–client ties between the dictator and Colorado Party chiefs.

In general, the commitment of the state's resources and the exploitation of the nation's natural resource endowment followed a predatory rather than a developmental logic. As long as there existed an abundance of such opportunities relative to the demands made on them by the key constituents and agents of the PS, the state was able to successfully manage any potential challenge to its rule. Little effort was expended to increase the productivity of the masses of small agricultural holders, for example. While some effort was made to relocate small-scale cultivators to the relatively under-populated regions outside the nation's central department, support services were inadequate and the lack of land titles made ownership claims tenuous.

Instability in Paraguay's PS

As established under H2, to maintain its stability the predatory state must have the ability to maintain the five conditions described under H1. Since new stakeholders and civil society institutions are likely to emerge as a result of underlying structural changes in the political economy, such as demographic shifts or technical change, the PS must have the ability (D1) to co-opt or repress emerging new stakeholders and organizations, (D2) maintain or replace opportunities for the exploitation of rent havens, and (D3) meet new political and economic demands. We argue here that by the 1980s the ability of the Stroessner regime to maintain these dynamic conditions was seriously weakened.

Certainly, by the middle of the twentieth century when Stroessner came to power, the PS sought to turn its historical and geographic paths to best use. Rather than promote development, Paraguay's leadership sought to take advantage of a set of geographical circumstances that otherwise constrained its economic autonomy. The construction of the east–west highway referred to earlier, for example, reduced Paraguay's historical dependency on Argentina while promoting its economic and political relations with a rapidly growing Brazil. The rapid rates of growth and development in neighboring Argentina, and later Brazil, served Paraguay as an outlet for the latter's unemployed (Richards, 1987) as well as its agricultural surplus. Exports of cotton and soybeans in the 1970s and 1980s propelled Paraguay to among Latin America's economic growth leaders during these decades (Richards, 1994).

There is no necessary contradiction between the facts of Paraguay's high absolute and relative growth rates during this period and the state's essentially predatory behavior. The search for and extraction of rents by state and private sector actors did not preclude entirely productive private sector activity.

In an important sense the predatory state encouraged economic growth, especially in the agro-export and construction sectors of the economy. The ill consequences of the PS, however, revealed themselves in the extreme imbalance of the resulting growth, its limited and temporary impact on the economy's structure, its failure to impart productivity-increasing linkages to the rest of the economy, and its failure to alleviate absolute and relative poverty.[4]

It was during the 1980s that the limits to the dictator's predatory strategy became apparent. By this time the dams had been constructed and the agricultural frontier had been reached. The realization of these limits meant a drying up of important sources of benefits to be shared between the state and its agents and constituents. Growing restlessness among the country's landless peasant class erupted into more frequent conflicts with large landowners. Table 6.1 provides a summary of the sources of exploitable rent opportunities available to the PS and the rough dates over which they operated effectively as a source of political leverage.[5]

The external situation was also changing in ways that made it more difficult for Paraguay's predatory state to maintain political stability. Economic crisis in the region meant a dwindling demand for Paraguayan labor in the traditional centers of attraction for migrant workers. The large cities in Argentina, for example, could no longer play the role of a political economy safety valve as they had done in previous decades. Political crisis in the region also meant the transition from authoritarian to democratic rule in both Argentina and Brazil, and these changes could not be ignored in Paraguay.

Table 6.1:   Major types of rent havens and their periods of effectiveness

Type of resource	Description	Period of effectiveness
Land	Distribution and settlement of lands along country's eastern frontier regions	From creation of the Instituto de Bienestar Rural (IBR) in 1963 until early 1980s
Dam construction	Contracts related to the construction of the Itaipu Dam along the Brazilian border and the Yacyreta Dam on the border with Argentina	Itaipu construction, 1973–83 Yacyreta construction, 1983–94
Contraband trade	Smuggling of illegal imports and exports including money, illegal drugs, and arms	Continuously during the period of the predatory state
State-owned enterprises	Use of SOEs as a means of dispensing patronage	Continuously since the establishment of SOEs and up through the period of privatization in the 1990s

A particularly momentous political development in the region was the formation of the *Mercado Comun del Cono Sur* (MERCOSUR) in 1991. This common market initiative began as a bilateral effort between Argentina and Brazil, but soon was broadened to include Uruguay and Paraguay. The latter, smaller, countries pressed for membership as they could hardly afford to stand outside an agreement that included the two largest trading countries and markets in the region.

Under the combined weight of changing internal and external circumstances – changes that radically altered both the PS's control over resources and the contending potential claimants on those resources – the dictator could not maintain stability. Paraguay's own transition therefore was inevitable. Once the predatory state had exhausted the rents associated with the activities enumerated in Table 6.1, it could not reward the military and party elites and, consequently, could not maintain control over the party and the armed forces. By the end of the 1980s the dissatisfaction of army officers, the disenchantment of business sectors, the increasing international support for democracy and, after the mid-1980s, an awakening of civil society, backed notably by the Roman Catholic Church, added to the mounting economic frustration. All these factors contributed to the momentum that ended with the *coup d'état* that toppled the dictatorship in February 1989. From this point the country began to consider a package of reforms and initiatives oriented to democratizing the country and to building a developmental state.

The predatory state as an obstacle to the development state

As stated in H3, the predatory state operates as an obstacle to the emergence of the development state when it prevents the development of an efficient bureaucracy, constrains the development of civil society institutions and slows the accumulation of social capital.

Unfortunately, the same failure of civil society to develop effective organizational and institutional challenges to the PS inhibited the emergence of the institutions necessary for sustained economic growth and development. The reform proposals and initiatives of the 1990s suffered precisely from the lack of these institutions. Thus, the institutional legacy of the dictatorship lingered on after the fall of the dictator. Not only did Paraguay fail to develop the kinds of state bureaucratic institutions characteristic of the developmental state, but those features – including the habits of thought – typical of the predatory state continued to operate.

Two pillars of the predatory triad, the Colorado Party and the military, continued to dominate the political process during the transition period. In fact, the *coup d'état* that overthrew General Alfredo Stroessner was triggered by divisions over the spoils of government among the Colorado elite and the dissatisfaction of junior army officers. The reform process initiated in February 1989 faced not only the challenge of democratizing the country, an experience practically without historical precedent in Paraguay, but also of modernizing and decoupling the state apparatus and the Colorado Party. Considering the fact that the transition to democracy was led by the same political structure established by Stroessner, the reform process faced the enormous challenge of calling for new actors that could effectively carry it out.

The administration of General Andres Rodríguez was characterized by significant vertical control. Rodríguez's government established basic democratic institutions through an electoral reform and a rewriting of the national constitution in 1992 which called for presidential and parliamentary elections in the following year. The limits of the transition, however, became quite evident in the months preceding the 1993 presidential elections. The ruling establishment made massive use of state resources and warned public employees that they would lose their jobs if they did not vote for the Colorado Party. Similarly, sectors within the military indicated that they would not accept a Colorado defeat.

Despite victories by the Colorado Party in the three presidential elections held after 1989, new claimants to the social product have emerged at a time when economic growth has decelerated. The predatory party has been no more able than the predatory dictator to promote productivity improvements in established lines of economic activity, promote new lines of activity, or to help develop new external markets.[6] The elected governments have been forced to satisfy an increasing demand for benefits and patronage precisely when the old sources of these benefits were drying up. These demands have been met by excessive growth in public sector employment and correspondingly larger fiscal imbalances.

6.4　The impulse to reform in Paraguay

The impulse to reform in Paraguay derived from both political and economic factors. The political factors were largely tied to the regime change of 1989. While it is fair to say that the removal of the Stroessner dictatorship was widely welcomed by Paraguayan society, it is equally true that the new postdictatorial transition regimes were faced with the problem of establishing their own legitimacy. Bicanic et al. (2005) discuss the relationship between legitimacy and reform. In their interpretation legitimacy is a prerequisite to the execution and success of reform initiatives. In the case of Paraguay, by contrast, it could well be argued that reform initiatives were a means by which the transition regime could acquire legitimacy for itself.

The political climate both within and outside of the Southern Cone region during the late 1980s and 1990s was rife with reform. Brazil and Argentina, for example, had recently commenced the process of their own democratic transitions as well as structural reforms of their economies. Similar processes were also in the offing in Eastern Europe and the Soviet Union. Support for the authoritarian model of rule was disappearing at a pace that even the Paraguayan military and Colorado Party could not ignore. It seemed inevitable that any regime that hoped to claim the mantle of legitimacy in the eyes of the rest of the world would have to wrap itself in the rhetorical cloak of reform.

The problem of political legitimacy at the domestic level was complicated by the desire of certain elements of the Paraguayan military to retain partial, or total, control of the political machinery. Paraguay's post-coup constitution required that members of the armed forces withdraw from membership in the Colorado Party. This requirement was deemed unacceptable to a portion of the military hierarchy headed by General Lino Cesar Oviedo who supported a civilian, Juan Carlos Wasmosy, in the 1993 elections.[7] Wasmosy was elected president, but then had to walk a delicate political tightrope – enforcing the constitution on the one hand by limiting military involvement in politics, while on the other hand limiting the obvious political ambitions of his military patrons. This balancing act predictably failed in April 1996 when Oviedo attempted a military coup. The coup was unsuccessful but Oviedo retained a considerable degree of support among the *militante* faction of the Colorado Party until his subsequent exit to Brazil in 1999. He fled Paraguay in order to escape prosecution on charges for his alleged involvement in the assassination of Vice President Luis Argana.

Paraguay also suffered from mounting economic crisis at the time of and immediately after the 1989 coup. As shown in Table 6.2, economic growth had sharply decelerated from the high rates of the 1970s and early 1980s. Correspondingly, rates of open unemployment were on the rise.

A strong contributory factor to the deceleration of the Paraguayan economy in the 1980s was the completion of the construction of the hydroelectric project at Itaipu. The sheer size of Itaipu in relation to the Paraguayan economy is impressive. Its construction costs between 1973 and 1983 are estimated to have been four times Paraguay's GDP (Valdovinos and Naranjo, 2004). The ratio of Itaipu-related investment to total Paraguayan investment reached nearly 140 per cent at its peak in 1978 (Paez, 2001).

The completion of the dam construction resulted in a sharp deceleration in external finance and foreign exchange. Public and external deficits were growing without a corresponding increase in external finance. According to Borda (1997: 134), in the months leading up to the 1989 coup, the central

Table 6.2: Economic growth and unemployment, 1974–93 (average annual rates, %)

	1974–77	1978–81	1982–85	1986–89	1990–93
Growth of GDP	8.3	10.5	0.8	4.2	2.7
Growth of GDP per capita	5.1	6.5	−2.3	1.1	−0.2
Unemployment	6.1[a]	4.0	6.6	5.6	10.7

Note: [a] Data are for 1976–77 only.
Sources: Calculated from data provided by Borda (1997) and *Statistical Abstract of Latin America* (various issues).

bank had warned the public of an impending foreign exchange crisis. The Rodríguez government reacted to the impending crisis by executing a reform agenda which, while necessary from the perspective of short-run macroeconomic stabilization, fell far short of serving the goals of structural adjustment, long-run growth, and/or poverty alleviation. The centerpiece of this reform involved the elimination of a distortionary regime of fixed exchange rates. While this had the beneficial effect of increasing returns to the traded goods sector (for example, cotton and soybeans) it did little to control inflation. Neither was it a real solution to the nation's growing debt problem. As is apparent from the data provided by Table 6.3, the elimination of exchange market distortions helped borrowers service their external obligations, but only at a cost of borrowing heavily from the central bank (Borda, 1997: 134–5).

The growing belief that Paraguay was in need of economic reform extended to her external economic constituencies – such as foreign creditors and multinational development agencies – and further underscored the need to at least *appear* to be committed to the goals of a reform agenda. Given the growing fiscal and internal debt crises, policy-makers were faced with an imperative to attract new capital from any and all sources. International financial institutions such as the IMF, World Bank, and Inter-American Development Bank were increasingly calling for a variety of reforms that would reduce the size of the state's role in the economy. These included measures that would liberalize trade, eliminate domestic price distortions, reduce government spending, reform the tax system, and accelerate the process of privatization of state-owned enterprises.

As Rius and van de Walle (2005) note, external pressure can be a tenuous basis from which to launch a reform initiative. Insofar as the domestic agents of the reform are not fully 'on-board' with both the intermediate and ultimate goals of the reform package, there is increased danger that the effort will get stuck at the *de jure* level. The outcome of the process may involve a certain

Table 6.3: International trade and finance indicators, 1989–93

	1989	1990	1991	1992	1993
Inflation (%)	28.5	44.1	11.8	17.8	20.5
Exchange rate (guarani/US$)	1,144	1,230	1,325	1,499	1,753
International reserves ($m)	447	675	975	573	700
Foreign debt ($m)	2,076	1,700	1,758	1,249	1,227
Registered exports ($m)	1,009	959	713	649	727
Trade balance ($m)	348	−235	−538	−581	−372
Fiscal surplus/GNP (%)	2.4	4.6	1.8	0.9	0.3
Central bank credit to the public sector ($m)	136	374	264	1,038	1,183

Source: Borda (1997).

amount of cosmetic change designed to appease external aid providers but lack a real commitment to the kind or level of change that is necessary to realize more fundamental objectives. That is to say, externally motivated reforms may face a serious constraint of political will.

Notwithstanding a clear need for a reorientation of the Paraguayan political economy, the transition regimes that came to power were ultimately no more dedicated or better equipped to pursue economic development and sustainable economic growth than their autocratic predecessor. Transition politics was far more about state capture than it was about building state capacity.[8] Talk of economic reform became a standard expectation of Paraguayan politicians, even among those who fully intended to pursue public office in the anticipation of harvesting and distributing rents in the traditional clientelist fashion. Such talk, however, was understood more as a means of obtaining immediate electoral legitimacy than as a true expression of a mandate for the goals of a reform aimed at transformation and development. Paradoxically, rather than regarding legitimacy as a sine qua non for successful reform (Bicanic et al., 2005), in Paraguay the rhetoric of reform became a pre-condition for political legitimacy.[9]

Ultimately the external constituencies, especially the IMF, which provided the effective stimulus for Paraguay's incipient reform movement made two critical mistakes. The first was in overestimating the sufficiency of its Washington Consensus-style package of reform measures. As shall be argued in the sections to follow, without changes in the breadth and technical capacity of a variety of its development and regulatory institutions, Paraguay's 'impulse' to reform would stagnate. The second mistake lay in its overestimation of the depth of political commitment of Paraguay's lingering predatory state to pursue a meaningful developmental reform agenda of any sort.

6.5   An analysis of Paraguay's reforms

Market reforms

Integral to the post-1989 transition was a basket of market-oriented reforms stimulated in no small part by a variety of external agencies such as the International Monetary Fund, the World Bank, and the international financial community. These institutions advocated a familiar menu of reform measures – for example, trade liberalization, financial deregulation, privatization of state-owned enterprises, and so on – that had been widely urged on the so-called transition economies and had become popularly identified as the 'Washington Consensus' (WC). There are two fundamental reasons to doubt the appropriateness of the recipe of reforms advocated by the WC for Paraguay. First as argued by Borda and Masi (2002), for the larger part of the twentieth century the Paraguayan economy had never been characterized by the kinds of price distortions typical of transition economies as well as many other reforming economies both within and outside of Latin America. Paraguay's trade policy was generally a liberal one. It had not pursued a policy of import substitution industrialization. The state sector in fact was small relative to the size of the overall economy. Neither did Paraguay suffer from large fiscal imbalances or excessive inflationary pressures. Paraguay's predatory state relied on more direct means of providing its clients and supporters with rewards, such as the distribution of state-controlled lands and its acquiescence in the contraband trade. In other words, the WC recipe for economic reform was not designed with Paraguay in mind.[10]

The second reason for agnosticism as regards the usefulness of the WC resides in the limitations of the doctrine itself. As Joseph Stiglitz (2002) has so persuasively argued, the uncritical application of liberalization measures, regardless of the affected nation's institutional capacity to absorb the new reforms, often results in the onset, or exacerbation, of economic crisis. We shall argue below that the 'Stiglitz critique' applies with particular force in the Paraguayan case.

Trade policy reforms

As noted earlier Paraguay is one of the few Latin American countries which did not pursue an import substitution industrialization strategy during the 1960s and 1970s. Consequently, its trade has reflected its comparative advantage, with exports being generally land- and resource-based primary commodities and imports generally consisting of capital-intensive manufactured goods. Prior to its 1989 trade liberalization, average tariff rates were low, though customs collected internal taxes of about 16 per cent. Tax evasion, however, was rampant.

The Treaty of Asunción of March 1991, ratified in July 1991, substantially improved the tariff regime. Paraguay agreed to an automatic schedule of tariff reduction as well as a reduction in its list of exceptions so as to become part of the MERCOSUR free trade zone by 31 December 1995. The trade reforms reduced both tariff levels and internal taxes on imports. Common external tariff (CET) rates increased from a range of 3 to 8.6 per cent prior to the reform, to 9.6 per cent for manufactures, 6.9 per cent for agriculture, and 3.4 per cent for mining and quarrying. Paraguay also eliminated all quantitative restrictions and non-tariff barriers on imports, making it perhaps the most liberal trade regime in Latin America. Between 1990 and 1999, Paraguay's average tariff rate declined from 16 per cent to 9 per cent, a tariff regime actually lower than those for either Argentina or Brazil.

MERCOSUR poses delicate challenges to Paraguay because of its openness and the size of its informal economy. The latter is closely linked to trade on goods imported by Paraguay and exported to Argentina and Brazil. Such 'triangular trade' continues to be a source of rent-seeking and corruption in the Paraguayan economy (Smith, 2003). Triangular trade occurs when traders seek to capture rents associated with goods arbitrage within the customs union. This occurs in the case of the MERCOSUR since internal taxes are higher in

Brazil and Argentina than they are in Paraguay. Consequently, traders in Brazil and Argentina find it profitable to export to Paraguay and avoid the burden of higher sales taxes in the formal economies. A second form of this trade occurs when goods are smuggled into Paraguay from outside the customs union and then re-exported to Argentina and Brazil, thus evading the CET.

Obviously, triangular trade is a source of official irritation between Paraguay and its Southern Cone neighbors. Paraguay's trade in illegal, stolen, and counterfeit goods is likewise a source of irritation between Paraguay and the rest of the world.[11] Until Paraguay can gain control over its illicit trade problem the country will continue to be regarded as an international economic pariah. The consequences of this include its continued avoidance by international investors. Moreover, as long as illegal trade continues to flourish, so will the rent-seeking mentality that has driven the nation's business culture for decades. Finally, as long as the state, including the court system, is complicit in the illegal trading system, the predatory ethos will continue to prevail and serve as an obstacle to meaningful political and economic reform.

Financial reforms

Again at the urging of its international constituencies, after 1989 a number of financial reforms were implemented to grant greater operating freedom to financial intermediaries. Liberalization consisted of lowering reserve ratios, eliminating controls on interest rates, and dismantling mechanisms for obligatory investments and mandated lending.

Reserve requirements on both local and foreign currency deposit accounts were substantially reduced by 1996. Interest rates were liberalized in 1990. Ceilings on interest rates (active and passive) were eliminated. In 1993, public funds were permitted to be deposited in the private financial sector. In 1994, law 34/94 permitted all contracts to be expressed in foreign currencies. Between 1991 and 1998 the government embarked on an effort to change the financial and regulatory infrastructure. In 1991, the National Value Commission (CNV, *Comisión Nacional de Valores*) was established, creating the legal framework for the development of the capital market. While the new institutional framework has been an important step in modernizing legal norms, it has not been very successful in developing the capital market. As of 1997 only 60 firms opened their capital to the stock exchange.

In general, financial reform in Paraguay provides a textbook example of the perils of financial liberalization in the absence of an adequate regulatory superstructure. Liberalization took place before strengthening the supervisory body and improving the regulatory framework. Regulatory capacity has been constrained by the lack of qualified personnel and by weak institutions incapable of applying necessary sanctions (Schreiner, 2005). It is hardly surprising then that a financial crisis struck in the immediate aftermath of the first wave of reform.

The first crisis occurred in May 1995 when the central bank intervened in four insolvent banks and a number of smaller financial institutions due to their inability to clear overdrafts with the central bank. The interventions uncovered many fraudulent activities, including lending to related parties and sizable unrecorded deposits. The central bank action led to a substantial withdrawal of deposits from private domestic banks. A run on the system was avoided only due to the presence of other, largely foreign-owned, banks that were perceived to be safe, and also thanks to a large injection of liquidity by the central bank. However, the clean-up of the financial system was left incomplete and institutions with significant deficiencies were allowed to continue operating.

A second crisis erupted in June 1997. This time the central bank was forced to intervene in the largest savings and loan institution and in the largest domestic private commercial bank due to the latter's inability to honor depositor claims and cover overdrafts. These interventions once again triggered a run on deposits. Calm returned only after passage of legislation raising deposit insurance limits. Supervision was increased and some banks were re-capitalized, but regulation continued to be lax. In September 1998 the central bank was once again forced to intervene in three more banks because of liquidity problems. The IMF estimated the total cost of bank rescue operations to be one billion dollars (more than 11 per cent of GDP) with the crisis still not fully resolved.

The banking crises of 1995, 1997, and 1998 wiped out many domestic banks, leaving only the foreign banks in a relatively strong position. By December 2002, a majority of bank deposits were held in branches of foreign banks. The system was also highly dollarized, with dollars accounting for about 69 per cent of deposits and 58 per cent of lending. De facto dollarization, however, was hardly a panacea for the highly vulnerable system as contagion from the Argentine currency crisis affected Paraguay. The system started losing deposits from early 2002 (February). In June, the third largest bank, the Banco Alemán, owned by an Argentine-Uruguayan conglomerate, was closed. As a consequence, the outflow of foreign currency deposits accelerated. Recently established mutual funds companies (Banaleman and Garantia) also closed, leaving many investors unable to recover the full amount of their deposits. Between the end of 2001 and July 2002, the system lost US$420 million in foreign currency deposits, about one-third of the total.

The ill-considered sequencing of Paraguay's financial reform is essentially a result of political, economic, and technical factors. The availability of external sources of finance required that the state demonstrate progress in the process of reform. It was comparatively easy to execute decrees related to such issues as reserve requirements and interest rate regulation. More difficult were the tasks associated with bank supervision. Here the Paraguayan banking supervisory authority lacked either the political will or technical expertise, or both, to gain control over a system that showed a strong tendency to engage in high-risk lending behavior, lack of sufficient capitalization, and fraudulent practices (Borda and Masi, 1998: 76–80).

Recently a financial sector reform law has been passed that provides Paraguayan firms with a substantial tax break when they undertake measures designed to promote their participation in the broad capital market via the public issuance of stocks and bonds. Such firms are required to comply with new regulations requiring that they submit to independent financial auditing. To date, however, few firms have entered the formal, public capital market with stock or bond issues. Curiously, however, many family owned firms have managed to acquire the new legal status to qualify for the tax break.

Recurrent crisis in the Paraguayan financial system not only provides evidence of poor sequencing in the reform process, it also illustrates once again, two of the fundamental themes of the present analysis. These are (1) the continuing predatory nature of the system (for example, fraudulent lending practices) and (2) the consequences of a lack of appropriate institutional and state capacity (H4). The second of these failings is particularly evident in the nation's lack of adequate regulatory law and technical expertise in the area of bank and capital market regulation. The financial sector reform law alluded to in the previous paragraph was supported by an IDB loan worth US$81 million and modeled on similar legislation passed in Chile, a country with far more developed institutions than those prevailing in Paraguay. In addition, the moral hazard problem of reliance on central bank intervention does nothing to strengthen ultimate confidence in the domestic banking system and, as we shall see below, otherwise renders the central bank far less capable of pursuing its traditional and primary function of macroeconomic stabilization.

Exchange rate and monetary policy

Monetary and exchange rate policy during the 1990s can be divided into three distinct periods. Prior to 1995, Paraguayan monetary policy was basically passive, following the rules of a crawling peg similar to Chile's (La Tablita), but with the difference that the rate of devaluation was not pre-announced. From the middle of 1995 to the end of 1997, the central bank, as noted above, was forced to absorb the costs of the crisis in the financial sector. In order to mitigate the inflationary impact of the credits awarded to troubled financial institutions, the growth in the monetary base was reduced and the exchange rate was defended by central bank intervention.

Following December 1997 the central bank reached a critically low level of reserves and opted to stop selling foreign exchange. The nominal exchange rate depreciated by close to 10 per cent from December to January. From January through September 1998 the guarani depreciated an additional 14 per cent. This was followed by another wave of closings in the financial sector that forced the central bank to inject additional liquidity.

Mid-2001 saw yet a third approach to monetary and exchange rate policy. The crawling exchange rate peg was discarded. The central bank relied more on interest rate manipulation to manage liquidity in the system and moved to a more flexible management of the guarani. Also reserve requirements were temporarily increased. The closure of Banco Alemán and the panic it induced put enormous pressure on the exchange rate and inflation. The authorities responded with a tightened monetary policy combining money market operations with temporary reserve requirement increases. The bank also intervened frequently in the foreign exchange market during the year to stop rapid depreciation of the guarani.

In summary, monetary and exchange rate policies during the transition period can best be characterized as reactive rather than autonomous. In particular, they were attempts to respond to other disequilibria in the economy, which were themselves the consequences of other partial, or failed, reform measures. It is relevant to comment on the role of Paraguay's central bank in this regard. The Banco Central de Paraguay (BCP) is probably the nation's strongest economic institution in terms of its technical and bureaucratic expertise. For most of the post-1954 period the BCP had done an admirable job of providing Paraguay with a degree of macroeconomic stability largely absent from many of the other nations on the South American continent. Given Paraguay's small size and external openness, this has been no small accomplishment. As we have seen, however, the continued ability of the BCP to maintain macro stability has been cast into doubt due to the erosion of its policy autonomy.

There are two sources of this erosion. The first derives from the kind of dilemma, discussed by Fanelli and Popov (2005), faced by small, less developed countries situated in an increasingly global financial system. As these authors make clear, this system functions in an extremely asymmetrical fashion. The typical problems of such small nations are compounded in Paraguay's case by the fact that the larger countries that constitute its regional economy have themselves recent histories of extreme exchange rate and macro instability. Optimal exchange rate policy then becomes extremely complicated. Pegging the guarani to the dollar renders Paraguay vulnerable to fluctuations in that currency as well as making autonomous monetary policy far more problematical as a demand management tool. Floating the guarani carries the risk that sudden domestic currency depreciation will have a dramatic negative impact on the nation's trade – a risk that may be unacceptable for a highly trade dependent nation. Pegging the guarani to the Argentine or Brazilian currency, or to a regional monetary unit, carries equally serious risks in the absence of the ability of these countries to solve their own macro stabilization problems.

The BCP also faces a second challenge to its autonomy. Prior to the 1980s when the economy was in its boom period, it could focus on maintaining price stability and was unlikely to be forced to address crises emanating from other state-induced disequilibria. Once the economy began to generate substantial twin deficits, however, the BCP became captive to the need to address crises at the cost of yielding to macroeconomic instability.

This is not to say that the BCP has ever been characterized by the sort of institutional autonomy characteristic of central banks in the industrialized democracies. Bank administrators, including the president and board of directors, are political appointees and serve at the pleasure of the president of the republic. This fact by itself is not remarkable, but considering the nature of the Paraguayan economy – that is, small, open, dependent, and highly vulnerable to a variety of internal and external shocks – it is clear that BCP is in no position to turn away from addressing crises from whatever source they emanate and whenever they emerge. The bank's unique (by Latin American standards) ability during most of the post-war period to steer a course of macroeconomic stability was precisely due to the lack of a need to confront such crises.

It is tempting to conclude from Paraguay's recent experience that the future ability of the BCP to pursue macroeconomic stability would be met by building into the institution adequate insulation from the pressures of other kinds and sources of economic and political crises. This is hardly realistic, however, particularly given the low level of Paraguay's financial development. More realistic is the conclusion that more general reform of Paraguay's economic and political institutions, especially those charged with oversight of its financial institutions, will be needed in order to allow the BCP to pursue its more fundamental macroeconomic responsibilities. In this sense then, institutional reform cannot proceed on a piecemeal basis – it must rather proceed comprehensively.

Tax reform and fiscal policy

A tax reform law implemented in 1991 sought to implement a number of principles of sound public finance including efficiency, non-distortion, and revenue sufficiency. To a considerable extent two of these goals (efficiency and non-distortion) were accomplished by the reform (Richards, 2001). The new law eliminated a long list of non-remunerative and distortionary taxes including those on exports.

The centerpiece of the reform law was the introduction of a broad-based value added tax (VAT). Paraguay's VAT is levied at a general rate of 10 per cent with exemptions granted to agriculture and small enterprises. The VAT soon became the single most important source of revenue accounting for nearly 40 per cent of the total by 1993. Sales taxes in general account for over 50 per cent of central government revenue.

The important shortcoming of the 1991 tax reform concerns the issue of revenue sufficiency. Paraguay experienced a growing problem of public sector deficits during the 1990s. Given the country's desperate need for public goods and its extremely limited ability to attract foreign capital, ways have to be found to expand the tax base. Ideally, the revenue shortfall would be made up via a combination of income taxes and taxation of the agricultural sector (for example, on land holdings), which otherwise remains relatively unburdened. The implementation of these forms of taxation, however, presupposes the existence of precisely the sort of efficient, honest, and technically capable bureaucracy that we have argued is absent in Paraguay.[12]

A related problem concerns the high rate of tax evasion, which characterizes the present system. Even the VAT, a relatively easy tax to administer and collect, is said to suffer from an evasion rate in the order of 30 to 35 per cent.

Also, the following point should be noted about the application of the VAT tax. While the tax is applied at a general rate of 10 per cent, a special preferential rate of 7 per cent is given to cigarettes and a selective list of so-called 'goods of tourist consumption'. While these provisions at first glance may appear to be rather innocuous exceptions designed to promote Paraguay's tourist trade, closer consideration suggests that they are further evidence of the state's continuing predatory tendencies. Cigarettes and 'goods of tourist consumption' are at the center of Paraguay's illicit contraband commerce. The failure of the state to eliminate their exceptional status must be taken as implicit consent, and even complicity, in such activity.

On the expenditures side of the budget, state performance during the transition period is hardly more encouraging. Even as the size and frequency of the public sector deficit has grown, Paraguay lags well behind the norm for South America in the provision of basic social services and infrastructure as Table 6.4 indicates.

Public employment, on the other hand, has certainly grown. But, as argued earlier, this growth has followed the logic of clientelism rather than a logic we would associate with the development of an efficient, professional bureaucracy. Predictably, current expenditure has outpaced capital expenditure in the state's budget, and expenditure at the level of the central government has grown at a much more rapid rate than at the department and municipal levels (Borda and Masi, 2002: 18–20). In general, as older sources of rents became exhausted, the public budget came to be seen as the replacement source of official patronage with very negative consequences for the nation's fiscal health.

Privatization of state-owned enterprises

Allied to the increase in public sector employment and current public expenditure is the status of Paraguay's state-owned enterprises (SOEs). The continuing predatory character of the Paraguayan state is perhaps nowhere more obvious than in its SOEs. Not surprisingly, its external stakeholders (IMF, World Bank, Inter-American Development Bank, USAID and European Union) also recognized this fact since, in true WC fashion, they made privatization of SOEs a necessary condition for continued financial support.

As a result of this external pressure, two privatization initiatives were pursued. The first of these was undertaken during the rule of President Wasmosy (1993–98). The government established a priority list of five SOEs to privatize of which four enterprises were eventually sold off: the state airline, Líneas Aéreas Paraguayas SA (LAPSA), the state steel-making plant, Aceros del Paraguay (ACEPAR), the state shipping line, Flota Mercante Paraguaya (FLOMERPASA) and the state alcohol plant, APAL. The remaining enterprise on the priority list, the state national railway, Ferrocarril Central Carlos Antonio López (FCCAL), remains under state control, although it ceased operations in 2000.

Controversy surrounding the manner and terms of the privatization, and accusations of mismanagement and corruption leveled against President

Table 6.4: Selected indicators of infrastructure and social services, 1995

Country	Telephones per hundred inhabitants	Total commercial energy consumption per inhabitant (kW)	Population with access to safe drinking water (%)	Length of railway network (km)	Length of roads (km)	Percent of paved roads	Population with access to sanitation (%)
Argentina	15.9	2,197	65	35,753	218,276	29.1	75
Bolivia	4.0	608	70	3,440	53,259	5.6	41
Brazil	8.5	913	69	30,403	1,840,000	9.3	67
Chile	13.2	1,533	91	6,445	79,359	19.0	81
Colombia	11.0	830	75	2,100	114,912	11.9	59
Ecuador	6.5	804	55	956	43,249	13.3	53
Paraguay	3.5	465	39	441	29,901	11.8	44
Peru	4.7	500	66	2,121	78,901	12.9	61
Uruguay	19.5	857	89	3,002	8,679	76.4	61
Venezuela	11.4	4,494	79	627	95,676	36.4	72

Source: Statistical Abstract of Latin America, volume 38.

Wasmosy, provoked opposition to the program. LAPSA's asset value was grossly undervalued at the time of its sale for $26 million in 1994. ACEPAR was sold in 1997 for $35 million to be paid over 10 years. In May 2000 the state prosecutor demanded the cancellation of the agreement. FLOMERPASA was auctioned off in 1996 for US$4.8 million. In 2001 the state prosecutor brought corruption charges against Wasmosy, alleging that the auction was carried out without the authorization of the privatization council and the state audit office and that the $15 million proceeds were never transferred to the state treasury. APAL was converted into a commercial venture, Cañas Paraguayas (CAPASA), in 1993. In 1997 the state retook control of the company, which has been operating at a massive loss ever since. In mid-2001 it was requested that the company, which had debts of US$1.5 m, be declared bankrupt (Nickson and Lambert, 2002).

The second privatization initiative was conducted during the González Macchi government, which set up a state reform secretariat, Secretaría Nacional de Reforma del Estado (SNRE). In March 2000 President González sought congressional approval for a law granting executive 'fast-track' powers to privatize Antelco, the state telecom company, and Corposana, the state water company, within a 180-day period (Ley EPERT).[13] The law was finally approved by Congress on 24 October 2000.

On 3 November 2000 President González decreed intervention in the case of three loss-making SOEs: Antelco, Corposana, and the railway company, Ferrocarril Central Carlos Antonio López (FCCAL). Results on these initiatives are still pending. Overall, however, the prospects for successful privatization are slim. Two factors are likely to adversely affect its legitimacy. First, it is highly unlikely that the tendering and adjudication process will be fair and transparent, given the lucrative nature of the assets involved, the potential for corruption, and the high level of politicization surrounding the process. Second, the dangers of 'regulatory capture' are rife, given the lack of any tradition of professional ethics in the senior levels of the public administration. A regulatory commission has yet to be appointed for the urban water sector, despite advanced plans for introducing private sector participation in Corposana. Fears of undue political influence in the process were heightened when, in a flagrant and revealing violation of regulatory independence, the director of CONATEL (the telecom regulatory body), was elected to the ruling council (*Junta de Gobierno*) of the Colorado Party in May 2001 (Nickson and Lambert, 2002).

An additional obstacle to privatization of SOEs in Paraguay concerns the legal framework within which the process is currently conducted. As noted by Sohn (2005), Law 636 requires that workers in SOEs must be given an opportunity to acquire an 80 per cent share of their enterprises on a preferential basis. The same law in fact makes it difficult for any other party, other than current or previous workers, or others directly associated with the firm, to acquire ownership. The effective result of this legal constraint is to ensure that ownership of SOEs remains in the hands of 'insiders', with the further result that they continue to be used for the political advantage of established elites.

The lack of institutional prerequisites for successful privatization makes these initiatives subject to the Stiglitz critique. This lack has also generated substantial popular suspicion of and resistance to the privatization movement. Future success for this sort of reform will depend on both a more general effort at state institution-building and the ability to endow institutions with the necessary legitimacy. Of course, as Liew et al. (2005) argue, democratic institution-building is a long-term process. These authors counsel a gradualist approach to the privatization process in order to avoid adding further incentives to opportunistic behavior. In the case where opportunistic behavior might already be said to operate within the SOE, as in Paraguay, they advocate the involvement of external actors (for example, international organizations) in the timing and method of privatization.

A second motivation for a gradualist approach to privatization speaks to the need to overcome popular resistance both to privatization and economic reform more generally. This concerns the general macroeconomic climate within which reform measures are implemented. In an economy like Paraguay's, in which private sector employment opportunities are still few, 'successful' privatization which results in massive lay-offs of public sector employees will encounter substantial resistance.[14] The point here is not that inefficient and corrupt SOEs should be tolerated in the interests of social peace. It is rather that privatization is not itself a panacea. Where a premature privatization threatens to derail other, more fundamental reforms, or a popular mandate for reform, it is probably preferable that it be delayed.

Land reform: the reform that wasn't

Conspicuously absent from Paraguay's reform initiatives during the 1990s was any serious effort to rectify the highly unequal distribution of agricultural holdings in this still highly agrarian society.[15] Pressure for such reform grew markedly during the 1980s and 1990s when a number of new peasant organizations were formed and began working for a visible role in an increasingly liberal political environment (Fogel, 1997; Nagel, 1999). While the increase in peasant activism was often met with violence, especially in cases where land disputes were involved, on the whole there seemed to be growing support for land reform and redistribution both as restitution for prior illegal land seizures and as a means to exercise greater nationalist control over Paraguayan resources (Nagel, 1999: 153–8).[16]

Nevertheless, the National Constitutional Assembly in June 1992 pursued a land reform agenda that largely conformed to the interests of large landowners. In particular, the assembly enacted legislation that required full and prior indemnization for any expropriated lands. This law effectively put a brake on land redistribution given the limited financial and legal resources of the landless peasantry.

While the new law is frequently defended in terms of rational land use, it is doubtful that it has had this effect. Fogel (1997: 101) argues that some large landowners, fearing further attempts to expropriate underutilized holdings, have deforested large tracts of land and turned them over to use as cattle pasture. The result is neither environmentally sound, nor does it represent a productivity-increasing strategy for land use. Perhaps, most importantly, it does little or nothing to provide rural employment or alleviate poverty.

Land conflict in Paraguay, as noted by Nagel (1999), has in recent years been described by the Paraguayan press as a struggle between a landless but otherwise tradition-bound peasantry and a modernizing capitalist rural elite. The latter is taken to include both domestic and foreign investors in Paraguay's agricultural sector. While there is an element of such a division in rural Paraguay, as a generalization it highly over-simplifies the reality. Closer to the truth is Nagel's argument that the class divisions in Paraguay's rural sector reveal four distinct categories. In addition to the two mentioned above, there are at least two additional sectors. The first of these is a peasant sector that, while having a strong social and cultural attachment to the land, is also characterized by a strong profit motive and a desire for accumulation and material improvement. The second is a distinctively rentier class. Such a class seeks and holds land not for the purposes of capitalist production but rather as a symbol of its social status and political power. This rentier class was established and supported by Paraguay's predatory state under the Stroessner dictatorship. It continues to rely on its clientelist relationships with the state, which it employs to control not only land itself but also the political space that peasant and rural worker organizations have to press their interests.

In Section 6.2 we posed the hypothesis (H2) that the stability of the predatory state requires that new social actors who represent a challenge to the organizational effectiveness of the PS be either co-opted or repressed. Repression, of course can take a variety of forms. Under the predatory dictator, repression was swift, overt, and unapologetic. Under the transition regimes of Rodríguez and Wasmosy, repression of new contenders took legalistic and ideological forms in addition to violence. Wasmosy's interpretation of the new constitution placed a great deal of stress on the inviolability of private property without reference to competing values of productive efficiency, social stability, or economic development. While land conflicts were often met with violent reactions, they were just as frequently settled via judicial and executive decrees in favor of the established claims of traditional elites. The press played an ancillary role in depicting landless movement as itself violent and opportunistic (Nagel, 1999).

Civil service and decentralization reforms

It has been argued in previous sections that a serious weakness of the Paraguayan state is the absence of what we termed a Weberian bureaucracy. The lack of this feature of the development state places severe constraints on the state's technical and administrative capacities to initiate and execute meaningful reforms. It also acts as an obstacle to inspire social capital accumulation across the highest levels of the state apparatus and society at large. Insofar as state bureaucrats act and are perceived as self-serving rent-seekers, they will fail to engender trust in their institutions and in the state as a whole. Civil service reform designed to construct a state bureaucracy with Weberian characteristics would then seem to be a necessary prerequisite to meaningful economic reform.

If social capital is more easily produced at the local level, then appropriate decentralization of state functions and resources would seem to play a useful role in the more general reform process. Decentralization can also play a useful function insofar as it helps to reduce the power and discretion of the central state that stands opposed to reforms. Finally, to the extent that decentralization brings budgetary authority and responsibility closer to those who are directly served, it may also bring efficiency benefits.

Civil service reform

Paraguay's first civil service law was instituted in 1970. The law was never actually implemented, however. It was not until 1996, seven years into the transition, that the Chamber of Deputies passed a new civil service bill, which then languished in the senate until December 2000. At that point it only passed into law after overcoming a partial veto from the executive.

From the outset, the reform never mustered any real enthusiasm. The new law was designed to replace the patronage system with a career civil service based on merit. Within weeks of its promulgation, the law was challenged in the courts by the chief public prosecutor and a coalition of public sector trade unions. Key features of the law were suspended by a supreme court ruling that declared 40 of its articles to be unconstitutional, including the introduction of an eight-hour work day, the merit-based system for selection and promotion of public administrators, and two-year minimum service before granting job security.[17] The lack of political support or an organized pro-reform constituency suggests that the new civil service law could, like its 1970 predecessor, simply not be implemented (Nickson and Lambert, 2002).

Furthermore, the management of public personnel is in a state of chaos. In the central administration alone there are 2500 job categories, with unjustifiable salary differences among them. Many public appointments and promotions are essentially based on political loyalty and personal relations. A public salary is rarely viewed as providing a single source of income. Thus, given the low wages and six-hour workdays, state employees tend to hold second jobs. Many accept bribes as a form of salary supplement. On average, public employees in Paraguay augment their income by 30 per cent thanks to bribe taking (Gobierno de la República del Paraguay, undated).

At the center of the resistance to reform of the civil service stand Paraguay's established political institutions, especially its political parties. This is especially true of the dominant Colorado Party. Opposition political parties have pushed half-heartedly for some measures of state reform, but have avoided advocating privatization or professionalization of the public administration. While the public sector is a bastion of electoral support for the Colorado Party, it is widely seen on all levels – local, departmental, and national – as part of the spoils of electoral competition, a political reward that accompanies electoral success. When opposition parties have won elections, the trend has been not to initiate public sector reform, but to use parts of the public sector as a potential party fiefdom in the same manner as the Colorado Party (Gobierno de la República del Paraguay, undated: 167).[18]

The spiral of predatory rent-seeking, inefficiency, and corruption has now brought Paraguay to the brink of fiscal collapse. The country's historically small tax base and low levels of revenue collection, coupled with a bloated public roll, have put an unprecedented strain on the national purse. Between 1989 and 2002, the state's workforce increased by nearly 49,000, a 32 per cent rise over 14 years. At present, close to 95 per cent of state expenditures are for salaries and pensions alone. By the end of 2002, state administrators were actually scrambling to find funds to pay their staff.

In sum then, while the basis of predatory state behavior has substantially changed from resource-based rent-seeking to other forms, the predatory instinct continues to function as a defining feature of the state apparatus during the transition period. Moreover, this predatory instinct operates as a major obstacle to substantial reform of the state and its institutions beyond the merely pro forma stage.

This not to say that real progress has not been made. Even pro forma reforms provide a necessary beginning to the reform process. Unless, however, the basis for the predatory state continues to be undermined, advance to the second stage of genuine reform leading to sustainable economic growth and development will be tenuous and uncertain.

Decentralization

The reform effort aimed at decentralization of state functions and powers begun after 1989 has followed essentially the same pattern as that for the civil service and the general political infrastructure. That is, some *de jure* modifications have been made and have subsequently been rendered impotent by a lack of executive, congressional, and judicial support. This lack of support is once again best understood as an effort by the established political interests to maintain control over sources of revenue and patronage.

In 1996, a new municipal law was passed by Congress several parts of which were subsequently vetoed by President Wasmosy. The new law, however, did transfer control over urban and rural property taxes from central to local administration. No independent sources of revenue were established for the departments. Instead, they were allotted 15 per cent of local property tax proceeds, 15 per cent of VAT revenue, and 30 per cent of the tax monies collected from gambling and lottery sources in their jurisdiction (Nickson and Lambert, 2002). After a determined lobbying effort by the national association of municipalities and the council of departmental governors, a law was passed in 1998 that gave departments and municipalities a 50 per cent share in the royalties of Paraguay's two binational (with Argentina and Brazil) hydro-electric plants. The gradual implementation of the law, however, has stumbled into predictable obstacles, with municipal leaders complaining in 2001 that the Ministry of Finance was shirking their obligations for actual budget allocations (Nickson and Lambert, 2002).

As noted, despite the legal changes that would devolve more rights and responsibilities to department and local government, in practice the country continues to concentrate the bulk of state services, resources, and decisions in Asunción. Less than 3 per cent of the entire state budget and fewer than 4 per cent of all public staff are responsible for running 226 municipalities and 17 departments (Morley and Vos, 2001). Health services and public works, for example, remain highly dependent on ministerial authorities in Asunción.

Political participation, civic engagement, and social capital

For the reform movement to gain momentum it is especially important that ordinary Paraguayans believe that they have a stake in the process and that they are able to influence its course and its outcomes. In the absence of such a belief there is no reason to believe that reform that challenges the prerogatives of the established elites will be undertaken, or if it is initiated, that it will progress beyond a pro forma, *de jure* character.[19] These observations then suggest the following additional hypothesis:

The process of acquiring the institutional infrastructure characteristic of the developmental state requires first that the predatory state be undermined.[20] This subversive process is aided by the development of an active civil society (H5).

The overall political situation in Paraguay since 1989 has contributed to a heightened sense of civic fatigue and growing popular disenchantment with politics. With the increase in electoral options, formal political participation in elections increased from 53.3 per cent in the presidential elections of 1989 to 80.5 per cent in 1998, but then declined to 64.2 per cent in 2003. Asked in a recent poll if they would agree to suspend national elections for ten years, almost half of the national respondents said yes (Vial, 2002). What is more, close to two-thirds said they would favor freezing all political party activities for a similar period of time.

Despite a decrease in formal political participation through elections, civic engagement in different forms has seen a notable increase over the 1990s. Freedoms of association and expression have contributed to a notable expansion and innovation in such activity. Most noticeably, it has contributed to a discernable growth and mobilization of popular sector organizations, especially among the peasantry and urban workforce. Popular protest is nowadays broadly accepted as commonplace activity.

In recent years there have been a number of disruptive civil society mobilizations. The March 1999 civic revolt was a clear manifestation of popular disappointment over the country's meager political leadership. A growing sense of empowerment can be discerned in the assertiveness that has taken hold of certain civil society sectors, as does the toughness of their protest measures. Though quite disorderly in style and mostly reactive in content, these episodes reveal a new dynamic and temper within civil society.

At the same time, however, civil society development may be blocked by the continuing functioning of the predatory state. The discretionary patterns of authority of a PS blur distinctions between public and private goods, undercut predictable rules, invite impromptu arrangements, and stir a sense of recurrent flux and confusion. Societal organizing efforts become more complicated and less resilient in such settings. What is more, predatory or patrimonial states nurture an opportunistic ethos that undermines social norms of trust and cooperation (social capital). This ethos, in turn, perpetuates the problem of state corruption.

In many ways, civil society mirrors the forms of conduct that are found in the state – namely, organizational informality and improvisation, personalist leadership, internal factionalism, nepotism, and corruption. This is hardly surprising given the near total dominance of civil society by the ruling Colorado Party during the Stroessner dictatorship. As described by Barreto (1996), the dictatorship infiltrated civil society organizations as a means of both political control and dispensing patronage. Key industries, producers' organizations, and labor and peasant organizations were used to form dyadic contracts between party bosses, or members of the military, and subordinates within the organization. In this way, writes Barreto, most Paraguayans came to view politics as a means of manipulating people so as to achieve their personal or group ends. Political life in virtually all specific contexts is motivated by these same individualistic or group desires rather than by ideology, much less public ideals. The task of creating public institutions that can claim a popular legitimacy faces the daunting need to transform the popular consciousness about the meaning of politics as an insiders' game.

The best hope for this transformation, perhaps, involves the provision of external support for those civil society organizations that heretofore have not been the traditional objects of party infiltration and dominance. Selectively supported civil society organizations can be a fruitful mechanism by which to improve the material well-being of large numbers of people, especially the poor, as well as to develop the social capital needed for a wholesale reform project. Costa and Molinas (2003) of the Inter-American Development Bank advocate that support be provided to specific civil society organizations working in concert with state organizations that address the felt needs of affected communities for security and to combat corruption. At the same time, however, they emphasize the need to provide careful oversight over the distribution and use of IDB resources via the maintenance of administrative mechanisms, for example, Consejo Asesor de la Sociedad Civil, that empower participation at the local level and among the intended beneficiaries of the programs.

6.6   Conclusions

If it is true, as we have argued, that sustainable, growth-promoting reform is blocked in Paraguay by a set of inappropriate institutions, the relevant question then becomes, how can institutions appropriate for a predatory state be replaced by those appropriate for a development state?

Logically, the first insight that follows from our analytical discussion in relation to this question is that insofar as the predatory state relies on the exploitation of rent havens, anything that undermines the opportunity for rent-seeking and capture will also undermine the PS and its institutions. Recent history supports this observation inasmuch as crisis and instability in Paraguay have occurred precisely when the traditional sources of resource-based rents have come under increasing pressure. The closing of the agricultural frontier and the completion of the dam-related construction projects signaled the closing of important sources of 'easy' returns for the PS. In the absence of replacements for these rent havens, the institutions supporting the traditional power hierarchy have come under pressure.

A second insight that follows from our model is that additional instability derives from the emergence of new and competing demands on the social product. The long period of political and social quiescence that began in 1954 has ended with increases in worker, peasant, and civil society demands for greater participation in all aspects of the nation's political economy. Institutions predicated on low transaction costs of social control are no longer viable. Repression, forced exile and easy co-optation are no longer effective means of enforcing regime stability.

Finally, a third important insight concerns the international environment within which the Paraguayan PS has traditionally operated. As long as the PS could operate under conditions of relative autonomy, there were lower costs of conducting business that was conducive to stability. With the increased tendencies to regional economic opening and democratic transition, however, have come increased pressures brought by additional, external constituencies. Brazil and Argentina in particular are no longer as inclined to ignore events in their Southern Cone neighbor as in previous decades. For that matter, neither are the United States and Europe willing to ignore Paraguay's tendencies to flout international standards and conventions as they were earlier in the twentieth century. Each of these factors then contributes to our understanding of the dysfunctional relationship between Paraguay's lingering hangover of PS-type institutions and its ability to attain self-sustaining economic growth and democratic stability.

Notes

We would like to thank Fernando Masi, Nelson Aguilera-Alfred and all members of CADEP for their contributions to this chapter.

1. In framing the issues in this fashion, we place ourselves squarely on the side of what Fanelli and Popov (2005) describe as the procedural approach (PA) to reform analysis in contradistinction to what they term as the substantive approach (SA). We agree with these authors in their position that actual reforms are a combination of both procedures and substance. In giving priority to the PA, however, we hold that in cases such as Paraguay, where institutions are highly dysfunctional to the promotion of sustainable economic growth and poverty alleviation, the emphasis on the creation of new rules of the game is essentially pragmatic.

2. See Moselle and Polak (2001) for a good example of the rational choice approach to the predatory state based on its authority to tax and provide public goods.

3. As a result of this war, Paraguay lost 26 per cent of its national territory, almost 58 per cent of its pre-war population and 90 per cent of its male population (Lambert, 1997: 19).

4. This view is shared by several other commentators including Barreto (1996) and Borda and Masi (2002).

5. The interested reader should consult the following sources for details. For a discussion of the Instituto de Bienestar Rural (IBR) and Paraguay's land reform and colonization projects see Kleinpenning (1987). Discussion of the dam projects is provided by Miranda (1983). Contraband trade is discussed by Luis (1992) and Miranda (2001).

6. The MERCOSUR markets associated with Argentina and Brazil were well established before the advent of MERCOSUR. Paraguay was compelled to affiliate with MERCOSUR and pursue a program of *de jure* reform in order not to lose these markets. The failure of Paraguay's predatory state to pursue new markets in other countries in or near the Southern Cone region accounts for the smaller nation's continued dependency on these two dominant economies and its vulnerability to their instability.

7. Wasmosy himself had risen to prominence in Paraguay as a result of his participation in the lucrative contracting surrounding the construction of the Itaipu project (Abente-Brun, 1999).

8. In this respect Nickson and Lambert (2002) aptly characterize Paraguay's reform movement as an exercise in 'state privatization'.

9. Liew et al. (2005) coin the term 'preventive democratization' to describe the attitude of the entrenched elites in former Eastern European countries that sought to salvage their power in the face of a fundamental political challenge. The same term also applies well to Paraguay's political transition.

10. This is not to suggest that all of the WC recommendations were irrelevant to the Paraguayan case. Paraguay's system of multiple exchange rates, discussed in detail below, is an example of the sort of price distortions the WC seeks to rectify. The critical mistake, however, is to assume that the WC is applicable *in general* to Paraguay and sufficient as a remedy to its (fundamentally) institutional distortions.

11. Smith (2003) reports that since 1997 the Nintendo corporation has brought 36 cases in the Paraguayan courts over counterfeiting or smuggling of its goods. None of these cases had been resolved at the time of his report.

12. A substantial fiscal reform has since been implemented and introduces among other measures a moderately progressive income tax.

13. 'Ley EPERT' refers to the Ley General de Reorganización y Transformación de Entidades Públicas Descentralizadas y de Reforma y Modernización de Organismos de la Administración Central.
14. This was precisely what happened in June 2000, when protesters clashed with police in the streets of Asunción over the planned privatization of the telephone, water, and railway companies.
15. Fogel (1997: 104) reports that toward the end of the 1990s, of the 450,000 families residing in rural areas, at least 143,000 do not have access to land of their own. Of the rest, 1,230,000 work plots of less than two hectares. At the other extreme, 1 per cent of landholdings cover 77 per cent of the country.
16. Brazilian encroachment on the eastern Paraguayan border first became a source of nationalist concern during the 1970s, giving impulse to the Stroessner regime's colonization efforts.
17. It would be tempting to cite this as evidence in support of Rius and van de Walle's (2005: 187) thesis that a proliferation of 'veto points' decreases the likelihood of reform initiatives. In the Paraguayan case, however, such an interpretation would overlook the clientelist character of the state as a whole and ascribe a level of inter-branch autonomy to the several components of the state apparatus that they do not possess.
18. Fidrmuc and Noury (2005) have developed a simple theoretical model that predicts the absence of an organized lobbying effort on behalf of civil service reform. One of the circumstances where this occurs is when the state's utility function does not include social welfare. This would seem to describe rather well the predatory state.
19. Fidrmuc and Noury (2005) provide a review of the incentives to block reforms in terms of protecting rents and political power.
20. Subverting the predatory state should not be confused with our advocating anarchy. Rather, we mean the institutional basis for predatory state behavior should be replaced by a new foundation that provides an incentive set to promote productive behavior. The internal agent for this change we believe is civil society.

7
Pro-Market Reform in Uruguay: Gradual Reform and Political Pluralism

Alvaro Forteza, Daniel Buquet, Mario Ibarburu, Jorge Lanzaro,
Andrés Pereyra, Eduardo Siandra, and Marcel Vaillant

7.1 Introduction

Over the last few decades, the countries of Latin America have gone through a 'double' transition. Even though this process was idiosyncratic to the region in many respects, it also resembles what happened in Eastern Europe after the collapse of 'real' socialism, and is comparable to what the southern regions of the Old World had to face in the mid-1970s. The first dimension of these dual transitions has to do with the process of democratization and its chances of gaining in strength. The second transition has to do with the processes of reform and structural change in politics, in the state and in the economy, and in modes of regulation and of public management. These are big changes in society on a nationwide scale, and also in international relations and in the integrated regional blocs.

This chapter involves an analysis of the relation between politics and reforms – politics and policies – in Uruguay. It shows the ways in which the institutions, the political processes and the games of the different power brokers impact on the path of the reforms – promoting them, limiting them, or blocking them; modeling the rhythms, the initiatives, and the characteristics of the solutions which have come to be adopted, their implementation and their effectiveness; and illustrating the strengths and weaknesses which have emerged. In turn, following recent literature on political economy, the chapter distinguishes between institutions or policy rules and specific policies or policy acts. The focus is on the former.

Much progress has been made in this line of research but further study is needed. For a while, the debate was centered on the reforms themselves and on their suitability, principally with regard to political institutions, the economy, the state, public management, and social policies. Subsequently attention turned to politics, to its rules and its specific development, as a determinant factor in the dynamic of these reforms within the fabric of national and international conditioning factors. In our study we adopt this second perspective.

We aim to provide answers to the three main questions posed in Fanelli and Popov (2005) for the Uruguayan case. The first question is, why did the reform take place? Our short answer is that it depends on the reform: some were heavily conditioned by external influences (like the role of Brazil and Argentina in moving towards regional trade integration); others were based on internal politics (like the social security reform). The second question is, what kind of reform was better suited to the country? Our answer is a gradual one, which is an optimal approach to reform given the characteristics of the political parties and the general lack of enthusiasm of the population towards market economies. The third question is, how well did the reform perform? We found mixed results and a number of incomplete reforms, with even the possibility of some reversals.

This chapter focuses on a series of structural pro-market reforms implemented in recent years, mainly during the 1990s, in the areas of foreign trade, social security, public utilities, legal infrastructure, and electoral and government systems. Although it is not an exhaustive list of reformist initiatives, it covers the core of the process, instances where sustained political action in a specific direction can be identified.[1] A chronicle of the main changes in political economy in the 1990s has been brought up to date, and there is a detailed account of the positions of the different actors involved.

Uruguay is often regarded as a reluctant reformer. This view is to some extent supported by some indexes of economic reform. Lora (2001) computes an index of pro-market structural reform in 19 Latin American and Caribbean countries. In this group, Uruguay is the country whose index of economic reform changed least between 1985 and 1999, the period of most intense reform in the region. According to the same index, Uruguay was the fourth top reformer in 1985, surpassed only by Chile, Jamaica, and Trinidad and Tobago, but it plummeted to last position in 1999 (Table 7.1). This period coincides with the first three democratic administrations after Uruguay returned to democracy in 1985.

According to Lora (1998), it is not that Uruguay did not reform, but that it did so gradually. Using values from the structural reform index of 1985 and 1995, Lora classified Latin American and Caribbean countries in four groups: early reformers, gradual reformers, late reformers, and slow reformers. Uruguay is one of the two gradual reformers (Colombia is the other). Lora and Olivera's (2004) index of 'unbundling' reinforces this view. The index of reform-unbundling registers its maximum value when reform takes place only in one area at a time, and its minimum value when it takes place simultaneously in all areas to an equal extent. Uruguay has the second highest value for unbundling in the region.

The stance of economic reform varies considerably from one area to another. According to Lora (2001), trade and finance are the areas in which Latin America and the Caribbean have reformed the most, while privatization and tax and labor policies are the areas in which there has been the least progress.

Table 7.1: Structural reforms index in Latin America and the Caribbean

	1985	1986	1987	1988	1989	1990	1991	1992	1993	1994	1995	1996	1997	1998	1999
Argentina	0.338	0.326	0.327	0.311	0.366	0.468	0.551	0.574	0.602	0.598	0.595	0.597	0.607	0.604	0.616
Bolivia	0.290	0.348	0.390	0.406	0.403	0.466	0.487	0.485	0.474	0.475	0.614	0.711	0.705	0.699	0.690
Brazil	0.259	0.301	0.301	0.344	0.419	0.430	0.431	0.449	0.468	0.489	0.515	0.530	0.551	0.580	0.610
Chile	0.488	0.512	0.513	0.549	0.580	0.570	0.572	0.564	0.565	0.570	0.577	0.586	0.585	0.585	0.606
Colombia	0.291	0.386	0.386	0.383	0.383	0.413	0.477	0.540	0.525	0.534	0.524	0.529	0.555	0.560	0.562
Costa Rica	0.306	0.387	0.428	0.421	0.420	0.425	0.420	0.440	0.446	0.453	0.536	0.533	0.542	0.557	0.557
Dominican Rep.	–	–	–	–	–	0.384	0.378	0.432	0.436	0.447	0.439	0.441	0.454	0.490	0.599
Ecuador	0.309	0.317	0.320	0.321	0.323	0.405	0.399	0.456	0.461	0.484	0.536	0.535	0.539	0.536	0.528
El Salvador	0.349	0.353	0.351	0.348	0.362	0.399	0.401	0.416	0.494	0.505	0.488	0.497	0.489	0.572	0.566
Guatemala	0.344	0.344	0.410	0.425	0.447	0.445	0.444	0.450	0.462	0.475	0.513	0.505	0.509	0.570	0.592
Honduras	–	–	–	–	0.354	–	–	–	–	–	0.489	0.500	0.490	0.540	0.511
Jamaica	0.397	0.410	0.494	0.495	0.498	0.500	0.524	0.549	0.539	0.545	0.554	0.557	0.586	0.652	0.666
Mexico	0.290	0.308	0.340	0.392	0.403	0.424	0.453	0.479	0.474	0.540	0.531	0.500	0.510	0.501	0.511
Nicaragua	–	–	–	–	–	–	–	–	–	0.574	0.574	0.580	0.623	0.617	0.598
Paraguay	0.355	0.351	0.350	0.348	0.371	0.437	0.510	0.542	0.555	0.562	0.563	0.562	0.564	0.563	0.566
Peru	0.279	0.313	0.308	0.295	0.286	0.335	0.399	0.459	0.526	0.590	0.598	0.632	0.625	0.643	0.659
Trin. and Tobago	0.520	0.515	0.521	0.533	0.538	0.567	0.548	0.539	0.540	0.628	0.640	0.640	0.626	0.625	0.631
Uruguay	0.369	0.346	0.345	0.363	0.361	0.372	0.375	0.434	0.437	0.442	0.451	0.452	0.460	0.460	0.477
Venezuela	0.284	0.270	0.270	0.265	0.289	0.343	0.370	0.384	0.461	0.480	0.477	0.504	0.501	0.516	0.514
Regional average*	0.341	0.360	0.377	0.384	0.399	0.436	0.455	0.484	0.503	0.522	0.539	0.548	0.554	0.573	0.583

Note: * The regional average does not include the Dominican Republic, Honduras, or Nicaragua.
Source: Lora (2001).

By 1999 (the last year in Lora's study), Uruguay was the country in the region that had privatized the least, and was the second least flexible in terms of labor institutions. Forteza and Rama (2006) compute an index of labor rigidity and it shows that Uruguay is the most rigid country in Latin America.[2] On the other hand, Uruguay has one of the highest values in the (free) trade index in Lora's computations, and has intermediate values for financial and tax policies.

The above-mentioned studies are useful to put the country in a regional perspective, but they inevitably leave some aspects out of the picture. First, reform is the outcome of a political process, which is only laterally addressed in the cross-country studies. Without this ingredient, it is not possible to provide a satisfactory answer to the type of questions that guided this research. The political process is not just a context variable, but a central object of analysis in this chapter. We want to advance hypotheses, for instance, about why the Uruguayan reform process was so gradual. More generally, we want to know what kind of political process shaped this type of reform. Second, the cross-country approach provides some useful stylized facts, but as such they do not strictly apply in each and every country. The reform indexes are proxies used to study complex phenomena. More detailed narratives of specific experiences, such as those presented in this research program, can thus be a useful complement. To this end, we adopted an analytic narrative methodology (Bates et al., 1998).

Our narrative of the Uruguayan reform process was guided by some general hypotheses. An important one is that the gradualism that characterized this process was more the result of the interplay of several actors with different interests and views on the reform process in a pluralist political system than a deliberate strategy pursued and imposed by a dominant player. A second related hypothesis is that gradualism and socio-political inclusion were two sides of the same coin. Third, we maintain that the intensive use of instruments of direct democracy, while reducing the speed and conditioning the content of the reform, contributed to legitimizing the political system. Referendums and plebiscites were highly effective devices for the resolution of conflicts. We also discuss to what extent some hypotheses that have played a prominent role in the economic reform literature can help us to understand the Uruguayan case. Among them, the ideas that relate reforms to crisis receive significant attention in this chapter. Uruguay is also a good case for the study of hypotheses on the influence that other countries may have on the domestic reform process, for it is a small country enclosed by two much larger and highly unstable countries.

This chapter is organized in five sections. Section 7.2 addresses the issue of why the reforms have been undertaken, focusing on goals and incentives. In Section 7.3, the chapter turns to the what-kind-of-reform question. A wide range of policies can be listed under the general heading of market-friendly reforms. The outcome of the reform process is highly sensitive to the specific mix of policies that are being pursued in each particular historical context. Hence, it is crucial to identify the specific characteristics of the reform package in each country case. To this end, we try to identify the values and ideas involved in the reforms, the way they have been formulated, the decision-making process, and issues of implementation. Section 7.4 provides a brief account of existing evidence on the performance of the reforms. In Section 7.5, we present some concluding remarks. Appendix 7.1 gives a general chronology of the Uruguayan reform process.

7.2 Why have reforms been implemented?

The electoral campaign of 1989 reshaped the Uruguayan policy agenda and was the point of departure of the main pro-market reform cycle in the democratic period initiated in 1985. In the National Party, the candidate who eventually won the election made a point of the need to continue the pro-market reform agenda and criticized the former president for not doing so. Even in the party of the former president, the fraction that received most votes criticized the previous government for being too gradualist. The impulse that the 'Washington Consensus' gave to the pro-market agenda throughout Latin America in the 1990s contributed to this domestic political turn.

The political competition among parties and among fractions within parties sometimes reduced the speed of reforms or even blocked them. But this same competition often provided incentives for reformist politicians to propose new initiatives for reform. The two most intense reformist periods of the 1990s can be analyzed in terms of the tensions and trade-offs that politicians faced between electoral considerations (vote-seeking and blame avoidance) and the profile of public policies (policy-seeking).

An analysis of the reasons behind the reforms answers the question of the objectives and the incentives of the actors in the process. Economic and social development is invariably a declared goal for everyone involved in processes of structural reform. More specific objectives, on the other hand, vary from one actor to another and from one reform to another. The actors in the process are subject to different conditioning factors which affect their incentives with regard to reform. Factors such as the current economic crisis, and external pressure and internal feedback, which the process of reform itself can generate, are usually important incentives. In this section we propose to shed some light on the reasons for the reforms in Uruguay by exploring the objectives and incentives of the actors involved in the process.[3]

7.2.1 Objectives

As in other countries, the most enthusiastic Uruguayan reformers argued that the market economy, if allowed to function freely, would lead to economically efficient results. On a very general level, the low rates of growth that the country had in the twentieth century were attributed to strong state intervention, which isolated Uruguay via trade protectionism, eliminated competition by introducing monopolies in key sectors of the economy, expanded the size of the state excessively, caused macroeconomic instability, and generated legal uncertainty by governmental interference in private contracts. In line with this diagnosis, the solutions proposed included opening the economy to foreign competition, reducing the role of the state in the economy, and adopting orthodox macroeconomic policies that would guarantee stability. However, in Uruguay, the sectors that most enthusiastically favor pro-market reform have never had enough power to carry their reform program through by themselves. Consequently, the proposals for reform were usually moderate and recognized country idiosyncrasies and specificities in each reform area. In addition, local debate fed on different contributions and to a large extent mirrored the universal academic debates and proposals that were going on in the rest of the region.

The declared objectives of the reforms were ambitious and wide-ranging. They included promoting growth, increasing efficiency, strengthening social policies, and consolidating and strengthening democratic institutions. However, the specificity of the reform program analyzed in this chapter does not lie in these general postulates but in the more specific proposals for reform that, in turn, stem from a particular diagnosis of the country's situation.

The general objectives of the reform process conformed to the Washington Consensus and were relatively fixed in the period under consideration, but there was a certain evolution in the more specific or instrumental objectives. These changes were induced by the reform process itself. In the area of trade policy, a strategy that favored unilateral opening gave way to a strategy of regional integration. This change was clearly determined by the evolution of the regional integration process, and this in turn was determined basically by the large countries in the region. In the area of public enterprises, the attempt at privatization in the first half of the 1990s failed, and this caused adjustments to the reformist proposal, which tended to emphasize the removal of monopolies, the possibility of public enterprises associating with private companies, and the creation of independent regulatory bodies.

After the dictatorship ended, several political changes took place which involved the consolidation of democracy. Although the democratic transition affected virtually every area of politics, the analysis in this chapter is centered specifically on the process leading to the constitutional reform, which was approved in 1996. According to their proponents, the new dispositions sought to foster the formation of majorities to govern, while at the same time promoting transparency in the electoral system.[4] On the first point, the new constitution seeks to incorporate norms that will stimulate political agreements and negotiation, the forming of coalitions, stability in cabinets, and legislative majorities. Moreover, it was maintained that the second round in elections would stimulate the making of agreements to govern.[5] In addition, the mechanisms for replacing the directors of the public enterprises were modified so as to increase the costs for a political party to abandon a coalition government. As to the transparency of the electoral system, the intention was to give the voter greater certainty and freedom by limiting the application of the double simultaneous vote and permitting voters to opt for different parties in the different sections that make up the electoral process (primary, national, and local elections).

7.2.2 Incentives

The literature about the political economy of the reforms has identified factors that usually affect the incentives of agents to promote or to put a brake on reform. In this section, we analyze the incidence of three of these factors: crisis, external pressure, and internal feedback.

The crisis of the system

There has been much debate in the literature on political economy about the role of crises in reform processes, but no consensus has been reached (Drazen, 2000: 444–54; Sturzenegger and Tommasi, 1998: 9–11).[6] The experience of reform in Uruguay does not allow firm conclusions on this question to be drawn. Crises may have been a factor in triggering reform in some areas (trade) and a brake in other areas (financial, public services). The Uruguayan experience also shows that not only the current crisis matters for reform. The perception that there may be more crises to come, and that these perceptions are the object of political action are also important aspects of the reform process.

In 1974, the first oil crisis contributed to the termination of the import substitution model, which had been showing clear signs of exhaustion. The increase in the price of petrol (which Uruguay does not produce), the loss of markets for meat and the fall in the prices of traditional export products brought about a change of model. This episode fits in with the stylized fact, emphasized by Cardoso and Galal (2002), that crises characterized by falls in real income and negative rates of growth facilitate the adoption of trade reform. The subsequent move to opening, which took place at the start of the 1990s with the creation of the MERCOSUR, was not connected to any crisis with these characteristics. Quite the contrary, it was a period of significant economic growth and of rising income.

When it comes to public enterprises, it can be said in a very general way that there was no objective sign of crisis that called for reforms. The provision of public services in Uruguay has the not very common characteristic of running without big deficits and providing very wide cover, especially when compared with the indicators of other developing countries. However, at the start of the 1990s, there were broad deficiencies in the quality of services. But the situation was (and is) not seen as critical either by public opinion, by the political system, or by the business sector.

In some specific moments, crises not only did not trigger reform but they rather acted as a brake on the reform process. In the 1980s, the protracted financial crisis made it very difficult to introduce changes in the legislation to develop financial markets. It was not until the second half of the 1990s, when the worst of that crisis had been left behind, that the authorities could promote a legislative agenda to update the financial legislation of the country. However, a few years later, a new crisis negatively impacted on the reform process. According to some government spokesmen, the administration of the crisis that the Uruguayan economy went through from 1999 until 2002 occupied a lot of the government's energy, thus limiting its capacity to push forward with its reform program (*Búsqueda* 1216, 28 August 2003: 12). There are clear signs that the government was weakened politically by the crisis, and it had to make concessions under pressure from different groups that resisted attempts at reform. Particularly telling are the referendum processes that were successfully launched during this period by the unions of three public enterprises operating in telecommunications (ANTEL), petrol (ANCAP), and water and sewage (OSE).

The constitutional reform that was approved in 1996 sought to resolve the problem of governability. The experience of the two previous administrations had shown that the government was finding it increasingly difficult to obtain parliamentary majorities. In particular, the plebiscite that in 1992 overturned the law of public enterprises by an overwhelming majority left the National Party government isolated politically. The rise of the left coalition in the 1994 elections, which could be seen as a crisis for the traditional parties, motivated them to promote a change in the electoral rules. However, the reform was not directly triggered by a government crisis. Quite the contrary in fact, when the constitutional reform of 1996 was passed, the government had the most solid coalition in the recent history of the country.

The experience of social security reform brings to light two more facets of the complex relation between crisis and reform. First, it is not the crisis in itself but perception of the crisis that often prompts action for or against reform. Second, this perception is not something exogenous that the players cannot influence; the players undertook specific action geared to modifying this perception.

The reforms in social security have been strongly conditioned by the long-term problems of solvency in the system. The trend towards growing expenditure in social security was reinforced in Uruguay by the increase in payments that came about after the plebiscite of 1989, which introduced a system of pension indexing into the constitution of the republic. The lagged indexation of pensions to wages and the disinflation process that took place in the first half of the 1990s led to a big rise in the purchasing power of pensions in the subsequent years (expenditure on retirement pensions and benefits increased by approximately 4 points of GDP between 1990 and 1994), and prevented the government from attacking the fiscal deficit by reducing the value of retirement pensions and benefits, which had been the traditional remedy. In some sense, the plebiscite itself made a deeper reform inevitable (de Oliveira et al., 1994: 21; Filgueira et al., 1999; Saldain, 1999: 3; Rius, 2003). However, the crisis had not yet struck, at least not to the extent that the Social Security Administration (BPS) or the government, which assisted it financially, were in imminent danger of not being able to make the payments. The crisis could have been anticipated insofar as different studies show that the financial accounts could only deteriorate in subsequent years, but in any case it was the perception of future crises rather than the reality of a present crisis which triggered action leading to reform.

The perception of crisis is also an arena of political competition. Luján (2003) shows how the promoters of reform try to transmit a sense of emergency to the population, while those who oppose it resist. According to Luján (2003: 14), 'One of President Julio María Sanguinetti's successes was to generate the perception that financial crisis was inevitable in the middle term if reform of the social security system was not undertaken.' Against this, an opposition Senator said, 'Although there is a problem in the social security system, it is not as serious nor is it at the level of crisis which the Presidency claims' (Senator Alberto Couriel, *Búsqueda* 804, 10 August 1995: 8–9).

External factors: multilateral institutions and the reform in the region

As in other developing countries, multilateral institutions have contributed to pushing forward the market-friendly reform process in Uruguay. The institutions contributed proposals, technical assistance, and finance to carry out various reforms. But the rhythm and many specific details of the reforms were largely conditioned by internal factors. The process was marked by the presence of political and social forces with conflicting visions of the reforms, and this had the effect of slowing them down and limiting their scope. At times, the action of the multilateral institutions themselves seemed somewhat uncertain and contradictory, possibly because of the need to negotiate solutions with a variety of different internal actors.

On more than one occasion, both government spokesmen and representatives of the multilateral institutions said that these institutions had played a secondary role in fostering reform. For example, Luján (2003: 211) cites declarations made by the presidential secretary during the Sanguinetti administration (1995–2000), which claimed that the reform agenda had been established internally, without external influence, 'According to the secretary of the President, the structuring of the reform proposal came from endogenous sources and had more to do with the national limits of the coalition than with external guidelines from international or regional credit institutions.' The president of the Inter-American Development Bank (IDB) made declarations in the press to the same effect. It seems evident that with public statements such as these, the IDB and the Uruguayan government wished to convey the idea that the reform had been designed in Uruguay, without foreign influence. However, such declarations do not prove that the agenda was in fact established by parties independently of multilateral institutions. Rather, bearing in mind the prevailing preoccupation with national political autonomy and the low status of multilateral credit institutions in local public opinion such statements might be expected. Nonetheless, the content of the Uruguayan reforms, and some details of the negotiation process, suggest that the institutions had to make considerable concessions.

The mission documents of the international institutions and the commitments made by the country, for example, the letters of intent with the IMF, maintain a reformist rhetoric, but the goals set are not necessarily met in the time period agreed where this would cause grave consequences for the country or financial restrictions. Multilateral organizations have recognized the restrictions to reform stemming from internal political processes, despite a government's efforts to move forward. For example, in November 2000, a report from the World Bank supported the government's efforts to allow the private sector a greater stake in activities traditionally undertaken by the public sector, '. . . given the political mandate against privatization of public enterprises' (a clear reference to the plebiscite that overturned the proposed law of public enterprises). What is more, the IDB and the World Bank (WB) financed expansion projects in some public enterprises in the 1990s without imposing, as a prior requirement, structural reforms, such as privatization or the imposition of regulatory frameworks. In the social security reform, the IDB and the WB adopted positions that were very far apart. At the beginning of 1995 the WB questioned the reform proposal being negotiated by the political parties and withdrew its support.[7] The IDB, on the other hand, supported the reform from the beginning, contributed funding and provided technical and political backing.

These apparent contradictions, and the margins of flexibility that are evident, seem to be explicable in a strategic context in which the multilateral institution recognizes itself to be one of many 'principals' who are struggling to influence the policy implemented by the government.[8] In this context, the rational thing to do is concede something if, in exchange, the reform process can be unblocked.

The situation in trade reform is somewhat different. The multilateral credit institutions have not played an active role in the process of trade reform in Uruguay. If there was some kind of imposition of conditions, it was more global and more on the level of ideas than anything else. But in this instance we cannot talk about a concession on the part of the multilateral institutions since, beyond certain deviations in trade policy, Uruguay is recognized in the international community as a member of the club of Latin American countries that implemented trade reform and opened the economy (Rajapatirana, 1995).

Events in other countries in the region also played a key role in shaping the agenda of internal reforms in Uruguay. There is no doubt that, apart from local idiosyncrasies, reforms such as the 1992 public enterprises law, the 1995 pension systems law, and the 1997 law of the regulatory framework for electrical energy followed general guidelines present in the reform processes being implemented in the region. Also the impulse to trade opening, which was present in Uruguay at the start of the 1990s, was favored by a change in the trade policy orientation of the countries in the region. During those years, the import substitution model was tending to be replaced by a model of trade opening and orientation to exports. The most significant change was that, from the late 1980s and especially at the start of the 1990s, Brazil intensified the process of opening its economy unilaterally. Brazil has about 40 times the economic weight of Uruguay, and this policy change on the part of her biggest neighbor altered the domestic equilibrium in Uruguay in favor of pro-export groups (Krishna and Mitra, 2005).[9] Clearly, in the period 1990–94, the National Party government in Uruguay was conscious of this change. The MERCOSUR should be understood in the context of this change of model and paradigm because it was an instrument that supported and consolidated this strategy of unilateral opening. All the economies in the region without exception adopted this strategy, although each went at its own pace. In this sense, regionalism was not a substitute for unilateralism.

Even though the constitutional reform of 1996 has many autochthonous characteristics, it follows the general pattern in the region. The introduction of the majority run-off system, the limitation to one presidential candidate per party, the primary elections and the separation of the local and national elections are in line with the changes that several countries in Latin America were implementing in those years. In turn, multilateral institutions did not play an active role in the process of political reform.

The Chilean experience had an evident influence and was widely debated in Uruguay. Reform in Argentina also had an effect on Uruguay, but with changing sign. In the first half of the 1990s, the Argentine model was presented by the reformist political sectors as the road to be followed. But afterwards, to the extent that economic results in Argentina turned sour and reports of corruption spread, the experience of its closest neighbor tended more to serve the political interests of opponents of pro-market reform in Uruguay.

Internal factors: public opinion, parties, and social organizations

Public opinion has had a decisive influence on the reform process in Uruguay, conditioning its rhythm and specific content. The opinion of the people has not only made itself felt in national elections but also in a number of referendums and plebiscites about the reforms that took place during the period. The intense use of mechanisms of direct democracy meant that, on the question of reform, the battle for public opinion was central to the activities of the political parties and of the social organizations involved.

In general, Uruguayan public opinion has been reluctant to support market-friendly reforms, and this seems to have deep roots in values and ideology. According to Latinobarometer (poll series 1995–2002), Uruguay's approval of the free-market economy is by far the lowest in Latin America, 35 per cent versus a continental average of 57 per cent. It is among the four countries that are least satisfied with this system (10 per cent satisfaction versus the Latin

American average of 24 per cent). Only Argentina has a more negative view of privatization than Uruguay: the former has an approval rating of 14 per cent and the latter of 16 per cent. This evidence raises at least two related questions: (i) Why do Uruguayan citizens seem to dislike market institutions? (ii) Is this ideology relevant to explain the reform process?

As to the first question, it has been argued that the initial success of the welfare model developed a century ago and often named as the 'Batllist model' explains the current statist ideology of Uruguayans. According to this view, many citizens find it difficult to understand why the model should be changed, since it was successful. The international conditions and technology have changed, the argument goes, in ways that make pro-market reforms convenient and even necessary in several fields. However, there is no simple way to prove it a priori. Furthermore, if there is no simple mapping from policies to outcomes, and some reforms involve initial costs and benefits that only come later, many citizens might continue resisting reform. If all this means that the reform never takes off, the learning will never take place.

The 'curse of success' does not seem to be just a nostalgic view of the past. In fact, current performance of the Uruguayan public sector is not bad by Latin American standards (Kaufmann et al., 2003). Hence, it is no wonder that Uruguayans value their public sector more highly than other Latin Americans do. There is also some cross-sectoral evidence that supports this view. We argue in this chapter that the market-friendly reforms were resisted more strongly in those public utilities perceived by the population to be working well, than in services that were working less well.

As to the second question, it could be argued that opposition to reform is just a self-interested position that has little to do with ideology. The literature provides several theories of resistance to reform that do not rest on ideology. In the Uruguayan case, this view finds support in the fact that referendums and plebiscites launched to stop the reform process were organized by groups with direct interests in the subjects submitted to vote. Nevertheless, and without ruling these theories out, we do think that values and ideas have also played a prominent role in this experience. The campaigns organized for plebiscites and referendums strongly appealed to the anti-market and anti-profit-seeking feelings of Uruguayan citizens. Right or wrong, the view that the privatization of public utilities would have a negative effect on the general interests of the country is strongly rooted in the population and there seems to be little doubt that it played a key role in the process. Obviously, the campaigns were organized by groups who directly benefited from the current state of affairs, so it is difficult to accept that ideology was their only motivation. But the interesting part is that, while this was obvious, they still managed on several occasions to convince other citizens that the reforms should be stopped. Without this underlying ideology, it seems difficult to understand how the unions of public employees managed to convince significant parts of the population to vote against some reforms.

More often than not public opinion opposed reform, but there were exceptions. An outstanding example of the latter is the regional trade liberalization. Although there was debate about the modality of the negotiations, the general principle that Uruguay should become integrated into the region was widely supported by the people. In other cases, rather than support for reform, there was discontent with the prior situation, which the proponents of reform were able to take advantage of. This is what happened with respect to the social security and constitutional reforms.[10]

Uruguayan political parties have internal factions that hold a relatively wide range of positions on the question of market-friendly reform. In the traditional parties, these positions range from radical reformists to moderate reformists. In the leftist coalition, the dominant positions are strongly against reform that has its roots in neo-liberalism, but there are factions that have shown some disposition to negotiate moderate reforms.

The traditional parties have occupied the presidency throughout the period under study, but the dominant factions have varied considerably. The four administrations in power from the return to democracy in 1985 to 2005, when a left-wing party took office for the first time, included two that could be called moderate (1985–90 and 1995–2000) and two administrations of a more definite pro-market orientation (1990–95 and 2000–05). However, there is no simple or direct relation between the ideological position of the presidency and the rhythm and extent of the reforms carried out. There was a first significant liberalizing push during the Lacalle administration, in the period 1990–95, but the stiff resistance which this provoked considerably limited the extent of reform in those years. The next administration was based on a coalition of center factions, and it managed to carry out some important reforms, including the social security and constitutional reforms.

The composition of the coalition government in 1995 is the key to explaining the reforms of that period. The two previous democratic governments negotiated governability agreements, but neither of them managed to make an agreement with the scope and duration of the coalition in power between 1995 and 2000 (Buquet and Piñeiro, 2000). In the literature, it is possible to identify two hypotheses that attempt to explain why the traditional parties succeeded in maintaining a particularly solid government coalition in the period 1995–2000. Both hypotheses have to do with the 1994 elections, in which the political left wing grew considerably and the center factions of the traditional parties emerged dominant. The growth of the left wing in the 1994 elections was a definite threat to the traditional parties, and it led them to form a more solid coalition than had been the case in the two previous administrations (Filgueira et al., 1999; Buquet and Piñeiro, 2000; Luján, 2003). Also, it has been argued that the triumph of moderate or center factions in the traditional parties in these elections contributed to making the coalition government of the 1995–2000 period viable (Lanzaro, 2000a: 173–6; 2000b: 291–2).

Some authors have maintained that there is a trend for reforms to be initiated when a new government begins its term (Haggard and Webb, 1994; Lora and Olivera, 2004). According to press statements, local politicians seem to share this idea.[11] One possible explanation is that governments have high discount rates as they come to care increasingly about their own term or, at best, re-elections of themselves or their coalition (Drazen, 2000; Sturzenegger and Tommasi, 1998).[12] Buquet et al. (1998) have argued that Uruguayan governments have been more able to pass laws during the first half of the term, when a cooperation strategy among members of the government coalition prevails, than in the second half of the term, when party factions that do not lead the coalition find it electorally more costly to support the executive.

The positions adopted by Uruguayan political parties on the question of reform were not only conditioned by their ideological posture, but also by links with the bureaucracy. In some cases, public enterprises allow their directors to maintain a high profile in the public eye and a certain capacity to influence the communication media, and this can enable these people to set up platforms for launching political campaigns.[13] A leader with this kind of background is naturally inclined towards a moderate position on the question of reform. For a politician, the creation of an image of leadership and capability in management is incompatible with a process of reduction and limitation in the management of the public enterprise which he directs, as would result from a radical reform, from privatization, or even from a significant reduction in the economic weight of the enterprise in that sector.

Various interest groups were intensively active in the matter of the reform process. What stands out here is the militant opposition to reforms shown by the unions in the public enterprises and the associations of pensioners. This was the classic case of groups made up of people with relatively uniform interests, and with the capacity to resolve the problems of internal free-riding, involved in collective action (Olson, 1965). They aimed to win over public opinion so as to block the reforms through plebiscites and referendums. They organized campaigns to convince the public, and they set legal mechanisms in motion which led to the exercise of direct democracy. In some instances, the changes caused by their activity, and the political situation that they created by submitting certain laws to direct popular vote, prompted some political sectors to change their position. This experience seems to indicate that obtaining backing from the left was a necessary but not sufficient condition for success in plebiscite campaigns.[14]

As a rule, organizations of entrepreneurs adopted a favorable position on the question of structural change because they thought that this would reduce both the weight of the state in the economy and charges for public services. But, in general, they have not been important actors in the reform process, probably because they were not able to overcome the problem of internal free-riding because of the relatively diffuse character of the advantages that they would obtain from a reduction in the costs of the state. Government efficiency certainly has the nature of a public good, so it is not easy to over-come the temptation to free-ride. There has been active lobbying in favor of state reform in other countries in the region, particularly when it comes to privatization. The entrepreneurs who actively participated in these activities insisted on the general benefits of a smaller and more efficient public sector, but they usually had more direct and private interests as well. In the case of Uruguay, however, this reform was blocked by a referendum. The reform of the ports is the only case in which a (smallish) group of businessmen had a keen interest in reform, and they organized themselves to exert influence in the situation. It is also likely that some banks exerted pressure to keep the capital account open. In the late 1970s, regional offshore banking took off, grounded on a strict banking secrecy regime and lack of personal income tax. Not surprisingly, the local banking system has had strong stakes in unfettered capital mobility, which tradable sectors blame partly for pro-tracted spells of domestic currency overvaluation.

The fact that entrepreneurial groups have been so little involved in reform could also be due to their having divergent positions and interests that do not always coincide with the reforms. Unlike the workers' unions, which had a single central organization, entrepreneurs were grouped in a number of dif-ferent business associations whose positions were different if not totally opposed to each other on the question of the reforms. Banks, for example, maintained a low profile, and their position with regard to laws geared to pro-moting the development of the capital market was ambiguous because the cap-ital market is a competitor of bank credit. In this ambit, only the administrators of retirement savings funds seemed to take an interest in the development of the capital market and in its legal instruments.

More generally, the reform reduced the scope for rent-seeking, an activity in which some leading Uruguayan entrepreneurs had become quite skillful. Finally, the reform involved a considerable degree of individual uncertainty, and many firms could not tell for sure whether they would be among the winners.

Political reform is an area in which interest groups were not seen to par-ticipate actively. Since it does not affect specific groups with well-defined interests, the debate about electoral and governmental reform remained in the specific ambit of party political activity. We can suppose that this non-intervention on the part of the social organizations benefited reformist sectors because the groups with the greatest capacity for organization invariably line up with the positions of the left wing, and the majority of the left coalition opposed political reform as it would negatively affect their chances in the elections.

In some areas the government was able to effect reforms without needing to have recourse to support in parliament. The outstanding example is trade policy, which was changed mainly by decrees and resolutions without par-liamentary participation.[15] Besides this, the government was able to take a number of infrastructure construction works out of the state sphere through mechanisms of awarding contracts for highways, airports, and water and sewage system concessions to private enterprise.

Another instrument of trade policy was conventions and treaties, and in this area the president is relatively autonomous of parliament. In the period, there was the MERCOSUR treaty of Asunción (1991) and the World Trade Organization Act of Marrakech (1994). In both instances, in spite of debate about approval, the ratification laws constituted a package which was approved without being opened. These two agreements constrained the scope for government discretion in trade policy.

7.3　What kind of reform is best adapted to achieving its objectives?

7.3.1　Politics and policies in democratic Uruguay

Since the return to democracy in 1985, Uruguay has shown a high degree of political inclusion, and political and social participation. Intensive negotiations have taken place between political parties and social organizations, with each holding a considerable degree of power. It has not been easy to arrive at agreements in a number of important policy areas. Contrasting views and different interests have made the negotiations rigid and often harsh, and as a result the reform process in Uruguay may look sluggish and incomplete. At the same time, and despite serious disagreements in this field, the country exhibits a remarkable degree of political and social cohesion. A general hypothesis of this research project is that the gradualism of the Uruguayan reform process and political and social inclusion go hand in hand.

The central proposition of this study is that in Uruguay there is not simply a blocking of reforms, as some have argued, but a manner of implementing reforms which permits progress to be made in a peculiar and distinctive way. What in fact comes out is gradualist and moderate political engineering, which sets the mode of the reform processes with respect to itineraries and also with respect to results.

As a basic hypothesis, we maintain that this gradualist and moderate logic is a result of political competition in a pluralist democracy like that which took over in Uruguay after the authoritarian regime ended. It sprang specifically from the characteristics of the government regime, the electoral rules, and the transformation of the party system. This gradualist and moderate 'incremental' logic is the result of the political dynamic. In concrete terms, it stems from the competition between parties and factions within the parties which shapes the course the government takes, regulates innovative initiatives, and mobilizes the 'veto players', setting certain parameters as to styles of leadership and reform coalitions, building consensus, and reducing dissent.

What we have here is a 'modal pattern', characteristic of pluralist democracies such as Uruguay, which generates a process of 'muddling through' (Lindblom,

1965) with continual compromises and adjustments in the implementation of public policies.[16] This pattern is typical of institutional settings that require broad consensus and special majorities for policy-making. These are democracies that induce plurality and a certain balance of power, both among political parties and among social actors. The culture and the behavior of the elites and the political culture of the citizenship show these pluralistic features as well, and this is so because the pluralist organization is a long-run phenomenon, rooted in the foundation of the country and with the original characteristics of a 'polyarchy' (Dahl, 1971).

It is important to note that, generally speaking, gradualism is not necessarily the result of any determinate political will. It is rather the objective resultant that emerges from the conflict of interests of the forces in play, and in particular from the competition between parties and factions within parties. In this general outline, gradualism is also the law of the game, proposing a kind of legality of change – that is, the model to which the proponents of reform have to adjust in order for their proposals to be workable, efficient and legitimate (building consensus and reducing dissent). Therefore, these factors determine the structure of opportunities for innovation in a system, the so-called political window (Kingdom, 1995) – certainly narrow – that reformers must find through continual compromises and adjustments. This is what 'the intelligence of democracy' (Lindblom, 1965) imposes in these scenarios.

This is also the key to being able to go through the 'eye of the needle' in the Uruguayan system (Lanzaro, 2000a). With these rules of change, gradualism and moderation in the reform process may stem from a political will and a style of leadership that adopts this strategy to avoid blocking, but it can also stem from an ex-post regulation: political initiatives that do not start with this approach face resistance and have to be changed or run a serious risk of being turned down. In fact, as we shall see in different sections of this study, the most successful initiatives are those that mold themselves to this model and meet at least two requirements: (i) presidential leadership which is both innovative and transactional, and (ii) a centrist, moderate, reform coalition, which makes progress by proposals for compromise.

As Lindblom (1965) would say, it is the science (wisdom indeed) of muddling through. The reform of the social security system and the reform of the electoral system with the constitution of 1996 provide two good cases for the discussion of these premises, and comparison with other, less successful initiatives. It is no coincidence that both these examples come from President Sanguinetti's second administration.

In all cases, the government took the initiative for the reform. The attitude and performance of the president was key and showed different styles of leadership. While Lacalle was relatively more ideological or pathbreaking, Sanguinetti was more pragmatic or pathfinding (Lanzaro, 2000a: 140–9).[17] These styles partially stem from the idiosyncratic characteristics of the presidents, but they also emerged as a result of a process of political learning. Sanguinetti in his second presidency (1995–2000) had to accentuate his moderation with respect to the reform process. After 2000, President Batlle had to postpone some of his previous plans when he had to rule the country in extremely adverse conditions. Also in this period and as a member of the government coalition, former President Lacalle also recognized the constraints imposed by the juncture, albeit demanding a more decisive pro-market orientation from the government (Lanzaro, 2000b). This political learning is based on the analysis of his own as well as others' mistakes.

In terms of comparative politics of reforms, these observations can be linked to two distinctions: (i) relating to the authoritarian or democratic regime; and (ii) relating to different types of democracy and styles of government. Some of the reform processes in Latin America have been undertaken under authoritarian regimes. The paradigmatic example of this is Chile under the Pinochet dictatorship, a period when there was radical liberalization of the economy, changes in the structure and in the functions of the state, and also constitutional reform which, to a large extent, still holds sway. Uruguayan reform also took place under the dictatorship and under democracy. The milestones of financial, domestic, and foreign liberalization, and the first steps to trade liberalization, were established during the dictatorship, but the Uruguayan dictatorship did not have the foundational style of that in Chile. As to the types of democracy and styles of government, we can distinguish majority regimes, populist or neo-populist formulas, and pluralist systems. Uruguay can be considered as a leading case in the last category.

7.3.2 Basic knowledge: values and information

Values and ideology

The values and ideology that made it difficult for the pro-market reforms to progress quickly also conditioned the contents of the reform. Public opinion has been a decisive factor in shaping the reform process, and politicians have to pay heed to it, regardless of their constituencies.

Although this is hard to document, swathes of public opinion have a negative perception of the financial sector and show some distrust of financial globalization. Not surprisingly, while the general public tends to favor financial regulation and supervision, some actual and would-be market participants demand less regulation and more freedom to operate. A part of the legal profession, sometimes with center-left leanings, voiced sovereignty concerns about concrete legislative proposals such as allowing private parties' choice of jurisdictions in particular instances of financial contracting, normally considered a protection to foreign investors (De Posadas, 1996).

A considerable proportion of the population does not trust private enterprise and they tend to associate it with corruption, profits taken out of the country, excessive charges and bad service. There is a perception that the large enterprises which operate public services in the world would have too much power relative to the small size of the country, and Uruguay would not be able to 'defend itself'.

By the middle of the last century, the idea of protecting the domestic market as a way of protecting national employment from the rest of the world was very popular in Uruguay. Proposals to liberalize foreign trade often faced resistance based on the fear of losing jobs. But in recent decades, the notion that economic growth must be led by exports has gained increasing support in the country. More generally, there seems to be a growing awareness among the Uruguayan population that a country the size of theirs must integrate with the world to enjoy economic and social progress.

Social security policy tends to be strongly conditioned by values and ideology. In the debate about reform there are at least two dimensions with powerful ideological connotations, the state versus the market, and equality versus efficiency. On the one hand, the fact that public opinion in the country does not trust the market makes it unlikely that a sweeping privatization reform could be successful. Therefore, the reform should reserve a dominating role to the public pillar in that system. On the other hand, although all the political and social actors involved in the reform process agree that the social security system ought to be redistributive and efficient, the promoters of reform see these objectives as causing a political dilemma, while opponents do not see it the same way. The parties and technicians who support the reform maintain that the tenuous correlation between contributions and payments in the old system generated powerful incentives for evasion and informality. The goal of the reform, therefore, was to give greater financial equity to the system in the expectation that this would increase incentives towards formalization. Opponents of the reform tended to attribute the inefficiency of the system, including evasion and informality in the labor market, to poor management in the administration of social security. In any case, and going beyond the differences noted here, the shared objective to developing redistributive policies through the pension system meant that the PAYG pillar had to continue as the basis, with the pillar of individual accounts as a complementary component.

Information and uncertainty

Uruguay is a relatively simple and homogeneous country and it has a relatively good statistical information base by Latin American standards. However, opponents of reform and various independent analysts have argued that the lack of information, transparency, and experience, particularly in regulatory matters, increased uncertainty with regard to the way some reforms could function.

In the sphere of foreign trade, there are no restrictions on the implementation of reform that stem from lack of knowledge. Many national and international studies have identified the costs of protectionism in the country.

Among these a number of studies made in the framework of different World Bank projects stand out (Corbo and De Melo, 1987; Connolly and De Melo, 1994; Rajapatirana, 1995; Shatz and Tarr, 2000).

In other areas there is a lack of information and transparency which could have had an influence on the success of the reforms. There was no experience of regulating public services before the attempt at reform began. The opposition claims that the impact of the reform was to a large extent ignored in most areas.

Absent or poor disclosure is the landmark of domestic corporate and financial sectors, often operating under weak regulation and supervision.[18] Databases from López-de-Silanes (2002) show that the ratings of Uruguayan accounting standards are clearly below the developing countries' average.

There are large areas in the social security system where information is lacking. Like the other countries in the region, Uruguay did not have records of work histories when the reforms began.[19] This lack has a serious effect on the quality of the financial projections that were made, and generates uncertainty about the extent of evasion (Caristo and Forteza, 2003).

A number of politicians and social actors who resisted the reforms, or who recommended greater prudence in implementation, based their arguments on these information problems, and in particular on the state's lack of experience and capacity to regulate the private sector.

7.3.3   Implementation, initial conditions, and gradualism

In a way, the implementation phase is the moment of truth for reforms. It is the stage in which reformist forces must demonstrate their capacity to go from words to deeds. It has been pointed out that reforms often become bogged down at this stage because governments lack the capability to carry through public policies. The implementation of reforms can also be complicated by opposition from interest groups who find opportunities at this stage to block changes they do not agree with. Grindle and Thomas (1990) argue that in low-income countries participatory pressures emerge mainly in the implementation phase. Because of the weakness of interest groups and the low administrative capacity of the government, the decision-making process tends to be closed, non-participatory, and elitist. As a result, the argument goes, interest groups try to block policies they oppose at the time of implementation, bringing about a wide gap between *de jure* or official policy and de facto or actual policy.

In our view, the Uruguayan case does not exactly fit this pattern. Since 1985, the reforms in Uruguay have been extensively debated, with active participation of all political parties and many social groups. Referendums and plebiscites have provided vocal groups with a powerful opportunity to let their voice be heard. These tools of direct democracy have been used on a number of occasions to block reforms, but even when it did not come to this, the threat of referendum hung over the design of the reform. Its influence, then, was considerably greater than one might suppose from counting up the number of successful plebiscites. This does not mean that the interest groups opposed to reform would not have tried to block reforms which reached the implementation stage, but in any case there does not seem to be a clear bias towards blocking reforms at this final stage of the process.[20] Be that as it may, many of the difficulties which the reform programs faced made themselves strongly felt at this stage.

Not only were the reforms in Uruguay adopted slowly, but they were also implemented gradually. Several factors led to this outcome. In some cases, changing international factors conditioned the speed and orientation of the process (trade). In other cases, the existence of different views and interests in the reformist coalition and the decentralization of the process made it possible for several quite different projects to coexist (public services). Finally, in other cases the reform was designed to be implemented gradually, both for political and economic reasons (pensions).

Trade reform is a clear example of a policy that had a number of ups and downs caused by the changing conditions of the situation. Before the 1990s, trade reform made progress as unilateral opening. The opening process increased in the first half of the 1990s, but now in the framework of a process of regional integration. In 1994, the Marrakech agreement was ratified in the framework of the World Trade Organization, in what can be characterized as reciprocal multilateral opening. However, the MERCOSUR agreement had greater scope for Uruguay than the Marrakech agreements. The 1995 to 1999 period was a time of convergence towards both a common trade policy in the MERCO-SUR and general rules of the World Trade Organization. Finally, from 2000 to 2003, there was a move back towards protectionism, stemming from the serious crisis that affected the country and its main trade partners in the region.

The reform of public services has varied considerably from one area of activity to another, and has changed during the period being studied. In part, this diversity is due to different initial conditions, but more important than this is the fact that there seems to have been a lack of a clear dominant model. In Uruguay, various political sectors were competing to impose their different visions of reform, and there was no single and consistent leadership of the process as there had been in Britain under Margaret Thatcher or with Felipe González in Spain. The referendum that overturned the public enterprises law in 1992 forced the reformist sectors to abandon privatization. But even before that episode, the same administrations that undertook some privatization and outsourcing in some areas of the state promoted new investment and developed new activities in other areas.

There are a number of examples of this policy of attempting to strengthen Uruguayan public enterprises just when the privatization model was at its apogee. The public electricity enterprise was restructured between 1995 and 2000 in a transition that involved considerable investment. More significant still is the case of the state petrol enterprise, which in the 1990s invested in an overhaul and an expansion of its refining capacity, bought a distribution company for petroleum products in Argentina, and shifted the distribution of petroleum products in Uruguay to a private company that traditionally distributed fuel under the trademark of the public enterprise. In this period, no progress was made in opening the sector to competition. The area of mobile telephony is another example of a public enterprise that continued to extend its activities during the period. The mobile telephony service was first offered in Uruguay in 1992 by a private company, but two years later the public telecommunications enterprise came into the cellular phone market. From that time until the end of 2001, the mobile telephone market was a duopoly in which the private company is a contractor of the public one. This means that there was no real competition between the firms since, to a large extent, decisions about technology were taken by the state enterprise, and the private company fell into line.

At the same time, successive governments have been promoting reforms involving privatization, the breaking up of monopolies, and the design of regulatory systems. However, no significant progress was made in privatization after the 1992 law of public enterprises was overturned by referendum, which rapidly blocked that road. Then, norms were enacted which dismantled monopolies in a number of public services including electricity generating, long-distance and cellular telephony, and the refining and importing of petroleum products. But there have not been big changes in competition in these areas, except for long-distance international telephony. This is either because private investors have not come forward (the generation of electricity), or because the norms were later abolished. Lastly, during the Batlle administration (2000–05), bodies to regulate competition in a number of public service areas were established. However, the lack of progress in privatization and dismantling of monopolies has led to uncertainty as to what scope these bodies will have in practice.

The reform of the Uruguayan social security system is clearly gradualist. A first sign of this can be found in the full recognition of the rights acquired by retired people in the previous system. Besides this, the new norms modify only slightly the conditions for access to benefits for those workers who had acquired the right to retire but had not yet begun the retirement procedure when the reform started. Another sign of gradualism is the introduction of the so-called 'transition regime', a reformed pay-as-you-go regime applicable to workers who were 40 years old or over when the reform began. Lastly, various changes in the parameters of the pay-as-you-go pillar were programmed for gradual implementation over a period of several years.

It does not seem possible to identify one single reason for this gradualism in the reform of the Uruguayan social security system, although President Sanguinetti, in general, defended a gradualist strategy rather than shock strategies, quite apart from the specific reform of social security that took place during his mandate. To this we can add that the other leading partner in the coalition government also had a clear preference for gradualism. The government coalition was in the political center, and it was gradualist.

Concern with mitigating the financial costs of the transition also contributed to the choice of a gradual strategy. The fact that when the reform began only those under 40 years old would be fully incorporated into the mixed regime considerably reduced the deficit of the transition. Statements by Saldain (1999), who was one of the architects of the reform, indicate that this effect was expressly sought by the reformers. The transition was designed to be long in order to distribute the costs of the adjustment over time. Lastly, gradualism was to some extent a by-product of the strategy of de-activating blockages caused by opponents. There was an attempt to reduce opposition by excluding different generations and some groups of workers from the reform.

The constitutional reform was implemented without much difficulty. The rules for primary and local elections generated some political confrontation, but the reformists managed to get reform through. It is not an area of reform in which it seems possible that opposition blocs might form in the implementation stage. This does not mean, however, that the reform can be called successful in terms of achieving its declared objectives, that is to say in bestowing greater governability and transparency on the electoral system.

7.4 How well did the reform perform?

Uruguay has recently left behind one of the deepest economic crises in its history. From 1999 to 2002, the country went through one of the longest recessions ever experienced, and a very serious fiscal and financial crisis came to a head in 2002. Economic activity is now making a strong recovery, but the fiscal situation is still delicate; the banking sector suffered a tremendous shock; earnings have not yet recovered; and the rate of unemployment continues high. There is no doubt that this crisis will have far-reaching negative consequences for the Uruguayan economy. The question naturally arises as to the extent to which the market-oriented reforms may be responsible for these recent developments. Of course, the fact that the crisis followed some attempts at reform does not mean that these policies should be blamed for the negative situation. Some analysts even claim the opposite, that is, 'that the problem was not too much reform but too little' (Cardoso and Galal, 2002: 10). Nevertheless, even if the problem was 'too little reform', it can be argued that the failure to change traditional policies that badly needed a complete redefinition is a 'reform failure' (if not in the narrow technical sense, it is indeed a failure in a broader political sense).

It is not difficult to identify external, basically regional, factors that triggered the recent crisis in Uruguay (spillover effect). However, this is not the end of the story. On several fronts, Uruguay showed only limited ability to deal with the external shocks. First, the country was not able to escape from the currency overvaluation that characterized the whole region during the 1990s. Given the size of Uruguay and its links with neighboring countries, it was not easy to avoid this regional phenomenon, but some analysts argue that the country could have done more to reduce its high vulnerability to the exchange rate adjustment (see Licandro and Licandro, 2004, among others). More could have been done, the argument goes, in terms of promoting indexed financial instruments to substitute for assets denominated in dollars. The Uruguayan experience during the 1990s shows that reducing inflation may not be sufficient to significantly reduce the extent of dollarization in the economy. Although this is not the only explanation behind continued high levels of dollarization, it does provide some support to the idea that the government must actively promote financial intermediation in domestic currency and in indexed instruments.[21] The government budget was a second front of vulnerability. Fiscal performance looked quite good during the 1990s, but subsequent events proved that the Uruguayan fiscal stance was not strong enough for a country of this size located in the Southern Cone of Latin America (the 'bad neighborhood' issue). To some extent, currency overvaluation disguised the actual extent of the public debt, which is mostly denominated in dollars. Besides, public expenditure was pro-cyclical, aggravating the currency overvaluation problem. Finally, the financial crisis revealed some important weaknesses in bank supervision and in the management of public commercial banks.

In light of recent experience, the Uruguayan pro-market reforms program does not seem to have emphasized fiscal and financial institutions as much as it should have. On the fiscal front, the government could not avoid repeating the traditionally pro-cyclical pattern of public finances: public expenditure grew more than GDP during the expansionary 1990s and was reduced even more than GDP in 2002, when economic activity plummeted. This pro-cyclical behavior not only accentuated the economic cycle, but it eventually contributed to the risky situation with respect to fiscal sustainability.

It is not that Uruguayan governments did not realize that fiscal policy could and should be improved upon. The reform of the pensions system was to a large extent motivated by fiscal concerns, but the positive effects were not expected to arrive immediately. Reforms that introduce individual savings accounts in a previously fully pay-as-you-go system, such as that passed in 1995, are known to temporarily raise the deficit of social security institutions. It is only after the new norms have been in place for several years that this type of reform contributes to the reduction of the deficit. Also during the 1990s and like other Latin American countries, Uruguay made attempts at improving fiscal performance by adopting fiscal responsibility rules (Licandro, 2000; Brum et al., 2001). The parliament passed a first debt-ceiling law in 1994, well before neighboring countries passed their better known fiscal responsibility laws. However, the debt-ceilings were soon modified and some issuances of public debt were explicitly excluded from the ceilings. Therefore, even though this legislation shows that the political system was aware of the problem, it also shows that Uruguayan political parties could not agree on a strong, well designed, and enforceable fiscal responsibility law.

Bank supervision and management of public commercial banks showed weaknesses that eventually proved extremely damaging for the whole economy. During the 2002 bank run, only the foreign banks could fully and normally turn the money back to their clients (with the exception of the Argentinian Banco Galicia). Uruguayan private and public commercial banks could not resist the bank run, and the authorities had to close several private institutions and reschedule deposits in public ones. After the crisis, the parliament passed some laws to reorganize the system and improve supervision.

With the background of this brief analysis of the recent macroeconomic performance of the country, we turn now to the more structural reform issues that are the specific object of this research project.

The Uruguayan economy underwent a significant trade liberalization process, with almost no reversions, between the mid-1970s and the late 1990s. Tariffs were reduced on average and made more uniform (Table 7.2). Foreign trade flows rose significantly. Even though the trade openness coefficient computed at current prices does not show a clear positive trend in this period, the picture looks completely different, and a significant upward trend emerges when the coefficient is computed at constant prices. The gap can be explained in terms of the domestic currency overvaluation that took place during the late 1970s and the early 1980s and 1990s (Figure 7.1). The ratios of imports to demand and of exports to production rose, indicating the increasing specialization of the Uruguayan economy. In the 1990s, the structure of production and employment significantly changed. Total employment grew slowly in a context of intense reallocation across sectors. While the import substitution industries reduced employment, in some export industries and the service sector employment increased. There was a big increase in labor productivity (Casacuberta and Vaillant, 2002) and in total factor productivity (Casacuberta et al., 2003). The rewards for skilled workers increased, but jobs were lost among unskilled workers.

These changes in the structure of the economy are consistent with the liberalization of foreign trade that took place during this period. Needless to say, other factors must have also contributed to determining this performance (technological progress, for example), but the consistent, albeit gradual liberalization of trade policy across several decades played a key role in the described reorientation of the Uruguayan productive sectors. In turn, this policy could be sustained and perceived to be mostly permanent (which is obviously crucial to its effectiveness) because of the support it received from an unusually wide spectrum of the political system and social organizations. Soon after the country recovered democracy in the mid-1980s, it was generally accepted that there was no way back to the old import substitution model. It was just too obvious that a country with a population of three million could not afford to remain in isolation. Besides, the change in Brazilian trade policy and the MERCOSUR agreement in the early 1990s reduced internal resistance to trade liberalization.

Table 7.2: Custom global tax structure, 1982–95 (%)

	Jan. 82	Jan. 83	Jun. 85	Aug. 86	Aug. 87	Jun. 89	Apr. 90	Sep. 91	Apr. 92	Jan. 93	Jan. 95
Raw materials	10–15	10	15	10	10	10	15	10	10	6	0–14
Intermediate goods (1)	25–35	20	25	20	20	20	25	–	–	–	–
Intermediate goods (2)	45–55	35	40	35	30	30	35	20	17	15	0–20
Intermediate goods (3)	65	45	50	45	40	35	35	–	–	–	–
Final goods	75	55	60	50	45	40	40	30	24	20	0–20

Note: Intermediate goods were classified in three different categories.
Source: Vaillant (2000).

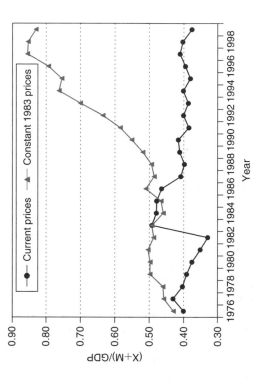

Figure 7.1 Trade openness coefficient
Source: Own computations with data from BCU.

The reform in public utilities and in some services formerly monopolized by public companies has been uneven, both in terms of the progress achieved in modifying the policies and in terms of the economic impact of the policy changes that did manage to get through. The reform in the port of Montevideo and the liberalization of the insurance markets seem to be two of the most successful stories. In both cases, the reform was implemented, brought about competition in markets formerly controlled by monopolies, and prices went down. Between 1992 and 1994, the National Port Administration (ANP) spent 10 per cent of its revenues in severance payments (Beato, 1996), but the number of employees dropped from 3200 to 1900 and to 1022 in 1991, 1994, and 2002, respectively. At the other extreme, there was basically no progress in the petroleum, water and sewage sectors, and little progress in telecommunications. The public enterprise unions led referendum campaigns that blocked the reform in petroleum and telecommunications, and the reform project in water and sewage faced so much internal opposition that it never took off. The results were more mixed in electricity and gas.

In spite of the progress made in legal capital market reforms in the 1990s, recent experience shows serious weaknesses. Stock or share markets have been insignificant during the last 60 or 70 years. Corporate bonds capitalization and investment funds grew significantly during the first years after the legislation was passed in 1996, but they decreased sharply after 1998–99 (Table 7.3). Poor security market regulation and supervision helped the bubble. Crises in Asia (1997) and Russia (1998), mixed with a homemade corporate scandal in 1998 and the Brazilian currency depreciation in 1999, brought the primary market activity to a halt from 2000 onwards. Part of the breeding

Table 7.3:   Public issues of corporate securities 1993–6/2003 in primary market

	Shares		Bonds		Others		Total	
	No.	Amount*	No.	Amount*	No.	Amount*	No.	Amount*
1993	0	–	1	4	0	–	1	4
1994	1	11	7	31	6	22	14	63
1995	0	–	6	14	4	43	10	57
1996	0	–	19	111	1	10	20	121
1997	0	–	30	212	0	–	30	212
1998	1	10	6	25	2	20	9	55
1999	3	14	11	132	4	23	18	169
2000	0	–	9	30	6	78	15	108
2001	1	17	8	29	4	30	13	76
2002	0	–	6	11	1	26	7	37
Jun-03	0	–	4	8	1	2	5	11
Total		52		607		253		912

Note: * In US$ million.
Source: Central Bank of Uruguay.

ground for the domestic scandal were the poorly defined civil (and possibly criminal) liabilities of auditing firms (PriceWaterhouse) and rating agencies. Also, the accounting standards in Uruguay seem to be deficient compared to other countries (López-de-Silanes, 2002). The legislation on securitization was poorly prepared and approved in 1999 under the tight deadline of a legislative period nearing its end. Since the legal instrument of trust was not then available, the legislator put in place a 'credit close ended investment fund', but this never took off. Finally, the outdated Uruguayan corporate law was left virtually unreformed, and therefore nothing was attempted with regard to equity markets. Moreover, failures to enact a new bankruptcy code contributed to the underdevelopment of this sector.

Pension expenditures were expected gradually to reduce as a percentage of GDP after the reform. However, expenditure did not decrease and it has even risen in recent years (Table 7.4). Also, the deficit of the Social Security Bank was initially smaller and later larger than some previous projections had suggested. The discrepancies seem to be the outcome of the profound economic cycle the Uruguayan economy went through after the reform (Forteza, 2004). A careful monitoring of the situation will be crucial in the near future to determine to what extent this is just a temporary phenomenon. A second dimension that is worth analyzing is the coverage of the population. Coverage of employees has not significantly increased on average after the reform (Table 7.4) as should have been the case according to the reformers. According to Bucheli (2003), the share of private dependent workers who contribute to social security rose from 62 per cent in 1995 to 67 per cent in 2002.[22] In turn, the proportion of independent workers who contribute decreased in the same period. The coverage among the elderly was already high when the reform began and continued to be so afterwards. In this respect, Uruguay is no exception in Latin America, for there is no consistent evidence of increasing formalization after the reforms (Gill et al., 2003). Coverage did increase in Chile (Schmidt-Hebbel, 2001), but it did not increase in most countries, and in some countries, such as Argentina, it decreased significantly. Finally, there is some evidence that the management of the social security system has improved. For one thing, there has been a considerable reduction in the time it takes to receive awarded benefits. In addition, in the area of contributions, a system for recording individual work histories is being implemented.

From the political point of view, it can be said that the reform of the pension system was initially very successful and, to some extent, given the sensitivity of the subject, better than might have been expected. First, low-paid workers opted massively for the individual accounts pillar.[23] Second, as Ramos (1999: 143) notes, a number of public opinion surveys between 1995 and 1999 showed an increase in satisfaction with the BPS on the part of the general public. Lastly, in 1999, various retired people's organizations and the PIT-CNT union federation failed in an attempt to initiate a plebiscite to modify substantial aspects of the new system. It is worth remembering that these

Table 7.4: Selected social security indicators

	1985	1990	1995	1996	1997	1998	1999	2000	2001	2002	2003
Coverage (contributors/employed, %)[a,b]	na	59.4	57.6	57.3	56.5	56.5	56.7	56.9	58.1	58.3	na
Population above 65 years old (% of total population)	10.9	11.5	12.3	12.8	12.9	13.0	13.1	13.2	13.2	13.3	13.3
Population aged 65 and above contributing or receiving pensions (%)[a]	na	91.1	90.9	90.8	90.9	90.3	90.2	90.0	89.1	90.4	89.2
Number of pensions paid by BPS[c]	609,846	627,317	640,715	646,807	660,900	664,109	660,514	656,493	652,580	651,310	649,365
Average pension paid by BPS (in pesos of Dec/2002)	2243	3042	4240	4356	4452	4558	4712	4662	4609	4225	3660
Public expenditure in pensions (% of GDP)	8.9	10.4	13.9	14.0	13.8	13.8	15.6	15.8	15.9	15.9	na
Total public expenditure (% of GDP)	20.8	22.4	25.6	25.0	25.1	25.4	28.6	29.0	30.8	31.3	na

Notes:
[a] The number in column '1990' corresponds to 1991.
[b] Source: Bucheli (2003). There was a change in the survey in 2001 which might affect comparability with previous years.
[c] Contributory pensions only.
Source: Own computations based on BCU, BPS and INE.

same organizations had in 1989 and in 1994 overturned attempts at reform using this recourse to plebiscite. It seems unlikely that the system will be substantially modified in the near future.

The reform of the electoral system, while fostering more fragmented political configurations than the previous system, did not give the government effective instruments which would serve to neutralize this fragmentation. The only ambit in which the new rules could have some impact is in the legislative discipline of factions and parties, a phenomenon which, in any case, was present before the reform. All things considered, the changes which may occur in the future will depend more than anything else on election results which might (or might not) give legislative majorities to those who govern, and favor (or do not favor) changes in their political orientation. Nevertheless, there appears to be some relative satisfaction with the consequences of the constitutional reform among the Uruguayan elite, though adherents of the National Party and, specially, of the Encuentro Progresista consider that the reform harmed their interests (Table 7.5).

Corruption and lack of transparency have been stumbling blocks in the reform process in many countries.[24] Uruguay does not seem to be one of these cases. According to the indexes computed by Kaufmann et al. (2003), Uruguay outperforms its neighboring countries, Argentina and Brazil, in terms of accountability, political stability, government effectiveness, regulatory capacity, rule of law, and control of corruption. However, Chile presents better ratings in the six areas. There is also some evidence that clientelism affected the implementation of social policies in Uruguay in the past (Saldain, 1999; Forteza, 2003), but we are not aware of any international comparative study on this.

Table 7.5:   Opinion poll conducted among elites, 2001. Answers to the question: Do you think that the reform of the constitution improved the working of the Uruguayan political system? (%)

	Party identification of the respondent					
	Undefined	NE	PN	PC	EP-FA	Total
Don't know/no answer	0.0	0.0	0.0	3.0	0.0	0.9
It deteriorated a lot	10.0	0.0	9.5	3.0	17.9	10.1
It deteriorated	20.0	0.0	14.3	9.1	38.5	21.1
It did not improve or deteriorate	20.0	16.7	14.3	3.0	10.3	10.1
It improved	40.0	66.7	57.1	57.6	30.8	46.8
It improved a lot	10.0	16.7	4.8	24.2	2.6	11.0
Total	100.0	100.0	100.0	100.0	100.0	100.0

Notes: NE = Nuevo Espacio; PN = Partido Nacional; PC = Partido Colorado; EP-FA = Encuentro Progresista-Frente Amplio.
Source: Instituto de Ciencia Política, FCS-Universidad de la República.

7.5   Concluding remarks

The model of market-friendly reforms is far from being consolidated in Uruguay. There is no perceptible reduction in resistance to change as the reform process goes forward.[25] The reformist sectors do not seem to have been able to make political capital out of the successes that reform had in areas such as foreign trade, the port, and social security. Rather, the macroeconomic crisis has dominated the national scene since 1999. Also, events in Argentina have worked strongly towards undermining the perceived legitimacy of reforms in Uruguay.

Although it is quite a number of years now since reform in Uruguay was initiated, there is still no consensus about how well it is going, nor is it possible to discard the possibility of a reversal of some aspects of the model. Various social organizations and some factions of the left-wing coalition that won the last national elections continue to question the basic premises of reform. But other factions of the same coalition and the new president do not seem willing to initiate a deep reversion of the reform process. Some political analysts think that political competition in Uruguay today necessarily leads to moderation, with a move to the center, and that this would limit the scope for reversing the pro-market reform.

Gradualism and moderation are the hallmarks of Uruguayan reforms. The market-friendly agenda faced the opposition of strong and well-organized parties and vocal groups that managed to voice strong anti-market feelings which are also deeply rooted in Uruguayan public opinion. The political competition in a pluralist democracy generated a process of muddling through with continual compromises and adjustments in the implementation of public policies. The reforms that managed to get through did so only after long periods of negotiation.

Political inclusion was the other side of this coin. Opponents to the reform could make good use of Uruguayan political institutions – particularly institutions of direct democracy – to achieve their goals. They managed to slow down and limit the scope of the reform process within the formal democratic institutions. The operation of these channels for political participation was crucial for the health and strength that the political system showed throughout the recent severe economic crisis that affected Uruguay.

The political and social movement opposed to the pro-market reforms countered with an invaluable weapon – the referendums and plebiscites. In several cases, opponents to the reform managed to block the process by voting the reform laws down in referendums and plebiscites. In other cases, the credible threat of the usage of these instruments of direct democracy obliged the reformist parties to moderate their proposals. Even though some vocal groups opposed to reform railed against the negotiation process, claiming low participation, there is ample evidence that reformers could not safely ignore them. When they did, they failed (for example, the law of public enterprises).

International financial institutions (IFIs) showed unstable support for reform and often competed among themselves (for example, the WB and IDB regarding pension reform). These contradictions, combined with the density of the domestic negotiation process, determined that the IFIs played a secondary role as agents for reform. With all its strengths and weaknesses, the Uruguayan pro-market reform was mostly a home-grown process.

Grindle and Thomas (1990) assert that in developing countries reform-opposing interest groups block policies at the implementation, not at the decision stage, hence there is a wide gap between *de jure* and de facto policies. The Uruguayan case contradicts this: reforms were designed with the active participation of many groups – and hence were partial or moderate – and yet, there is no apparent gap between *de jure* and de facto policies. The sources of this gap must thus be looked for in other places.

In sum, reformists have not won the battle for public opinion in most policy areas in Uruguay. The resistance to market-friendly reform has been strong and shows no signs of diminishing. The disappointing economic performance of the country in the late 1990s and early 2000s and the collapse of Argentina, after the IFIs insisted that this was the model to follow, contributed to discrediting the pro-market reform agenda. However, at the same time, social and political unrest in Uruguay have been very limited during the crisis, and the political system continues to look strong. These facts are the more remarkable considering the depth and duration of the crisis, and the 'bad press' of the economic policies pursued by recent governments. We argued in this chapter that political pluralism explains the puzzle. The Uruguayan institutions provided channels for vocal groups to express disagreement, and gave them legal weapons (referendums and plebiscites above all) effectively to oppose the reform, limiting its speed and scope. Hence, these groups were politically included, so that their activity did not undermine the legitimacy of the political and the party systems. Finally, the existence of a large political party that systematically opposed reform, having significant probabilities of winning the elections, at least since 1994 with victory in 2004, contributed to the stability and legitimacy of the political system.

Notes

1. The aim of this research project was to understand reform rather than to provide a comprehensive assessment of the Uruguayan reform process. Therefore, the list of reforms covered in this study is not exhaustive: the reform of the central administration was not analyzed and the reform of the ports and the insurance sector were only briefly considered. The choice was mostly dictated by the availability of data and previous studies on the reforms.
2. It should be mentioned here that several local experts strongly disagree that Uruguayan labor markets are more rigid than other labor markets in the region. This opinion has been personally communicated to the authors of this study by Ricardo Zerbino (former finance minister), Juan Manuel Rodríguez (expert on labor

relations), and Adriana Cassoni (labor economist), among others. We are not aware of comparative studies supporting this view, save for Heckman and Pagés (2000) who specifically show that separation costs in Uruguay are not particularly high by Latin American standards.

3. A fundamental aspect of the reform process is who takes part and who is excluded. This process of inclusion and exclusion can be partially endogenous, and some players may have the capacity to include or to exclude other players. For this reason, when we speak of the actors involved in reform we are referring both to those who are included and to those excluded. Luján (2003) has analyzed this aspect of the negotiation process in social security reform in Uruguay.

4. In the exposition of the reasons for the projected constitutional law, we read that, 'substantial modifications to the prevailing electoral system are proposed so as to make it more transparent and suitable to the current situation . . . and also to make the relation between the executive power and the legislative power more fluid, thus making it easier for government agreements between the different parties with parliamentary representation to emerge and be consolidated' (Record of the sessions of the Senate Chamber No. 103, volume 376, 13 August 1996: 33).

5. 'To create, therefore, greater political representativeness, and consequently facilitate the indispensable task of allowing agreements and political help from outside parties in order to establish stable government. This is what is embodied in the stipulation of a second round of voting in elections in cases in which no candidate has obtained more than 50% of the total votes cast in the first round' (Record of the sessions of the Senate Chamber No. 103, volume 376, 13 August 1996: 33).

6. Some authors maintain that crises have been factors that triggered reform (Bresser Pereira et al., 1993; Bates and Krueger, 1993; Cardoso and Galal, 2002), while others have questioned this hypothesis. Rodrik (1996) argued that this idea is a tautology, for reforms become an issue only when current policies are not working. Some models indicate that reforms might be more likely in good times than in bad (Orphanides, 1996). More recently, there has been emphasis on the idea that crises may be costly and may destroy institutions, affecting the quality of reforms and perhaps even leading to their abolition (Fanelli and Popov, 2005; Rius and van de Walle, 2005; Tommasi, 2002). The empirical evidence on crisis and reform is scarce and mixed. Drazen and Easterly (2001) found that countries that showed very high inflation and black market premiums enacted reforms that reduced inflation and black market premiums below the level of countries that did not suffer from inflation or exchange rate shocks. They did not find evidence of crises triggering reform when there were fiscal and current account deficits and low GDP growth.

7. At that time, the mission of the World Bank believed that the reform was not sufficiently far-reaching (Ramos, 1999). In the following years, the WB revised this vision and saw the situation in a more favorable light.

8. This hypothesis fits in with the common agency model developed by Grossman and Helpman (2001), among others.

9. Krishna and Mitra's (2005) paper concludes with the following statement: 'We find that such unilateral liberalization induces reciprocal tariff reduction by the partner country. Intuitively, unilateral liberalization by one country has the effect of increasing the incentives for the export lobby in the partner country to form and to lobby effectively against the import competing lobbies there for lower protection. The results stand in contrast to the policy arguments that suggest that closing (or threatening to close) one's market would help pry open the markets of others as well as some recent results in the literature which emphasize institutional reciprocity as an essential means of getting to efficient outcomes.'

10. Shortly before the social security reform law was passed, public opinion polls indicated that the majority of the population was not satisfied with the prevailing system and that a reform was considered to be necessary. The Ministry of Public Health cited the results of surveys, which they considered 'promising'. According to these, 70 per cent of the population thought that the prevailing system was unjust or very unjust, 68 per cent felt little or very little protected by the social security regime, and 73 per cent thought it reasonable or very reasonable that the country should undertake reform in this area. Nevertheless, the same survey indicated that Uruguayans did not consider this matter to be a priority (*Búsqueda* 786, 30 March 1995).

11. The President, Julio María Sanguinetti, expressed this idea in the following terms, 'What is not done in the first year of government is not done in the other four' (President Julio María Sanguinetti, *Búsqueda* 788, 20 April 1995: 3).

12. There was an additional more idiosyncratic explanation for passing the reform of the Uruguayan pension system at the beginning of the term. By constitutional ruling, the reform law for the social security system cannot be overturned by referendum because it is a matter exclusively for the presidency. The only instrument of direct democracy that opponents of the reform could have recourse to is a plebiscite on constitutional reform. Through a reform of the constitution, the main dispositions of the reform law could be rendered ineffective. But plebiscites can only be called along with national elections. Therefore, by pushing a reform through at the beginning of its period of administration, a government is assured of more than four years in which to organize the new system before it can be put to the test of a plebiscite.

13. For the elections of November 1994 and November 1999, the directorships of the big public enterprises with the greatest economic importance were platforms for the launch of preliminary candidate nominations from the Colorado and National (Blanco) parties. For the elections of 1999, this path was taken by several members of the Colorado Party, namely Ricardo Lombardo, president of the management board of ANTEL (the state telecommunications enterprise), Mario Carminatti, president of UTE (the state electrical power utility) (*Búsqueda*, 13 November 1997), and Ronald Pais, member of the management board of UTE (*Búsqueda*, 11 December 1997). But the most famous and most pioneering case was Alberto Volonté, president of the UTE board in the period, who, in effect, competed in the national elections of 1994, and whose only previous political role had been as president of UTE.

14. In that period, there were a number of interesting cases in the country of lobbying activity based on the transmission of information in a way that Grossman and Helpman (2001) analyze in Part 2 of their book.

15. Rajapatirana (1995) identifies this same pattern of trade policy in many countries.

16. Bergara et al. (2004) present a similar view of the policy-making process in Uruguay.

17. The distinction between 'styles of leadership', with typologies similar to the ones we use, can be found in several studies in political science (for example, Kavanagh, 1997) and particularly in the comparative analysis on presidential leadership (for example, Neudstadt, 1990; Greenstein, 2004).

18. We distinguish banking secrecy from poor disclosure and lack of transparency problems. Banking secrecy is a legitimate protection of a customer's private information. Problems of disclosure and transparency refer to unlawful hiding of financially distressed firms. For a long time, much of the corporate private sector had some degree of state sponsorship (protectionist trade policies are a glaring case). Therefore, some government forbearance of nearly failing firms to save jobs (and

entrepreneurs) is hardly surprising. Interestingly, a legally enforced banking secrecy was key to keeping jobs in a then buoyant banking system.

19. Work history is a record of contributions paid by workers to social security.
20. Bergara et al. (2004: 43) express a similar view: 'Both the most visible and account-able veto mechanisms via plebiscites and the obscure veto at the implementation stage are being observed in recent years in the Uruguayan political process.'
21. The resilience of dollarization despite the drop in the rates of inflation during the 1990s could be a reaction to the lack of credibility of the government budget path. If this were the right diagnostic, then the solution should be looked for on the fiscal front, rather than on the development of new financial instruments. Recent events seem to provide some ground for this hypothetical skepticism about the fiscal trends. However, by the mid-1990s, most analysts thought that the budget was on a safe and sustainable path (see for instance Borchardt et al., 1998), which renders the lack-of-credibility story less compelling. Therefore, the hypothesis that there might also be market failures behind the lack of financial intermediation denominated in domestic currency or in a domestic unit of account (such as CPI) cannot be dismissed. Furthermore, as the main issuer of bonds, the government cannot avoid making specific decisions on the type of financial instruments to use that significantly affect the market.
22. It must be mentioned here, however, that this evidence could be affected by changes in the household survey questionnaire introduced in 2001.
23. The reform law establishes that workers with income of less than approximately US$800 per month as of May 1995 would in principle continue to be covered exclusively by the public pillar, but they were given the option of paying half of their personal contribution to the individual accounts pillar. More than 90 per cent of workers in this situation took up this option.
24. See the studies for Ukraine and Indonesia in the Understanding Reform Project (Dubrovskiy et al., 2004; Kuncoro and Resosudarmo, 2004).
25. As Lora and Olivera (2004) point out, some political economy models suggest that experiences of reform can facilitate the acceptance of following reforms if they reduce general uncertainty about the distribution of the costs and benefits, and the government's uncertainty about their ability to implement the reform. Fernández and Rodrik (1991) argue that uncertainty about who will be the winners and who will be the losers generates a bias in favor of the status quo. Milesi-Ferretti (1991) shows that reform may be slowed down if the government has to cope with uncertainty about its own ability to carry it through at low cost. The reform process could itself have the effect of reducing such uncertainty and the resistance it generates, but this does not seem to have been a dominant factor in the Uruguayan case.

Appendix 7.1   Chronology of the reform

1985	A government elected by popular vote assumes power after 12 years of military dictatorship. Julio María Sanguinetti of the Colorado Party is elected president.
1989	There is a plebiscite on a reform measure that introduces the indexing of pensions in the Constitution of the Republic. The proposal is passed with an 82 per cent majority.
1990	A new government comes to power, under Luis Alberto Lacalle of the National (Blanco) Party.
1990	The presidency submits a project for reform of the pension system to parliament. It proposes modifications of some parameters in the system, while maintaining a pure payments regime. It is not passed by parliament.
1991	Agreement for the creation of the MERCOSUR (Treaty of Asunción). The Program of Trade Liberalization is created. This fixes a timetable for the dismantling of tariffs on intra-regional trade which will culminate in January 1995 with the creation of a free trade area. Procedures to eliminate non-tariff barriers on intra-regional trade are proposed. There is recognition of the need for a common external tariff.
1991	The government issues a decree which contains a program for the unilateral liberalization of tariffs with respect to third markets. In the last third of 1991, the highest tariffs are reduced. Additional reductions are programmed for 1992 and 1993, and they are effectively implemented.
1992	The presidency presents a new pension reform project to parliament. It is proposed to maintain the pure pay-as-you-go regime but introducing 'notional accounts', similar to what was later introduced in Italy and Sweden. Parliament rejected it.
1992	The law for the rendering of accounts is passed. It includes a number of articles that modify parameters in the pension system. Thirty years is fixed as the minimum period of contributions for the right to a pension; labor history is regulated; it is established that paid contributions will be the only valid base for receiving a pension. These dispositions will be overturned in 1994 (see below).
1992	Parliament passes the public enterprises law, which opens the door to total or partial privatization of the main public enterprises.
1992	Revocation by referendum of the articles in the law of public enterprises that have to do with the privatization of the public telephony enterprise (ANTEL).

1992	IDB technical assistance on 'Investment Sector Reforms Program'. Purpose: to improve 'investment climate' by identifying stumbling blocks and suggesting instruments to overcome them.
1993	Inter-party group submits for consideration by parliament a constitutional reform project, which would modify the electoral regime and the relation between the executive and the legislative powers ('maxi-reform'). In 1994 it receives a negative vote.
1993	First concession of water and sewage services (Aguas de la Costa).
1993	The law for the de-monopolization of the insurance market (Law 16426) is promulgated.
1993	The presidency presents a project for the reform of the social security system to parliament (third proposal in the National Party administration). It is bogged down in a parliamentary commission.
1994	Inter-party group proposes to parliament a constitutional reform centered on questions that have to do with local government ('mini-reform'). The parliament approves this proposal by an ample majority of votes. It is then presented to the people in a plebiscite, but fails to gain the necessary majority.
1994	The presidency submits to parliament a social security reform project 'for urgent consideration' (fourth proposal in the National Party administration). It does not pass in parliament.
1994	A consortium headed by Gaz de France is awarded the concession to supply piped gas in Montevideo, privatizing the public gas enterprise, which had been nationalized in 1975.
1994	A constitutional reform is passed by plebiscite. It lays down that pension norms cannot be included in budget laws, thus nullifying the articles connected to the BPS (Banco de Previsión Social) in the law of the rendering of accounts passed in November 1992.
1994	The Uruguayan parliament ratifies the Treaty of Marrakech, signed in the framework of Uruguay's joining the new World Trade Organization.
1994	Summit of MERCOSUR presidents (Ouro Preto) redefines the objectives of the regional agreement. The MERCOSUR Adjustment Regime is created, which fixes the program to set up a Free Trade Area in a longer period (2000), and also agrees a common external tariff along with a trajectory to establish this. In this way the objective of creating a customs union is crystallized.
1995	A new government comes to power under Julio María Sanguinetti of the Colorado Party.
1995	Parliament passes the social security reform law which introduces a mixed pensions system (Law 16713).

1996	The presidency issues decrees with new rules for multilateral trade (anti-dumping and safeguards) in the framework of the World Trade Organization membership law.
1996	Laws are passed to foster the development of the capital market: Exchanges and Corporate Bonds Law 16749 and Investment Funds Law 16774.
1996	Parliament passed a constitutional reform law (requiring a special majority of two-thirds) which modified the electoral regime and was confirmed in a plebiscite by the citizenry.
1997	Transitory increase in the MERCOSUR common external tariff.
1997	Law 16832 of the Electricity Industry Regulatory Framework is passed.
1998	The government awards the concession for the construction of a gas pipeline between Buenos Aires and Montevideo and the distribution of piped gas in the provinces in Uruguay to private enterprise.
1998	Second concession for water and sewage services (Uragua).
1998	Failed attempt to overturn by referendum the Electricity Industry Regulatory Framework Law.
1998	The Investment Act 16906 is passed.
1998	The Executive Power submits a General Bankruptcy Code Bill, but it never leaves a Congress Commission.
1999	Parliament passes the Securitization and Factoring Law 17202.
1999	Pensioners' associations collect signatures for a plebiscite on a new constitutional reform aimed at nullifying the social security reform law passed in 1995, but they fail to obtain the necessary number of signatures.
2000	A new government under Jorge Batlle of the Colorado Party assumes power.
2000	Regulatory offices for electrical energy (UREE) and communications (URSEC) are set up.
2000	MERCOSUR extends the period for exceptions to the common external tariff, and extends the increased common external tariff passed in 1997.
2000	Legal authorization of competition in communications (long distance international, mobile telephony, and data transmission).
2000	Parliament passes the Movable Property Collateral Law 17228.
2001	The creation of the Regulatory Unit for Energy and Water Services (URSEA) is passed by law. This regulatory body inherits the role of the UREE (which disappears) for the electricity sector, and assumes control in the other energy sectors and in water and sewage services.
2001	Parliament passes the Amendment to Bankruptcy Regime Law 17292.

2001–2002	In a situation of severe economic crisis, the MERCOSUR countries set up various extra- and intra-regional non-tariff barriers to trade. In particular, the Uruguayan government also changes its trade policy with respect to extra-regional third markets through a collection of protectionist instruments.
2002	Parliament passes the reform law for the notaries' pension system. It is a reform of parameters, without individual accounts being introduced.
2002	A law authorizing the public fuel enterprise (ANCAP) to associate with private companies is promulgated.
2002	The presidency approves the regulations for the wholesale market in transport and electricity distribution.
2002	The Buenos Aires–Montevideo gas pipeline is inaugurated.
2002	The legal base which supported the liberalization of telecommunications is abolished in parliament.
2002	Failed attempt by the government to auction off mobile telephony.
2002	The presidency submits a Trust Bill to the Congress.
2003	The Administration of the Wholesale Electricity Market is set up.
2003	The ANCAP Association Law is voted down in a referendum.
2003	Trust Law is approved.

8

The Difficulties of Reforming an Oil Dependent Economy: the Case of Venezuela

Ricardo Villasmil, Francisco Monaldi, Germán Ríos, and Marino González

8.1 Introduction

The main purpose of this chapter is to provide a comprehensive yet concise analysis of Venezuela's limited but revealing experience with market-oriented reform. We devote the bulk of our efforts to the study of *El Gran Viraje* (the Great Turnaround), an ambitious agenda of macroeconomic and structural reforms led by President Carlos Andrés Pérez during his second presidency (1989–93). The other reform attempt included in our study is the 'Agenda Venezuela', carried out during the Caldera administration in 1996 and generally regarded as far too timid to be classified as a reform program. We nevertheless include it in our work, not only for the sake of completeness but mostly in order to explore the aftermath of the 1989 reform program to the fullest possible extent.[1]

For the purposes of the Understanding Reform Project, analyzing Venezuela's experience is worthwhile for at least two reasons. The first is the apparent paradox embedded in its failure to reform. Even within the academic community, there is a tendency to ascribe Venezuela's political and economic woes to a lack of political will, given that from a financial standpoint at least, its massive oil revenues *should* help ease the burden that accompanies reform. The experience of resource-rich nations with reform has shown, however, that policy-makers in these countries tend to face *stronger* opposition in their attempts to reform. This apparent paradox has found some explanation in the institutional literature, where many empirical studies have concluded that the political economy of resource wealth seems to have a strong and negative effect over institutional development, generating untenable expectations and promoting rent-seeking behavior.[2] The general failure of the two reform initiatives that took place in Venezuela between 1989 and 1998 indeed suggests the overriding importance of political and institutional constraints in determining the likelihood of success of economic reform.[3] It follows that more thorough research may prove valuable, not only for resource-rich nations, but for all countries contemplating reform.

The second reason is that Venezuela's experience with reform has not been analyzed nearly as well as that of other Latin American countries. Aside from the studies by Naím (1993), Navarro (1993), Hidalgo (2002), and the comparative studies by Corrales (2002) and Weyland (2004a), the academic literature devoted to analyzing the 1989 reform program, for instance, is quite thin and written shortly after the events took place, too soon perhaps to perform an adequate assessment of the reasons behind its demise. The 1996 reform program has received even less attention, maybe because it was not nearly as ambitious or as profound as the previous one.

One of the most salient conclusions of our work is the omnipresence of oil as an ultimate or deep explanatory variable of the crisis that led to reform and of the fate of the reform program and its aftermath. We present and discuss the validity of a series of hypotheses regarding what we consider to be more proximate explanatory variables of the crisis, the reform process, and its aftermath. These include the incompatibility of Venezuela's institutions – shaped as they are by oil wealth – and a radical program of adjustment and reform, the lack of awareness of the population of an impending crisis, the deconsolidation of the party system, the lack of government-party support, the front-loaded nature of the adjustment costs and the lack of an adequate communication and negotiation strategy. We also conclude that some interest groups – particularly the media and to a lesser extent labor unions and some financial groups – played their part in undermining the 1989 reform program, but that political parties, and the president's party in particular, dealt much more devastating blows.

We have structured the chapter in four sections. Section 8.2, intended mainly for those not wholly familiar with Venezuela, provides a brief description of the country's political and economic history, concentrating on the economic and political conditions leading up to Pérez's 1989 reform program. In Section 8.3 we try to rationalize the events through the presentation, discussion and validation of testable hypotheses in a setting of rational political and economic agents. We also provide some answers to the three main questions this project wishes to address: (1) what motivated the executive in power to undertake market-oriented reforms? (2) How, in terms of speed and content, were the reforms planned and carried out? And (3) how well did the reform programs perform? In Section 8.4 we summarize our findings and conclude with some thoughts on the lessons learned from the Venezuelan experience.

8.2 A brief political and economic history

8.2.1 Introduction

By the turn of the twentieth century, Venezuela was one of the most backward countries in Latin America.[4] In contrast with the US experience, the independence wars of the early 1800s did not lead to civil and political order, but were instead followed by more than two centuries of internal strife, civil warfare, and economic stagnation.

The consolidation of a central authority did not come about until the early 1900s (under the iron hand of General Juan Vicente Gómez), and as late as 1941, three-quarters of the adult population remained illiterate, the school enrolment ratio stood at a paltry 35 per cent and only 3 per cent of Venezuelan households had access to improved water sources.[5]

Around this time, however, this relatively new setting of civil and political order combined with the discovery and subsequent exploitation of huge oil deposits, allowing for the possibility of channeling growing fiscal revenues into much needed public goods and services. Although not always wisely spent, the growth in government spending during the 1920–70 period allowed Venezuela to become one of the top economic and social performers in Latin America and the world. Incomes grew eightfold in per capita terms, life expectancy increased from 31 to 65 years, and literacy rates went from 32 to 77 per cent (see Table 8.1). In addition, after the overthrow of its last dictator in 1958, the country became a model of a stable democracy in a region marred by open violations of basic civil and political rights.

Crucial to stability after 1958 was the 'Pacto de Punto Fijo', an agreement between the three main political parties at the time to respect electoral outcomes, build coalition governments, and pursue broad development goals under private property.[6] This economic, political and social 'miracle' began to unravel, however, in the late 1970s (see Figure 8.1), and the causes underlying such a drastic reversal of fortune are still being hotly debated. Still, there

Table 8.1:   Social and economic performance, 1920–70

	Literacy (%)		Life expectancy (years)		GDP per head*		
	1920	1970	1920	1970	1920	1970	Cumulative growth 1920–70 (%)
Argentina	68	93	49	67	586	620	106
Brazil	35	68	32	59	155	316	204
Chile	63	88	31	62	318	544	171
Colombia	44	78	32	61	236	309	131
Costa Rica	58	88	37	67	370	285	77
El Salvador	27	58	28	57	109	298	273
Guatemala	15	45	25	52	169	284	168
Honduras	32	53	29	53	145	140	97
Mexico	35	75	34	61	330	547	166
Nicaragua	39	57	24	54	115	313	272
Venezuela	32	77	31	65	128	1,070	836
US	94	99	57	71	1,886	3,239	172

Note: * US$ 1970 PPP adjusted.
Source: Astorga et al. (2003).

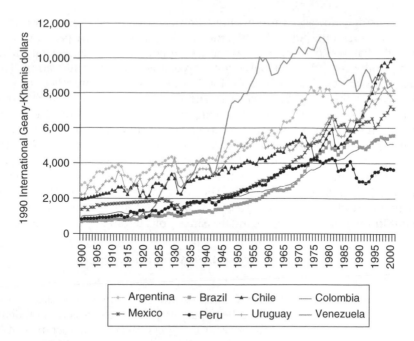

Figure 8.1 GDP per head, 1900–2001
Source: Maddison (2001).

seems to be some degree of consensus on the notion that the financial excesses triggered by the misinterpretation of the temporary oil shock as a permanent one, coupled with a dramatic decline in production capacity in the late 1970s, made the country vulnerable to the US interest rate hike of the early 1980s that plunged Venezuela into a fiscal and balance of payment crisis that received only palliative treatment until 1989.[7]

8.2.2 Economic conditions at the outset of the 1989 reform program

President Pérez took office on 2 February 1989. The strong countercyclical policy followed by his predecessor during the last three years of his term brought strong economic performance in terms of output and employment, but the financial figures underlying such performance revealed sizable imbalances growing at an alarming rate.[8] To contain inflationary pressures and currency outflows, the administration had relied on a multi-tiered exchange rate system coupled with price and import controls, but by the end of 1988 the dam was clearly overrun: the external current account deficit hovered around 8 per cent of GDP, the public sector deficit had reached 9.3 per cent of GDP and delays in the approval of price adjustments for items under price control were causing significant shortages of basic foodstuffs and medicines.[9]

Surprisingly however, the outgoing administration faced a relatively unruffled situation on the political front. Enjoying the largest ever one-party majority in both chambers of Congress, it was able to appoint as attorney general and as comptroller general individuals openly favorable to the administration. The faction of President Lusinchi in Acción Democrática (AD) controlled the vast majority of the party. Regional party heads (state secretary generals) were appointed governors of the states, making it the most party-centered administration in the nation's history. In addition, and in spite of the rocky economic situation described above, the country lived through a period of relative calm on the labor front. The administration had a very close relationship with the labor union bureau of his party, which in turn, controlled the Confederación de Trabajadores de Venezuela (CTV), the umbrella workers union. The government ended with a favorable rating of 37 per cent, the highest of any government in the final year of its mandate (since polls began in the late 1960s).[10]

8.2.3   Description of the 1989 and 1996 reform programs

The Gran Viraje (1989–93)

On 4 December 1988, Carlos Andrés Pérez became President of Venezuela for the second time, with 52.8 per cent of the popular vote. The newly elected president, however, did not enjoy a majority in Congress. Acción Democrática (AD) obtained 97 seats in the house and 24 seats in the senate (48.3 and 46.2 per cent of the total seats, respectively). Most importantly, AD's establishment supported his candidacy only grudgingly after his crushing victory in the party primaries in October 1987 over Lusinchi's chosen successor. The anti-Pérez old guard controlled the party's leadership and machinery, but they could not stop his candidacy in the internal party primaries due to his high popularity.

Pérez's campaign was based on the promise of a return to better times, and those of the *Gran Venezuela* in particular (the oil and debt financed bonanza that characterized his first presidency in 1973–78). In an impressive display of Pérez's international status, more than twenty heads of state, ranging from Felipe González and Lech Walesa to Fidel Castro and Daniel Ortega, showed up for his inauguration. The event took place in the most luxurious concert hall in the capital and came to be known as 'Pérez's Coronation'. In his speech, Pérez outlined vague policy orientations for his new government, stressing the significance of inter-American and international relations in the overall strategy for building a way out of the political and fiscal crisis, as well as the notion that his government's political formula for dealing once and for all with Venezuela's debt burden would be based on solidarity among debtor countries.

Two weeks later, President Pérez addressed the nation to announce his decision to engage, under IMF supervision, in a macroeconomic adjustment program formally known as *El Gran Viraje*.[11] The agreed-upon program was designed to restore fiscal and balance of payments viability as well as to promote a sound development of the Venezuelan economy over the medium term by moving from a state-led, inward-oriented strategy to one led by export growth. For these purposes, it entailed a number of major structural reforms in the fiscal, exchange, trade, and financial sectors. The government also consented to improve the performance, revenue collection, and cost efficiency of a number of deficit-ridden enterprises, and as part of this program, an aggressive program of privatization was expected to take place over the next few years. On the expenditure side, central government expenditure would be reoriented from large investment projects and general subsidies in favor of direct transfers and social services for the poor and towards the modernization of public infrastructure and maintenance outlays in order to support the private sector in their ability to respond to international prices. Most of the measures contained in the *'paquete económico'*, as it came to be known, were to be executed immediately or in the coming months. Among them, the abolishment of the multi-tiered foreign exchange apparatus in favor of a unified, market determined exchange rate and a 110 per cent increase in the average price of domestic fossil fuel derivatives effective from 26 February.

In response to this and other price adjustments, public transportation prices were set to increase 30 per cent, stay at that level for 3 months, and afterwards rise again up to 100 per cent of their original levels. Dissatisfied with the government's proposal, public transportation unions called for a strike effective on 27 February. That same morning, bus drivers serving a key intercity service in the outskirts of Caracas, decided to impose their demands on the public instead. The indignation triggered a spontaneous, unanticipated, and massive outbreak of violence that began with torched buses and general pillage, particularly in food markets. Television images and other media sources spread the news to other cities, and with it, the pattern of violence. By noon the next day, the president decided that the disorder had surpassed the containment capacity of regular police forces, called the national guard and the army for support, suspended constitutional guarantees for ten days, and imposed curfews. At its end, official figures of *'El Caracazo'*, as it came to be known, revealed enormous losses for the owners of the shops and transportation units looted or otherwise destroyed in the events, more than 1000 people injured and over 300 dead.

Venezuelan authorities corresponded with IMF authorities on 24 May that same year to report on the progress made on the commitments specified in the 28 February memorandum (see Appendix 8.1) and to discuss the performance criteria by which the program was to be evaluated by IMF authorities for the approval of subsequent disbursements. The government recognized the price and exchange rate adjustments as the immediate cause of the *Caracazo* and stated the need to continue making efforts to soften the economic and social impact of the program over the most vulnerable segments of the population. Nevertheless, authorities emphasized their intention to carry on with the original program's content and course of execution.

Accordingly, the authorities put into effect on 1 April, a 65 per cent increase in commercial and industrial electricity tariffs and a 35 per cent increase in residential tariffs, and later that month, significantly raised the domestic prices of aluminum, steel, iron ore, and petrochemical products, setting up mechanisms to carry on their transition towards international levels. The Venezuelan government also made advances in the negotiations with the Bank Advisory Committee for a financing package that would include US$2 billion in new money in 1989 and a menu of options for debt and debt service reduction.[12]

The program significantly underestimated the price and aggregate demand effects of the adjustment measures. The projected decline of GDP was 2.7 per cent, but it fell 8.3 per cent, with non-oil GDP taking the hardest hit with a 10.6 per cent drop. Reflecting the price and exchange rate corrections, the 12-month change in consumer prices reached 140 per cent during the second quarter of 1989, and closed the year at 81 per cent, compared with a program target of 62.2 per cent. Not surprisingly, perhaps, the social and political tensions continued unabated throughout the year. On 18 May the main worker's union (CTV), led by the government, convened a general strike against the '*paquete económico*', and one month later, reacting to the irony behind the imposition of economic adjustments by a president perceived as corrupt, the people took to the streets in a peaceful protest dubbed '*la marcha de los pendejos*' (the march of the fools).

On the political front, some significant reforms were also implemented in 1989. The country had its first direct elections of governors and mayors, who until then were freely appointed and removed by the president. Given the harsh economic situation, AD had an acceptable performance in the regional elections of December 1989, obtaining 11 of the 20 governors being elected. For a party that had won a plurality in almost all regions in the two previous national elections (1983 and 1988), however, losing nine governorships represented a significant decline.[13] Moreover, the abstention rate of 54.4 per cent was the highest in any type of election in Venezuela's democratic history.

Throughout the first half of 1990, economic activity remained weak. The failure to achieve the programmed objectives, particularly in the fiscal area, was driven mainly by a strongly adverse political and social climate. Domestic revenues were impaired by delays in the congressional approval of new tax legislation, depressed domestic demand, delays in the execution of programmed increases in the price of domestic fossil fuels, and a longstanding problem of compliance. In addition, the resulting substitution of domestic for foreign borrowing significantly increased interest payments of the central government, thus contributing to a significant infringement of the ceiling on the public sector borrowing requirements set by the program.

In the second half of 1990, the financial and economic circumstances of the country improved considerably as a result of a sudden increase in oil prices following Iraq's invasion of Kuwait and the completion of commercial debt negotiations between Venezuela and its Bank Advisory Committee. The strengthening in oil prices, together with a 25 per cent increase in export volumes over 1989, boosted international reserves and public sector revenues.[14]

The multi-year financing package was concluded with the Bank Advisory Committee on 25 June, and by October US$1.9 billion of outstanding debt was extinguished and US$10 billion stood to benefit from interest rate reduction. Significant reflows of private capital followed, and by the end of 1990, GDP had grown 6.5 per cent in real terms (14 per cent for oil GDP and 4.5 per cent for non-oil GDP). Inflation, responding to a stabilization of the exchange rate and further liberalization of agricultural imports, slowed down to 37 per cent.

There were additional reforms in the political system that year. A reform of the electoral system to elect the legislature was approved to take effect in 1993. The pure proportional representation system was changed to a personalized proportional one in which 35 per cent of the deputies were elected by plurality in single member districts.

In 1991 the fiscal accounts suffered as a result of the combined effect of a sharp decline in oil prices, a larger than programmed increase in capital spending by PDVSA, and the failure to obtain congressional support for the introduction of a VAT, the single most important source of non-oil revenue projected in the program. In addition, the income tax reform was passed by Congress in June, lowering personal and corporate income tax rates, but the new legislation failed to expand the tax base as planned through the elimination of exemptions and deductions. The privatization of 40 per cent of the shares of CANTV, the state telephone monopoly, brought in US$1.85 billion, four times the amount originally envisaged, but under the program, revenues in excess of projected receipts were to be saved. Aside from that privatization, structural reforms did not advance much, and the severance payment system reform was shelved after signs of public outrage. Social unrest continued throughout the year, and during the second half, classes in public high schools had to be suspended for several weeks as riots intensified. At the year's end, the president announced '*El Megaproyecto Social*', a collection of social programs directed towards the poor with technical and financial assistance from multilateral institutions.

In the late hours of 3 February 1992 the president returned from the annual meeting of the World Economic Forum held in Davos to find a coup attempt in progress. Miraculously, the president managed to escape to a local television station, and from there, he addressed the nation, reported the events and called for the support of the general population. In a few hours, the loyal forces managed to regain partial control of the situation. Early that afternoon, Hugo Chávez, the lieutenant colonel in charge of the coup operations in Caracas, surrendered. Fighting between coup forces and those loyal to the president were still taking place in some parts of the country, so in an effort to prevent further violence, Chávez was allowed to address his comrades through national television. In a brief speech that would propel him to stardom, he recognized that '*por ahora*' (for now) the coup's objectives had not been achieved, and asked his comrades to lay down their arms.

Despite its failure to topple the president, the coup caused significant damage to the government's image. On 5 February a joint session of Congress was convened to approve a presidential decree that would suspend constitutional guarantees and impose a curfew on the population. Parliamentary groups representing both parties had agreed not to discuss the matter but to issue a statement condemning the coup attempt instead. Nevertheless, former President Caldera took to the podium. He began his speech disputing some aspects of the decree, mainly that it could not be asserted that assassinating the president was the intention of the coup, for that would not explain, among other things, the fighting in other parts of the country. Afterwards, he highlighted the lack of popular support for the democratic government during the coup as an indication of a growing discontent with the political establishment. He argued that leaders could not expect support from the people in the name of liberty and democracy when such values could neither feed them nor prevent the rampant and widespread corruption they witnessed every day. Condemning the coup but at the same time legitimizing the reasons behind it, he claimed that political leaders in the developed world should understand that external debt should be revised, that in the words of Pope John Paul II, 'it is not right to demand or expect payment when the effect would be the imposition of political choices leading to hunger and despair for entire peoples'.[15] Linking the coup to the *Caracazo*, he pointed to the failure of the state in providing public services and on the economic adjustment measures as reasonable causes for social discontent, and criticized privatization as a way out of this problem. He ended his speech by calling on the president to face this issue in all its depth and its different dimensions.

Caldera capitalized on a political and social sentiment somewhat sympathetic towards the coup leaders and their intentions. Pérez, politically weakened by the events, was forced to make concessions. Miguel Rodríguez, chief architect and most visible spokesman of the economic program, was replaced and a *Consejo de Notables* was created to advise the president on important policy matters. Composed of eight mostly independent and intellectually recognized public figures, the council presented in early March of that same year a report advocating more strenuous efforts in the fight against corruption, a clean-up of the judicial system, the continuation of the decentralization process and a constitutional reform consistent with the expectations of the Venezuelan people. The report also recommended significant changes in the economic program, including the suspension of gasoline price increases, the introduction of price stabilization measures for basic goods and services, and a halt on the removal of trade restrictions in agricultural goods pending a revision that would take into account the specific circumstances of the country.

In March, the government announced the reintroduction of temporary price controls for foodstuffs and medicine staples as well as the suspension of the scheduled monthly increases in fuel and electricity prices. The VAT remained shelved in Congress and exchange rate flexibility was compromised in order to contain inflationary pressures, albeit with a cost in international reserves of over US$1 billion during the year. Political pressures continued however, and on the morning of 27 November a second coup attempt took place, this one headed by high ranking officers from the three branches of the armed forces. The rebels managed to take control of the state controlled television station and of the transmission station of the other three networks in order to broadcast a video of Chávez inciting the people to rebel against the government. Before noon, however, loyal forces had regained control of the situation.

Under these circumstances, very little was done in terms of economic reforms. In December, a new charter for the central bank was approved into law, giving more independence to the monetary authorities and creating a new board of directors with staggered terms. The most consequential institutional change however, proved to be a change in the composition of the supreme court that would pave the way for Pérez's impeachment one year later. In the regional elections of 1992, just a few days after the November coup attempt, AD suffered a very significant defeat. Of the 22 governors being elected, AD took only seven, one of the worst performances in its history. The abstention rate was 50.7 per cent, a slight improvement from the one in 1989.

As part of an attempt to recover the political initiative, in early March the president proposed a constitutional reform and called for a constitutional assembly. These efforts proved futile. One week later, the attorney general presented a case of misuse and appropriation of US$17 million in public funds against Pérez.[16] Two months later, the supreme court stated that it had found sufficient evidence to process Pérez, despite his insistence that the case was a fabrication directed by his political opponents, Shortly afterwards, the Senate decided to remove Pérez from office, and on 5 June, Ramón J. Velásquez, Head of the *Consejo de Notables,* was sworn in to complete Pérez's term in office.

Economic and political conditions at the outset of the Agenda Venezuela

Ramón J. Velásquez, a prominent historian and head of the *Consejo de Notables,* was appointed by Congress to complete the remainder of Pérez's presidency (8 months). He faced a particularly difficult political situation. After the two coups of 1992, several polls indicated that more than 70 per cent of the population did not have faith in the democratic system.[17] Velásquez was supposed to lead the country through a short transition period, but he managed to implement some important reforms in the fiscal and financial areas and to push forward the decentralization process as well. To this end, Congress granted him special powers to approve laws through decrees (Ley Habilitante).

Velásquez's administration passed the creation of the VAT, something Pérez could not do during his tenure. His government also created a special ministry for decentralization and put in place a mechanism for fiscal co-participation of the VAT proceeds between the central government and local administrations. In addition, a decentralization fund was implemented (FIDES) to promote the transfer of functions from the central government to states and municipalities.[18] The banking law was also reformed to improve supervision, but too late to prevent the oncoming banking crisis. Nevertheless, other measures such as further increases in gasoline prices were not approved by Velásquez in order to avoid additional social unrest.

In the meantime, Rafael Caldera was busy campaigning for the upcoming presidential elections. Having left COPEI, he set up a new party, Convergencia, and obtained support from *'el chiripero'*, a collection of smaller parties that included Movimiento al Socialismo (MAS), Movimiento Electoral del Pueblo (MEP), and Partido Comunista de Venezuela (PCV). He based his campaign on the virtues of a sincere and morally strong leadership as well as on the repudiation of the hardship imposed by the economic adjustment program of 1989. In clear reference to Pérez's adjustment program, he signed a 'Letter of Intent with the Venezuelan People', a somewhat vague policy document committing himself among other things, to the fight against poverty, to the implementation of constitutional reform and to the elimination of the recently created VAT. The VAT was an issue in Caldera's campaign because it represented one of the most emblematic components of the *paquete económico* and the cornerstone of the fiscal reform. Caldera opposed the reform mainly on the grounds of the perverse effect of indirect taxation on the poor.

Caldera took office on 2 February 1994 after winning the December elections with 30.5 per cent of the national vote, although with a very small representation in Congress (see Table 8.2).[19] He inherited a complicated macroeconomic situation characterized by a fiscal imbalance, increasing inflation, declining international reserves, and a mild economic recession. In addition, the severe banking crisis that began in January with the government's intervention in the second largest bank of the country affected an important part of the financial system, becoming eventually a heavy fiscal burden. To make matters worse, the delay by the administration in announcing a strategy to deal with the banking and fiscal crisis resulted in mounting uncertainty.

Table 8.2: Outcome of the 1993 congressional elections

	House		Senate	
	Seats	(%)	Seats	(%)
AD	55	27.1	16	32.0
Copei	53	26.1	14	28.0
MAS	24	11.8	5	10.0
Causa R	40	19.7	9	18.0
Convergencia	26	12.8	6	12.0
Others	5	2.5	–	0.0
Totals	**203**	**100**	**50**	**100**

Source: Consejo Nacional Electoral (CNE).

Although Caldera was not a big fan of decentralization, his political weaknesses and the support he received from small parties with strong regional ties forced him to continue, albeit slowly, the decentralization process. He abolished the VAT, but a few weeks afterwards implemented a very similar tax (general sales and luxury tax) due to the increasing fiscal imbalance and pressure on the part of regional authorities.

The banking crisis deserves special attention because it deeply affected the macroeconomic environment in which Caldera operated. It also exemplifies the way economics, politics, and oil intertwined in Venezuela. For decades, bank supervision was poor, bank practices were not among the best and the financial system was weak, functioning in a heavily controlled and volatile economy. In addition, the macroeconomic conditions before the crisis started contributed to the erosion of banks' assets and deposit flights. Bankers were powerful lobbyists and enjoyed important political ties. Once the oil bonanza started to recede at the end of the 1970s and the beginning of the 1980s, the difficulties became apparent. Lack of adequate supervision, corruption and bad management led to, among other things, unlawful accounting practices to hide bad loans and insufficient reserves, poor investments, and loans to related businesses (Garcia et al., 1997; Krivoy, 2002).[20]

As a consequence of the weak macroeconomic and fiscal stance and the banking crisis, international reserves were depleted, the currency suffered a significant depreciation, and inflation accelerated. In late 1994, Caldera faced the situation with heterodox adjustment policies. He fixed the exchange rate, established a strict exchange rate control, and imposed widespread price controls.

These policies allowed international reserves to recover somewhat, but the uncertainty regarding the resolution of the banking crisis and the exchange rate control slowed down the foreign exchange flows to the private sector, thereby weakening non-oil activity. At end of 1994, inflation was 70 per cent, non-oil GDP declined by 5 per cent, unemployment increased, and real salaries plummeted. The current account went from a deficit in 1993 to a surplus in 1994 as restrictions in the foreign exchange market caused a severe contraction in imports. The Caldera administration tried to keep the fiscal situation under control through expenditure cuts, a temporary financial transaction tax, and the introduction of a general sales and luxury tax, but the massive financial assistance to banks in trouble produced a considerable fiscal deficit. A mix of central bank credit, domestic debt, and accumulation of arrears was used to finance this deficit.

In 1995 the continuation of the banking crisis coupled with a decline in oil revenues and increasing public expenditure put further pressure on the fiscal accounts. Negative expectations persisted during the year due to the exchange rate controls, inhibiting private investment, and the continuation of an expansive monetary policy contributed to the maintenance of negative real interest rates. Inflation closed the year at 57 per cent due mainly to public sector wage increases and expectations of increasing prices. GDP growth reached 2 per cent, but this was mainly fueled by the oil sector.

The deficit of the consolidated public sector dropped from 14 per cent of GDP in 1994 to 8.5 per cent in 1995. However, if assistance to troubled banks is excluded (13 per cent of GDP in 1994 and 4 per cent in 1995), the underlying fiscal deficit worsened by 3 points of GDP. This was mainly due to declining revenues and an increase in interest payments. Regarding the external accounts, in 1995 the current account surplus fell to 2.5 per cent of GDP from 5 per cent the previous year.

The Agenda Venezuela program

At the beginning of 1996, the political environment was characterized by increasing unrest and rumors of discontent within the armed forces. In fact, many political analysts argued that Caldera's term was coming to an end. There was also a perception that the government did not have a coherent strategy to deal with the impending crisis, and there were several changes in the economic cabinet, particularly in the planning ministry, that did not improve expectations.

In this context, Caldera appointed a savvy politician, Teodoro Petkoff, as minister of planning. Petkoff, a former leftist guerilla leader, was an outspoken critic of Caldera's economic policies and founder of the MAS party, one of the main political organizations of the *chiripero* coalition that supported the government. With the help of technocrats from PDVSA, the state oil company, and in coordination with the finance ministry and the central bank, Petkoff led the design and implementation of a stabilization and adjustment program known as the Agenda Venezuela.

In April 1996 the government began to implement a medium-term economic adjustment program with IMF support. The main objectives of the Agenda Venezuela were to reduce inflation, restore confidence, set the conditions for renewed and sustained growth, and reduce poverty. The program was designed to be implemented in two phases. During the first part, from the second semester of 1996 to April of 1997, the Caldera administration committed itself to reducing macroeconomic imbalances, stabilizing the economy, strengthening the banking system, improving the current social safety net, re-establishing normal financial relations with external and domestic creditors, reforming the severance payment system, resuming the privatization program, and paving the way for other structural reforms needed to achieve sustained growth.

The second phase was designed to consolidate macroeconomic stabilization, to continue the strengthening of the financial system, to deepen privatization efforts, to engage in a widespread public administration reform and to revamp social security. To support the program, the government requested financial assistance from the IMF in the form of a 12-month stand-by agreement for the first phase of the program, and an extended IMF facility to help the implementation of the second phase. The government never used the IMF's available resources, among other things because of the oil bonanza of this period. However, the 'seal of approval' of the IMF was considered very important as a way of regaining confidence and obtaining, if needed, additional external funding.

Caldera did not agree with the program, but because of the increasing deterioration in economic, social, and political conditions he allowed his economic team to proceed. In fact, during the announcement of the Agenda Venezuela on national TV, he said that 'only God knows how much this costs me'. One of the main differences between the Agenda Venezuela and the Pérez program was an aggressive strategy of communication undertaken by the economic team. This was done to convey to the public the idea that the program was necessary and painful, but that the results would improve the living conditions of the population, mainly through the reduction of inflation, which was reaching levels never seen in Venezuela before. To this end, members of the economic cabinet held periodic meetings with business leaders, congressmen, unions, and civil society at large. They appeared frequently on TV and radio programs to explain the reasons, the effects, and the benefits of the program to the population. There was also an important effort to implement a set of compensatory social policies to offset the initial effect of the economic liberalization.

Part of the strategy of the economic team was to convey the idea that IMF participation in the program was as a mere financer and not as an active player. In fact, the Agenda Venezuela was sold as a domestic program with the blessing of the IMF. This allowed the government to claim sole ownership of the program and differentiate itself from Pérez's IMF supported program.

The program in practice

The main objective of Agenda Venezuela was to obtain a quick reduction in inflation and recover confidence. The authorities' target was to reduce monthly inflation to 2 per cent by the third quarter of 1996 (inflation was 8.5 per cent in April and 12.5 per cent in May), 1.5 per cent by the fourth quarter, and 1 per cent in the first six months of 1997. The program envisaged that real GDP would decline by 1 per cent in 1996 due to a decline of 3.5 per cent in non-oil GDP and positive growth of 6 per cent in oil GDP.

Agenda Venezuela recognized that strong fiscal measures were needed to reduce inflation, decrease the public debt, and restore confidence. The program stated that the fiscal deficit of the public sector would be reduced from −4.3 per cent in 1995 to −1.2 per cent in 1996 and a small fiscal surplus would be obtained in 1997. The government argued that non-interest expenditures had decreased significantly since 1991; therefore further reduction would be very difficult in the short term, especially taking into account expenditure rigidities and social demands. This implied that the fiscal effort would focus on increasing domestic revenues. To this end, the government planned to raise the general sale and luxury tax (GSLT) from 12.5 per cent to 16.5 per cent, and to increase domestic fuel prices. These measures were expected to produce additional annual revenues of 1 per cent and 2.5 per cent of GDP respectively.

Domestic gasoline prices were increased tenfold. To reduce the unpopular impact of this measure, the administration implemented a communication strategy which explained the reasons behind the adjustment, and negotiated with public transport unions to prevent exaggerated transportation fare increases. In this regard, a clever subsidy scheme was implemented. This was an important achievement for the economic team, which was aware of the problems that Pérez had faced in increasing gasoline prices in the 1989 reform program, and the enormous opposition and social unrest which the increase had provoked.

Due to the distortions caused by the exchange rate control and the increasing gap between the parallel and the official market, the government decided to liberalize the exchange rate regime and introduce a credible exchange rate system. On 22 April 1996, the authorities eliminated all exchange rate restrictions under the assumption that a full liberalization accompanied with prudent financial policies would help to regain confidence quickly. Furthermore, the new exchange rate system unified the different exchange rates that existed in the controlled system.

Before the change in the exchange rate system, the Caldera administration tightened credit policies and liberalized interest rates. Interest rates on BCV papers (monetary stabilization papers or TEMs according to its Spanish acronym) went from 35 per cent in March to 60 per cent in mid-April. In addition, on 15 April ceilings on lending rates and floors on deposit rates were abolished. After an initial overshooting, the Bolivar stabilized with limited intervention by the central bank. In early July, the central bank decided to implement a band system with the idea of lowering inflationary pressures while preserving a certain degree of flexibility.

As mentioned above, the banking crisis of 1994 put enormous fiscal pressure on the government and contributed to macroeconomic instability. Therefore, the government sought to strengthen the banking system and improve the efficiency of financial intermediation, with high priority to improving banking supervision and the capital base of financial institutions. Additionally, the government announced its decision to privatize nationalized banks and sell the assets of liquidated banks.

Another important element of the program was the re-establishment of normal financial relations with all creditors. In this regard, the government was committed to clear arrears by December 1996 through a quarterly schedule of payments of both domestic and external arrears. A prudent debt management policy was announced, which imposed restrictions on contracting and guaranteeing of external debt by the public sector. A debt redemption fund was designed with the objective of being capitalized with the proceeds of privatization and oil exports in excess of the program estimates. These resources were intended to be used to amortize and repay central government domestic and external debt.

In order to strengthen the fiscal position and achieve sustained economic growth, the Agenda Venezuela moved to carry out structural reforms. In terms of the privatization effort, and besides the selling of the banks that were nationalized during the banking crisis, the government sold its remaining shares in the telecommunication company (CANTV), the public steel company (SIDOR), and several small enterprises such as hotels and utilities. Regarding labor issues, the Caldera administration reformed the severance payment system eliminating retroactivity and limiting payments within reasonable levels.

The government decided to increase expenditures on the social safety net by 1 per cent in 1996. A program called 'family subsidy' which provides a cash transfer to poor families with children was implemented. Old age pensions were doubled in May 1996, and a transport subsidy was implemented in April 1996 to compensate for the increase in transportation fares after the increase in gasoline prices.

State governors continued to influence the policy-making process of the fiscal policy during these years. In particular, in late 1996, new legislation established the minimum level of transfers (about 15–20 per cent) from the value added tax revenues to FIDES and, at the beginning of 1998, the legislature approved a law (*Ley de Asignaciones Especiales*) in which a share of oil royalties had to be transferred to the states.

The impact of the Agenda Venezuela

The main economic impacts of the reform program materialized in 1997. Following a decline of 0.2 per cent in 1996, real GDP grew by 6.4 per cent in 1997, fueled by a strong performance in the non-tradable sector. From the demand side, GDP expanded mainly because of an increase in domestic expenditures due to an increase in real wages, an expansion in public expenditures, a surge in investment, and the recovery of private sector credit.

During 1996, inflation reached 103 per cent due in part to the devaluation of the bolivar and the price liberalization. During the first part of 1997 the annualized rate of inflation receded to 30 per cent, but a relaxation of fiscal policy accelerated price increases during the second part of 1997, bringing inflation for the whole year to 37.5 per cent.

The current account of the balance of payments went from a surplus of 12.5 per cent of GDP in 1996 to a surplus of 3.9 per cent of GDP in 1997 as private demand recovered, government expenditures increased and the bolivar appreciated in real terms. Foreign direct investment (FDI) increased significantly due to the opening up of the oil sector and the privatization program. Net international reserves reflected the strong external position, recovering from US$12 billion in 1996 to US$15.7 billion in 1997.

A prudent fiscal policy in 1996, the reduction in non-recurrent expenditures due to the banking crisis, and favorable conditions in the oil market, helped shift the fiscal balance of the central government from a deficit of 4.3 per cent of GDP in 1995 to a surplus of 0.6 per cent of GDP in 1997. That same year, fiscal policy became expansionary due to increases in the wage bill and higher transfers to local governments and decentralized agencies. The real appreciation of the exchange rate contributed to a reduction of fiscal oil receipts. Nonetheless, the central government registered a surplus of 2.2 per cent of GDP because of important revenue from the sale of participation rights in the oil sector.

The exchange rate band system implemented after the elimination of controls was used as a nominal anchor to keep inflation under control. During 1997, the bolivar depreciated by 6 per cent against the US dollar, but it appreciated in real terms by more than 35 per cent. The relative stability of the domestic currency was mainly due to the favorable external position.

Monetary policy was determined, in part, by the exchange rate arrangement, but in the first nine months of 1997 the central bank used open market operations of TEMs in order to reduce liquidity brought about by the monetary expansion. The excess liquidity was caused by increasing government expenditure in the wake of high oil revenues and international reserves. Starting in September, monetary policy turned expansionary as the central bank decided to start redeeming TEMs because of growing concerns regarding the stock of these papers and the quasi-fiscal losses of the central bank. In parallel, the monetary authority relied on the sale of foreign exchange to absorb excess liquidity.

In terms of structural policies, the economy was substantially liberalized by the abolishment of exchange, interest rate and price controls, by the privatization program, and by the reduction of energy subsidies. Labor legislation was improved through the reform of the severance payments system, which eliminated the double indexation present in the old system and lowered uncertainty in the labor market.

Some analysts estimated labor liabilities of around US$7 billion, which was a heavy fiscal burden for the government and negatively affected firms' competitiveness. Previous attempts to reform labor laws were fiercely opposed by the CTV. The government decided to initiate negotiations with FEDECAMARAS and CTV through a mechanism of structured meetings known as *'tripartita'*. The key element of this negotiation was the elimination of the costly severance payments system, but accompanied by more flexibility in the labor market and an improvement in real salaries. On the part of the government, the minister of planning, Teodoro Petkoff, coordinated the group and led the political negotiations with workers and business representatives.

One of the biggest successes of Caldera's reform program was the opening of the oil sector. PDVSA played a key role in convincing the executive and legislative branches of the need to allow private investment in the oil sector within the parameters set forth by the hydrocarbon law, which reserved the property and exploitation of oil to the government, but permitted associations between PDVSA and private companies with approval by Congress. This process started in the early 1990s, but it was in 1996 that results finally materialized through the signing of contracts between PDVSA and foreign companies to operate marginal fields for a fee. Also, joint ventures were formed to explore selected areas at the risk of the private companies while sharing profits with PDVSA if oil was discovered and produced. In 1997, new joint ventures were created to produce in heavy oil fields.

The opening of the oil sector generated a steady increase in oil production and employment as well as technology transfers, funds for new investments, and a rise in proven reserves. This process exceeded all expectations and implied extra revenues for the government of about US$2 billion. The government intended to save this additional income to prevent future oil shocks or repay debt, but mounting pressures by labor unions led the government to sign overly generous labor contracts that absorbed the extra resources.

Some reforms were not approved or as advanced as the program envisaged. For example, the oil stabilization fund was submitted to Congress in May 1997 but was approved later. The establishment of the oil stabilization fund earlier in the program would have helped to reduce pressures for higher public expenditure in 1997 and would have facilitated monetary management by the central bank. The Caldera administration also started to reform the social security system, and although a new law was approved in late 1997, it was never implemented. Other areas in which little progress was made were the restructuring of the public sector, a better targeting of the social safety net, the liberalization of domestic fuel prices, and the privatization of the aluminum complex.

Poverty increased during the implementation of the Agenda Venezuela program to the highest level yet recorded in Venezuelan history (Riutort and Balza, 2001) and inequality worsened slightly as measured by the Gini coefficient (Ortega, 2003). As discussed later, this could have contributed to strengthening the arguments against market reforms used by Hugo Chávez, and may have helped pave the way for his subsequent triumph. The main economic indicators for the period are summarized in Table 8.3.

Table 8.3:　Macroeconomic framework, 1993–97

Indicator	1993	1994	1995	1996	1997
Real GDP growth (%)	0.3	−2.4	3.7	−0.2	6.4
Consumer price index (annual % change)	45.9	70.8	56.6	103.2	37.6
Current account balance (% of GDP)	−3.7	5.3	3.4	12.5	3.9
Central government fiscal balance (% of GDP)	−2.9	−7.3	−4.3	1.3	2.2
Oil export price (in US$ per barrel)	13.3	13.3	14.8	18.4	16.4

Source: IMF.

8.3   Analysis of the 1989 and 1996 reform programs

We begin our analysis by addressing the reform programs in terms of the three major issues this project wishes to address: why reform, how to reform, and how well did the reform perform. Afterwards, we present and discuss a series of hypotheses in an attempt to explain why reform attempts – and the Gran Viraje in particular – have not been successful in Venezuela. Given the overriding importance of oil wealth for the Venezuelan economy, we then proceed briefly to analyze the different ways in which oil wealth has influenced the Venezuelan crisis, the reform attempts, and their aftermath. Finally, we discuss the role that the ubiquitous interest groups played throughout this process.

The analysis of reform attempts in terms of questions such as why reform, how to reform, and how well have the reforms performed does not mean to imply that they can be understood as separate and unrelated issues. By definition, a forward looking policy-maker facing the decision to reform (the why issue) will consider beforehand which of the different policy responses (the how issue) is the one with the highest probability of success based on a prior probability distribution (the how well issue). The analysis is of course complicated by the presence of uncertainty in the link between policy selection and policy outcomes as a result of: (a) the fact that the policy-maker sees the link between policy selection and policy outcomes based on his particular model of how the world works; and (b) the fact that the policy-maker is not in full control of policy selection, for other players (nature, political parties, public opinion, courts) also participate in the game.

The message we are trying to convey before we proceed with our analysis is that the decision to reform is inextricably linked to the decision on how to carry it out, which in turn hinges on the likely pay-offs of each alternative. The fact that there is an analytical distinction to be made between the factors that determine whether to reform or not and those that determined the particular design of the reform package should never obliterate the intrinsic connection between them.

8.3.1   Why reform?

The reform literature identifies three distinct yet sometimes related reasons to engage in market-oriented reform: crisis, external events, and policy feedback. We will argue that all three causes played a part in the 1989 reform program.

As discussed in Chapter 1, the economic situation was critical in many respects when Pérez took office in February 1989. The external position of the country demanded the most immediate attention, since the depletion of international reserves left little room to maneuver. Simply put, the exchange controls had to be dismantled, given that the government had no way to intervene in the foreign exchange market. In addition, and given the grossly overvalued exchange rate implicit in the exchange control mechanism, a significant devaluation was to be expected.

Addressing the huge fiscal imbalances would be no picnic, either. The previous year showed a central government deficit of 7.4 per cent of GDP and a consolidated public sector deficit of 9.4 per cent. Given the fiscal importance of oil receipts, the devaluation would improve the fiscal accounts considerably in the short run, of course, but clearly not enough to finance the deficit in the coming years given the heavily frontloaded profile of the foreign debt service schedule. Therefore, a more structural and integral response to the issue would be necessary to return to a fiscally sustainable path.

Pérez and his economic team were unaware of the real magnitude of the external imbalance until one month before taking office. The amount of exchange guarantees offered by the central bank to the private sector proved to be much more than originally envisaged, thereby limiting even more the room to consider other policy options. Nevertheless, one can argue that foreign events and policy feedback played a part *before* the extent of the crisis was known, most notably in deciding the policy direction of his presidency and the composition of his cabinet.

The basic question here is what led Pérez, a big spender and a state-oriented developer in his first term, to convince himself of the virtues of adhering to the Washington Consensus even before knowing the extent of the crisis. To answer this question, one needs to go back a few years.

During his first presidency, Pérez gained international recognition and prestige as a champion of democracy in Latin America through the execution of a very active foreign policy. In 1980, after leaving the presidency, he continued to travel extensively, meeting with key political figures around the world. In 1985, he approached Miguel Rodríguez, a young US-trained economist with a PhD from Yale University, who had written a paper about the Venezuelan foreign debt that Pérez found quite revealing. As a researcher at IESA, Rodríguez had been actively voicing his opposition to Lusinchi's economic policy, and in 1987, he was chosen to conduct research at the Institute for International Economics (IIE) in Washington, DC. Through close contact with John Williamson and other members of the IIE staff as well as with other economists from Washington-based IFIs, Rodríguez convinced himself of the need to address Venezuela's longstanding economic malaise through the implementation of a radical shift in economic policy along the lines of what Chile was doing.

In October of 1987, Pérez obtained the presidential nomination of his party, AD, by beating Octavio Lepage in the primaries.[21] In the meantime, Pérez's close friendship with Felipe González and Alan García gave him backstage passes to two radically different approaches to economic policy and to the consequences of each. He saw Felipe González opt for an orthodox program of fiscal restraint and a less interventionist role for the state that would set the stage for Spain's stellar economic performance of the second half of the 1980s. At the same time, he saw Alan García's unorthodox approach to economic policy plunge Peru into one of the worst economic crises ever recorded, with inflation reaching 114 per cent in September of 1988 and a 9 per cent fall in GDP that same year. In order to get a better assessment of the issue, he had Eglee Iturbe, a long-time friend and future finance minister, join Miguel Rodríguez and visit both countries in mid-1988. That same year in September, Miguel Rodríguez attended a meeting in Caracas hosted by Pérez's closest political aide and future chief of staff. The short guest list was determined directly by Pérez, and included other technocrats who would later hold key government positions.

The official economic program did not espouse, at least publicly, the kind of reforms that Rodríguez proposed. After winning the elections of December 1988, Pérez finally offered Rodríguez the job of Minister of Cordiplan (economic planning) and then the two of them convinced the rest to join the new government. The selection of the team, however, was made directly by Pérez.

To sum up, the main determinant of the decision to reform seems to be the fact that the government had few policy options other than to abandon the currency controls and attack the fiscal deficit through a combination of expenditure cuts and new sources of revenue. Nevertheless, other more structural components of the program, such as the trade reform, were not forced by the crisis. In addition, the personal involvement of Pérez in deciding the economic direction of his presidency and the composition of the cabinet that would design and implement the reforms, even before the true extent of the crisis became known, points towards the importance of external influences and policy feedback as determinants of the decision to embark on the reform program.

8.3.2   How to reform?

The question of how to reform can be understood as two separate yet related issues. The first one relates to the particular contents of the reform program, and the second to the way in which such contents were carried out, that is, the sequence and speed of the reform program.

Contents of the reform program

By the time Pérez and his cabinet took office, it is clear that they had reached a definite conclusion in terms of the economic policy course of the new government. Rodríguez's stay at the IIE had convinced him that addressing the deep-rooted problems of the Venezuelan economy and reversing the trend of growing poverty and inequality required strong economic growth and job creation, and that these would not appear without structural economic reforms. The comparative experiences of Spain and Peru, the consequences of Lusinchi's policies and the success of the Chilean economy also served to convince the economic team that the only sensible thing to do was to engage in a comprehensive reform program from the start, one that would, so to speak, 'take advantage of the crisis' to go after the deep determinants of the dismal performance of the Venezuelan economy.[22]

The composition of the cabinet is in itself evidence of this 'all or nothing approach'. Unconvinced of this approach, Pérez would not have chosen Rodríguez, Naím, Martínez Mottola and other technocrats, and neither would they have taken the job. The personality traits of Pérez and his cabinet were quite consistent with this quest. Throughout his political life Pérez gained a reputation of a man with the desire to become an important figure in Venezuelan history. His energetic personality, his craving for international recognition, and his penchant for audacious, grandiose and, more often than not, outrageous development projects became indeed the trademarks of his first presidency. In retrospect, one should not be surprised at the idea that Pérez would embrace the new international paradigm of development during his second presidency with the same energy as he did the state-led model of industrialization during his first one.

In terms of the social components of the reform program, the economic team repeatedly stressed the notion that the resumption of economic growth and the job creation that came with it would be the core elements of social policy. Some indirect subsidies were removed with the reduction of the items under price controls, and the general idea was to gradually remove all of them in favor of direct subsidies towards the poor. It is clear however, that the political and social discontent that began with the *Caracazo* induced a more active social policy.

In sum, there is no doubt that the critical situation of the country in 1989, both in the external and fiscal accounts, demanded immediate policy responses. The Gran Viraje, however, was much more than a response to an impending balance of payments crisis. It was a comprehensive reform program motivated by the desire to thrust Venezuela into a path of high, sustainable, and equitable growth, not surprisingly, the same objective that (mis)guided Pérez's policies during his first presidency.

Speed and sequence

In order to explore the issue of how, in terms of speed and sequence, the different components of reform would go into the implementation stage, it is necessary to distinguish between the blueprint (the way the policy-makers envisaged the implementation process) and the events in the field (the way in which the reform was eventually carried out).

In terms of the blueprint, the decisions regarding the way in which the contents of the program were to be implemented – or introduced to Congress for their consideration – rested on both technical and political considerations. From a technical standpoint, and based mainly on the experience of Chile in the 1970s and 1980s, the economic team had strong opinions regarding the particular sequence in which the different components of the reform were to be carried out. The economic benefits brought about by trade reform, for instance, would only be captured in the presence of a competitive real exchange rate and in the absence of significant distortions in the price of inputs. Therefore, the first order of business would be to deal with relative price imbalances (the exchange rate overvaluation in particular), remove price distortions and correct fiscal disequilibria.

In terms of the speed of the reforms, and again, from a technical standpoint, a gradual implementation of each component of the reform program seemed very difficult. In the case of the dismantling of the exchange rate and price controls, for instance, the impediments rested mainly on the lack of international reserves to defend the currency and the absence of a state apparatus efficient enough to administer a gradual approach to price liberalization.[23] Regarding the fiscal reforms, the issue was further complicated by the fact that resources coming from the introduction of the VAT as well as those coming from the income tax reform would not be available in the short run, given that they required congressional approval and institutional build-up. The executive was therefore forced to plan on other ways to solve the fiscal imbalance in the first two years at least. The devaluation would of course be a significant source of fiscal revenue which would become available immediately, and so would the additional resources resulting from the initial increase in the price of fossil fuel derivatives and other goods and services provided by the public sector.

Again, institutional weaknesses convinced policy-makers that a big bang-cum-shock therapy approach would be the only feasible way to implement these measures. In addition, Pérez himself argued that the alternatives would give the opposition better chances to mobilize against them, in particular, after the *Caracazo*. But this is, of course, a generalization. The case of trade reform, for instance, was designed from the beginning as a gradual process given that it was relatively easy to administer. Nevertheless, it ended up being less gradual than planned, something that could be attributed to: (a) the fact that the opposition from the industrial sectors was not as fierce as originally envisaged; and (b) the fact that this piece of legislation did not require congressional approval.[24]

The fiscal reform, on the other hand, was not only significantly delayed (the VAT legislation was approved after Pérez's removal from office), but was substantially distorted by Congress to the point where the income tax legislation (the only tax component approved during Pérez's term in office) ended up extracting potentially less revenue than the original one. Another component of reform, that involving the financial sector, did not advance as planned, either. The government put the blame on Congress, but the industrial elite in particular expressed significant suspicion, implying connections between the government and the banking sector through Tinoco, head of the central bank and former president of Banco Latino, the largest bank in Venezuela at the time. The lack of adequate banking supervision during this period proved costly later on when a large-scale banking crisis hit the country in 1994.

But not all of the blame can be attributed to the reluctance of Congress to go along with the government's timetable. As noted earlier, the programmed increases in fossil fuel prices and those of other state-provided goods and services could not advance as planned due to an unfavorable social, economic, and political environment.

8.3.3 How well did it perform?

Evaluating the performance of a particular reform program is difficult, for it can be understood in a variety of ways. One possible interpretation, for instance, is to compare the degree of success in achieving the intermediate objectives set forth in the original program, that is, exchange rate and price liberalization, trade reform, privatizations, fiscal reform, and so forth. A second yet related interpretation would be to look at the degree of success in achieving the ultimate objectives of the reform program, that is, macroeconomic stabilization, economic growth, poverty reduction, political freedom, and so on. And yet a third interpretation, given the time constraints forced upon a democratic government, would be to ascertain after a few years have passed, the longevity or sustainability of the reforms.

In the first interpretation, the performance of Pérez's reform program is mixed. In some areas the reforms advanced quite smoothly. That is the case, for instance, of exchange rate and price liberalization, trade reform, debt reduction and rescheduling, and privatizations. In other areas, such as fiscal reform, it failed miserably. Taking the second interpretation, the performance is also mixed, a result that can be attributed to the above-mentioned partial success in consolidating basic intermediate objectives. Macroeconomic stabilization, for instance, was not achieved due to the lack of congressional approval of the fiscal measures and to the presence of a political and social environment strongly against further fiscal adjustments. The program did achieve, however, significant success in reviving economic growth, at least in the short run.

In the third interpretation, our assessment of the program is less benign, in spite of the fact that many reform components have been maintained (such as the trade liberalization or the privatization of the telephone monopoly) and others that were not approved were implemented later on (VAT, privatization of SIDOR, macroeconomic stabilization fund, and so on). Most importantly, however, the program was an abject failure in political terms and its philosophical orientation fell into disrepute. Pérez generated a reform backlash and a degree of animosity towards the political system he was part of that ultimately served to put him in jail, bring Caldera back from political oblivion, and advance Chávez's political ambitions. As we have seen in the discussion of the Agenda Venezuela program above, in his first two years in office Caldera managed to reverse many of the reforms implemented by Pérez, and only after an impending crisis did he grudgingly accept to implement palliative measures. In Section 8.3.4, we present and discuss some hypotheses that try to explain the reasons behind these events.

8.3.4 The political economy of backlash and reversal of reforms

The Venezuelan case of reform backlash stands in sharp contrast with the immediate political success of other reform programs implemented contemporaneously. In the case of Latin America in particular, most reform programs led to political victories for the reform promoters, at least in the short and medium term. The electoral victories of Menem in Argentina, Sanchez de Losada in Bolivia, Cardoso in Brazil, and Fujimori in Peru are probably the best examples (Gervasoni, 1995).

In Venezuela, which used to be the most stable democracy in the region, President Pérez suffered two military coup attempts and ended as the first and only president impeached in the country's forty-five year democratic history. President Caldera's reform attempt also ended with extremely low popular support and the election of radical leftist and former coup leader Hugo Chávez. There are only a few other examples of early failure in Latin America. One of them is the case of President Collor de Mello, who led an unorthodox reform program in Brazil that ended with his impeachment.

Even though by the early 2000s the majority of countries had experienced at least some symptoms of reform fatigue, the Venezuelan case is one of the earliest reversals and the most dramatic backlash against reforms. This occurred despite some significant economic successes in the two years preceding Pérez's program's derailment in 1992 and Chávez's victory in 1998. This section offers an explanation for this puzzling result. It is organized in terms of separate hypotheses. The separation is made for analytical tractability, but the hypotheses and their argumentation are inextricably linked. The order does not reflect their relative importance, but an attempt not to be too repetitive with the arguments. Throughout these hypotheses, the importance of the abundance of oil as a structural explanatory variable becomes more than evident. Moreover, at the end of this discussion a section is devoted to explicitly connecting the analysis to the political economy of oil wealth.

1. *The 'rentist' political institutions that successfully facilitated the consolidation of Venezuela's democracy made it very difficult to accept the implementation of an adjustment program*

This hypothesis may seem almost tautological, for it is awfully hard to imagine elected politicians happily engaging in an adjustment program. The question remains, however, on the *degree* of resistance to reform in the face of the alternative of further deterioration. We argue that ideology, and more importantly, the largely successful implementation of its basic tenets from the 1930s until the late 1970s, gave the polity little reason to believe, let alone be convinced, that a radical change of course (a Gran Viraje, in fact) would be wise not only politically, but in economic terms as well.[25]

From its beginnings in the 1930s, one of Acción Democrática's strongest political messages hinged on the absurdity of imposing hardship on a mostly poor, uneducated, and politically neglected population through ever-increasing forms of indirect taxation. As an alternative, it argued that fair and viable revisions of the terms under which the oil companies operated would increase fiscal revenues to levels that would not only render such measures unnecessary, but allow the means to finance a vast array of public goods and services that would significantly improve the living conditions of the people and serve as a catalyst to the formation of a strong and productive non-oil economy (Karl, 1986). What seemed to be a free lunch, proved true – at least for a long while – when AD did just that.

The oil companies acquiesced, not without significant confrontations, to continue operating under increasingly less favorable terms, and fiscal revenues – and expenditures – rose accordingly[26] (Monaldi, 2001). Acción Democrática became immensely popular, taking the presidential elections of 1946 with almost 80 per cent of the popular vote. After the ten-year dictatorship of Pérez Jímenez, Acción Democrática won the following two elections as well, and the build-up and maintenance of a patronage network made possible by oil revenues was crucial to the remarkable stability Venezuelans were able to enjoy until the 1980s, the famous 'illusion of harmony' described in Naím and Piñango (1984).

Problems with the oil-rent financing strategy began to surface in the early 1970s when oil production capacity fell sharply. The systematic increase in oil taxes during the 1960s and the non-renewal of the oil lease contracts (setting an end to oil concessions in 1983) had created the conditions for private dis-investment (since 1958) including the virtual abandonment of exploration activities (Monaldi, 2001). This phenomenon was eclipsed, however, by the temporary yet dramatic increase in oil prices caused by the 1973 oil crisis – perceived incorrectly at the time as a permanent one – fueling this patronage network and the fiscal needs accompanying it. Expenditures were significantly expanded and with them, the dependence on high oil prices. By the time the temporary nature of the oil bonanza became evident (late 1970s–early 1980s), the polity had painted itself into a corner. Politically unable to retrace its steps through an orthodox fiscal adjustment program, it opted for partial and palliative measures, that is, exchange rate and price controls, devaluations, and so on, slowly debilitating its power base without destroying it altogether. Rather than continuing down this path, in 1989 Pérez decided against the polity and the patronage network built around it (most importantly perhaps, against his own party, see below), to embark on a radical solution to Venezuela's economic problems. In doing so, he unveiled the long-hidden ills of the Venezuelan economy, thereby destroying the popular support for the two-party system and for his party in particular.

2. The majority of the Venezuelan population was not prepared for economic adjustment and did not perceive the need for structural reform

Running even deeper than the rentist program, Venezuelans' cultural beliefs have also been significantly shaped by the importance of oil wealth throughout the last century. As a result, the vast majority of the population was generally unprepared to face the harsh adjustments necessary to cope with a decline in oil rents to less than half their 1981 per-capita peak level.[27] Moreover, the public has been generally dubious of the need for drastic economic reforms. Throughout Venezuela's democratic history, oil income had allowed policy-makers to soften, or escape altogether, the tough political and economic choices normally faced by developing countries. As explained above, oil fiscal income permitted a clear trend of increasing fiscal expenditures without the correspondent increase in domestic taxation. This 'favorable' economic environment was a major factor in allowing Venezuela to have one of the most stable, least polarized polities in the region as well as its second oldest democracy (Karl, 1986; Rey, 1972).

The existence of significant oil resources has also promoted a static perception of wealth in which efficiency and wealth creation are given less importance than oil rent distribution. According to a poll conducted at the outset of the reform program, 91 per cent of Venezuelans considered that the country was 'very rich', 82 per cent said that oil wealth 'should be distributed equally among the population', 75 per cent agreed that 'oil wealth is sufficient to satisfy all the needs of the population', but 77 per cent felt they 'had not received much of the oil wealth' (Keller, 1992). The 'rich country' myth has had significant implications. There seemed to be little awareness of the dramatic decline in oil income per-capita or of the fact that oil wealth alone was not capable of delivering well-being levels comparable to those that prevailed from 1950–80 or even to those achieved by the more developed countries in the region.

Moreover, the perception of abundance combined with the (generally correct) perception that oil wealth had not been equitably distributed, led to the conclusion that corruption must have been the main source of society's ailments.[28] Widespread corruption has represented a major obstacle for Venezuela's development. According to the World Bank Institute and Transparency International's indicators, the country fares among the worst in the region and the world.[29] However, the notion that the cause of the decline in the well-being of the majority can be traced primarily to the capture by a corrupt elite of the largest share of the pie (oil wealth) is, to say the least, naive. As recent studies show, income distribution has not significantly worsened in the last two decades (Riutort, 2000). In contrast, income has dramatically declined for Venezuelan society as a whole. In the last 25 years only Nicaragua has had a worse income per-capita performance in the region (IDB, 2002).

After decades of systematic improvements in welfare it was difficult for Venezuelans to face the new realities of relative scarcity. In particular, the perceptions of abundance that still prevailed represented a major obstacle for convincing Venezuelans of the need for major reform and adjustment in 1989.[30] The populist credentials of President Pérez and his campaign promises of returning to the times of abundance created conditions for high frustration with adjustment. Pérez's first presidency (1974–79) in the middle of the oil price hike had been characterized by runaway spending in massive state projects and profligate subsidies. The country remembered this and also the general perception of widespread corruption. After he ended his presidency in 1979, Pérez faced corruption charges and he was only acquitted by an extremely narrow margin in Congress. In fact, the majority of voters in 1988 considered Pérez corrupt, but many of those were willing to vote for him again (Datos Polls; Templeton, 1995). In the campaign Pérez did not prepare the population for a reform program. Like many other eventual reformers in Latin America he did not campaign for reform. Moreover, the opposition candidate Eduardo Fernández had a much more pro-reform platform. Pérez's platform was based on vague social-democratic ideas, plans for 'modernizing' the country, and open references of a return to past abundance (Hidalgo, 2002).

Another crucial factor that differentiates Venezuela from other countries where reforms fared politically better is that in Venezuela the previous two years had been characterized by relatively high growth and low unemployment (1987–88). The large imbalances and hidden costs of President Lusinchi's fiscally expansionary policies were not evident to the population. Notice the difference from countries such as Argentina, Bolivia, or Peru where adjustment and reform followed a period of hyperinflation in which the high costs of not reforming became evident for the majority of the population. In Venezuela reformers had only the abstract counterfactual of what would have happened if reforms were not implemented to convince the public of their necessity (Naím, 1993).

The shock of Venezuelans at the sudden adjustment program can be traced back using polling data. In the last quarter of 1988, only 35 per cent of the population expected to be worse off in the next six months (Datos Pulso Nacional Polls). In contrast, in the third quarter of 1989, 68 per cent felt worse off than six months before. Moreover, from 1989 to 1992 between 51 per cent and 56 per cent expected to be worse off in the next six months. Venezuelans clearly did not vote for a reform program along the lines of what was implemented and did not perceive the costs of not adjusting.

The large front-loaded costs in terms of income decline, devaluation, and increase in poverty paid by the population in 1989 resulted in a rapid decline in the administration's popularity. Eight months after winning the elections with 53 per cent of the popular vote, the popularity of President Pérez was 22 per cent, the lowest of any previous president since polls began in 1968. Moreover, the good economic performance of 1990–92 did not translate into significant political support for the government (Table 8.4).

Table 8.4: Presidential approval ratings, 1988–92

Nov. 1988	Nov. 1989	Nov. 1990	Nov. 1991	Aug. 1992
37%	14%	22%	19%	13%

Source: Datos Pulso Nacional Polls; Templeton (1995).

Despite popular dissatisfaction, the reform effort was favored by the fact that discontent and opposition to it was relatively unorganized, at least in the beginning. For example, business groups did not play a significant role in trying to oppose key reforms that negatively affected them, such as trade reform (Naím, 1993).[31] However, neither was support for the program organized. No political party or social movement of significance openly embraced the program, not even the ruling party, as will be shown below. Oddly, there appeared to be no other credible alternative plan on the table, providing a big advantage to the technocrats.

As was explained, political backlash was the main cause of the derailment of the program. The coup attempt of February 1992 was surprisingly very popular. The majority of the population supported the anti-reform backlash led by Caldera (particularly in his speech in Congress just after the coup). Another coup attempt in November 1992 and the impeachment of Pérez in 1993 put an end to the program.

Caldera's political discourse (as Chávez's later on) perfectly captured the popular sentiment about the situation of the country. He claimed that the origin of the decline in welfare could be traced firstly to corruption and the poor use of the national wealth; and secondly to the neo-liberal reform program that had impoverished the population and given away strategic assets. An honest government giving good use to the state's resources could, argued Caldera, bring back the good old days of the first decades of democracy. Chávez's discourse in 1998 went a step further arguing that the whole political system was corrupt and that Caldera did not and could not change that because he was part of the oligarchy that benefited from it.

3. *The reform was front-loaded in terms of its costs, and back-loaded in terms of its benefits*

A classical argument explaining the difficulties faced by market-oriented reformers is that reform is akin to 'tough love' or to 'a bitter pill' – that is, a course of action that will, after a costly but temporary slump, bring about significant and sustainable increases in welfare. This line of reasoning has been used by Przeworski (1991) – and most forcibly by former Singaporean Prime Minister Lee Kuan Yew (2000) – to explain the apparent lack of success democratic regimes have had, relative to authoritarian ones, in implementing reform.[32] Recent empirical evidence, however, coming particularly from Latin America, seems to point in a very different direction, with the most striking counter-examples provided by Menem in Argentina and Fujimori in Peru, both of whom saw their economies, together with their popular support, soar shortly after announcing and implementing orthodox market-oriented reform programs.

The explanation behind this apparent contradiction seems to be directly related to pre-reform economic conditions, the specific contents of the program, and in particular, the type of stabilization pursued, that is, money-based or exchange-rate based. Prior to reforms, Argentinians and Peruvians were facing hyperinflation with strong declines in consumption levels. Venezuelans, on the other hand, were not. GDP, in fact, had grown 6.3, 4.5, and 6.2 per cent, respectively, in the three years prior to the announcement of the reform program. More relevant is the fact that the stabilization programs in Peru and Argentina were exchange-rate based, which boosts consumption levels in the short run (Calvo and Vegh, 1994). The Venezuelan program, on the other hand, was money-based, required a sizable devaluation as policy-makers allowed the exchange rate to respond to market forces, and entailed other significant short-term costs.

Pérez's economic team argued that a significant short-term fall in consumption was inevitably imposed by the circumstances. An exchange-rate-based stabilization was not a feasible option; the exchange rate was grossly over-valued and international reserves were depleted. The fiscal situation, characterized by a huge deficit and significant foreign debt obligations, demanded more than could be expected from the additional inflow provided by the conversion of oil revenues at the new and higher exchange rate. In the absence of other sources of revenue, the price of gasoline and other fossil fuel derivatives had to be raised significantly, as well as that of other goods provided by the state. Furthermore, all but a reduced number of items under price control had to be lifted, contributing to a significant jump in the price index (the annualized change in consumer prices reached 140 per cent during the second quarter of 1989).

The program was, indeed, a textbook case of a bitter pill. Based on a particular model of how the Venezuelan economy would respond to this new incentive structure, the program promised significant benefits in return for these short-term costs. The problem was that the program demanded patience and trust, both from the polity and from the population at large, neither of whom had any faith – or any real understanding, for that matter – in this new economic paradigm espoused by the authorities.

4. *Despite being a candidate from the left carrying out an orthodox economic adjustment program, Pérez was widely perceived as corrupt, and therefore ill-suited to carry the torch of austerity and hardship*

The issue of how the political affiliation of the reformers affects the probability of success of the program is one that has spurred considerable debate in recent years. On one side of the fence, there are those who argue that it takes a Nixon to go to China (Cukierman and Tommasi's, 1998a, metaphor); on the other side, there are those who stress the difficulties a government faces when its actions betray its core constituencies.

As mentioned in Section 8.2, Pérez fits the description of a candidate from the left, chosen on a populist platform, but who shortly before taking office convinces himself of the need to implement radical market-oriented economic reforms. And furthermore, as in the case of Menem or Fujimori, he takes voters by surprise by doing so.[33] So why did Pérez fail in doing what Menem and Fujimori were so successful at?

We argue that one of the reasons Pérez could not capitalize on the Nixon-in-China advantage was that the program's call for austerity and stoic hardship just didn't sound convincing coming from a politician widely perceived as corrupt. And aside from his image, there were symbolic events which served to highlight the stinging contradiction between the austerity he expected from Venezuelans and the example he gave with his own actions; the most salient one, of course, his imperial presidential inauguration, followed two weeks later by the announcement of the *paquete económico*.

The Nixon-in-China argument applies quite well, however, to Caldera, who – a symbol of moral rectitude able to profit from the popular anger against reforms – won the presidency after Pérez's demise, and eventually implemented an IMF-sponsored economic adjustment program without generating a single outburst of violence.

5. *The lack of governing-party support was a key determinant of the fate of the reform program*

One crucial factor that distinguishes Venezuela's reform attempts from other politically more successful programs is the lack of significant government-party support for Pérez's program and overall political support for Caldera's. Historically, Venezuela's party system was stable, strong, and disciplined, conditions that generally are supposed to favor reform. Parties provided significant political backing to their president with relatively little dissent. In Section 8.3.5 a structural and institutional explanation for the decline in the Venezuelan party system will be presented. Here, however, we analyze how the conflict between Pérez and his party affected the reform program and ultimately contributed to its demise.

Despite winning the 1988 presidential election with the largest margin in twenty-five years, from the beginning Pérez faced significant opposition from within his own political party. Acción Democrática was controlled by a faction of the 'old guard', which had strongly opposed Pérez in the internal primaries of 1988. After the Lusinchi administration, which had governed in complete symbiosis with the party leadership, with Pérez the old guard faced an administration led by the leader of the minority 'out' faction of the party (Corrales, 2002).[34]

There were a variety of factors that would have created conflict between Pérez and AD, even if he had not implemented a market-oriented reform program. However, these factors were compounded by the launching of a radical program that was not supported by key members of the leadership of AD.

The animosity between Pérez and some of the leaders of his party started with his first administration (1974–79), in which Pérez ruled with significant autonomy, bringing many outsiders into his cabinet who were not linked to the party and in fact had been opponents of AD in the recent past. Pérez obtained the windfall from the oil boom of the early 1970s and launched an ambitious transformation strategy using special decree powers provided by Congress. The lack of party involvement in many key decisions and the impression that Pérez was attempting to create for himself an independent power base alienated the leadership, including AD's founder Rómulo Betancourt. Moreover, the first Pérez administration faced many corruption charges, including some coming from important leaders of AD, such as Luis Piñerua, the party's presidential candidate in the elections to find Pérez's succesor.[35] In fact, after ending his presidency he faced corruption charges that were only dismissed after a close vote in Congress.

During the next AD presidency of Lusinchi (1984–89), the party became much more involved in the government, controlling the patronage network through which rents were distributed. The regional secretary generals of the party were appointed governors, merging the party completely with the administration. Perceiving that the party leadership would oppose his run for the presidency, Pérez attempted to promote a radical change in the leadership to take control of the party. However, after some partial successes, his attempt failed and only two members of his faction entered the forty-odd member party board. The victory of Pérez in the presidential primaries against Octavio Lepage – the choice of the party leadership and Lusinchi – did little to improve relations. However, in order to retain the presidency for the party, they helped in the campaign.

Relations between the party and the new administration had a rocky start when the commission to coordinate the smooth transition between the two administrations could barely function. This lack of cooperation was surprising given that the ruling party was unchanged.

The appointment of a technocratic elite not related to AD in key cabinet positions further alienated AD's leadership from the new Pérez administration. Neither Miguel Rodríguez – the architect of the reform program – nor other key members of the economic team had any past relationship with AD.[36] Pérez included some AD members to guarantee some support from the party, but most of them were from his own faction in the party.

In addition, in order to justify his harsh adjustment program, Pérez blamed the Lusinchi administration, which had ended with high popularity, for leaving him a ticking time-bomb. More generally, in order to justify the reform program Pérez's ministers openly criticized the past policies that were the symbol of AD. Pérez's discourse justified the program as one that was made inevitable by the circumstances, but that he did not embrace ideologically; at times even arguing that the IMF was imposing the new policies. This way he tried to reassure the party that he had not changed his ideological views.

However, this ambiguous position did little to convince party leaders of the advantages of reform. Later on the president assumed the reform ideas much more forcefully in his discourse. Another cause for confrontation were the many corruption charges against Lusinchi's government that surfaced in 1989–90. The party felt that Pérez was doing little to support his fellow party members and some even accused him of promoting the corruption scandals.

The coldness between Pérez and his party was one of the leading causes of the lack of support for his legislative agenda. To begin with, the party decided it was not going to give Pérez special decree powers as they had done in his previous administration and in Lusinchi's. As could be seen in the description of the reform program, most of the reforms that did not require new legislation (commercial reform) were rapidly implemented, while the ones that had to pass through Congress lagged or were completely obstructed. Moreover, Congress promoted and passed some legislation that ran in the opposite direction to the reform effort.

The fiscal reforms, one of the pillars of the reform effort, constitute the best example of the obstruction to the program. The key element, the value added tax, was discussed but never even voted. The income tax law proposed by the government was significantly modified adding additional loopholes instead of reducing them, making it ineffective. The crucial spending laws of 1989, required to implement the World Bank structural reform loans, were postponed for half a year, and the oil stabilization fund law did not move forward. This legislative obstruction cannot be attributed to the opposition parties. Acción Democrática had a large plurality of 48.3 per cent in the Chamber of Deputies. They also had allies such as F1 (1 per cent), NGD (3 per cent) and ORA (1 per cent), with which they could have easily passed the laws. In the Senate it was more difficult, but with NGD (1 senator) they had 25 of the 51 senators. Former president Lusinchi, life member of the Senate, could have been used to get the majority, but was used only a couple of times. Moreover, the main opposition party, COPEI, in many instances was more willing to cooperate with the reform legislation than AD.[37] Clearly there were other factors that obstructed the approval of reform legislation, but the lack of support by some key leaders of AD was crucial.

The approval of the labor law promoted by former President Caldera in Congress went in the opposite direction to the reform. This law made labor markets more inflexible, increasing the costs of hiring and firing workers. Acción Democrática supported the law with even more enthusiasm than COPEI, Caldera's party. Similarly, Congress approved the law of the mortgage debtor, which among other things, controlled the interest rates of this type of loan, diminishing significantly the issue of new loans in the years to come. It was initiated by COPEI, but was not obstructed by AD despite the president's rejection.

There was one area in which reform did pass in Congress: privatization. In particular the legislature approved the privatization of the telephone monopoly. This case offers some evidence that very controversial reforms that were not supported by key leaders of AD could be pushed through Congress if there was enough will of the government and an effective campaign to negotiate with opponents. It required significant compensation for the losers, in particular for the workers of the company. Some leaders in Congress argued that the same was not done in negotiations of the fiscal laws. Nevertheless, even in the privatization process major elements of the reform agenda were disrupted. For example, the privatization law proposed by the executive established that all resources obtained from the sale of public assets had to be used to pay external debt. Luis Raul Matos Azocar, a key leader of the labor movement of AD and chairman of the committee in charge of this law, demanded the elimination of this clause in exchange for his approval. As Corrales (2002: 132) puts it: 'The Venezuelan Congress did everything to delay as many reform-supportive bills as possible.'

There were other areas in which the confrontation with AD made a big difference. The labor union confederation (CTV), controlled by the old guard of AD, had from the beginning a confrontational attitude towards the government. This contrasted with their absolute support for Lusinchi's administration, even when it took unpopular measures such as cutting spending in the first two years. The national strike of 1989, organized by CTV, set the tone for a rocky relationship that resulted in a record number of strikes. In the past, CTV had had a very different stance towards AD governments (favorable) than COPEI's (unfavorable); this changed with the Pérez reform package.

After its disappointing performance in the regional elections of December 1989, leaders of the party began criticizing the government more openly. Most of the technocratic members of the cabinet were the targets of bitter criticism and faced scrutiny by Congress commissions. Party discipline clearly weakened. Many times AD governors did not cooperate with the reform program (Corrales, 2002: 126–7). Even some of the few AD ministers actively blocked reform initiatives. For example, the minister in charge of Guayana heavy industries, Leopoldo Sucre Figarella, blocked privatization.

The impeachment of Pérez in 1993 received the support of AD. At that point it could be argued that the party simply wanted to deflect the costs of having such an unpopular president. However, it is still very significant that key members of the party facilitated the process of impeachment in the supreme court and the attorney general's office.

6. *The Pérez administration conveyed the idea that adopting the proposed measures was the only sensible course of action, one that should not be subject to political negotiation*

One of the most common criticisms of the Pérez administration was that they failed adequately to explain, both to the polity and the population at large, the need to embark on a radical change in economic policy, and to negotiate the contents and implementation of the program with the relevant actors.

The validity of this criticism was largely confirmed, in the case of the polity, throughout our interview process. As argued in hypothesis 5, the lack of political maneuvering came out quite clearly with members of Pérez's own party, who perceived no real intention to negotiate with them or with Congress on crucial issues such as the VAT legislation. But the thrust of this argument is perhaps better conveyed through the analysis of a successful component of the reform program, since doing so may serve to compare both the omissions and the mistakes in those components that failed. For this purpose, we choose the privatization of CANTV, the state telephone monopoly, as a case study of a successful reform. Note that this case represents a highly sensitive and thorny reform component, one that by nature threatened the privileges of an array of entrenched interest groups operating comfortably and wielding their power as syndicate heads or providers of a state monopoly. Moreover, it was likely to involve massive lay-offs, bring about substantial increases in rates and – an issue of particular importance in a developing country with a highly interventionist state like Venezuela – was hotly contested on ideological grounds.

It is important to recall that the privatization of CANTV was not part of the original reform program. In fact, Pérez himself remained vehemently opposed to it as late as 1990, when Fernando Martínez Mottola (FMM, hereafter), head of negotiations with the World Bank at the time and future president of the company, expressed his thoughts regarding the future of the state monopoly. More surprisingly, the rest of the economic team and the World Bank also opposed privatization, mainly on two grounds: (1) that the company did not represent a fiscal burden (it actually had a positive cash flow); and (2) that the privatization process would be very costly from a political standpoint. FMM disagreed. He argued that modernizing the telecoms industry was crucial to the country's competitiveness and for that purpose it required around US$1 billion a year in new investments that the fiscal coffers could not provide.

FMM's negotiating strategy during the restructuring-cum-privatization period was strikingly simple: the only item that was non-negotiable was the privatization date. He arranged to have regular meetings with all the relevant players, that is, congressmen, labor union bosses, the press, media moguls, business leaders, and so on. In these meetings, he carefully explained his plans for the company by presenting the pros and cons of all possible options, trying to push his ideas as far as possible without causing alienation.[38]

Finally, on 6 December 1991, two months before the first coup attempt, the winning consortium made official its purchase of 40 per cent of the shares of CANTV for US$1.8 billion dollars.[39] But the virtues of the privatization process were not limited to the relatively large sum obtained in return, and the industry statistics are revealing. In 1991 CANTV had 1.5 million subscribers, today it has over 8 million; the average waiting time to obtain a phone line was 8 months, today it is less than a month; average repair time was between 30 and 40 days, today it is less than a day. And all this was achieved while cutting jobs from 23,000 in 1991 to fewer than 8,000 in 2005.

The experience faced by the Pérez administration, and particularly in regard to the importance of a well thought-out communication strategy, was not lost on Petkoff, head of the Agenda Venezuela program during the Caldera administration. Having witnessed the demise of Pérez's attempt to reform, Petkoff became convinced that an adequate communication strategy was a key element of the implementation strategy. He personally took on the task of explaining the program's inherent logic and intentions, traveling extensively throughout the country to meet with local labor and business leaders and the media.

7. The deconsolidation of the Venezuelan party system

In many ways the lack of party support for the reform programs of the 1990s reflected a more structural phenomenon that became evident in 1989: the deconsolidation of the Venezuelan party system. Until the 1980s Venezuela had one of the strongest, most stable, disciplined, and cooperative party systems on the continent. However, during the 1990s the party system imploded, setting the stage for Chávez's radical revolutionary project. Poor economic performance in the 1980s induced the political upheaval, which in turn contributed to instability and further economic decline. The increasing fragmentation, volatility, decline in party discipline, political instability, and authoritarianism, which has characterized Venezuelan politics since 1989, made the successful advancement of reform difficult, and are key ingredients in understanding the backlash and reform reversal.

The Venezuelan democracy in the period 1958–88 was generally considered a regional model. While most other Latin American countries suffered democratic breakdown and high instability, in Venezuela the political system consolidated into an uneventful two-party alternation of power. Four presidents were members of AD and two of COPEI. Political fragmentation was low. In 1973–88 the number of effective parties in the legislature was 2.6, below the Latin American regional average.[40] Polarization was relatively low and both parties converged to a moderate set of policies. The party system was stable. Party volatility was below the regional average.[41] Party discipline was very high and parties were highly institutionalized (Crisp, 2000; Monaldi et al., 2004; Shugart and Carey, 1992).

The features of the party system described above were to a significant degree the result of the political institutions set up by the 1961 constitution. This constitution institutionalized the elite agreement that established the bases for democracy in 1958 (the Pact of 'Punto Fijo'). Among the key institutional features were: (1) Venezuelan presidents were formally weak. In comparison with most presidents in the region, they did not have significant legislative powers.[42] For example, a simple majority could override the president's veto. However, in other dimensions presidents were powerful, they had significant control over the expenditure of oil rents and could appoint all state governors. Moreover, Congress could delegate significant law-decree powers to the president (Shugart and Carey, 1992). (2) The electoral system of proportional representation (PR) with closed lists allowed national party leaders to control the nominations and exert a high level of discipline. (3) The full concurrency between winner-takes-all presidential elections (plurality) and legislative elections maximized the *coattail* effect. Concurrency, combined with the fact that there were only two votes – one for the president and the other for the legislature – and no regional offices were elected, tended to minimize the fragmentation produced by the PR system (Monaldi et al., 2004). (4) The umbrella groups of labor and business groups were incorporated into the policy process through presidential commissions (Crisp, 2000).

The institutional framework described above, combined with a favorable environment provided by increasing rents, allowed for a high degree of cooperation among a few key political actors: the national party leaders of AD and COPEI, the two leading corporatist groups (CTV and Fedecámaras), and the president. Conversely, the conciliation mechanisms that were so effective in the consolidation of democracy proved ill-suited for adjusting to new political and economic circumstances, for example, the decline in oil rents. The institutional arrangement blocked popular participation (increasing abstention rates), cartelized the party system (high barriers to entry), promoted clientelism, and was slow to respond to exogenous shocks (inflexible). The patronage system created by the parties resulted in high levels of corruption and inefficiency. In addition to the negative political consequences of the institutional framework, the appalling economic performance from 1978–88 weakened popular support for the political system (Templeton, 1995). To revitalize the polity, the government of Lusinchi (1984–89) appointed a commission to come up with proposals for political reform and public administration reform (the 'COPRE'). The proposals included the direct elections of governors and mayors and a change in the proportional representation system to include a direct connection between voters and representatives (COPRE, 1986).

These propositions confronted an immediate resistance from AD (the president's party), which had an absolute majority in the legislature. They thought that COPRE's recommendations were too radical. Gonzalo Barrios, AD's president, publicly rejected these reforms, particularly the direct election of governors, 'because the country is not historically prepared for this type of reform'.[43] AD was not willing to withdraw its control over the patronage network that regional and local bureaucracies offered the party. AD's national party leaders perceived COPRE's propositions as directly aimed at undermining their political power. As a result, the reforms were not even discussed in Congress.

It was only during the 1988 presidential campaign, due to the attention that the candidates Eduardo Fernández of COPEI and Carlos Andrés Pérez of AD, paid to these issues, that AD's national party leaders were forced to pass some of these reforms. Pérez had won the party nomination against the fierce opposition of AD national party leaders and he wanted to weaken their centralized control of the party. Fernández used COPRE as a campaign tool against AD, which had been publicly opposed to any opening to the political process, possibly expecting that AD would continue blocking the reforms. Pérez's campaign in favor of the reforms forced AD to approve some of them in Congress: the mayors' election and the electoral reform to be implemented in 1993. But the election of governors, which AD feared the most, did not pass.

The riots of 1989 created the political circumstance for the approval of the rest of the political reforms. In 1989 the first direct election of governors and mayors generated the movement towards decentralization. Also the electoral system to select the legislature was changed to a mixed system in which a portion of the members is elected by plurality and the rest by PR (IDB, 2002; Penfold, 2001).

The implementation of political reforms, combined with the weakening effects of market reforms over the patronage system, induced a dramatic transformation in the incentives provided by the political system, increasing the transaction costs of creating a political consensus for market reforms. A polity formerly characterized by few effective parties, high party discipline, and party control by national leadership, progressively transformed into a fragmented system, with less internal discipline, and an increasing power of the regional authorities in national policy-making.

In the period 1989–2003, the effective number of parties jumped to an average of 4.6, reaching a high in 1994–99 of 6.0 (from an average of 2.6 in 1973–88). The volatility of the parties' share in the legislature also increased dramatically.[44] Party discipline declined as the control of national party leaders over the party members' careers, including nominations, diminished dramatically. For the first time parties other than AD and COPEI held executive elected office as governors and mayors. There were many significant party splits and defections. Regional parties surfaced and became relevant players. Governors of large states became prominent political leaders with a real option for the presidency (Monaldi et al., 2004; Penfold, 2001). The structure of parties changed and regional leaders gained more power. Having regional elections every three years modified the electoral cycle shortening the politicians' horizons. All these transformations made it more difficult for the leadership of AD and COPEI openly to support unpopular reforms. It also made negotiations much more complex.

In addition, the declining oil rents, the reduction of clientelistic programs, and the direct election of regional authorities diminished the president's negotiating tools. As a result, presidents, who had been historically weak in terms of legislative powers, became even weaker in their capacity to lead policy change (IDB, 2002; Monaldi et al., 2004).

Even though other factors were operating, to a large degree the transformation of the political system can be attributed to the reforms. The career incentives of politicians were radically changed. Not following the orders of the national party leadership often became politically profitable. Veto players increased dramatically (Monaldi et al., 2004).

The system imploded, losing political stability and weakening the capacity to implement reforms. The instability that ensued manifested itself in a variety of ways. As described above, the 'original sin' of the reform program was the explosion of massive riots in February 1989, which could only be controlled by the use of brutal repression by the armed forces. These events signaled the incapacity of the parties and corporatist groups to control the situation. This 'shattered glass effect' inaugurated a new era, in which the role of the masses, the military, and many smaller political players was to be decisive. Even though the riots should not be read mainly as a protest against the reform package, these events shattered the foundations of Venezuela's political equilibrium, complicating the successful advancement of a reform program.

The military coup attempts of 1992, the presidential victory of one of the former coup leaders (Hugo Chávez) in 1998, the radical institutional change implemented by his administration, and the rising polarization and political instability that have prevailed since, provide further evidence of the implosion of Venezuela's democracy. According to the index of political instability provided by the World Bank Institute since 1996, Venezuela is amongst the most unstable countries in the region and in the world.[45] Even though it is difficult to disentangle the causality between economic decline, political reform, economic reform and instability, it seems safe to argue that the political reforms implemented weakened the political system and made reform more difficult.

8.3.5 A note on oil dependence and the political economy of reform

As should be clear at this point we ascribe significant relevance to the role that oil wealth has played in the fate of reforms in Venezuela. In many of the hypotheses oil enters in one way or another. Here we will briefly review the role of oil and add some further comments on its impact over the political economy of reform.

Oil wealth has entered the analysis of reform in the following ways: (1) Influencing political ideology by shaping the historically successful rentist program. (2) Shaping the cultural beliefs of the population. Creating the myth of the rich country that only has to distribute oil wealth equitably to attain development. (3) Inducing a patronage and clientelistic state that promoted corruption and inefficiency. (4) Allowing the country to avoid a full-blown fiscal crisis (that is, hyperinflation), a major precedent of politically successful reform attempts. (5) Creating more economic distortions than those present in other countries of the regions that did not have oil rents. (6) Making fiscal reform much harder.

The difficulties for fiscal reform deserve some additional attention. Pérez's administration was not the first to fail in an attempt to implement some significant tax reform. The Venezuelan political system has had a systematic tendency to avoid and block fiscal reform. For example, in the period 1964–68, President Raúl Leoni attempted a major fiscal reform to expand the non-oil tax base and also increase oil taxation. In the end he could only pass the oil tax hike (Monaldi, 2002). As Navarro (1994: 22) puts it:

Historically, oil taxes have relieved individuals and firms of significant contributions to the financing of governmental activities, simultaneously creating a preference for high levels of public expenditure and low willingness to pay for publicly produced goods . . . this adds to the difficulty of any major tax reform . . . runs against beliefs deeply ingrained in the political and economic culture . . . the difficulties were reinforced in 1990, 1991, when both Congress and the Executive were unable to avoid the impression that tax reform was not a priority – or not necessary at all – given the oil prices due to the Gulf War.

The fiscal reform attempt of 1990–92 fits neatly into a pattern of the political economy of oil booms and busts, in which in periods of boom reform attempts are easily derailed and spending is increased to unsustainable levels and in periods of bust it becomes politically difficult and economically undesirable to cut spending and raise taxes.

Also it is worth emphasizing how oil rents allowed for a magnification of the inefficiencies generally induced by the import substitution model. Consequently, Venezuela's industrialization forged an economy with more distortions than the ones existing in most other developing countries. Moreover, as mentioned before, the political system was based on the distribution of oil rents and patronage. As a result, the reduction of subsidies and the elimination of large distortions were politically more costly than was the case in other countries. For example, the price of fertilizer produced by a subsidiary of the state-owned oil company was around one-tenth of market value. The elimination of this subsidy faced tremendous opposition from agricultural producers (Naím, 1993).

The literature on the political economy of oil-dependent countries has emphasized the weak state capacity of such states (Karl, 1997). Naím (1993) argues that one of the key weaknesses of the reform effort in Venezuela was the state's incapacity to implement policies. As a result, at times the optimal speed or sequence of reform was not implementable. Moreover, the programs to compensate vulnerable populations and losers of the reforms took too much time to execute. Similarly, the government did not have an effective information and communication strategy. Naím attributes the degree of these weaknesses to the fact that the Venezuelan state had been shaped by oil wealth. Supporting that view, there is a literature arguing that the presence of oil induces a low institutional quality (Sala-i-Martin and Subramanian, 2003). The World Bank Institute data show that Venezuela in general has institutional indicators below those of countries with similar per-capita GDP (Kaufmann et al., 2003).

8.3.6   The role of interest groups in the fate of Venezuela's reforms

Contrary to the extensive literature giving a prominent role to interest groups in the approval and sustainability of reforms, in the Venezuelan case interest group pressures had a relatively insignificant role in the passing and reversal of major reforms. However, in some instances specific groups, such as labor and media outlets, did have a significant role in opposing certain reforms that affected them directly.

Authors such as Frieden (1992) have argued that interest groups with high asset specificity, which benefited from the state-led development strategy, were partly responsible for the postponement of reform in the 1980s. However, their capacity to block reforms can be questioned in light of the events of the 1990s. For example, one area in which the literature has emphasized the blockage of reforms by interest groups is trade reform. To the surprise of most analysts and the government (including trade minister Naím) business groups did not present a fierce opposition to trade liberalization. Tariffs were dramatically reduced from one of the highest in the region to among the lowest, but the beneficiaries of import substitution did not use their influence to block it (Naím, 1993). One possible explanation, specific to this reform, is that the very high real depreciation that accompanied the reform compensated them for the reduction in tariffs. However, the lack of significance of interest groups appears to be the general case rather than the exception.

Venezuela had one of the most corporatist political arrangements in the region (Crisp, 1997). Both labor and business groups had a key role in the policy-making process under the political structure that evolved from the power sharing Pact of Punto Fijo. The largest labor unions were grouped under the umbrella association, CTV, which was controlled by the AD labor group. CTV, as well as the business umbrella group (Fedecámaras), were involved in most presidential commissions created to draft economic and social legislation. Similarly, the boards of the state bureaus and companies, through which a large portion of public spending was allocated, generally included members of both CTV and Fedecamaras. In practice, this resulted in significant rents being distributed to these privileged corporatists groups (Monaldi et al., 2004). Organized labor was financed by the state and unionized workers were generally given above opportunity-cost salaries. The rents created by import substitution industrialization financed by oil revenues allowed both capital and labor to obtain abnormally high returns in the sectors sheltered by high tariffs and subsidies (Frieden, 1991).

Reforms, for example, trade liberalization and privatization, eroded the rents earned by organized labor. As a result, labor unions opposed the reform programs. However, they were not a major force inducing the postponement, derailment, or reversal of them. They staged two national strikes and rallies, but in most instances reformers were able to negotiate with them to pass specific reforms such as the privatization of CANTV and VIASA. It is true that labor obtained major concessions, but none that made privatization unviable.[46]

Also labor unions approved the reform of severance payments and of pensions during Caldera's tenure.

One possible general explanation for the apparent lack of significant opposition from business and labor groups refers to their lack of autonomy in a country in which the largest portion of the economy is controlled by the state (that is, oil revenues). Organized labor was mostly financed by the state. Its rent-seeking leaders were generally perceived as a corrupt part of the establishment and had lost legitimacy with their grassroots. By the early 1990s, these once-powerful political machines were substantially diminished. In that sense the decline of the corporatist political groups and party system that supported Venezuela's democracy might have allowed the passage of some reforms without strong opposition, but it also undermined their future sustainability.

Another possible explanation for the lack of opposition to certain specific reforms is that very influential groups, such as importers or participants in the privatization process, were among the beneficiaries of reform. However, in the case of privatization only a few national private groups participated with a very minor proportion of shares. The privatization program was not like Russia's, a case of major transfers of wealth to some local oligarchs.

One area in which interest groups seem to have played a significant role in postponing reforms is the financial sector. Once the oil bonanza started to recede at the end of the 1970s and the beginning of the 1980s, the difficulties in the financial sector became apparent. Lack of adequate supervision, corruption, and bad management led to, among other things, unlawful accounting practices to hide bad loans and insufficient reserves, poor investments, and loans to related businesses (Garcia et al., 1997; Krivoy, 2002). Bankers constituted a strong interest group that lobbied against the financial sector reform proposed during the Pérez administration. In particular, the proposed banking law required increases in capital requirements, opened the banking business to foreign competition and strengthened regulation and supervision. Clearly, if these measures had been approved, they would have negatively affected the profitability of some banks. In addition, former bankers headed the two agencies responsible for drafting and implementing the law, the Ministry of Finance and the central bank.

The arguments used by bankers to oppose and postpone the new banking law were that they needed more time to abide by the new capital requirements, and that foreign competition would cause loss of jobs and contribute to the denationalization of the country started by Pérez and the Gran Viraje program. Politicians and regulators bought the argument, causing delays on the approval of the law. In fact, the law was originally proposed in 1989, and only approved in December 1993, a month before the crisis started.

The media campaign against the government deserves separate attention. Some media outlets continuously accused the government of corruption and promoted a campaign against Pérez. They feared that Pérez would favor some business groups that had been close to him since his first administration (for example, in the privatization of CANTV). Most analysts, and the ministers we interviewed, considered that the media campaign opposing the government (not necessarily the reform program) played a key role in shaping the country's perception of the program and the government.

8.4 Concluding thoughts

It is said that Sigmund Freud, when asked by a young scholar how to become a successful academic, simply said 'exaggerate'.[47] Regardless of our success, we have certainly exaggerated the role of oil wealth in this work by singling it out as *the* ultimate or deep determinant behind economic adjustment and reform, the tragic fate of the reform program, and its aftermath. We have done so by arguing that the distribution of massive oil wealth in a backward, highly unequal, mostly illiterate, and poor country gave way to an economic, fiscal, political, and institutional structure increasingly dependent on the vicissitudes of the oil market.

Obviously, the strong similarities between Venezuela's crisis and its aftermath and those taking place at the same time throughout Latin America are unambiguous signs that there were other factors in play.[48] In this chapter however, we argue that the peculiarities of Venezuela's case were – and continue to be – deeply shaped by oil riches.[49] The presence of high rents and the high sunk-cost nature of the oil industry allowed for the possibility of imposing a path of increasing taxation, thereby creating a path of growing fiscal income, even in times of declining oil income in per-capita terms. This fiscal strategy, coupled with a drastic reduction of non-oil taxes, proved to be a very popular move, but one that caused not only over-exploitation and a virtual abandonment of exploration activities, but diminished pressures for transparency and accountability in the administration of government as well. Furthermore, oil revenues allowed policy-makers to maintain an 'illusion of harmony' by financing an increasingly subsidized and distorted economic system managed through an ever more complex patronage-based political system.

In the early 1970s, however, production capacity began to decline rapidly, heightening the dependency on high oil prices. Foreign financing filled the gaps, but made the country vulnerable to the interest rate hike of the early 1980s that plunged the country into fiscal and balance of payments crises that received only partial and palliative treatment until 1989 (Figure 8.2).

When in 1989 the government found itself financially unable to prolong this state of affairs and decided to advance an ambitious reform agenda to reverse the economic, social, and political decline, both the public and the polity reacted harshly. The authorities tried to push adjustment and structural reform as the only sensible course of action, but to no avail. With the benefit of hindsight, we explain such behavior by arguing that cultural attitudes could not be expected to change overnight. The true state of the Venezuelan economy had been kept hidden from the public for decades through a complex web of

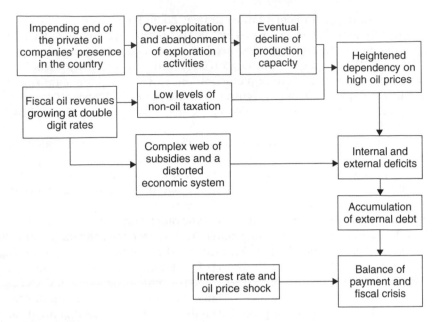

Figure 8.2 A simplified narrative of the events leading up to economic adjustment and reform

subsidies financed with oil revenues. Immersed in an apparently successful economic model with limited exposure to the ubiquitous trade-offs of a market economy, Venezuelans were ill-prepared to understand, much less to accept, the rigors of adjustment and reform.

We believe that our approach allows us to understand not only the immediate reaction to the reform program and its architects, but its aftermath as well. Well aware of the animosity towards reform, the polity, and AD in particular, tried to deflect the astonishment, anger, and frustration of the people towards Pérez and his collaborators; but the people did not buy this and punished AD with a significant defeat in the regional elections of 1992. Caldera capitalized on this sentiment by campaigning on an anti-reform platform and by effectively reversing many of Pérez's reforms during his first two years in office. But when economic circumstances forced him to impose a limited but still market-oriented adjustment program, the population turned towards the leader of the first coup against Pérez, Lt. Col. Hugo Chávez, who carries on an aggressive and successful campaign against Venezuela's traditional parties, against neo-liberalism, and in favor of participatory – as opposed to representative – democracy.

8.4.1 Was there a better alternative?

This question deals with the lessons learned from the experience with reform, and can be divided into two. The first one asks if with the information set at the time, that is, without the benefit of hindsight, different approaches either in the design or in the implementation strategy could have given the program significantly better chances of success. In this regard, we conclude that in terms of design, the Pérez team followed a textbook version of the paradigm of the times, the ubiquitous 'Washington Consensus' espoused by the IFIs. The same applies with regards to implementation, where a big bang-cum-shock therapy approach was chosen, arguing that institutional constraints coupled with political economy considerations gave gradualism and sequencing little chance of success.

As mentioned above, the overall communication and negotiation strategy of the government was deficient, particularly with regards to making the polity and the people understand the need to embark on an adjustment and reform program. The authorities transmitted the idea that the proposed measures were the only sensible course of action, that divergent opinions implied ignorance. The contrasting experiences of the fiscal measures and the privatization of CANTV illustrate this notion. More generally, however, after the initial measures were taken, and despite the *Caracazo* and the overall animosity towards the president and his program, the praise of the financial markets, and perhaps more importantly, the high price paid for 40 per cent of the shares of CANTV, was a clear indication that the financial markets, at least, were very optimistic about the country's future prospects. Given that one may assume that financial markets have every incentive and sufficient resources to acquire and process all relevant information when making their investment decisions, we argue that at least until early 1992 (prior to 4 February coup led by Chávez, which may be considered as an unexpected shock), the overall program was considered a success.

Taking the second part of the question now, with the benefit of hindsight, our analysis leads us to believe that the program's architects – and the financial markets as well – underestimated the role of history and culture in shaping beliefs, institutional constraints, and organizational and individual resistance to reforms. By doing so, it failed to consider the destabilizing effects of the strong internal opposition coming from the polity (and AD in particular) and from the population at large. This lesson was not lost on Petkoff, head of the Agenda Venezuela, and should be remembered vividly by all future reformers.

8.4.2 Rationality and culture

One of the main premises on which reform process are analyzed in the current literature is that which assumes perfect rationality on behalf of all players. Assuming otherwise not only makes the analysis a much less grounded and precise enterprise, but more importantly, begs the question of why certain players are irrational while others are not.[50] At the same time however, the evidence seems to be inconsistent with rationality-based theories. As we discussed in hypotheses 1 and 2, for instance, on the eve of the crisis the Venezuelan population remained blatantly ignorant not only of the dire situation of the macroeconomy, but more importantly, still perceived that

Venezuela was a rich country, and that its problems were rooted in the corrupt nature of political parties.

The crucial question is: are Venezuelans rational individuals in terms of their understanding of the economic forces that shape their lives? UCAB (2004) tries to answer this question. Based on a national survey, this study shows that a majority of Venezuelans have cultural values that are consistent with a traditional culture as opposed to a modern one. They feel, for instance, that they cannot control their fate and see their welfare as a result of forces beyond their control, such as luck, destiny, a divine plan, or the government. In light of this result, the idea that Venezuelans should have had a thorough understanding of the need for reform seems foolish indeed.

A growing number of social scientists have argued forcefully against the neoclassical assumption of perfect rationality and perfect foresight, stressing the evidence that mental models vary substantially across individuals and across cultures.[51] Robert Edgerton (2000), for instance, argues that most societies survive despite not being rational entities in search of optimal solutions, and that fundamental deviations from traditional behavior are very rare. Important changes, if they occur, are a result of external shocks, and in their absence, people tend to base their actions on traditional solutions that appeared in response to past circumstances. In addition, as Daniel Kahneman and Amos Tversky (1995) and others have shown, humans are not very good at calculating risks, particularly when the threat is new, and tend to underestimate the future effects of technical and economic change.

Given that reform is precisely about change, we feel that the recent interest within the economic profession in examining the links between culture and development is a welcome addition to our quest for a more thorough understanding of the general failure of reform in developing countries.

Notes

1. In Forteza and Rama (2002), the Gran Viraje is classified as the only economic reform program implemented in Venezuela, at least since 1980.
2. See, for instance, Karl (1997) and Sala-i-Martin and Subramanian (2003).
3. According to Lora (2001), Venezuela ranks among the laggards in structural reform within Latin America.
4. In Appendix 8.1 we provide a brief description of the geographic and demographic characteristics of the country.
5. 1941 national census data cited in Betancourt (1958).
6. For further details on its contents and relevance, see Rey (1972), Sosa (1987), and Przeworski (1991).
7. A similar argument is developed in Manzano and Rigobón (2001).
8. One of the main objectives of such a policy was to increase the chances of Acción Democrática in the upcoming elections.
9. Unless an alternative source is specified, all macroeconomic performance data in this chapter are taken from IMF Financial Statistics.

10. Templeton (1995) and Datos Pulso Nacional 1968–2003.
11. Later that year, the government produced a 154-page document under that title describing the program and its rationale.
12. Discussions were also moving along with World Bank authorities for a Structural Adjustment Loan (SAL) in support of the economic program and a Sector Adjustment Loan (SECAL) in support of the trade reform.
13. COPEI won 6 governorships, MAS 2, and Causa R 1. Source: Consejo Nacional Electoral (CNE).
14. On 30 November the Venezuelan authorities requested waivers from the IMF for the nonobservance of quantitative performance criteria for end-March and end-June for public sector borrowing requirements, net international reserves, and net domestic assets of the central bank. Authorities also expressed 'extreme concern about the deep economic recession and the need to return to a strong growth path in the near future', stating that the continued shortfall in foreign financing, the substitution of domestic for foreign financing in public sector operations and the reduction in domestic tax revenues as a result of the economic contraction conspired against this objective. In addition, authorities recognized the temporary nature of the oil price shock, stating their intention to sterilize a substantial share of the windfall through the creation of a stabilization fund and to cushion its impact on the Venezuelan economy. Moreover, and in spite of the recent change in Venezuela's balance of payment prospects, Venezuelan authorities once again emphasized their interest to continue with the extended arrangement program with the Fund.
15. *Centesimus Annus*, 35.4, 1991. For more details see: http://www.osjspm.org/debt.htm.
16. The case was supported by investigations made by two journalists, José Vicente Rangel (currently serving as Chávez's Vice-President) and Andrés Galdo. According to the attorney general, the resources were used to finance the presidential campaigns of Chamorro in Nicaragua, Zamora in Bolivia, and Aristide in Haiti.
17. See Otálvora (1994).
18. As will be shown in the analytical section, the reforms implemented under the Velásquez interim administration revealed the significant transformation in the policy-making process introduced by the political reforms of 1989, that is, the direct election of governors and mayors and the introduction of a mixed-member electoral system for the legislature. The newly elected governors became a powerful and influential force in the legislative arena, pushing for fiscal and administrative decentralization. Legislators had now more incentives to cater to their constituencies and to the regional party bosses. In order to pass the VAT law a significant share of its revenues had to be transferred to the regional and local governments. Similar episodes would occur under Caldera's administration, for example, with the approval of a law to distribute part of the royalties from the new oil projects to the states.
19. The election results were not only close but controversial as well. Claudio Fermín from AD took 23.6 per cent, Oswaldo Alvarez Paz from COPEI took 22.7 per cent and Andrés Velásquez from Causa R took 22 per cent.
20. In the analytical section of this chapter we will argue that bankers constituted a strong interest group that lobbied against the financial sector reform proposed during Pérez's administration.
21. By that time, Pérez was traveling twice a month to the US to visit a relative on cancer treatment, and took advantage of his presence there by having the Venezuelan ambassador in the Organization of American States (OAS) arrange meetings with key politicians and policy-makers such as Michel Camdessus, Director General of the IMF. Miguel Rodríguez attended some of these meetings.

22. In the words of Naím (1993: 49), 'to move from a state-led, inward-oriented strategy to one led by export growth'.
23. This latter argument is forcefully stressed in Naím (1993).
24. A thorough analysis of this point is made in Naím (1993).
25. This argument is particularly forceful when we relax the neoclassical assumptions and consider instead that agents are unclear how policies map into outcomes, that learning takes place over time as a gradual process of updating beliefs, and that the pattern and speed of this process depends on the particular circumstances and experiences of the agents involved. See Harberger (1993a) and North (1994). At the end of the chapter we deal briefly with this issue.
26. The fact that the oil industry operates with significant sunk costs is crucial in explaining the success of this policy, at least in the short run. It proved deleterious in the long run, however, inhibiting further additions to the capital stock (including oil reserves in particular) and promoting over-exploitation of the existing one. For further discussion, see Monaldi (2001).
27. In contrast to a 'war of attrition' explanation for opposition to reform, according to which interest groups try to postpone the adjustment so that its costs are borne by other groups, here we argue that a large majority of the population did not even perceive the need to implement a costly adjustment program. In other countries the 'war of attrition' resulted in hyperinflation or other easily identifiable costs. In the Venezuelan case, to a large majority the costs of not implementing reform were not easily identifiable.
28. One interesting implication of the focus on rent distribution and the lack of perceived scarcity is the relatively minor role that economists played in Venezuela's society until 1989. In contrast lawyers were the leading profession in the country in terms of both prominence (not necessarily so any more) and per-capita numbers (still true today).
29. In 2002 Venezuela ranked in the 18 per cent percentile of the countries with less 'corruption control' using the index developed by the World Bank Institute (Kaufmann et al., 2003). Only Ecuador and Paraguay fare worse in the region. Since the start of this index in 1996 this rank has been relatively stable. Similarly, in the Transparency International corruption perception index Venezuela ranks in the lower third of the countries in Latin America.
30. We discuss this notion at the end of the chapter.
31. This issue will be discussed later.
32. It has also faced strong criticism, most notably by Sen (2000).
33. As argued by Przeworski et al. (1999), this may seem treacherous if voters care about policies, but the issue is not so clear if it is results that they care about in the end.
34. As President Lusinchi said, his administration was the most *adeca* (that is, AD-centered) in history.
35. According to the 1961 constitution, re-election was only possible 10 years after the end of the first presidential mandate.
36. The other 'technocrats' included Moises Naím, Minister of Industry, Eduardo Quintero, Minister of Investment (later privatization), and Pedro Tinoco in the central bank.
37. As one leader of COPEI put it: 'We told Pérez here are the votes of COPEI, put the votes of AD and we can approve the Value Added Tax . . . it is not easy to ask the opposition to pay the political costs of the reform when they are not assumed by the governing party' (interview with Gustavo Tarre Briceño, 2003).
38. An unexpected supporter of the process was AD's party boss, Alfaro Ucero. His coming on board came as a shock even to Pérez, who aware of the significance of

Alfaro's support not only gave FMM the job, but more importantly, allowed him to remove important members of AD's inner circle from the company, substitute them with his own technical staff, and proceed with his plans to privatize the company.

39. The account of the privatization process is drawn from interviews conducted by us with the policy-makers involved in the process. More details can be found in Umérez (2001) and Francés and Aguerrevere (1993).

40. The number of effective parties is a measure of fragmentation that weights the number of parties by their share of the legislature's seats. It is equivalent to the inverse of the Herfindahl concentration index (Monaldi et al., 2004).

41. The Index of Volatility in 1958–88 was 18 per cent while the regional average was 22 per cent.

42. The Venezuelan president had the lowest legislative powers of all Latin American presidents according to an index designed by Shugart and Carey (1992).

43. Cited in Monaldi et al. (2004).

44. The Index of Volatility increased to 28 per cent in 1989–2003 from 18 per cent in 1958–98.

45. In 2002 Venezuela was in the 17 per cent percentile rank in the world, and only Colombia and Paraguay fared worse in Latin America (Kaufmann et al., 2003).

46. It is true that the onerous labor contracts of VIASA played a role in its bankruptcy, after being bought by IBERIA.

47. Quoted in Heckman (1995: 1092).

48. A recent yet growing literature stresses the role of geography, history, culture, and institutions in explaining Latin America's economic underperformance. See, for instance, Haber (1997).

49. Chief among these peculiarities are the stronger rise prior to the 1983 crisis, the rougher fall that comes as a result of such crisis, and the more prolonged stagnation and decline that has followed since.

50. This point is made forcefully in Alesina (1994).

51. Notable among them are Douglass North, Joseph Stiglitz, David Landes, Samuel Huntington, and Francis Fukuyama. In cognition, the term mental model refers to 'deeply ingrained assumptions, generalizations, or even pictures or images that influence how we understand the world and how we take action'. They reflect both the semi-permanent 'tacit maps' of the world which people hold in their long-term memory, and the short-term perceptions which people build up as part of their everyday reasoning processes. According to some cognitive theorists, changes in short-term everyday mental models accumulating over time will gradually be reflected in changes in long-term deep-seated beliefs (Senge et al., 1994: 237).

Appendix 8.1 Geographic and demographic characteristics of Venezuela

Venezuela is located in the northern part of South America, occupying a territory of 912,050 square kilometers, approximately twice the size of California. Largely forgotten by the Spanish conquistadors due to the lack of precious metals, this tropical country was occupied by a geographically dispersed, rural population well until the 1930s, when the discovery and exploitation of large oil deposits gave way to large urban centers located near the Caribbean coastline and in the Andean mountain region, leaving the rest of its territory, comprised of the Orinoco plains, the Guayana highlands and the northern part of the Amazon jungle, largely uninhabited.

The great majority of the population qualifies as *mestizo*, a heterogeneous group with widely varying proportions of European, African, and Native American heritage. Few in number prior to European arrival, the original Native American population fell sharply afterwards as a result of conflict, displacement, and, most importantly, infections against which they had no immunity. The remaining native population, together with the more resistant African slaves who were brought in from neighboring islands to work in agriculture, mixed early on with Spanish conquistadors and began to form a complex class structure along ethnic lines.[1] Independence brought few changes, as the elite *criollo* class merely took over the privileges of the Spanish rulers, and as a result, significant inequalities in terms of economic, social, and political opportunities persisted virtually unchanged until the 1930s, when oil money provided the means and the political pressure to provide the poor, illiterate and rural majority with basic education and health services in growing urban communities, as well as with increased political participation.[2] As of today, pure ethnic groups are rare and very small in number. Exact figures are not available, given that national censuses have not classified Venezuelans according to ethnicity since 1926, but according to one estimate, a credible break-down for 1990 would be 68 per cent *mestizo*, 21 per cent unmixed Caucasian, 10 per cent black, and 1 per cent Indian.[3]

In terms of age, the Venezuelan population is currently undergoing a demographic transition with rapidly falling birth rates adjusting to lower mortality rates, themselves a result of significant improvements in public sanitation and health, as well as much better overall living conditions. As a result, the Venezuelan population is predominantly young, but aging fast. As a proportion of the total population, the elderly (65 and older) represented in the year 2000 only 4 per cent of the total population, but are projected to reach 16 per cent by 2050.

Notes

1. In the 1800–09 period, the make up of the Venezuelan population was considered predominantly black (62 per cent), predominantly white (26 per cent), and predominantly Indian (13 per cent). See Engerman and Sokoloff (2002a).

2. The long-run consequences of the different paths of colonial development in the Americas, and more concretely, the way these different paths determined initial inequality and through it institutional and economic development is analyzed in Engerman and Sokoloff (2002b).
3. Venezuela Country Study, Federal Research Division of the Library of Congress under the Country Studies/Area Handbook Program sponsored by the Department of the Army, 1990.

Appendix 8.2   *El Gran Viraje* (the Great Turnaround)

On 28 February 1989, only 26 days after taking office, the Government of Venezuela addressed a Letter of Intent to IMF's Managing Director, Michael Camdessus, committing itself to a far-reaching economic adjustment program in exchange for Fund resources and better chances of reaching an agreement with private creditors that would bring new loans, a significant rescheduling of debt service obligations and a sizable reduction of outstanding commercial debt. The letter characterized the economic situation of the country as critical and stressed the need to reorient its economic adjustment strategy without delay.

The agreed-upon program was designed to restore balance of payments viability and promote a sound development of the Venezuelan economy over the medium term. For this purpose, it entailed a number of major structural reforms in the fiscal, exchange, trade, and financial sectors. A major element was the establishment of a unified, market-determined exchange rate to be implemented in March. The Central Bank was expected to intervene in the foreign exchange market in order to minimize erratic fluctuations, albeit in compliance with the program's net international reserves targets. As a complement to the exchange rate measures, a major reform of the trade system was to be implemented by the end of the year. A timetable for this reform was to be worked out with the World Bank, with an overall objective to rationalize the effective rate of protection and the system of tariff exemptions and quantitative restrictions in place at the time.

Together with the exchange and trade reforms, the authorities committed themselves to a significant reduction of existing price and interest rate controls. The previous three-tier system was to be eliminated in favor of a new system covering prices of 18 essential goods and services comprising around 10 per cent of the consumption basket used in the determination of the cost-of-living index. Prices for the goods and services subject to control were to be periodically adjusted with respect to changes in the consumer price index, and the price control policy as a whole was to be phased out in line with the expansion of social programs. Effective from 17 February 1989, all binding interest rate controls were removed, with the exemption of agriculture financing, which would fluctuate at 7 percentage points below the average bank lending rate for commercial activities, and special housing loan and mortgage programs set at a fixed rate of 15 per cent. The authorities also committed themselves to a medium-term program of financial reform with the objective of strengthening the financial system and improving its efficiency.

Due to their fiscal and political significance, fossil fuel derivatives stood out among the subsidized goods that were to see their domestic prices realigned with international markets. On 26 February the prices of 14 petroleum products sold in the domestic market were increased by 110 per cent. Over the following two years, these prices were set to be gradually raised up to those prevailing in international markets. In addition, the program called for significant increases in the domestic prices of state-provided goods such as aluminum and steel. Electricity and telephone tariffs were also targeted for significant price adjustments.

In order to maintain stability in the exchange market, reduce inflationary pressures, make room for an expansion in private activity, and achieve a reduction in absorption consistent with the programmed improvements in the external current account, the fiscal program called for a reduction in the overall public sector deficit. In 1989, this deficit was programmed to fall to 3 per cent of GDP from an estimated 6 per cent of GDP in 1988.[1] In order to achieve this target, the authorities were relying on the effects of the exchange rate liberalization and the increase in the domestic price of fuel derivatives. In order to strengthen the fiscal position of the country over time, the authorities were also planning significant legal and institutional changes in revenue collection, parametric changes in social security, and the introduction of a sales tax in 1989 to be converted into a value added tax later on.

On the expenditure side, central government expenditure would be reoriented from large investment projects in favor of the provision of social services, the modernization of public infrastructure, and maintenance outlays in order to support the private sector in their ability to respond to international prices. Public investment programs would include the completion of projects already in train in the aluminum, petrochemical, and electric power sectors. The investment burden however, was expected to be carried by the private sector, either by itself or through joint ventures with the public sector.

The government also consented to improve the performance, revenue collection, and cost efficiency of a number of deficit-ridden enterprises. As part of this program, an aggressive program of privatization was expected to take place over the next few years. The authorities also committed to a prudent wage policy, although on 1 March 1989 and in response to a sharp decline in real wages over the past three years, wages of general government employees were set to rise 30 per cent on average, including the effect of a 54 per cent increase in the minimum wage.

As additional compensation for the economic and social impact of the adjustment measures and as part of its new social policy strategy, the authorities were to implement a number of social programs. These were announced by President Pérez on 16 February 1989 when the adjustment program was revealed to the public. Among these social measures, were the following: (1) subsidies for the purchase of basic goods and services; (2) a direct monetary subsidy linked to school attendance; (3) the establishment of 42,000 daycare facilities for the poor; (4) a strengthening of the income support and health control program for breastfeeding mothers, their children and for infants; (4) a control program for diarrhea-related and respiratory-related illnesses as well as for those preventable through vaccination; (5) urban slum consolidation programs; (6) support programs for microenterprises; (7) a massive food transfer program directed to all children under 14 years of age, pregnant women, and breastfeeding mothers; (8) consolidation of primary care facilities; (9) reform of the social security system; and (10) the establishment of a Presidential Commission for the Fight against Poverty.

The overall rationale of the program was also explained in January 1990 in the Nation's 8th Plan,[2] titled *El Gran Viraje* (the Great Turnaround). In this document, the creation of a more productive and competitive economy with a more equitable distribution of wealth was stated as the program's primary objective. A particular emphasis was placed on improving the living conditions and income-generating capabilities of the poorest segments of the population, stressing the notion that sustained and stable rates of growth, international competitiveness, and the preservation of economic and financial equilibriums are of utmost importance in the fight against poverty and exclusion, both in their own right and as necessary conditions for a successful social policy.

The 154-page document begins by briefly discussing the legacy of the import substitution model in place since the beginning of Venezuelan democracy in 1958, its achievements, its pitfalls, and most importantly, its prolonged deterioration until utter exhaustion. After contrasting the benefits of the proposed policy turnaround with the consequences of inaction, the core sections of the document condense the main components of the proposed turnaround into six broad guidelines or policy objectives: (1) Social Commitment; (2) Growth with Low Inflation; (3) International Competitiveness; (4) Conservation of Natural Resources; (5) Institutional Change; and (6) Human Resource Capitalization.

Notes

1. As it turned out, the overall fiscal deficit in 1988 reached 9.3 per cent of GDP.
2. The Nation's Plan is presented by the president at the end of his first year in office in a Congressional Address.

References

Abente-Brun, D. (1999), 'People power in Paraguay', *Journal of Democracy*, 10(3): 93–100.

Abusada, R (ed.) (2003), *La Reforma Incompleta*, Lima, Peru: Universidad del Pacifico e Instituto Peruano de Economía.

Acuña, C.H. (1995a), 'Política y Economía en la Argentina de los 90 (O por qué el futuro ya no es lo que solía ser)', in Carlos H. Acuña (ed.), *La Nueva Matriz Política Argentina*, Buenos Aires: Nueva Visión, pp. 331–83.

Acuña, C.H. (1995b), 'Sobre los juegos, las gallinas y la lógica política de los pactos constitucionales', in Carlos H. Acuña (ed.), *La Nueva Matriz Política Argentina*, Buenos Aires: Nueva Visión, pp. 115–50.

Acuña, C.H. (2006), 'Transitional justice in Argentina and Chile: a never ending story?', in Jon Elster (ed.), *Retribution and Reparation in the Transition to Democracy*, New York: Cambridge University Press, 206–38.

Acuña, C.H. and M. Tommasi (2000), 'Some reflections on the institutional reforms required in Latin America', in *Institutional Reforms, Growth and Human Development in Latin America*, New Haven: The Yale Center for International and Area Studies.

Acuña, C.H. and W.C. Smith (1994), 'The politics of arms production and the arms race among the new democracies of Argentina, Brazil and Chile', *Political Power and Social Theory*, 9: 121–57.

Aedo, C. and L. Lagos (1984), 'Protección efectiva en el sector manufacturero', Universidad Católica de Chile Working Paper no. 94, Santiago, Chile.

Aizenman, J. and B. Pinto (2004), *Managing Economic Volatility and Crisis*, Cambridge, Mass.: Cambridge University Press.

Alarco, Germán (2003), 'Modificaciones económicas al marco estructural de la constitución Peruana', mimeo, Universidad Panamericana, Mexico.

Alesina, A. (1994), 'Political models of macroeconomic policy and fiscal reforms', in Stephan Haggard and Steven B. Webb (eds), *Voting for Reform: Democracy, Political Liberalization, and Economic Adjustment*, Oxford: Oxford University Press, pp. 37–60.

Alesina, A., R. Hommes, R. Hausmann and E. Stein (1996), 'Budget deficits and budget procedures in Latin America', NBER Working Paper no. 5586, Cambridge, Mass.

Alston, Lee, T. Eggertsson and D. North (eds) (1996), *Empirical Studies in Institutional Change*, London: Cambridge University Press.

Aninat, C., J. Londregan, P. Navia and J. Vial (2004), 'Political institutions, policymaking processes, and policy outcomes in Chile', mimeo, Universidad Adolfo Ibáñez, Santiago.

Aoki, M. (2000), 'Institutional evolution as punctuated equilibria', in Claude Menard (ed.), *Institutions, Contracts and Organizations*, Cheltenham, UK, and Northampton, MA, USA: Edward Elgar.

Aoki, M. (2001), *Toward a Comparative Institutional Analysis*, Cambridge, Mass.: MIT Press.

Apoyo Opinión y Mercado (1998, 1999), 'Encuestas de Poder en el Perú', Apoyo: Lima, Peru.

Arellano, J.P. (1985), *Políticas Sociales y de Desarrollo. Chile 1924–1984*, Santiago: CIEPLAN.

Arellano, J.P. and M. Marfán (1987), '25 Años de Política Fiscal en Chile', *Colección Estudios Cieplan*, 21: 129–62.

Arenas, A. and M. Marcel (1999), 'Fiscal effects of social security reform in Chile: the case of the minimum pension', mimeo, Ministerio de Hacienda, Santiago.

Aspe, P. (1993), *El camino mexicano de la transformación económica*, Fondo de Cultura Económica, México.

Astorga, P., A. Bergés and V. FitzGerald (2003), 'The standard of living in Latin America during the twentieth century', QEH Working Paper Series, Working Paper Number 103.

Baca, Jorge (2003), 'El ancla fiscal: la reforma tributaria', in Abusada (ed.), pp. 163–218.

Bambaci, J., T. Saront and M. Tommasi (2002), 'The political economy of economic reforms in Argentina', *Journal of Policy Reform*, 5(2): 75–88.

Baptista, Asdrúbal (2003), 'Las crisis económicas del siglo XX venezolano', in P. Márquez and R. Piñango (eds), *En esta Venezuela realidades y nuevos caminos*, Caracas: Ediciones IESA.

Barahona, P., M. Costabal and A. Vial (1993), *Mil días, mil por ciento: la economía Chilena durante el gobierno de Allende*, Santiago: Universidad Finis Terrae.

Barandarian, E. and L. Hernández (1999), 'Origins and resolution of a banking crisis: Chile 1982–86', Central Bank of Chile Working Paper no. 57, Santiago.

Bardalez, E., Martín Tanaka and Antonio Zapata (eds) (1999), *Repensando la Política en el Perú*, Lima, Peru: Red para el Desarrollo de las Ciencias Sociales en el Perú.

Barreto, R.A. (1996), 'Institutional corruption and Paraguayan economic development', mimeo, University of Colorado, Boulder.

Bates, R., A. Greif, M. Levi, J.L. Rosenthal and B. Weingast (1998), *Analytic Narratives*, Princeton, NJ: Princeton University Press.

Bates, R.H. and A.O. Krueger (1993), 'Generalizations arising from the case studies', in R.H. Bates and A.O. Krueger (eds), *Political and Economic Interactions in Economic Policy Reform: Evidence from Eight Countries*, Oxford: Blackwell.

Baumann, R., J. Rivero and Y. Zavattiero (1997), 'As tarifas de importações no plano real', *Pesquisa e Planejamento Econômico*, 27(3): 541–86.

Beato, Paulina (1996), 'Las reformas Portuarias Latinoamericanas. Estudios en tres puertos', IFM 96–102, Departamento de Programas Sociales y Desarrollo Sostenible, IDB: Washington, DC.

Bergara, M., Andrés Pereyra, Ruben Tansini, Adolfo Garcé, Daniel Chasquetti, Daniel Buquet and Juan Andrés Moraes (2004), 'Political institutions, policymaking processes and policy outcomes: the case of Uruguay', April, Universidad de la República, FCS, Uruguay.

Berlinksi, Julio (1998), 'El Sistema de Incentivos en la Argentina (de la liberalización unilateral al mercosur', Instituto Torcuato Di Tella, Centro de Investigaciones Económicas.

Betancourt, Rómulo (1958), *Venezuela, Política y Petróleo*, Caracas: Monte Avila Editores Latinoamericana, 2nd edn 1979.

Bicanic, I., V. Gligorov and I. Krastev (2005), 'State, public goods, and reform', in Fanelli and McMahon (eds) (2005a), pp. 242–72.

Boix, C. (1997), 'Privatizing the public business sector in the eighties: economic performance, partisan responses, and divided governments', *British Journal of Political Science*, 27(4): 473–96.

Bonelli, R. (2002), 'Labor Productivity in Brazil during the 1990s', Texto para Discussão IPEA n. 906, IPEA – Instituto de Pesquisa Econômica Aplicada, Rio de Janeiro, Brasil, September.

Bonelli, R. (1999), 'A reestruturação industrial Brasileira nos anos 90: reação empresarial e mercado de trabalho', *Brasil*, Organização Internacional do Trabalho (OIT) e Ministério do Trabalho e Emprego, Editora 34, São Paulo, SP.

Bonelli, R., P.L. da Motta Veiga and A. Fernandes de Britto (1997), 'As políticas Industrial e de Comércio Exterior no Brasil: Rumos e Indefinições', Texto para Discussão

IPEA n. 527, IPEA – Instituto de Pesquisa Econômica Aplicada, Rio de Janeiro, Brasil, November.

Borchardt, M., I. Rial and A. Sarmiento (1998), 'Sostenibilidad de la política fiscal en Uruguay', CERES, Distribuido como documento de trabajo R-320 del BID, January.

Borda, D. (1997), 'Economic policy', in Peter Lambert and Andrew Nickson (eds), *The Transition to Democracy in Paraguay*, New York: St Martin's Press.

Borda, D. and F. Masi (1998), *Los Limites de la Transición: Economia y Estado en el Paraguay en los anos 90*, Asunción: Centro Interdisciplinario de Derecho Social y Economia Politica.

Borda, D. and F. Masi (2002), 'Paraguay: estancamiento económico y desgaste político en los años de MERCOSUR', in Roberto Bouzas (ed.), *Realidades Nacionales Comparadas*, Buenos Aires: Altamira.

Borner, S., A. Brunetti and B. Weder (1993), 'Obstáculos Institucionales al Crecimiento de América Latina', CINDE Ensayo Ocasional 24, Santiago.

Bresser Pereira, L., J. Maravall and A. Przeworsky (1993), *Economic Reforms in New Democracies: a Social Democratic Approach*, New York: Cambridge University Press.

Brum, Conrado, Germán Tobler and Ximena Usher (2001), 'Aseguran la sostenibilidad de las cuentas públicas las reglas fiscales aplicadas en los países del Mercosur?' Trabajo de investigación monographic, Facultad de Ciencias Económicas y de Administración, Universidad de la República, Uruguay.

Bucheli, M. (2003), 'La cobertura de la seguridad social en el empleo', OIT, Santiago, Chile.

Buquet, Daniel and Rafael Piñeiro (2000), 'Coalición de gobierno y reforma constitucional. Un enlace estratégico', Instituto de Ciencia Política, FCS, UDELAR. Uruguay

Buquet, Daniel, Daniel Chasquetti and Juan Andrés Moraes (1998), 'Fragmentación política y gobierno en Uruguay: un enfermo imaginario?' Instituto de Ciencia Política, FCS, UDELAR, Uruguay.

Búsqueda, Weekly Magazine, various dates.

Bustamante Belaúnde, Alberto (2003), *Del Diablo Su País*, Lima, Peru: PEISA.

Butelman, A., H. Cortés and R. Videla (1981), 'Proteccionismo en Chile: una visión retrospectiva', *Cuadernos de Economía*, 54(18): 141–94.

Caballero, Manuel (1998), *Las crisis de la Venezuela contemporánea (1903–1992)*, Caracas: Alfadil Ediciones.

Calderón, C. and R. Fuentes (2005), 'Complementarities between institutions and openness in economic development: evidence for a panel of countries', mimeo, Central Bank of Chile, Santiago.

Calomiris, C. and A. Powell (2000), 'Can emerging market bank regulators establish credible discipline? The case of Argentina, 1992–1999', NBER Working Paper Series 7715, Cambridge, MA.

Calvo, G.A. and C. Vegh (1994), 'Inflation stabilization and nominal anchors', *Contemporary Economic Policy*, 12(2): 35–45.

Cameron, M. (1994), *Democracy and Authoritarianism in Peru, Political Coalitions and Social Change*, New York: St Martins Press.

Cardoso, E. and A. Galal (2002), 'External environment, globalization and reform', Working Paper, Georgetown University and the Egyptian Center for Economic Studies.

Caristo, Anna and Alvaro Forteza (2003), 'El déficit del Banco de Previsión Social y su impacto en las finanzas del gobierno', Documento de trabajo, Departamento de Economía, FCS-UDELAR, Uruguay.

Carpizo, R. (1978), *Las Atribuciones Meta-Consitucionales del Presidente de la Republica*, Mexico, DF: Fondo de Cultura Económica.

Casacuberta, C., G. Fachola and N. Gandelman (2003), 'Employment, capital and productivity dynamics: trade openness and unionization in the Uruguayan manufacturing sector', Working Paper, UDELAR-ORT, Uruguay, April.

Casacuberta, Carlos and Marcel Vaillant (2002), 'Trade and wages in Uruguay in the nineties', Working Paper No. 9, Departamento de Economía, Facultad de Ciencias Sociales.

Castro, N. (2000), 'Privatização no Setor de Transportes no Brasil', in Pinheiro and Fukasaku (eds).

Cauas, J. and S. De la Cuadra (1981), 'La Política Económica de la Apertura al Exterior en Chile', *Cuadernos de Economía*, 54(18): 195–230.

Centeno, M.A. (1996), *Democracy within Reason: Technocratic Revolution in Mexico*, University Park, Pennsylvania: Penn State University Press.

CEP (1994), *Bases de la política económica del gobierno militar Chileno* [popularly referred to as *El Ladrillo*], Santiago: CEP.

Cetrángolo, O. and J.P. Jiménez (2003), 'Política fiscal en la Argentina durante el régimen de convertibilidad', Working Paper CEPAL, Santiago, Chile.

Charap, J.C. and Christian Harm (1999), 'Institutionalized Corruption and the Kleptocratic State', in C. Menard (ed.), pp. 188–211.

Chudnovsky, D. and A. López (2001), *La transnacionalización de la economía Argentina*, Buenos Aires: Eudeba.

Chudnovsky, D., A. López and G. Rossi (2004), 'Foreign direct investment spillovers and the absorption capabilities of domestic firms in the Argentine manufacturing sector (1992–2001)', Working Paper No. 74, Dept. of Economics, Universidad de San Andrés, Buenos Aires.

Chumacero, R. and R. Fuentes (2002), 'On the determinants of the Chilean economic growth', Central Bank of Chile Working Paper no. 134, Santiago.

Cocchi, Angel (ed.) (1988), *Reforma Electoral y Voluntad Política*, FESUR/Banda Oriental, Montevideo.

Comisión Presidencial para la Reforma del Estado (1986), *Documentos para la Reforma del Estado*, Caracas: COPRE.

Congreso del Peru (2002), *Actas de la Comision Investigadora de Corrupción*, Lima, Peru: Congreso del Peru.

Connolly, M.B. and J. De Melo (1994), 'The effects of protectionism on a small country. The case of Uruguay', Regional and Sectoral Studies, World Bank.

Consejo Nacional Electoral (several years), Venezuelan Electoral Results (www.cne.gov.ve).

Coppedge, M. (1994), *Strong Parties and Lame Ducks: Presidential Patriarchy and Factionalism in Venezuela*, Palo Alto, CA: Stanford University Press.

Corbo, V. (1985), 'Chile economic policy and international economic relations since 1970', in G. Walton (ed.), *The National Economic Policies of Chile*, Greenwich, Conn.: JAI Press.

Corbo, V. and J. De Melo (1987), 'Lessons from the Southern Cone policy reforms', *World Bank Research Observer*, 2(2): 111–42.

Corbo, V., R. Lüders and P. Spiller (1997), 'The foundations of successful economic reforms: the case of Chile', mimeo, Pontifical Catholic University of Chile, Santiago.

CORDIPLAN (1990), *VIII Plan de la Nación: El Gran Viraje*, Caracas: CORDIPLAN.

Corrales, J. (2000), 'Presidents, ruling parties, and party rules. A theory on the politics of economic reform in Latin America', *Comparative Politics*, 32(2): 127–49.

Corrales, J. (2002), *Presidents without Parties: the Politics of Economic Reform in Argentina and Venezuela in the 1990s*, University Park: Pennsylvania State University Press.

Costa, J.M. and J.R. Molinas (2003), 'Capital social, gobernabilidad democratico y desarollo: en busdueda de relaciones entre el estado y la sociedad mas fructiferas en Paraguay', paper prepared for the Inter-American Development Bank, Instituto Desarrollo de Captacion y Estudios, Asuncion, Paraguay.

Crisp, Brian (1997), *El control institucional de la participación en la democraca venezolana*, Caracas: Jurídica Venezolana.

Crisp, Brian (2000), *Democratic Institutional Design: the Powers and Incentives of Venezuelan Politicians and Interest Groups*, Palo Alto, CA: Stanford University Press.

Cruzat, M. (1969), 'Algunas ideas sobre el mercado de capitales en Chile', *Cuadernos de Economía*, 17(6): 59–77.

Cukierman, A. and M. Tommasi (1998a), 'When does it take a Nixon to go to China?' *American Economic Review*, 88 (1): 180–97.

Cukierman, A. and M. Tommasi (1998b), 'Credibility of policymakers and economic reforms', in F. Sturzenegger and M. Tommasi (eds), *The Political Economy of Reform*, Cambridge, MA: MIT Press.

Dahl, Robert (1971), *Polyarchy: Participation and Opposition*, New Haven: Yale University Press.

Dammert Ego-Aguirre, M. (2002), *El Estado Mafioso: El Poder Imagocrático*, Lima, Peru: EL Virrey.

Dancourt, O. (1999), 'Ajuste Económico y Proceso de Largo Plazo en la Economía Peruana', mimeo, Facultad de Economía, Pontifica Universidad Católica del Perú, Lima, Peru.

Davis, T. (1967), 'Ocho Décadas de Inflación en Chile: 1879–1959, Una Interpretación Política', *Cuadernos de Economía*, 11(4): 65–74.

De la Cuadra, S. and S. Valdés (1992), 'Myths and facts about financial liberalization in Chile: 1974–1983', in Philip Brock (ed.), *If Texas were Chile: a Primer on Banking Reform*, San Francisco: ICS Press, pp. 11–101.

de Oliveira, Francisco Barreto, Kaizô Beltrão Iwakami, Gustavo Michelín, Leandro Maniero, María Teresa Pasinato and Milko Matijacic (1994), 'Viabilidad de la seguridad social', en *Diagnóstico y Perspectivas de la Seguridad Social en el Uruguay*, Programa de Cooperación Técnica BID 704-OC-UR, Montevideo, November.

De Posadas, I. (1996), *Mercado de Valores: Ley No. 16749 de 30 de mayo de 1996*. Montevideo: UCUDAL, pp. 44–80.

Degregori, I. (2000), *La Década de la Anti Política*, Lima, Peru: Instituto de Estudios Peruanos.

Denzau, A. and D. North (1994), 'Shared mental models: ideologies and institutions', *Kyklos*, 47: 3–31.

Dirección de Presupuestos (1974), *Administración Financiera del Estado*, Santiago: Dirección de Presupuestos.

Dirección de Presupuestos (2003), *Informe de Finanzas Públicas*, Santiago: Dirección de Presupuestos.

Dixit, Avinash K. (2004), *Lawlessness and Economics*, Princeton, NJ: Princeton University Press.

Drazen, A. (2000), *Political Economy in Macroeconomics*, Princeton, NJ: Princeton University Press.

Drazen, A. and W. Easterly (2001), 'Do crises induce reform? Simple empirical tests of conventional wisdom', *Economics and Politics*, 13(2): 129–157.

Dubrovskiy, V., W. Graves, E. Golovakha, O. Haran, R. Pavlenko and J. Szyrmer (2004), 'The reform driving forces in a captured state: lessons from the Ukrainian transition', paper prepared for GDN project on Understanding Reform.

ECLAC (2006), *Social Panorama of Latin America 2005*, Santiago, Chile: United Nations.

Edgerton, Robert (2000), 'Prácticas y creencias tradicionales: algunas mejores que otras?', in Samuel Huntington and Lawrence Harrison (eds), *La cultura es lo que importa*, Argentina: Editorial Planeta, pp. 185–202.

Edwards, A. and S. Edwards (1987), *Monetarism and Liberalization: the Chilean Experiment*, Chicago: University of Chicago Press.

Edwards, S. (1989), *Real Exchange Rates, Devaluation, and Adjustment: Exchange Rate Policy in Developing Countries*, Cambridge, Mass.: MIT Press.

Edwards, Sebastian (1995), *Crisis and Reform in Latin America: from Despair to Hope*, Oxford: Oxford University Press.

Edwards, Sebastian and R. Dornbusch (1991), *The Macroeconomics of Populism in Latin America*, Chicago: University of Chicago Press.

Encina, F. (1911), *Nuestra Inferioridad Económica*, Santiago: Editorial Universitaria.

Engerman, S. and K. Sokoloff (2002a), 'Inequality before and under the law: paths of long-run development in the Americas', paper presented at the Annual Bank Conference on Development, Oslo, June 24–26.

Engerman, S. and K. Sokoloff (2002b), 'Factor endowments, inequality, and paths of development among new world economies', NBER Working Paper no. 9259, Cambridge, MA.

Evans, P. (1989) 'Predatory, developmental, and other apparatuses: a comparative political economy perspective on the Third World state', *Sociological Forum*, 4(4): 561–87.

Evans, Peter (1995), *Embedded Autonomy: States and Industrial Transformation*, Princeton, NJ: Princeton University Press.

Fanelli, J.M. and G. McMahon (eds) (2005a), *Understanding Market Reforms, Vol. 1: Philosophy, Politics and Stakeholders*, Basingstoke: Palgrave Macmillan.

Fanelli, J.M. and G. McMahon (2005b), 'Introduction to Understanding Reforms', in Fanelli and McMahon (eds) (2005a), pp. 1–28.

Fanelli, J.M. and G. McMahon (eds) (2006a), *Understanding Market Reforms, Volume 2: Motivation, Implementation, and Sustainability*, Basingstoke: Palgrave Macmillan.

Fanelli, J.M. and G. McMahon (2006b), 'Introduction to the regional syntheses and country case studies', in Fanelli and McMahon (eds) (2006a).

Fanelli, J.M. and V. Popov (2005), 'On the philosophical, political, and methodological underpinnings of reform', in Fanelli and McMahon (eds) (2005a), pp. 29–77.

Feigenbaum, H., J. Henig and C. Hamnett (1999), *Shrinking the State*, Cambridge: Cambridge University Press.

Fernandez, R. and D. Rodrik (1991), 'Resistance to reform: status quo bias in the presence of individual-specific uncertainty', *American Economic Review*, 81(5): 1146–55.

Ferreira, P. and G. Facchini (2004), 'Trade liberalization and industrial concentration: evidence from Brazil', Ensaios Econômicos n. 531, Fundação Getúlio Vargas, Rio de Janeiro, Brazil.

Ffrench-Davis, R. (1973), *Políticas Económicas en Chile: 1952–1970*, Santiago: Ediciones Nueva Universidad.

Ffrench-Davis, R. (1981), 'Liberalización de Importaciones', *Estudios de Cieplan*, 4: 39–68.

Fidrmuc, J. and A.G. Noury (2005), 'Interest groups, stakeholders, and the distribution of benefits and costs of reform', in Fanelli and McMahon (eds) (2005a), pp. 153–75.

Figueiredo, A.C. and F. Limongi (1999), *Executivo e Legislativo na Nova Ordem Constitucional*, Rio de Janeiro: Fundação Getúlio Vargas.

Filgueira, Fernando, Juan Andrés Moraes and Constanza Moreira (1999), 'Efectos políticos de la reforma. Parte II', in Nelson Noya (ed.), *Efectos económicos y políticos de la reforma en la seguridad social en Uruguay*, Uruguay: Cinve.

Fishlow, A. (1990), 'The Latin American state', *Journal of Economic Perspectives*, 4(3): 61–74.

Fitzgerald, E.V.K. (1976), 'The state and economic development: Peru since 1968', DAE Ocasional Paper 49, Cambridge University Press.

Fogel, R. (1997), 'The peasantry', in P. Lambert and A. Nickson (eds), *The Transition to Democracy in Paraguay*, New York: St Martin's Press.

Fontaine, A. (1988), *La historia no contada de los economistas y el Presidente Pinochet*, Santiago: Editorial Zig-Zag.

Fortes, M. (1994), 'Integração competitiva e privatização', Folha de São Paulo, October 19.

Forteza, A. (2003), 'Lecciones de las reformas de la seguridad social en América Latina: el manejo de los riesgos', *Revista del Banco Central del Uruguay*, June: 151–61.

Forteza, A. (2004), Uruguay, options for pension reform, departamento de economía, FCS, Universidad de la República, Uruguay.

Forteza, A. and M. Rama (2002), 'Labor market rigidity and the success of economic reforms across more than one hundred countries', Policy Research Working Paper, Washington, DC: World Bank.

Forteza, A. and M. Rama (2006), 'Labor market "rigidity" and the success of economic reforms across more than one hundred countries', *Journal of Policy Reform*, 9(1): 75–105.

Forteza, A. and M. Tommasi (2006), 'Synthesis of country studies from Latin America', in Fanelli and McMahon (eds) (2006a).

Foxley, A. (1983), *Latin American Experiments in Neo-Conservative Economics*, Berkeley: University of California Press.

Foxley, A. (1996), 'Economic and social goals in the transition to democracy', in C. Pizarro, D. Raczynsky and J. Vial (eds), *Social and Economic Policies in Chile's Transition to Democracy*, Santiago: CIEPLAN, pp. 11–29.

Francés, Antonio and F. Aguerrevere (1993), *Aló Venezuela: apertura y privatización de las Telecomunicaciones*, Caracas, Venezuela: Ediciones IESA.

Frieden, Jeffrey (1992), *Debt, Development and Democracy*, Princeton, NJ: Princeton University Press.

Fuentes, R. (1995), 'Openness and economic efficiency: evidence from Chilean manufacturing industry', *Estudios de Economía*, 22(2): 375–87.

Fuentes, R. and C. Maquieira (2001), 'Why people pay: understanding high performance in Chile's financial market', in M. Pagano (ed.), *Defusing Default: Incentives and Institutions*, Washington: Inter-American Bank for Development, pp. 189–223.

Fuentes, R. and V. Mies (2005), 'Mirando el desarrollo económico de Chile: una comparación internacional', Central Bank of Chile Working Paper no. 308, Santiago.

Fuentes, R., M. Larraín and K. Schmidt-Hebbel (2004), 'Fuentes del crecimiento y comportamiento de la productividad total de factores en Chile', Central Bank of Chile Working Paper no. 287, Santiago.

Fundación Polar (1997), *Diccionario de Historia de Venezuela*, Caracas: Fundación Polar.

Galiani, S. and D. Petrecolla (2000), 'The Argentine privatization process and its aftermath: some preliminary conclusions', in M. Birch and J. Haar (eds), *The Impact of Privatization in the Americas*, Miami: North-South Center Press.

Galiani, S. and P. Gerchunoff (2003), 'The labor market', in G. Della Paolera and A. Taylor (eds), *A New Economic History of Argentina*, New York: Cambridge University Press.

Galiani, S., D. Heymann and M. Tommasi (2003), 'Great expectations and hard times: the Argentine convertibility plan', *Economia: Journal of the Latin American and Caribbean Economic Association*, 3(2): 109–60.

Galiani, S., P. Gertler and E. Schargrodsky (2005a), 'Water for life: the impact of the privatization of water supply on child mortality', *Journal of Political Economy*, 113: 83–120.

Galiani, S., P. Gertler, E. Schargrodsky and F. Sturzenegger (2005b), 'The benefits and costs of privatization in Argentina: a microeconomic analysis', in A. Chong and F. López-De-Silanes (eds), *Privatization in Latin America: Myths and Reality*, Palo Alto, CA: Stanford University Press.

Gallego, F. and N. Loayza (2002), 'The golden period for growth in Chile. Explanations and forecasts', in N. Loayza and R. Soto (eds), *Economic Growth: Sources, Trends and Cycles*, Santiago: Banco Central de Chile, pp. 417–63.

García Diego, J. (1994), *El TLC Día a Día: Crónica de una negociación*, México, DF: Miguel Ángel Porrúa.

García, G., R. Rodríguez and S. Salvato (1997), *Lecciones de la crisis bancaria en Venezuela*, Caracas: Ediciones IESA.

Garibaldi, J.A. (1999a), 'The institutions of corruption', paper presented at the III Annual Conference of the International Society for New Institutional Economics, Berkeley.

Garibaldi, J.A. (1999b), 'The lens through which we see: the impact of ideas on institutional performance', in Menard (ed.), pp. 254–78.

Garibaldi, J.A. (2000), 'The informal institutions of the upper Mexican civil service', McNamara Scholarship Paper, World Bank.

Gasparini, Leonardo (2003), 'Argentina's distributional failure: the role of integration and public policies', Working Paper no. 1, CEDLAS, UNLP, Argentina.

Gerchunoff, P. and L. Llach (2003), *El ciclo de la ilusión y el desencanto*, Buenos Aires: Ariel.

Gervasoni, Carlos (1995) 'El impacto electoral de las políticas de estabilización y ajuste estructural en América Latina', *Journal of Latin American Affairs*, 3(1): 46–50.

Gibson, E. (1997), 'The populist road to market reform: policy and electoral coalitions in Mexico and Argentina', *World Politics*, 49(3): 339–70.

Gibson, E.L. and E. Calvo (2001), 'Federalism and low-maintenance constituencies: territorial dimensions of economic reform in Argentina', *Studies in Comparative International Development*, 35(3): 32–55.

Gill, I., T. Packard and J. Yermo (2003), 'Keeping the promise of old age income security in Latin America', Background Paper for Regional Study on Social Security Reform, Office of the Chief Economist, World Bank, November.

Gobierno de la República del Paraguay (undated), 'Diagnóstico sobre los Patrones de Comportamiento y Desempeno Institucional, Gobernabilidad y Corrupción en el Sector Público del Paraguay', mimeo.

Gonzáles Arica, Guillermo (2001), *Los Escaños de Montesinos*, Lima, Peru: El Virrey.

Gonzáles de Olarte, Efraín (1994), *El Péndulo Peruano*, Lima Peru: Instituto de Estudios Peruanos.

Gonzáles de Olarte, Efraín (1998), *Neoliberalismo a la Peruana, Economía Política del Ajuste Estructural, 1990–1997*, Lima, Peru: Instituto de Estudios Peruanos.

Greenspan, Alan (2005), 'Reflections on central banking', Remarks by Chairman Alan Greenspan, at a symposium sponsored by the Federal Reserve Bank of Kansas City, Jackson Hole, Wyoming, 26 August.

Greenstein, Fred (2004), *The Presidential Difference. Leadership Style from FDR to George W. Bush*, Princeton, NJ: Princeton University Press.

Greif, A. (1994), 'Cultural beliefs and the organization of society: a historical and theoretical reflection on collectivist and individualist societies', *Journal of Political Economy*, 102: 912–50.

Greif, A. (2002), *Genoa and the Maghribi Traders: Historical and Comparative Institutional Analysis*, Cambridge: Cambridge University Press.

Greif, A. and D. Laitin (2004), 'A theory of endogenous institutional change', *American Political Science Review*, 98: 633–52.

Greif, A., R. Milgrom and B. Weingast (1994), 'Coordination, commitment, and enforcement, the case of the merchant guild', *Journal of Political Economy*, 102: 745–76.

Grindle, Merilee and John W. Thomas (1990), 'After the decision: implementing policy reform in developing countries', *World Development*, 18(8): 1163–81.

Grossman, G. and E. Helpman (1995), 'The politics of free trade agreements', *American Economic Review*, 85(4): 667–90.

Grossman, G. and E. Helpman (2001), *Special Interest Politics*, Cambridge, Mass.: MIT Press.

Guerra García, Gustavo (1999), *Reforma del Estado en el Perú, Pautas para Reestructurar el Ejecutivo, Agenda: Perú*, Lima, Peru: GRADE.

Haber, Stephen (ed.) (1997), *How Latin America Fell Behind: Essays in the Economic Histories of Brazil and Mexico, 1800–1914*, Palo Alto, CA: Stanford University Press.

Hachette, D. (2000), 'Privatizaciones: reforma estructural pero inconclusa', in F. Larraín and R. Vergara (eds), *La Transformación Económica de Chile*, Santiago: CEP, pp. 111–54.

Hachette, D. and R. Lüders (1993), *Privatization in Chile*, San Francisco: ICEG.

Haggard, S. (2000), 'Interests, institutions, and policy reform', in Anne Krueger (ed.), *Economic Policy Reform*, Chicago: University of Chicago Press.

Haggard, S. and R. Kaufman (1992), *The Politics of Economic Adjustment: International Constraints, Distributive Conflicts, and the State*, Princeton, NJ: Princeton University Press.

Haggard, S. and R. Kaufman (1995), *The Political Economy of Democratic Transitions*, Princeton: Princeton University Press.

Haggard, S. and M. McCubbins (2001), *Presidents, Parliaments, and Policy*, New York: Cambridge University Press.

Haggard, S. and S.B. Webb (eds) (1994), *Voting for Reform: Democracy, Political Liberalization, and Economic Adjustment*, Washington, DC: World Bank.

Harberger, A. (1959), 'Using the resources at hand more effectively', *American Economic Review*, 49(2): 134–46.

Harberger, A. (1985), 'Observations on the Chilean economy, 1973–1983', *Economic Development and Cultural Change*, 33: 451–62.

Harberger, A. (1993a), 'The search for relevance in economics' (Richard T. Ely Lecture), *American Economic Review*, 83(2): 1–16.

Harberger, A. (1993b), 'The other side of tax reform', in R. Dornbusch (ed.), *Policymaking in the Open Economy*, Oxford: Oxford University Press.

Hausmann, R. and R. Rigobon (2003), 'An alternative interpretation of the "Resource Curse": theory and policy implications', NBER Working Paper No. 9424, Cambridge, MA.

Heckman, James (1995), 'Lessons from the bell curve', *Journal of Political Economy*, 103 (5): 1091–120.

Heckman, James and Carmen Pagés (2000), 'The cost of job security regulation: evidence from Latin American labor markets', NBER Working Paper, 7773, Cambridge, MA: National Bureau of Economic Research.

Hepp, M. (1980), 'El antiguo sistema previsional: cómo era y adonde iba', mimeo, Dirección de Presupuestos, Santiago.

Hernández Rodríguez, Rogelio (1993), 'Preparación y movilidad de los funcionarios de la administración pública mexicana', *Estudios Sociológicos*, 11(32–33): 445–73.

Heskia, I. (1973), 'La distribución del ingreso en Chile', CIEPLAN Working Paper no. 31, Santiago.

Heymann, D. (2000), 'Políticas de reforma y comportamiento macroeconómica', in D. Heymann and B. Kosacoff (eds), *La Argentina de los Noventa. Desempeño económico en un contexto de reformas*, Buenos Aires: Eudeba.

Hidalgo, Manuel (2002), 'Liderazgo, reforma económica y cambio político en Venezuela: 1989–1998', in Ramos Jiménez A. (ed.), *La Transición Venezolana. Aproximaciones al fenómeno Chávez*, Mérida: Centro de Investigación de Política Comparada, Universidad de Los Andes.

Horta, M., G. Piani and H. Kume (1991), 'A política cambial e comercial', in IPEA (ed.), *Perspectivas da economia brasileira – 1992*, Rio de Janeiro: IPEA, http://www.worldbank.org/wbi/governance/pdf/paraguay/resultados.pdf.

Huntington, S. (2006), *Political Order in Changing Societies*, New Haven: Yale University Press.

IDB (Inter-American Development Bank) (2002), *Beyond Borders. The New Regionalism in Latin America*, Washington: IDB.

IDESP (Instituto de Estudos Sociais, Econômicos, e Políticos de São Paulo) (1990), 'As elites Brasileiras e a modernização do setor público', *Relatório de Pesquisa*, São Paulo.

INEI (various years), 'Series estadísticas', Lima, Perú, http://www.inei.gob.pe/.

International Monetary Fund (2001), *International Financial Statistics, CD Edition*, IMF: Washington, DC.

International Monetary Fund (various years), 'Venezuela: recent economic developments', Washington, DC.

Jones, M., P. Sanguinetti and M. Tommasi (2002a), 'Voters as fiscal liberals', mimeo, Universidad de San Andrés, Buenos Aires.

Jones, M., S. Saiegh, P. Spiller and M. Tommasi (2002b), 'Amateur legislators, professional politicians: the consequences of party-centered electoral rules in federal systems', *American Journal of Political Science*, 46(3): 656–69.

Jones, M., S. Saiegh, P. Spiller and M. Tommasi (forthcoming), 'Congress, political careers, and the provincial connection', in P. Spiller and M. Tommasi (eds).

Kahneman, Daniel and Amos Tversky (1979), 'Prospect theory: an analysis of decisions under risk', *Econometrica*, 47(2): 263–92.

Kamil, H. and A. Ons (2003), 'Formación de bloques comerciales regionales y determinantes del comercio bilateral: el caso del MERCOSUR', Instituto de Economía, Facultad de Ciencias Económicas y Administración, DT 2/02, Uruguay.

Karl, Terry (1986), 'Petroleum and political pacts: the transition to democracy in Venezuela', in G. O'Donnell, P. Schmitter and L. Whitehead (eds), *Transitions from Authoritarian Rule*, Baltimore: Johns Hopkins University Press, pp. 196–220.

Karl, Terry (1997), *The Paradox of Plenty: Oil Booms and Petro-States*, Berkeley: University of California Press.

Kaufman, R., C. Bazdresch and B. Heredia (1994), 'Mexico, radical reform in a dominant party system', in S. Haggard and S. Webb (eds), *Voting for Reform*, Oxford: Oxford University Press.

Kaufmann, D., A. Kraay and M. Mastruzzi (2003), *Governance Matters III: Governance Indicators for 1996–2002*, Washington, DC: The World Bank.

Kavanagh, Dennis (1997), *British Politics*, Oxford: Oxford University Press.

Kingdom, John (1995), *Agendas, Alternatives and Public Policy*, New York: HarperCollins.

Keller, Alfredo (1992), Consultores 21, Caracas.

Kingstone, Peter (1999), *Crafting Coalitions for Reform: Business Preferences, Political Institutions, and Neoliberal Reform in Brazil*, University Park, PA: Pennsylvania State University Press.

Kleinpenning, J.M.G. (1987), *Land and Man in Paraguay*, Amsterdam: Centre for Latin American Research and Documentation.

Kreps, D., Paul Milgrom, John Roberts and Robert Wilson (1982), 'Rational cooperation in the finitely repeated prisoners' dilemma', *Journal of Economic Theory*, 27: 245–52.

Krishna, P. and D. Mitra (2005), 'Reciprocated unilateralism in trade policy', *Journal of International Economics*, 65(2): 461–87.

Krivoy, Ruth (2002), *Colapso: la Crisis Bancaria Venezolana de 1994*, Caracas: Ediciones IESA.

Kuan Yew, Lee (2000), *From Third World to First: the Singapore Story, 1965–2000*, New York: HarperCollins.

Kume, H., G. Piani and C.F. Bráz de Souza (2003), 'A política brasileira de importação no período 1987–98: descrição e avaliação', in C.H. Corseuil and H. Kume (eds), *A Abertura Comercial Brasileira nos Anos 1990: Impactos sobre Emprego e Salário*, Rio de Janeiro, MTE/IPEA.

Kuncoro, A. and B. Resosudarmo (2004), 'Understanding Indonesian economic reforms 1983–2000', paper prepared for GDN project on Understanding Reform, mimeo, University of Indonesia and the Australian National University.

Lambert, P. (1997), 'The regime of Alfredo Stroessner', in Peter Lambert and Andrew Nickson (eds), *The Transition to Democracy in Paraguay*, New York: St Martin's Press.

Lanzaro, Jorge (2000a), *La 'segunda' transición en el Uruguay. Gobierno y partidos en un tiempo de reformas*, Montevideo: Fundación de Cultura Universitaria.

Lanzaro, Jorge (2000b), 'Autoridad presidencial, relaciones de partido y perfil de gobierno en los inicios del mandato de Jorge Batlle', in Instituto de Ciencia Política, *Elecciones 1999–2000*, Montevideo: Ediciones de la Banda Oriental.

Larraín, F. (1991), 'Public sector behavior in a highly indebted country: the contrasting Chilean experience', in F. Larraín and M. Selowsky (eds), *The Public Sector and the Latin American Crisis*, San Francisco: ICS Press, pp. 89–136.

Larraín, F. and P. Meller (1990), 'La experiencia socialista-populista Chilena: la unidad popular, 1970–1973', *Cuadernos de Economía*, 82(27): 317–56.

Larraín, F. and R. Vergara (2000), 'Un cuarto de siglo de reformas fiscales', in F. Larraín and R. Vergara (eds), *La Transformación Económica de Chile*, Santiago: CEP, pp. 79–109.

Larraín, M. (1989), 'How the 1981–83 Chilean banking crisis was handled', World Bank Working Paper no. 300, Washington, DC.

Le Fort, G. (1988), 'The relative price of nontraded goods, absorption, and exchange rate policy in Chile', *IMF Staff Papers*, 35(2): 336–70.

Levitsky, S. (2003), 'From labor politics to machine politics: the transformation of party-union linkages in Argentine Peronism, 1983–1999', *Latin American Research Review*, 38(3): 3–36.

Licandro, G. (2000), 'Las reglas de responsabilidad fiscal en el Uruguay', Documento de trabajo 01/2000, Banco Central del Uruguay.

Licandro, G. and J. Licandro (eds) (2004), *Una agenda de reformas para el sistema financiero uruguayo*, Montevideo, Uruguay: Universidad de la República y Universidad de la Paz.

Liew, L., L. Bruszt and L. He (2005), 'Causes, national costs, and timing of reforms', in Fanelli and McMahon (eds) (2005a), pp. 113–52.

Lindblom, Charles (1965), *The Intelligence of Democracy: Decision Making through Mutual Adjustment*, New York: The Free Press.

López Presa, J.O. and Jose Alberto Garibaldi (1999), *Corrupción y Cambio*, Mexico, DF: FCE.

López-de-Silanes, F. (2002), 'The politics of legal reform', mimeo, UNCTAD and Harvard University.

Lora, E. (1998), 'Una década de reformas estructurales en América Latina: qué se ha reformado y cómo medirlo', *Pensamiento Iberoamericano, Revista de Economía Política*, Volumen Extraordinario: 27–53.

Lora, E. (2001), 'Structural reforms in Latin America: what has been reformed and how to measure it', IDB, Working Paper 466, December.

Lora, E. and M. Olivera (2004), 'What makes reforms likely: political economy determinants of reforms in Latin America', *Journal of Applied Economics*, 7(1): 99–135.

Lora, E., U. Panizza and M. Quispe-Agnoli (2004), 'Reform fatigue: symptoms, reasons, implications', Inter-American Development Bank, Working Paper no. 1005.

Lüders, R. (1970), 'Una historia monetaria de Chile', *Cuadernos de Economía*, 20(7): 4–28.

Lüders, R. (1990), 'Veinte y cinco años de ingeniería social en Chile: un breve ensayo sobre la historia económica del período 1960–1988', *Cuadernos de Economía*, 76(25): 331–80.

Lüders, R. and G. Wagner (2003), 'Understanding development in Chile: are the 1930s a turning point?', *Cuadernos de Economía*, 121(40): 785.

Luis S.G.J. (1992), 'Drug addiction and trafficking in Paraguay: an approach to the problem during the transition', *Journal of Interamerican Studies and World Affairs*, 34(3): 155–200.

Luján, Carlos (2003), 'El proceso de negociación de la reforma de la seguridad social en Uruguay', tesis doctoral de la Universidad Católica del Uruguay.

Maddison, A. (2001), *The World Economy: a Millennial Perspective*, Paris: OECD.

Mahon, James (1996), *Mobile Capital and Latin American Development*, University Park: Pennsylvania State University Press.

Mallon, R., and J. Sourrouille (1975), *Economic Policymaking in a Conflict Society: the Argentine Case*, Cambridge: Harvard University Press.

Mallon, F. (1995), *Peasant and Nation: the Making of Post Colonial Mexico and Peru*, Berkeley: California University Press.

Manzano, O. and R. Rigobón (2001), 'Resource curse or debt overhang?', NBER Working Paper No. W8390.

Marcel, M. (2000), 'Aspectos macroeconómicos del Proyecto de Ley de Presupuestos del Sector Público del Año 2001', mimeo, Dirección de Presupuestos, Santiago.

Marcel, M. (2002), 'Aspectos Macroeconómicos del Proyecto de Ley de Presupuestos del Sector Público del Año 2003', mimeo, Dirección de Presupuestos, Santiago.

Marfán, M. (1998), 'El financiamiento fiscal en los años 90', in R. Cortázar and J. Vial (eds), *Construyendo Opciones. Propuestas Económicas y Sociales para el Cambio de Siglo*, Santiago: Dolmen editores, pp. 545–73.

McClintock, C. (1999), 'Peru: precarious regimes, authoritarian and democratic', in L. Diamond, Jonathan Hartlyn, Juan J. Linz and Seymour Martin Lipset, *Democracy in Developing Countries*, Boulder, Colorado: Lynne Rienner, pp. 309–66.

Mejia, D. (2003), 'Duration of ministers in Fujimori's government', mimeo, PUCP, Lima, Peru.

Menard, Claude (ed.) (1999), *Institutions, Contracts and Organizations*, Cheltenham, UK and Northampton, MA, USA: Edward Elgar.

Méndez, J.C. (ed.) (1979), *Chilean Economic Policy*, Santiago: Calderón.

Milesi-Ferretti, Giancarlo (1991), 'Dynamic models of strategic policy making', doctoral dissertation, Harvard University.

Miranda, A. (1983), *Paraguay y las obras hidroelectricas binacionales*, Asuncion: El Lector.

Miranda, A. (2001), *Crimen Organizado en Paraguay*, Asuncion: Miranda & Asociados.

Molinar Horcasitas, Juan (1991), *El tiempo de la legitimidad*, Mexico, DF: Ediciones Cal y Arena.

Molinet, Jonathan (2000), 'Desconcentración administrativa con autonomía técnica y operacional. La coalición del presidente en la reforma del Estado 1992–1996', in Rodolfo Vergara (ed.), *Reforma de las instituciones*, México: Colegio Nacional de Ciencia Política y Administración Pública.

Monaldi, Francisco (2001), 'The political economy of expropriation in high sunk cost industries', paper presented at the annual meeting of the American Political Science Association (APSA), San Francisco, California.

Monaldi, F., R. González, R. Obuchi and M. Penfold (2004), 'Political institutions, policymaking processes, and policy outcomes in Venezuela', paper presented at LACEA meeting 2004.

Mondino, G., F. Sturzenegger and M. Tommasi (1996), 'Recurrent high-inflation and stabilization: a dynamic game', *International Economic Review*, 37(4): 981–96.

Moreira, M.M. (2003), 'Abertura e crescimento no Brasil: deu errado?', paper presented at the seminar Brazil and the Risks and Opportunities of Integration into the World Economy, sponsored by the IDB and Getulio Vargas Foundation, São Paulo.

Morley, S. and R. Vos (2001), 'Pobreza y crecimiento dual en Paraguay', in Luis Galeano and Domingo Rivarola *Pobreza y Cambio Social*, Asunción: CPES.

Moselle, B. and B. Polak (2001), 'A model of a predatory state', *Journal of Law Economics & Organization*, 17(1): 1–33.

Muñoz, I. (2000), 'Privatizaciones y concesiones', in Abusada (ed.), pp. 449–82.

Muñoz, O. (ed.) (1990), *Transición a la Democracia. Marco Político y Económico*. Santiago: CIEPLAN.

Murillo, M.V. (1997), 'From populism to neoliberalism: labor unions and market-oriented reforms in Argentina, Mexico and Venezuela', doctoral thesis, Government Department, Harvard University.

Murillo, M.V. (2001), *Labor Unions, Partisan Coalitions, and Market Reforms in Latin America*, Cambridge: Cambridge University Press.

Murillo, M.V. (2002), 'Political bias in policy convergence: privatization choices in Latin America', *World Politics*, 54(4): 462–93.

Murillo, M.V. (2004), 'Policymakers' agency under globalization pressures: liberalizing public utilities in Latin America', paper prepared for the meeting of the Latin American Studies Association, Las Vegas, Nevada, October 7–9.

Nagel, B. (1999), ' "Unleashing the fury": the cultural discourse of rural violence and land rights in Paraguay', *Comparative Studies in Society and History*, 41(1): 148–81.

Naím, M. (1993), *Paper Tigers and Minotaurs: the Politics of Venezuela's Economic Reforms*, Washington DC: Carnegie Endowment.

Naím, M. and R. Piñango (1984), *El Caso Venezuela: Una Ilusión de Armonía*, Caracas: Ediciones IESA.

Navarro, Juan C. (1993), 'En busca del pacto perdido: la fallida Búsqueda del consenso en la Venezuela de los 80 y los 90', in A. Serbin, J. McCoy, A. Stambouli and W. Smith (eds), *Venezuela: la Democracia Bajo Presión*, Caracas: Editorial Nueva Sociedad, pp. 69–86.

Navarro, Juan C. (1994), 'Reversal of fortune: the ephemeral success of adjustment in Venezuela between 1989 and 1993', manuscript, Washington DC: World Bank.

Navia, P. and A. Velasco (2003), 'The politics of second-generation reforms', in J. Williamson and P. Kuczynski (eds), *After the Washington Consensus: Restarting Growth and Reform in Latin America*, Washington, DC: Institute for International Economics, pp. 265–303.

Neudstadt, Richard (1990), *Presidential Power and the Modern Presidency: the Politics of Leadership from Roosevelt to Reagan*, New York: Free Press.

Nickson R.A. and P. Lambert (2002), 'State reform and the "privatized" state in Paraguay', *Public Administration Development*, 22: 163–74.

North, Douglass (1979), *A Framework for Analyzing the State in Economic History*, in *Explorations in Economic History*, New York, Academic Press.

North, Douglass (1990), *Institutions, Institutional Change and Economic Performance*, New York: Cambridge University Press.

North, Douglass C. (1994), 'Economic performance through time', *American Economic Review*, 84(3): 359–68.

North, Douglass and Barry Weingast (1996), 'Constitutions and commitment, the evolution of institutions governing public choice in seventeenth century England', in Alston et al. (eds), pp. 129–34.

Nuñez, A. (1994), *La Reforma Electoral de 1989–1990, México*, Mexico, DF: Fondo de Cultura Económica.

O'Donnell, G. (1977), 'Estado y Alianzas en la Argentina, 1956–1976', *Desarrollo Económico*, 16(64): 523–54.

O'Donnell, G. (1994), 'Delegative democracy', *Journal of Democracy*, 5(1): 55–69.

Oliveira, G. and T. Fujiwara. (2005), 'Brazil's regulatory framework: predictability or uncertainty?', presented at conference on Brazil, a Sustainable Economic Success?, Paris, October.

Olson, Mancur (1965), *The Logic of Collective Action*, Cambridge: Harvard University Press.

Orphanides, A. (1996), 'The timing of stabilizations', *Journal of Economic Dynamics and Control*, 20: 257–79.

Ortega, A. (2003), 'Descripción y perfiles de desigualdad de ingresos en Venezuela, 1975–2002', PNUD, Documentos para la discusión, Caracas: Editorial Torino.

Otálvora, Edgar (1994), *La Paz Ramónica: Notas sobre un gobierno de transición*, Caracas: Editorial Pomaire.

Paez, B.D.R. (2001), *Itaipu y crecimineto economico de* Paraguay, Master's degree thesis, Universidad Nacional de Tucuman, Argentina.

Palanza, V. and G. Sin (1996), 'Estudios de caso: ley 23.696 (reforma del Estado), ley 23.697 (emergencia económica)', mimeo, Universidad del Salvador, Buenos Aires, Argentina.

Palanza, V. and G. Sin (1997), 'Partidos provinciales y gobierno nacional en el Congreso, 1983–1995', *Boletín de la Sociedad Argentina de Análisis Político*, 3(5): 46–94.

Palermo, V. and M. Novaro (1996), *Política y Poder en el Gobierno de Menem*, Buenos Aires: Norma.

Panizza, U. and M. Yañez (2006), 'Why are Latin Americans so unhappy about reforms', Inter-American Development Bank, Research Department Working Paper no. 567.

Payne, M., D. Zovatto, F. Carrillo-Flórez and A. Zavala (2002), *Democracies in Development: Politics and Reform in Latin America*, Washington, DC: Inter-American Development Bank.

Penfold, M. (2001), 'El colapso del sistema de partidos en Venezuela: una muerte anunciada', in J. Carrasquero, T. Maingon and F. Welsch (eds), *Venezuela en Transición*. Caracas: CDB publicaciones-RedPol.

Piñera, J. (1991), *El Cascabel al Gato, La Batalla por la Reforma Previsional*, Santiago: Editorial Zig-zag.

Pinheiro, A.C. (1996), 'Impactos microeconômicos da privatização', *Pesquisa e Planejamento Econômico*, 26(3): 357–97.

Pinheiro, A.C. (2004), 'Porque o Brasil cresce pouco?', in F. Giambiagi, J. Reis and A. Urani (eds), *Reformas no Brasil: Balanço e Agenda*, Rio de Janeiro: Nova Fronteira.

Pinheiro, A.C. (2005), 'Reforma regulatória na infra-estrutura Brasileira: em que pé estamos?', in Lucia Helena Salgado and Ronaldo Serôa da Motta (eds), *Marcos Regulatórios no Brasil – O que foi feito e o que falta fazer*, Rio de Janeiro: IPEA.

Pinheiro, A.C. and F. Giambiagi (2000), 'The macroeconomic background and institutional framework of Brazilian privatization', in Pinheiro and Fukasaku (eds), pp. 13–43.

Pinheiro, A.C. and K. Fukasaku (eds) (2000), *Privatization in Brazil: the Case of Public Utilities*, Rio de Janeiro: BNDES-OECD.

Posner, Richard (2003), *Law, Pragmatism, and Democracy*, Cambridge: Harvard University Press.

Prasad, E., K. Rogoff, S. Wei and M. Kose (2004), 'Financial globalization, growth, and volatility in developing countries', National Bureau of Economic Research, Working Paper 10942.

Prata, J., N. Beirão and T. Tomioka (1999), *Sergio Motta: O Trator Em Ação*, São Paulo: Geração.

Przeworski, A. (1991), *Democracy and the Market*, New York: Cambridge University Press.

Przeworski, Adam (2004), 'Institutions matter?', *Government and Opposition*, 39(4): 527–40.

Przeworski, A., S. Stokes and B. Maini (1999), *Democracy, Accountability, and Representation*, New York: Cambridge University Press.

Rajapatirana, S. (1995), 'Post trade liberalization policy and institutional challenges in Latin America and the Caribbean', Policy Research Working Paper 1465, World Bank.

Ramírez, G. and F. Rosende (1992), 'Responding to collapse: Chilean banking legislation after 1985', in P. Brock (ed.), *If Texas were Chile: a Primer on Banking Reform*, San Francisco: ICS Press, pp. 193–216.

Ramos Olivera, J. (1999), *Reforma de la previsión social. Piedra angular del gobierno de coalición*, Montevideo, Uruguay: Iconoprint.

Rey, Juan Carlos (1972), 'El sistema de partidos en Venezuela', Politeia 1, Instituto de Estudios Políticos, Universidad Central de Venezuela, Caracas.

Richards, D.G. (1987), 'Gender-related differences in Paraguayan migration to Buenos Aires, Argentina', *Social Science Quarterly*, 71(3): 628–38.

Richards, D.G. (1994), 'Booming-sector economic activity in Paraguay 1974–86', *Journal of Development Studies*, 31(2): 310–33.

Richards, D.G. (2001), 'Tax reform in a small open transition economy: the case of Paraguay', *Canadian Journal of Latin American and Caribbean Studies*, 20 (51): 27–47.

Riding, A. (1984), *Vecinos Distantes*, México, DF: Planeta.

Ritter, A., M. Cameron and D. Pollock (2000), *Latin America to 2000: Reactivating Growth, Improving Equity, Sustaining Democracy*, New York: Praeger.

Rius, A. (2003), 'Racionalidad limitada y "empaquetamiento" en los procesos de reforma: el caso de la seguridad social', in Aboal y Moraes, *Economía Política en Uruguay. Instituciones y actores políticos en el proceso económico*, Universidad de la República y Cinve, Uruguay.

Rius, A. and N. van de Walle (2005), 'Political institutions and economic policy reform', in Fanelli and McMahon (eds) (2005a), pp. 176–202.

Riutort, Matías (2000), 'Pobreza, desigualdad y crecimiento económico en Venezuela', Documentos del Proyecto Pobreza en Venezuela, Caracas: Instituto de Investigaciones Económicas y Sociales, Universidad Católica Andrés Bello y Asociación Civil para la Promoción de Estudios Sociales.

Riutort, M. and R. Balza (2001), 'Salario real, tipo de cambio real y pobreza en Venezuela: 1975–2000', Caracas: UCAB, IIES.

Rodrik, D. (1991), 'Policy uncertainty and private investment in developing countries', *Journal of Development Economics*, 36: 229–242.

Rodrik, D. (1993), 'The positive economics of policy reform', *American Economic Review*, 83(2): 356–61.

Rodrik, D. (1994), 'Getting interventions right: how South Korea and Taiwan grew rich', NBER Working Paper No. 4964, Cambridge, Mass.

Rodrik, D. (1996), 'Understanding economic policy reform', *Journal of Economic Literature*, March.

Rodrik, Dani (2005), 'Growth strategies', in A. Philippe, and S. Durlauf (eds), *Handbook of Economic Growth*, Amsterdam: North-Holland, pp. 967–1014.

Rojo, Pablo and Jeffrey Hoberman (1994), 'Deregulation in Argentina: a policymaker's view', *Quarterly Review of Economics and Finance*, 34: 151–77.

Rospigliosi, F. (2000), *Montesinos y las Fuerzas Armadas*, Lima, Peru: Instituto de Estudios Peruanos.

Rubio, L. (1992), *Como va a afectar a México el Tratado de libre Comercio?* Mexico, DF: Fondo de Cultura Económica.

Saavedra, J. (2002), 'La flexibilización del mercado laboral', in R. Abusada (ed.), pp. 379–428.

Saavedra, J. and A. Chong (1999), 'Structural reform, institutions and earnings: evidence from the formal and informal sectors in urban Peru', *Journal of Development Studies*, 50(5): 95–116.

Saez, S., J. Salazár and R. Vicuña (1995), 'Antecedentes y resultados de la estrategia comercial del Aylwin', *Colección de Estudios Cieplan*, 41: 41–66.

Sala-i-Martin, X. and A. Subramanian (2003), 'Addressing the natural resource curse: an illustration from Nigeria', NBER Working Paper no. 9804, Cambridge, MA.

Salas, F. (2001), *Incendiando la Pradera*, Lima, Peru: Planeta.

Saldain, Rodolfo (1999), 'Evolución de la seguridad social Uruguaya (1985–1999)', mimeo, October. unpublished.

Salinas de Gortari, C. (1994), *Sexto Informe de Gobierno, Anexo Estadístico*, Mexico, DF: Government Printers.

Salinas de Gortari, C. (2003), *México, un paso a la Modernidad*, Mexico, DF: Plaza y Janés.

Sanhueza, G. (2001), 'Chilean banking crisis of the 1980s: solution and estimation of the costs', Central Bank of Chile Working Paper no. 104, Santiago.

Santiso, Javier (2005), *Amérique Latine. Révolutionnaire, Libérale, Pragmatique*, Paris: Autrement/CERI.

Sawers, L. (1996), *The Other Argentina: the Interior and National Development*, Boulder: Westview Press.

Sawers, L. and R. Massacane (2001), 'Structural reform and industrial promotion in Argentina', *Journal of Latin American Studies*, 33: 101–32.

Schamis, Hector (2002), *Re-forming the State: the Politics of Privatization in Latin America and Europe*, Ann Arbor: University of Michigan Press.

Schmidt-Hebbel, K. (2001), 'Latin America's pension revolution: a review of approaches and experience', Central Bank of Chile, March.

Schneider, Ben Ross (1990), 'The politics of privatization in Brazil and Mexico: variations on a statist theme', in J. Waterbury and E. Suleiman (eds), *The Political Economy of Public Sector Reform and Privatization*, Boulder, CO: Westview Press.

Schneider, Ben Ross (1991), *Politics within the State: Elite Bureaucrats and Industrial Policy in Authoritarian Brazil*, Pittsburgh: University of Pittsburgh Press.

Schneider, Ben Ross (2004a), *Business Politics and the State in 20th Century Latin America*, New York: Cambridge University Press.

Schneider, Ben Ross (2004b), 'Organizing interests and coalitions in the politics of market reform in Latin America', *World Politics*, 56 (April): 456–79.

Schotter, A. (1981), *The Economic Theory of Social Institutions*, Cambridge: Cambridge University Press.

Schreiner, J. (2005), 'El credito y el sistema financieros en la generación de empleo', Working Paper, Centro de Análisis y Difusión de la Economia Paraguaya (CADEP)/ University of Toronto.

Scully, T. (1995), 'La reconstitución de la política de partidos en Chile', in S. Mainwaring and T. Scully (eds), *La Construcción de Instituciones Democráticas*, Santiago: CIEPLAN, 83–112.

Secretary of Finance (SHCP) (1995), *México: Informe Sobre la Situación Económica, las Finanzas Públicas y la Deuda Pública: Acciones y Resultados del 4to Trimestre de 1994,* Mexico: SHCP.

Sen, Amartya (2000), *Development as Freedom,* New York: Anchor Books.

Sen, Amartya (2004), Speech to open the Fifth Annual Global Development Conference, New Delhi, January.

Senge, P.M., R.B. Ross, B.J. Smith, C. Roberts and A. Kleiner (1994), *The Fifth Discipline Fieldbook,* London: Nicholas Brealey Publishing Limited.

Shatz, H. and D. Tarr (2000), 'Exchange rate overvaluation and trade protection. Lessons from experience', Policy Research Working Paper 2289, World Bank.

Shugart, M.S. and J.M. Carey (1992), *Presidents and Assemblies: Constitutional Design and Electoral Dynamics,* New York: Cambridge University Press.

Silva, Eduardo (1996), *The State and Capital in Chile,* Boulder, CO: Westview.

Smith, T. (2003), 'Contraband is big business in Paraguay', *New York Times,* 10 June: W.1.

Sohn, I. (2005), 'With all deliberate delay: economic and financial reform in Paraguay', International Trade and Finance Association 15th Annual Conference, Working Paper no. 51.

Sosa, Arturo (1987), 'De esta a otra democracia', *Revista SIC,* 50(500): 504–7, Centro Gumilla, Caracas.

Spiller, P.T. and M. Tommasi (2000), 'The institutional determinants of public policy: theory and the case of Argentine', paper presented at the IV Annual Conference of the International Society for New Institutional Economics, Heidelberg, Germany.

Spiller, P.T. and M. Tommasi (2003), 'The institutional determinants of public policy: a transaction approach with application to Argentina', *Journal of Law, Economics and Organization,* 19(2): 281–306.

Spiller, P.T. and M. Tommasi (forthcoming), *The Institutional Foundations of Public Policy in Argentina,* New York: Cambridge University Press.

Stallings, B. and W. Peres (2000), *Growth, Employment, and Equity: the Impact of the Economic Reforms in Latin America and the Caribbean,* Washington, DC: Brookings Institution Press.

Starr, P. (1999), 'Capital flows, fixed exchange rates, and political survival: Mexico and Argentina, 1994–1995', in P. Oxhorn and P. Starr (eds), *Markets and Democracy in Latin America. Conflict or Convergence?* Boulder: Lynne Rienner Publishers.

Statistical Abstract of Latin America (2002), J.W. Wilkie (ed.), UCLA Latin American Center Publications: Los Angeles, CA.

Stein, E., E. Talvi and A. Grisanti (1998), 'Institutional arrangements and fiscal perform-ance: the Latin American experience', NBER Working Paper no. 6358, Cambridge, Mass.

Stepan, A. (1999), 'Towards a new comparative analysis of democracy and federalism: demos constraining and demos enabling federations', mimeo, All Souls College, Oxford University.

Stiglitz, J.E. (2002), *Globalization and its Discontents,* Norton: New York.

Stokes, S. (2001), *Mandates and Democracy: Neoliberalism by Surprise in Latin America,* New York: Cambridge University Press.

Sturzenegger, F. and M. Tommasi (eds) (1998), *The Political Economy of Reform,* Cambridge, Mass.: MIT Press.

Superintendencia de Seguridad Social (1992), *El Costo de la Seguridad Social Chilena,* Santiago: Superintendencia de Seguridad Social.

Tanaka, M. (1998), *Los Espejismos de la Democracia: El colapso del Sistema de Partidos en el Perú,* Lima, Peru: Instituto de Estudios Peruanos.

Tanaka, M. (1999), 'La economia politica del ajuste y la reforma estructural en el Perú: el estado de la cuestion y la agenda pendiente', in Bardalez et al. (eds), pp. 121–64.

Tavares, M.H. (2004), 'Privatization: reform through negotiation', in M. Font and A. Spanakos (eds), *Reforming Brazil*, Lanham, MD: Lexington, pp. 53–70.

Teichman, Judith (2001), *The Politics of Freeing Markets in Latin America: Chile, Argentina, and Mexico*, Chapel Hill: University of North Carolina Press.

Templeton, Andrew (1995), 'The evolution of popular opinion', in L. Goodman, J. Mendelson, M. Naím and J. Tulchin (eds), *Lessons of the Venezuelan Experience*, Washington, DC: Woodrow Wilson Center Press, pp. 74–114.

Thorpe, R. and G. Bertram (1978), *Peru: Development in an Open Economy*, Oxford: Oxford University Press.

Thurner, M. (1997), *From Two Republics to One Divided: Contradictions of Postcolonial Nationmaking in Andean Peru*, Durham, NC: Duke University Press.

Tommasi, M. (2002), 'Crisis, political institutions, and policy reform', Working Paper, Universidad de San Andrés & Center of Studies for Institutional Development, Argentina.

Tommasi, M. (2004), 'Crisis, political institutions and policy reform: the good, the bad, and the ugly', in B. Tungodden, N. Stern and I. Kolstad (eds), *Toward Pro-Poor Policies. Aid, Institutions and Globalization*, Washington: World Bank.

Tommasi, M. (2006), 'Federalism in Argentina and the reforms of the 1990s', in T.N. Srinivasan and J.S. Wallak (eds), *The Dynamics of Federalism: the Political Economy Reality*, New York: Cambridge University Press.

Tommasi, M. and A. Velasco (1996), 'Where are we in the political economy of reform?' *Journal of Policy Reform*, 1(2): 187–238.

UCAB (2004), *Detrás de la Pobreza*, Caracas: Asociación civil para la promoción de estudios sociales (ACPES) and Universidad Católica Andrés Bello (UCAB).

Umérez, Julieta (2001), 'La reforma del sector telecomunicaciones en Venezuela: experiencias del ente regulador. CONATEL', CLAD, Documentos Estudios de Casos, Caracas.

Undurraga, S. (1974), 'Política de Desarrollo de un Mercado de Capitales Moderno y Eficiente para Chile', *Estudios Monetarios III*, Banco Central de Chile, Santiago.

Uslar Pietri, Arturo (1947), *De una a otra Venezuela*, Caracas: Monte Ávila Editores, 8th edn, 1996.

Vaillant, Marcel (2000), 'Limits to trade liberalization: a political economy approach', PhD thesis, University of Antwerp, UFSIA, Faculty of Applied Economics.

Valdés, J.G. (1995), *Pinochet's Economists. The Chicago School of Economics in Chile*, Cambridge: Cambridge University Press.

Valdovinos, C.G.F. and A.M. Naranjo (2004), 'Economic growth in Paraguay', Inter-American Development Bank Economic and Social Studies Series, RE 1-04-009, May.

Velasco, L. (1997a), 'A economia política das políticas públicas: fatores que favoreceram as privatizações no período 1985/94', Texto para Discussão 54, BNDES, Rio de Janeiro, Brazil.

Velasco, L. (1997b), 'A economia política das políticas públicas: as privatizações e a reforma do estado', Texto para Discussão 55, BNDES, Rio de Janeiro, Brazil.

Vial, S.A. (2002), 'Cultura política y prácticas de gobernabilidad democrática: la ciudadanía en su encrucijada', Resultados Preliminares, Asunción: CIRD.

Vial, J. (2001), 'Institucionalidad y Desempeño Fiscal. Una Mirada a la Experiencia Chilena en los 90', CIEPLAN Serie Estudios Socioeconómicos no. 5, Santiago.

Viguera, A. (1998), 'La política de la apertura comercial en la Argentina, 1987–1996', paper presented at 1998 Annual Conference of Latin American Studies Association, Chicago, September 24–26.

Waterbury, J. (1989), 'The political management of economic adjustment and reform', in J. Nelson (ed.), *Fragile Coalitions*, New Brunswick, NJ: Transaction.

Webb, R. (1972), 'The distribution of income in Peru', Discussion Paper No. 26, Princeton University: Woodrow Wilson School Research Program in Economic Development.

Webb, R. and G. Fernandez-Baca (1995), *Peru en Numeros*, Lima: Cuanto S.A. Ed.

Weingast, B. (1997), 'The political foundations of institutions and rule of law', *American Political Science Review*, 91: 245–63.

Weintraub, S. (1997), *El TLC cumple tres años: un informe de sus avances*, Mexico, DF: Fondo de Cultura Económica.

Weyland, K. (2004a), *The Politics of Market Reform in Fragile Democracies: Argentina, Brazil, Peru, and Venezuela*, Princeton, New Jersey: Princeton University Press.

Weyland, K. (ed.) (2004b), *Learning from Foreign Models in Latin American Policy Reform*, Baltimore: Johns Hopkins University Press.

Williamson, John (1990), 'What Washington means by policy reform', in John Williamson (ed.), *Latin American Adjustment: How Much has Happened?*, Washington DC: Institute for International Economics, pp. 7–20.

Williamson, J. (2003), 'Overview: an agenda for restarting growth and reform', in P.P. Kuczynski and J. Williamson (eds), *After the Washington Consensus. Restarting Growth and Reform in Latin America*, Washington: Institute for International Economics.

Winiecki, Jan (1996), 'Why economic reforms fail in the Soviet Union', in Alston et al. (eds), pp. 59–63.

Woldenberg, J., R. Becerra and P. Salazar (2000), *La Mecánica del cambio político en México: Elecciones, Partidos y Reformas*, Mexico, DF: Cal y Arena.

World Bank (1994), *Averting the Old Age Crisis*, Oxford: Oxford University Press.

World Bank (1996), 'Case study: restructuring and privatization of the Mexican steel industry', mimeo, World Bank, Washington, DC.

World Bank (2000a), 'Uruguay country assistance evaluation', Operations Evaluation Department Report No. 21353, November.

World Bank (2000b), 'Rehabilitation project in support of the first phase of the modernization & systems rehabilitation program', Report No: 20343-UR, May.

Young, H.P. (1998), *Individual Strategies and Social Structure, an Evolutionary Theory of Institutions*, Princeton, New Jersey: Princeton University Press.

Zaid, G. (1995), *Adios Al PRI, Colección con una cierta Mirada*, Mexico, DF: Océano.

Zedillo, Ponce de León, E. (1995), *Anexo Estadístico, Ier Informe de Gobierno*, Mexico, DF: Government Printers.

Index

Note: Bold entries refer to tables.